ETHICAL LAND USE

ETHICAL LAND USE

PRINCIPLES OF POLICY AND PLANNING

Timothy Beatley

The Johns Hopkins University Press

Baltimore and London

Published in cooperation with the Center for
American Places, Harrisonburg, Virginia

© 1994 The Johns Hopkins University Press

The Johns Hopkins University Press
2715 North Charles Street
Baltimore, Maryland 21218-4319
The Johns Hopkins Press Ltd., London

ISBN 0-8018-4698-6
ISBN 0-8018-4699-4 (pbk.)

Library of Congress Cataloging-in-Publication
Data will be found at the end of this book.

A catalog record for this book is available
from the British Library.

TO MY PARENTS,
FOR THEIR LOVE
AND INSPIRATION

That land is a community is the basic concept
of ecology, but that land is to be loved and
respected is an extension of ethics.

Aldo Leopold, 1933

If I am to impact the land for my survival,
I attempt to do so in such a way that
the land can heal as rapidly and as
aesthetically as possible. I consider
that to be ethical land use.

David R. Moyer, a Virginia
homesteader, 1993

CONTENTS

Part V. Conclusions

ABBREVIATIONS

AICP   American Institute of Certified Planners
APA   American Planning Association
ASLA   American Society of Landscape Architects
BMA   Beachfront Management Act
CBD   Central Business District
CEQA   California Environmental Quality Act
CORE   Congress on Racial Equality
DE   Deep Ecology
DP   Rawlsian Difference Principle
EPA   Environmental Protection Agency
ESA   Endangered Species Act
HCP   Habitat Conservation Plan
LULU   Locally Unwanted Land Uses
MB   Marginal Benefits
MC   Marginal Costs
NEPA   National Environmental Policy Act
NIMBY   Not in My Back Yard
TFE   Two Factor Egalitarianism
TFGQ   Take-for-Granted Quotient
TVA   Tennessee Valley Authority
ULI   Urban Land Institute
UN   United Nations

PREFACE AND ACKNOWLEDGMENTS

THIS BOOK IS ABOUT the ethical choices we make concerning land and the use of land. These choices—at both collective and personal levels—are pervasive and profound. It is the objective of this book to highlight these ethical choices and provide some guidance concerning the nature and content of our ethical obligations relative to land.

To illustrate the nature of the choices discussed in this book, we should begin with an example. You live and work in the coastal community of Beaufort, North Carolina. Near you lies a parcel of land which contains a large and pristine wetland area. These wetlands, most agree, are of tremendous ecological value and environmental importance. They are important for numerous reasons. They serve essential biological functions as nursery grounds for fish and other aquatic life. They serve as important habitat for wildlife and even several endangered species. They provide important regional hydrologic benefits, acting as natural sponges soaking up and holding floodwaters during storms—floodwaters that would perhaps be displaced onto other lands if the wetlands were not there. The wetlands serve significant pollution control and water quality enhancement functions as well, filtering sediment and absorbing pollutants from agricultural and urban runoff. But the community in which these lands are located has been growing rapidly in recent years, and the land has been increasingly attractive to developers. In fact, one developer, in particular, has recently purchased the land and has announced his intentions to fill the wetlands and convert the land to a shopping center.

Should you, from an ethical point of view, be concerned with such a result? Does the prospect of filling and destroying these wetlands raise questions of appropriate ethical conduct and policy? Do we have ethical obligations as a society, as a community, to these wetlands or relative to them?

I believe we do, but the extent and nature of these obligations will depend on several primary issues, including how we define the relevant moral community, and the appropriate ethical standards or principles we employ in resolving ethical dilemmas. Perhaps we have obligations to migratory waterfowl or other forms of life that depend on the wetlands for survival. Perhaps we have obligations to prevent the creation of harms to other people that will result from filling the wetlands; for example, the displacement of floodwaters, impacts of unabated pollutants on marine life, and, in turn, economic impacts on those who depend on harvesting aquatic resources for their livelihoods such as oystermen and fishermen. Perhaps we have obligations to future generations to protect these wetlands as part of our natural heritage; for example, as ecological treasures to be viewed, contemplated, and enjoyed by our descendants.

There are, consequently, a variety of specific ethical obligations that one can conceive of that will lead to the conclusion that filling the wetlands or allowing the wetlands to be filled is *morally wrong*. And here facts and empirical knowledge may be important and useful. It may influence this decision to know that annually as many as several hundred thousand acres of wetlands are lost to such activities, and that the base of natural wetlands has been critically reduced in many regions of the country. It may also be morally relevant to know that alternative development sites exist in the community, and that the desired use can be accommodated elsewhere with much less environmental damage.

Other people, using different processes of moral reasoning and different ethical standards, can arrive at different conclusions about the case at hand. For those who believe that no moral obligations exist to other forms of life, or to future generations, or to the land itself, there may, in turn, be no ethical obligation on their part to protect or avoid the wetlands. And, of course, a different interpretation of the facts may argue for a different ethical posture. Some observers might question, for instance, the published statistics about wetlands loss, or might question the impacts of these losses on fish and wildlife, water quality, and so on. The developer may argue that, while there are other sites for the shopping mall, these are inappropriate or less than ideal for a number of reasons such as potential impacts of traffic on adjoining residential neighborhoods, availability, and cost.

While some may only fail to acknowledge obligations to protect the wetlands in question, others may conclude that there is indeed an ethical obligation to *develop* the wetlands. If one believes, for instance, that the jobs and economic benefits to be generated by the mall are substantial, and important locally in terms of relieving unemployment and expanding the local tax base, this might argue for such a project almost regardless of the environmental impacts. It is clear that in this dilemma, as in most land-use disputes, the issues are complex, morally and factually, and preserving the wetlands in perpetuity is not the only logical ethical posture that can be embraced.

If ethical obligations do arise from this particular case—to the wetlands or relative to the wetlands—who must face up to them? Should the developer involved consider her or his obligations, even when all official permits have been received from all relevant local and state agencies? If so, how extensive are such obligations and how much personal sacrifice must be incurred? Should the developer, after careful ethical soul-searching, seek another site that does not involve wetlands or cause other serious environmental damage? Does he or she have the responsibility to find ways to minimize the filling of wetlands, perhaps by clustering development on any upland areas that may exist on the site? And what of the ethical responsibilities of professionals involved in the project, such as architects, engineers, landscape architects, and urban planners? After all, are they not just following orders, doing whatever the developer wishes, consistent, again, with the letter of the law? Does a landscape architect have a personal or professional ethical responsibility to walk away from such a project, if he or she feels the result is in some important way immoral? On the other hand, won't the developer simply hire someone else to do the necessary design work, someone who may not be as environmentally sensitive? Perhaps it is better for the designer to continue to work on the project and to look for ways to advocate for protection of the wetlands throughout the design process.

But can't it be argued fairly convincingly that the ethical judgment should be made at a public or collective level? That is, if the project violates important moral standards, is it not the responsibility of elected and appointed officials, and public sector planners, to acknowledge this and to withhold the necessary permits? After all, the issuance of permits sends the signal to developers, architects, and others in the community that this practice is socially acceptable.

This example illustrates the fact that numerous individuals and institutions are typically involved in land-use matters, and thus there are numerous opportunities for ethical choice-making. Moreover, these multiple points of decision-making further contribute to the moral complexity of these issues. This book is about these types of ethical dilemmas, and the different moral concepts and principles that can be used to resolve them. It is surprising that such a book has not been previously written. It has always been clear to me that decisions about the use of land—where we put houses and roads, how much growth we allow in our communities, and so on—are inherently value decisions and as such involve questions of ethical choice. Just as clear, however, is the difficulty with which we have been able to acknowledge the values aspect of such decisions and to deal with these issues explicitly as ethical concerns. This book has grown out of years of interest in the value-dimension in planning and land-use matters.

I have absolutely no delusions that what follows is "philosophically profound or deep." This book is not a work of philosophy, but the "ethics" involved are not the sole concern of the philosopher. My objectives are more expository in nature. I seek to expose the reader—whether a public planner, elected official, developer, or citizen—to the various ethical dimensions and considerations that *ought* to go into land-use decisions. I undoubtedly raise many more questions than I am able to answer, but in my view this is a clearly positive result.

I do intermix my own values and perspectives into the discussions that follow, and this may be a problem for some readers. I have taken the opportunity to put forth my own, albeit preliminary, vision of what ethical land use in fact is or might be, and this is especially articulated in the final chapter. My intent here is not to stifle further debate or conflicting views, but rather to stimulate and encourage it. Furthermore, I believe that, even if some readers find my conclusions unacceptable, the discussions from which they are derived will be useful and helpful in the formulation of their own notions of appropriate land-use policy and planning.

In the book I examine a variety of ethical positions and theories. I seek to illustrate the tangible implications of these different normative positions through numerous land-use examples, both hypothetical and actual. At times legal cases are discussed, not so much to convey to the reader an understanding of legal and judicial standards, but to illustrate complex land-use issues. The reader might notice a bias in favor of examples that deal with the natural environment, wetlands, coastlines, endangered species, and the like. This reflects, to a large extent, my other research and professional interests, as well as a special sense of concern I hold about the seriousness of our environmental predicament.

The chapters generally move us in our discussion of land-use ethics from the narrow to the broad, from the traditional to the contemporary. I begin in Chapter 2 with a few more basics about the ethical framework, describing in greater detail the nature of ethical concepts and theories and how they relate to the subject of land-use policy and planning. Chapters 3–14, the bulk of the book, each deal with a particular slice of the ethical pie, with substantive categories or components of a possible set of land-use ethics. I begin in Chapter 3 with a critical review and discussion of utilitarian and market views of land use, what I believe represents the dominant moral paradigm, to the extent that one exists, in the land-use policy arena. Each subsequent chapter attempts to expand our moral horizons, and the relevant factors and moral community to which we refer in making moral judgments about land use. These chapters address the central questions identified in Chapter 1. Chapter 4 examines the obligation to prevent and minimize harm as a moral basis for land-use policy, and the principle of culpability when land-use harms are created. Chapter 5 argues that utility maximization must be fundamentally constrained by individual land-use rights—legal, constitutional, or moral rights—which may be construed as inviolable. Chapter 6 acknowledges that land-use policy can have tremendous distributive effects, and considers the different distributive obligations that can be pursued through land-use policies. Ethical obligations to the environment are discussed in detail in Chapter 7, with special consideration given to non-anthropocentric ethics (i.e., to obligations to organisms, species, and ecosystems). Thus the relevant moral community is expanded to include other forms of life than human life, to the larger biological community. The moral community is further expanded in a temporal sense in Chapter 8, considering land-use obligations to future generations.

Many land-use issues involve questions of paternalism and the ethics of placing restrictions on individual liberties. These questions are examined in Chapter 9. Chapters 10 and 11 deal with expectations that arise in land-use matters. Chapter 10 examines the extent to which obligations exist to keep land-use promises, while Chapter 11 specifically applies these issues to the consideration of the sanctity of private property and the takings issue. Chapter 12 returns somewhat to the earlier discussions of personal freedom and considers the extent to which it is ethical for communities to regulate issues involving personal lifestyle and community character.

The moral community is further expanded geographically in Chapter 13, which considers the ethical obligations that one community may owe to another. Chapter 14 considers the extent to which ethical land use requires ethical politics, and the imperatives of ensuring political equality, participation, fair representation, and so on, in land-use decision-making. Finally, Chapter 15 summarizes the book's key points and presents a succinct and tentative listing of the principles of ethical land use.

This book represents a decade of my thinking and writing on land-use ethics, and several of the chapters draw heavily from earlier articles of mine. In particular, Chapter 10 draws extensively from "The Role of Expectations and Promises in Land Use Decisionmaking," published in *Policy Sciences* (vol. 22, 1989). Chapter 15 builds heavily upon "A Set of Ethical Principles to Guide Land Use Policy," published in *Land Use Policy* (vol. 1991).

There are many individuals who are directly or indirectly responsible for the ideas in this book. Much of my initial work and thinking about land-use ethics began when I entered the doctoral program in city and regional planning at the University of North Carolina in Chapel Hill. This proved to be an extremely stimulating environment in which to think about ethical and theoretical aspects of land-use policy and planning. A number of individuals provided support and encouragement. Most significant among them were Ed Bergman, David Brower, David Godschalk, Harvy Goldstein, Ed Kaiser, and Bill Rohe. Co-teaching a land-use policy course with Bill Rohe, a substantial component of which addressed ethical issues, helped me to further frame the important questions to be addressed by this subject.

Equally influential on my thinking has been my time at the University of Virginia in Charlottesville. The UVA Department of Urban and Environmental Planning has been an extremely supportive environment, and the chapters are in no small part a result of the stimulating dialogue with students and faculty there. I wish to thank the senior faculty for encouraging my work on ethical issues, and for allowing me the great pleasure of teaching a yearly seminar on environmental ethics. Rich Collins and Bill Lucy, on the planning faculty, have been particularly encouraging.

While the ideas and formulations presented here have developed over a number of years, special thanks go to the Lincoln Institute of Land Policy, which provided a sizeable grant specifically to write this book. This grant allowed me to take leave for a semester and to push this project along in a way that would otherwise have been quite difficult. Without its financial support the book would have undoubtedly remained in a series of uncompleted pieces. Special thanks to Ben Chinitz and Ron Smith at Lincoln for their confidence and support.

Over the course of developing this book, numerous individuals have read and commented upon various parts, and I wish to thank them. Among them are Phil Berke, Dave Brower, Rich Collins, Bill Lucy, Evelyn Martin, and Frederick R. Steiner.

Many thanks are also owed to Bettie Hall who tirelessly typed numerous drafts of the book, always with a cheerful disposition. Finally I wish to thank the staff of the Johns Hopkins University Press for their tremendous help along the way. George F. Thompson, president of the Center for American Places and a publishing consultant to the Johns Hopkins University Press, in particular has offered encouragement and valuable direction at numerous points and is to be commended for seeing the potential of this type of book.

PART I

THE ETHICAL FRAMEWORK

1

LAND-USE POLICY AND
ETHICAL CHOICES

It is axiomatic that public policy decisions are inherently ethical decisions as well. When we choose between expenditures for military defense and for social programs, we clearly make ethical choices. When we decide whether a woman should be able to have an abortion, we clearly make moral and ethical decisions. When we consider the extent to which developed nations have obligations to provide money, technology, and other forms of assistance to the developing world, we are making ethical judgments. In a myriad other public policy spheres it is commonly acknowledged that public policy decisions involve an ethical or moral choice.

Such a realization has been less forthcoming in the land-use policy and planning arena. Interestingly, this is illustrated by the common failure to include land-use ethics in major textbooks and readers on ethical issues in public policy. Failure to acknowledge the inherent ethical choices involved in land-use decisions and policies is grave when one considers the number and frequency of such decisions and the cumulative influence they have on people and the environment. If ever a policy sphere ought to consider its ethical and moral underpinnings, it is land-use policy. This book is an attempt to initiate a serious consideration of the ethical nature of land-use decisions and, in the process, to put forth the author's tentative views of what comprises *ethical land use*.

The central argument of this book is that the social allocation of land to different uses and activities is fundamentally and inextricably a problem of ethics. This is so because such land-use decisions have, both individually and cumulatively, tremendous social and environmental impacts. Land-use actions can destroy important elements of the natural environment, and today land development and urban growth are major causes of the loss of such areas as wetlands, habitat for endangered species, and forestlands, among others. Development patterns have much to do with the nature and extent of pollution generated by our society—ozone and carbon monoxide in urban areas due to land-use patterns that rely unduly on the automobile, nonpoint sources of water pollution generated by impervious surfaces, loss of natural vegetation, careless construction practices, and a variety of urban and rural uses such as underground storage tanks, landfills, and agricultural operations.

Land-use practices are even at the core of many of our global environmental problems. Worldwide, the emission of CO_2 and other greenhouse gases is in no small part the result of the heavy reliance of cities on inefficient auto-oriented transportation systems and heating and cooling systems that rely on fossil-fuel energy. The loss of global biodiversity, evidenced most dramatically by the rapid deforestation and degradation of tropical forests, is largely caused by inappropriate or ineffective land-use policies. In Brazil, for instance, deforestation of the Amazon River basin has been heavily influenced by government highway and development projects, resettlement programs, and a host of fiscal and other incentives promoting cattle ranching and other destructive land uses.

Land-use decisions have tremendous social and economic implications as well. Such decisions influence the distribution of basic goods and services in the society, including access to jobs, schools, transportation, and recreation facilities, among others. Land-use decisions also influence the distribution of *bads*, or hazards and threats to health and safety, including the extent to which individuals and families are placed at risk to cancer-causing toxic waste facilities; to floods, hurricanes, earthquakes, or other natural disasters; to hazardous air and water pollutants; or to dangerous traffic and road conditions. Land-use decisions, moreover, have the capability to isolate and segregate different social and economic groups, and to influence how people view themselves and the value of their lives.

In short, land-use decisions affect the condition and quality of the natural and built environment, and the basic quality of people's lives. Land-use decisions are thus not trivial, and should be the focus of careful and deliberative thought on the part of those individuals and institutions responsible for making or influencing them. All decisions about the use of land, then, are inherently ethical judgments, inherently ethical choices. Land-use decisions and policies raise questions of right and wrong, good and bad.

Those involved in land-use decision-making must realize that ethical judgments are not optional. That is, the failure to view a land-use decision as involving ethical choice is itself a de facto form of ethical judgment. Many land-use decisions, perhaps most, are of the de facto sort, because they are defined in narrow technical, economic, or legal terms.

Who Makes Ethical Choices about Land Use?

Moral judgments about land use are ultimately made by individuals, but they can occur at different social, governmental, or institutional levels. Land-use decisions occur not only at the level of the individual property owner (for example, decisions by a farmer or rancher concerning how to use his land), but also at a public or collective level (are the farmer's plans consistent with the community's zoning ordinance?). Consequently, individuals are faced with moral judgments concerning land uses at a number of levels, and in a number of different social roles or positions. While all individuals in a democratic society are confronted by and ought to be concerned about land-use issues, certain individuals will tend to be more directly involved in such issues. Landowners make a myriad of specific decisions about the use of their land, be they farmers determining how much fertilizer and pesticide to apply or owners of forestland determining the appropriate degree of forest harvesting. Land developers make numerous and significant decisions about the size, type, and configuration of housing development projects to undertake. It is important to recognize that no matter how aggressive or sophisticated public regulations concerning land use may be, they will also be imperfect—considerable responsibility will always lie with those who will directly use or control land.

Public land-use decisions occur at many governmental and jurisdictional levels, of course. In the United States, land-use control has been heavily directed to the local level through local comprehensive plans, zoning ordinances, and such decision-making instruments as the local planning commission. A variety of local officials, from elected city council members to appointed planning commissioners to staff planners, will typically have some degree of decision-making authority over land-use decisions. In recent years land-use controls have increasingly been applied at regional and state levels. Several states, such as Oregon, New Jersey, Florida, and California, have instituted significant controls over the use of land (see DeGrove, 1984). The state of Oregon, for instance, under Senate Bill 100, requires that all local plans and implementing ordinances must satisfy a set of statewide planning goals. While localities continue to have considerable local flexibility in making land-use decisions, they must also satisfy these minimum state standards. (Under goal 14, for instance, all incorporated cities and towns in Oregon must establish urban growth boundaries in which future urban development is to be contained and directed.)

State governments have enacted an increasing variety of environmental and resource management requirements. Many states, for instance, now have stringent regulations restricting activities in tidal and nontidal wetlands. Furthermore, states have primary implementation responsibility for many federal environmental laws, such as the Clean Water Act and Clean Air Act (see Rosenbaum, 1991). As another example, large state universities are often major landholders and face a myriad of land-use decisions. This has been vividly illustrated recently by the controversy over attempts by the University of Arizona (and a consortium of other universities and groups) to build an observatory on Graham Mountain in Arizona. This proposed project would take some of the last remaining habitat for the endangered Graham Mountain red squirrel. Other private and public universities have faced similarly difficult land-use questions, including how they should grow, whether they have obligations to be responsible neighbors, whether they should respect the integrity of surrounding neighborhoods, and whether they must strive to protect affordable housing.

Significant land-use decisions are also made at the federal level. This is perhaps a more important governmental or jurisdictional level than most readers might imagine. Many specific federal laws regulate, directly or indirectly, the use of land. The federal Endangered Species Act (ESA), for instance, serves as a major constraint on development proposed in the habitat areas of listed endangered and threatened species (see Defenders of Wildlife, 1989). Under section 404 of the federal Clean Water Act, significant restrictions are placed on the discharge of dredge and fill materials into wetlands (jointly implemented by the U.S. Army Corps of Engineers and the EPA; see Conservation Foundation, 1988). In addition to these types of direct control, the federal government has exerted, and continues to exert, significant influences on land use through more indirect means, such as the U.S. tax code.

The federal government, and to a lesser extent state governments, are also major landowners themselves, especially in the west, with some 700 million acres of public lands to manage in a complex system of national forests, parks, rangelands, wildlife refuges, recreation areas, monuments, and so on. At the federal level, responsibilities for planning and managing these public lands are spread across several agencies and departments, including the U.S. Forest Service (Department of Agriculture), the Bureau of Land Management (Department of Interior), and the National Park Service (Department of Interior). Disputes and conflicts over the use of national forest lands illustrate the tremendous ethical dilemmas faced by agencies such as the Forest Service. The recent controversy over the northern spotted owl is pitting those who view these resources as necessary to protect jobs in the northwest against environmentalists and others who believe, on the other hand, that the first objective ought to be to protect the biological and ecological integrity of these forestlands. While this specific issue has yet to be decided or resolved, it is essentially a question of land-use ethics.

Some of the types of individuals facing land-use decisions are identified in table 1.1. Some of them might not obviously be viewed as having opportunities for ethical choices. Decisions about housing are usually

Table 1.1 Individuals Faced with Ethical Judgments about Land Use

Landowners and landholders

Builders and land developers

Public land-users (off-road vehicle enthusiasts, hunters, fishermen, campers, birders, hikers, among others)

Citizens and representatives of particular community interests

Elected or appointed officials (members of a city council, planning commissioner, parks and recreation manager, sewers and streets managers, among others)

Land-use professionals and resource managers

Banks and lending institutions

Homeowners and renters

Environmental and conservation groups (local, regional, and national)

made exclusively for personal and economic reasons, without considering the collective and other impacts of such decisions. The examples of housing choices that raise ethical questions are innumerable. Is it ethical for a homebuyer to purchase a home located in a floodplain? It certainly may not be sensible, but, if the homebuyer is willing to assume the risks, is it still unethical to interrupt the natural hydrological system and to transfer flooding onto other lands not previously in the floodplain? In the case of the wetlands example, first mentioned in the preface, should the homebuyer research and ensure that his or her new home is not constructed at the expense of such an irreplaceable ecosystem? In a more urban context, does a prospective homebuyer have an ethical obligation to seek a residence in a racially and economically balanced community? While these types of ethical consideration require a major transformation in the way such decisions are made (and in the way people think), it is not inconceivable in the long run that we shall progress as human beings and as a society.

The scale and magnitude of land-use decisions faced by individuals will, of course, vary depending upon personal enlightenment and social responsibility as well as the particular social and professional roles and jurisdictional level at which decisions are made. The farmer or rancher has to make decisions about the appropriate use of the land (e.g., whether to use pesticides, or whether to employ soil conservation measures), but he or she is probably not in a position to make decisions about appropriate land-use patterns at the community or county level. Planning commissioners, on the other hand, often have the opportunity to influence such broader patterns. While the ethical concepts and principles discussed in this book apply in theory with equal force and relevance to the private or public landowner, the discussion is aimed heavily at the political/governmental realm and offers the greatest help to those involved in public land-use policymaking.

Ethics and the Land Professions

Just as land-use decisions occur at a number of social, jurisdictional, and governmental levels, different types of professions are also involved in such decisions. Broadly described as the "land professions" because of their involvement in the design, management, and planning of the land, this group includes urban and regional planners, landscape architects, foresters, soil conservationists, and conservation biologists, among others. While each profession has addressed ethical issues to some extent, through its literature and professional organizations, explicit attention has been limited, though it is on the rise.

In the urban and regional planning field, there has been a clear interest in ethics (see Barrett, 1989), though little attempt to formulate clear principles or ethical standards for guiding land-use policy. The American Institute of Certified Planners (AICP) has had a professional code of conduct for many years, but it offers relatively little substantive guidance. Much of the code deals with narrower questions of professional conduct, with little mention of the ultimate objectives of planning. A broad set of standards are included, however, which lay out the planner's responsibilities to the public and which begin to identify several ethical requirements.

One subject that has received considerable attention in urban planning is equity, or social justice. Concerns about the plight and condition of the least-advantaged members of society, and the need to expand social choice, have been central tenets in the planning field. The centrality of these concerns can be seen in the AICP Code, which states, for instance, the importance of expanding choices and advancing the interests of the disadvantaged: "A planner must strive to expand choice and opportunity for all persons, recognizing a special responsibility to plan for the needs of disadvantaged groups and persons, and must urge the alteration of policies, and decisions which oppose such needs" (AICP, 1989, p. 1).

The planning literature further reflects this concern with equity and social justice (see Beatley, 1984a; Davidoff, 1975; Feld, 1986; Krumholz, 1982). Explicit concern about obligations to the environment are much less clear. Very general standards in the AICP Code do also call on the planner to "strive to protect the integrity of the natural environment," and "to endeavor to conserve the heritage of the built environment."

The American Planning Association (APA) recently adopted a supplemental set of *Ethical Principles in Planning,* but the bulk of these similarly relate to the ethics of professional practice (e.g., avoiding conflicts of interest, rendering thorough and diligent planning service, ensuring access to public planning reports and studies on an equal basis, and maintaining public confidence). Again, few of the principles deal with the substantive content or direction of public land-use policy. Those that do are relatively general and vague. These call, as well, for the expansion of "choice and opportunity" and protection of the "integrity of the natural environment and the heritage of the built environment" (APA, 1992, p. 1).

The field of landscape architecture addresses, to a somewhat greater extent, professional obligations to the environment in its code of ethics, which is somewhat more specific in its direction than the AICP Code. Specifically, the American Society of Landscape Architects (ASLA) Code and Guidelines for Professional Conduct state, among other things, that members "shall exert every effort toward the presentation and protection of our natural resources and toward understanding the interaction of the economic and social systems with these resources"; and have a responsibility to "reconcile the public's needs and the natural environment with minimal disruption to the natural system" (ASLA, no date, p. 1).

The practice and thinking of a number of ecologically oriented landscape architects, Ian McHarg in particular, are further evidence of such environmental concerns. The landscape architecture literature increasingly addresses the subject of environmental ethics, focusing especially on the concept of stewardship (see Denig, 1985; Scarfo, 1986). Ecological planning and landscape design have also received considerable attention (see Steiner, Young, and Zabe, 1988).

The fields of silviculture and forestry have also given attention in recent years to ethical obligations (see Durwald, 1987; Rolston, 1988b; Sampson, 1992). Much of this debate has been prompted by, and centered around, the need to achieve sustainable forest use (see Norse, 1990; Postel and Ryan, 1991) and to protect nontimber functions of forests, such as biodiversity (see Franklin, 1989a, 1989b). Reflecting these concerns and the manner in which national forests in the United States have been managed, a new professional organization has recently been formed— the Association of Forest Service Employees for Environmental Ethics. With a membership that includes some 2,000 U.S. Forest Service employees, its stated vision is "to forge a socially responsible value system for the Forest Service based on a land ethic which ensures ecologically and economically sustainable management" (DeBonis, 1991, p. 1).

The field of soil conservation represents an additional set of professionals exercising a potentially significant influence over the use and management of land. Soil conservationists have worked with farmers, ranchers, and other landowners through federal, state, and local programs (e.g., soil conservation districts) to minimize erosive agricultural practices and to promote more sustainable approaches to farming. The soil conservation literature has, in recent years, been showing signs of a heightened concern to find a new ethic for relating to the land which would further support and defend such practices (e.g., Berry, 1991; Busby, 1990; Collins, 1991; Giltmier, 1990; Little, 1987; Meine, 1987; Steiner, 1991). Some discussions of ethical issues can also be found in other resource management areas, including fisheries management (Callicott, 1991) and conservation biology (Callicott, 1990; Salwasser, 1990), among others.

Many of the land professions, while only in recent years addressing questions of substantive land-use ethics, have in the past paid considerable attention to traditional "professional ethics," as we have already noted for urban and regional planning (Howe, 1980; Howe and Kaufman, 1979; Marcuse, 1976). Traditional professional ethics have largely to do with more various questions of the conduct and behavior of the professional. These issues, dealing with fairly narrow questions of practice and conduct, are heavily addressed in the professional codes. They relate to such things as the appropriate fees to charge; issues of client confidentiality; the ethics of lying, distorting, or otherwise failing to tell the complete truth. These ethical questions about professional behavior, while important, are not addressed in this book except as they relate to land use.

It is important to emphasize, though, that the connection between professional conduct and land-use ethics is often direct. Whether one believes certain types of professional conduct are ethical may depend largely on what one believes about the substantive land-use values being advanced. A local environmental planner may feel that distorting information about the potential impacts of a housing project on the water quality of a nearby river may be justified if this action results in a rallying of public opposition to stop the project. The planner's beliefs about what constitutes ethical land use—that there is an important ethical obligation to protect this pristine riverine ecosystem—may influence his or her beliefs about the ethics of professional practice. Others may, of course, believe that no matter how noble or worthy the end might be (i.e., the substantive land-use ethics), it can never justify compromising one's professional standards. (Let's hope they are in the majority.) Examples of situations where beliefs about land-use ethics can influence professional practice are innumerable. If a local public administrator, for instance, believes strongly that there is a basic right to minimum shelter, she may feel justified in doing all she can in her official capacity to support the candidacy of a mayor who has campaigned on a prohousing platform. Many might feel that such politicking by a public employee is inappropriate, but again if the ends are deemed sufficiently important, a violation or bending of professional rules of conduct may appear acceptable.

Empirical evidence suggests the importance of this link. In Howe and Kaufman's (1979) survey of the ethics of planners, they found that respondents were more likely to support a particular tactic or action (e.g., giving out draft recommendations of a plan) when the beneficiaries are environmental groups than when the beneficiaries are representatives of white homeowner groups or land developers (p. 247). The moral acceptability of certain professional practices, then, is influenced by the merits of the issue or cause being supported by such actions.

Theoretical Underpinnings of Land-Use Ethics

The subject of land-use ethics is a relatively new one. Although planners and other professionals involved in land-use matters have recognized the ethical nature and importance of land-use decisions for some time, there has been relatively little specific thought or writing in this area by either practitioners or academics. This lack gives me considerable freedom to construct an appropriate theoretical framework, appropriate terminology, and so on. I hope that this and subsequent work will help to solidify and establish the subject of land-use ethics as a practical and theoretically distinct area of knowledge and thought. I tentatively define land-use ethics, in a general way, as the study of the ethical and moral bases of actions and policies intended to influence the use and management of land and land resources.

There is a relatively small and undeveloped literature in the area of land-use ethics. The need for a land ethic has, of course, been cited for a number of decades, with relatively little work until recently on what such an ethic should consist of and what sort of theoretical and moral bases it might have. Aldo Leopold is often given credit for beginning in earnest the discussion of the land ethic, in an essay in his pioneering *A Sand County Almanac* (1949). There he issued this now famous admonition: "quit thinking about decent land-use as solely an economic problem. Examine each question in terms of what is ethically and esthetically right, as well as what is economically expedient. *A thing is right when it tends to preserve the integrity, stability, and beauty of the biotic community. It is wrong when it tends otherwise*" (pp. 224–25, emphasis added).

Leopold's vision was a strong one, suggesting the need to consider the ecological limits and characteristics of the land when using and managing it, and to consider human beings as but one member of a larger ecological community. Since Leopold's "The Land Ethic" was first published, he has been frequently cited in land-use literature and debates, and there have been many attempts to expand on Leopold's vision, which I examine more fully in subsequent chapters (see Callicott, 1989; Little, 1992; McHarg, 1969; North Carolina Land Stewardship Council, no date; Piedmont Environmental Council, 1981).

While such attempts at expounding the more specific elements and dimensions of a land-use ethic are to be commended, it is clear that they alone have been unable to take us very far, especially in terms of policy. A land-use ethic, or set of ethics, must be a tremendously broad thing; it must find application in resource and natural system settings (e.g., in the consideration of the appropriate use of wetlands or sensitive beach and dune areas) as well as more urban and highly developed areas (e.g., whether to permit a high-rise structure in a predominantly low-density residential area). It must often apply in circumstances where there are combinations of urban and resource conflicts (e.g., whether to permit new urban development in a region of prime agricultural land). Proposed land-use ethics are often not broad enough to encompass these different settings, and certainly not in a way which is in some sense unifying. The chapters that follow seek to elucidate and develop a body of normative theory—land-use ethics—which will seem familiar and applicable both to the rural environmental planner and the urban councilperson or policy analyst.

Recent efforts at espousing a set of land-use ethics can also be criticized on the grounds that they are not tied in any clear or direct way to specific moral theories or concepts that will help to both defend and justify them, and that will provide them with greater substantive meaning. An ethic or set of ethics may incorporate exhortations and encouragements (e.g., "Treat the land with respect"), but without a strong theoretical underpinning such statements will be questioned, and indeed should be. There must be morally rich theories and concepts to back up such exhortations. In this book I draw from a variety of theoretical areas and disciplines, including moral philosophy, economics, political science, and law. One area that offers particularly promising insights for land-use policy is the burgeoning topic of environmental ethics. The literature and discourse in this philosophical subdiscipline has become increasingly rich and fertile, and I have drawn heavily from it in developing a set of land-use ethics (see Attfield, 1983; Evernden, 1985; Oelschlaeger, 1991; Regan, 1984; Rolston, 1988a; Shepard, 1973, 1991; Stone, 1987; Taylor, 1986; and Van DeVeer and Pierce, 1986; this literature is examined more fully in Chap. 7).

Another criticism of past efforts at constructing a land-use ethic, as well as a criticism of the recent efforts in the area of environmental ethics, is that they are often presented at such a general level that their practical meaning is vague. What does it mean in a specific policy context to say, for instance, that land-use decisions must protect the interests of the least-advantaged members of society, or that land-use decisions must protect the integrity of a natural system, or must protect the rights and interests of future generations? I shall seek to overcome these problems through the use of specific land-use policy examples that will serve as focal points for ethical analysis and discussion.

Consequently, this book is necessarily eclectic and synthetic, drawing heavily upon the theories and concepts of a number of different disciplines. In particular I have drawn extensively from these: traditional ethics and moral philosophy (that branch of philosophy examining values, and questions of right and wrong); political philosophy (theories and concepts examining the forms of governance, relationships between the individual and the state); legal theory and ethics (the role of law in society, judicial theory used in resolving conflicts); and the relatively new, yet burgeoning, area of environmental ethics (or the examination of moral obligations to, or relative to, the natural environment).

Like traditional moral philosophy, land-use ethics deals with such concepts as obligations, rights and duties, social justice, and virtue. It deals primarily with matters of *ought,* rather than what *is.* It questions how we ought to act; how we ought to behave. It assumes, undoubtedly a debatable assumption in the minds of some, that as individuals we have the capacity to reason and contemplate, to engage in moral judgment, and in turn to be able to modify our decisions and behaviors according to the outcomes of such judgments. As human beings we can be said to be duty-bound; we can be said to have the capacity to be morally responsible. Exactly what constitutes morally responsible land-use decision-making is, of course, the major subject of this book, and my conclusions will obviously be open to considerable disagreement. Not everyone agrees, for instance, that the land has equal value to human existence.

Central Questions in Land-Use Ethics

There are a number of critical moral and ethical questions that emerge in the land-use policy arena and are explored in the chapters to follow. My discussion focuses on four questions in particular: (1) What is the extent of the moral community to which ethical consideration in land-use matters is due? (2) What are the extent and nature of the ethical obligations owed to members of this moral community? (3) What are the moral grounds or bases on which to defend or justify these moral positions? (4) How should we go about making decisions about the land and land use?

Defining the Relevant Moral Community

To resolve dilemmas about land-use policy it is important to determine what the relevant moral community is. There are at least three dimensions to this question. The first is *geographical.* Are we, on the one hand, obligated to consider the effects of a land-use decision or policy on the immediate neighborhood or community? Or should we consider the interests and well-being of broader publics—say, of the residents of the surrounding region, state, or nation? Perhaps we even have an obligation to consider the impacts of certain land-use decisions on the planet as a whole, as in the case of the cumulative impacts of fossil-fuel reliance in promoting global air and water pollution.

A second dimension to this question is *temporal*. Many land-use decisions and policies clearly have impacts that extend into the future. In considering whether to allow the destruction or degradation of some natural landscape, are we obligated to consider only the interests of the present human population? Or do we have an obligation to consider a much longer time frame, to factor into our moral calculations the effects of such an action on future generations? One might argue that, while a particular natural landscape is of little importance to the present generation, it will be important to future generations. But if there indeed are such intertemporal obligations, how far into the future must we (indeed, can we) consider? Fifty years? One hundred years? Five hundred years? Maybe a thousand years? The Amerindians often spoke of seven generations. Conservationists usually speak of our grandchildren's future.

A third dimension to the question of how to determine the relevant moral community is *biological*. Must we, when making land-use decisions, consider the interest and well-being of other forms of life? Some have argued that, morally, our only obligations extend to *Homo sapiens,* while others suggest that certain ethical obligations extend to all sentient life-forms. Still others argue that the moral community must include all forms of life, sentient and nonsentient alike, and that land-use and other societal decisions must reflect a certain level of ethical respect for this life.

The Ethical Obligations

Once conclusions are reached about the extent and parameters of the moral community, the question then becomes, What are the actual ethical obligations owed to the various members of this moral community? There are numerous ethical principles, standards, and concepts that have been considered and argued for in areas such as moral philosophy and environmental ethics. Is our moral obligation to decide land-use policy dilemmas through the use of utilitarian and economic concepts—choosing those policies or actions which maximize social utility? Or do we have moral obligations that extend beyond economical utilitarian efficiency? Leopold (1949) and Little (1992) clearly argue for aesthetics, for beauty and community. Do we have obligations to prevent actions and policies that impose harms on individuals and their community? Do we have obligations to protect and promote the *rights* of individuals, regardless of how economically inefficient the result may be? Do we have obligations to keep our promises?

The Moral Grounds of Our Ethical Standards

This question of defining the moral grounds that support our ethical standards is sometimes described as *metaethics* or *critical ethics,* and it involves the reasoning and methodology employed to arrive at and defend an ethical theory or principle. Do we seek to derive and defend ethical principles by reverting, for example, to some theoretical neutral point (what John Rawls [1971] describes as the "original position") where individuals agree to such principles in the absence of specific biasing information about their own personal life circumstances? Or do we defend and argue for ethical principles on the basis that they are intuitively pleasing to us— that is, they seem to satisfy our personal and collective sense of what is right and wrong? Defending and justifying ethical concepts remain controversial and contentious in philosophical circles, and I devote less attention to the question of metaethics than to the other categories of questions. Those involved in discourse about ethical land use will undoubtedly be called upon from time to time to defend their positions, and they should at least be aware of the importance of these issues.

Making Decisions about the Land and Land Use

It is at the stage of making decisions about land use that actual discourse about alternative ethical standards and concepts, and their implication for land-use policy, typically occurs. Several questions arise here, many revolving around alternative notions of what constitutes a democratic process for land-use decision-making. Questions include these: What is the correct role to be played by citizens in the land-use decision-making process (e.g., direct decision-making, as through referenda and public participation)? Must all individuals affected by land-use decisions be involved in the decision-making process? What theory of representation should elected officials involved in land-use matters adhere to?

Much in this book is an exposition and elaboration of these important questions. I examine in considerable detail alternative approaches to defining the moral community, and the variety of specific ethical and moral concepts and principles that can be embraced in deciding land-use policy issues.

The Relationship between What Is Ethical and What Is Legal

The relationship between ethics and the law will come into question at a number of points in this book, and I briefly attempt to clarify here my view of this relationship. For the casual observer, ethics and legality seem to be synonymous. Indeed, the nightly television news is replete with statements by public officials (e.g., congressmen or cabinet members) that some action or other is "not against the law." Not breaking a law is often tendered as a moral or ethical defense for a particular cause of action. My discussion assumes that ethics and legality are, in fact, clearly not synonymous; indeed, they are distinct from each other in important ways. First, what is legal is not necessarily ethical in the land-use arena. Historically, government control or regulation in the United States has been minimal and has often been aimed at curtailing only the most blatant and repulsive land-use practices. While federal and state regulations substantially regulate development in sensitive wetlands, for instance, they clearly do not prevent development, and estimates are that we continue to lose some several hundred thousand acres of natural wetlands yearly, as a nation. To many, the destruction of natural wetlands is morally and ethically wrong, despite its being legally permissible. Thus, what is *ethical* land-use may indeed conflict with what is *legal* land-use. Moreover, I do not assume that what is required or mandated through the passage of certain laws or through court interpretations of constitutions or laws is necessarily ethical. For instance, while the U.S. Supreme Court may have established certain principles that apply in resolving so-called takings cases (cases in which public regulation of land is said to be so onerous as to require just compensation), I will not be bound by these cases in examining what comprises an ethically just relationship between private property and public regulation. My position reflects the reality that laws and legal opinions change over time, and I hope the ethical discussion that follows will inform the legislative and judicial process.

On the other hand, I do believe that there is, in general, an a priori ethical obligation to respect and obey land-use laws. Short of extraordinary circumstances, there is a moral duty to abide by existing collective rules. Recent examples illustrate how existing rules can be violated and how the legitimate social sanctions can be imposed. Considerable attention, for example, has been given in the media in recent years to criminal convictions of landowners who have illegally filled wetlands (i.e., without approval from the U.S. Army Corps of Engineers). The laws were clear, and landowners wrongly and willfully violated the land-use rules established by society. Ethical land use requires that such rules be followed and, when they are not, society has the right and obligation to impose appropriate penalties.

The Assumption of Moral Pluralism

This book is intended to provide both a theoretical and a practical view. On the one hand I include a thorough examination of the alternative ethical theories, concepts, and principles that can form the basis of land-use decisions. On the other hand, I have provided these conceptual and theoretical bases in the context of tangible and specific land-use conflicts or questions. I have made considerable use throughout the book of actual or hypothetical land-use scenarios which more effectively highlight the nature of land-use decisions and how particular ethical concepts or principles might apply in these practical situations. In this way what follows can be considered applied ethics in its focus on action and policy.

Unlike other books about ethics, I do not embrace or argue for a single ethical viewpoint or paradigm. Some authors seek to take utilitarianism or variations on Rawlsian contract theory and to argue that these grand and unified theories can guide us effectively in resolving almost any ethical quandary. I believe that land-use circumstances and ethical dilemmas are too varied and complex to lend themselves to resolution through such unified approaches. Rather, different situations call into play different subsets of ethical concepts and principles. Thus, I assume a kind of moral pluralism, which suggests that no single paradigm is applicable in all circumstances. Indeed, I seek to lay out and describe critically the ethical terrain—the various possible components of a set of land-use ethics, including aesthetics. Whether particular components of this ethical terrain will be determinitive depends on the specifics of each land-use case.

This work also differs from some ethical treatises in my unwillingness to construct extremely specific ethical rules and standards. While the discussions here will take us much further than much of the earlier work in the area of land-use ethics (e.g., Leopold's very general exhortations), they fall short (intentionally) of laying out a set of detailed operational standards for resolving specific land-use conflicts. The complexity of such an undertaking is beyond this book. Moreover, in many ways it is too early in the development of the theory of land-use ethics for such an endeavor. What follows from each of the chapters is a set of ethical orientations, rather than a detailed set of operational standards. I hope these orientations will provide readers with substantial direction in making ethical judgments about land use, albeit without a detailed blueprint for how to behave in every situation.

I should note that, while the ethical orientations—or ethical principles—summarized at the conclusion of each chapter are my own personal statements, there is no assumption or expectation that they will be embraced wholly by all readers. On the contrary, readers should critically consider the issues and the tangible illustrations and reach their own conclusions. Indeed, my primary purpose with this book is to stimulate debate and contemplation about an important but largely ignored area. Over the course of each chapter I attempt to summarize the major theories and points of view, and even if the reader disagrees with my conclusions, he or she should receive substantial fodder for the intellectual mill.

2

THE NATURE OF ETHICAL
DISCOURSE ABOUT LAND USE

Before we discuss specific ethical theories and positions with relevance to land-use policy, it is important to establish an understanding of
the basic theoretical framework in which these subsequent discussions
will occur. What are land-use values and where do they originate? Are
there differences between land values and attitudes about the land? Are
principles or theories of environmental ethics different than environmental values and attitudes? Are there basic or fundamental ways of
classifying or categorizing the ethical principles and positions which will
be discussed in considerable detail in later chapters? In this chapter I
briefly discuss the nature of ethics, ethical principles, and the alternative
moral grounds available to defend one's ethical position.

An initial distinction of some importance is between *values* and *attitudes* about land and land use, and land-use *ethics*. Rokeach (1968) defines
a value as "an enduring belief that a specific mode of conduct or end-state
of existence is personally or socially preferable to an opposite or converse
mode of conduct or end-state of existence." He goes on to distinguish
between instrumental values (such as honesty, responsibility, and courage) and terminal values (such as freedom, equality, and inner harmony).
Many of these fundamental values influence significantly one's views
about ethical land use. Strong values concerning personal freedom may
suggest the unacceptability of certain government restrictions on what
individuals can do with their land. Strong views about equality, on the
other hand, might translate into support for redistributive objectives in
land-use policy. Moreover, we can identify a number of land-use values—
that is, fundamentally held personal values concerning land and the use
of land. For example, one may feel deeply that rivers, wetlands, and
wildlife habitat ought to be preserved for posterity. This position can be
described as a land-use value that is held by an individual or group of
individuals (see also Tuan, 1974).

There are subtle but important distinctions between land-use *values*
and land-use *ethics*. Ethics involves making and defending moral choices.
Ethics generally, and land-use ethics here, assumes that individuals have

the capacity to examine critically their current values and attitudes—and to examine their consistency and their defensibility. Moreover, ethics is the process by which values are applied to decision-making, and consequently is not static but dynamic. Values can be empirically described ("He believes . . . ," "She feels . . ."), but ethics is the broader endeavor of applying, testing, and critically examining these values in the public arena.

The term *attitudes* is sometimes used to describe what people think about particular things. Attitudes are usually thought to be more specific and numerous (compared with values) and not as central or "core" to an individual's belief system. The 1986 Urban Land Institute "It's Your Land" national public poll, for example, uncovered a number of specific land-use attitudes (Urban Land Institute, 1986). For instance, a majority of respondents indicated support for government subsidies for such programs as mass transit, low-income housing, and the preservation of farmland and open space. While these land-use positions express people's specific moral inclinations, they usually derive from deeper, more fundamental values. While it is helpful to know that one supports subsidies for low-income housing, what is the underlying reason or moral argument for such a position? Is it because one feels that all individuals have an inviolable right to minimum decent housing? Is it, rather, because one feels that such minimum goals are necessary to facilitate national economic growth and productivity (e.g., we will have a more productive society, less unemployment, and better communities, only if we satisfy such basic human conditions)?

It is important to remember the classic distinction between fact and value, between ought and is. Many attitudinal expressions are actually expressions of factual or empirical understanding, and are perhaps better described as *beliefs*. An individual in a public land-use debate might make the statement, "I believe you have the right to do whatever you wish with your land." This statement, without further exploring its meaning with the individual who makes it, could be either a factual or value statement. On the one hand, the individual might intend to express the value that the government *ought* not to interfere with a property owner; that by virtue of one's ownership of land one ought to be free to use it as he or she wishes. On the other hand, the individual could intend to express a factual or empirical assessment—namely, that under our existing legal system a property owner *has* certain legal rights to do with land what he or she wishes (a clearly false impression, I might add).

Most ethical judgments about land and land use involve a commingling of fact and value. Let's go back, for example, to the view held by some individuals that public subsidies ought to be provided—say, in the form of preferential tax assessment—to preserve farmland and open space.

Two individuals can disagree with such a position for different reasons, one factual, the other normative. One individual may simply question the premise that such lands ought to be protected, believing, for example, that members of society have no moral right to the visual and other enjoyment of such areas. Another individual may believe strongly that an ethical obligation exists to preserve such areas, but believes as a fact that adopting preferential tax assessment will be ineffective at advancing this social goal or value. It is important in land-use debates to keep factual and normative distinctions in mind.

Sources of Land-Use Values

Particular values, land-use values included, can be attributed to many sources, including parents and family, church, school, publications and the media, and political organizations. Research suggests, for instance, that parents influence to a considerable extent the political views and social outlooks of their offspring (see Dawson et al., 1977). And, clearly, one's basic political and social views will, in turn, influence one's views about ethical land use.

There is also considerable validity to the old saying that where you stand depends upon where you sit. One's values and attitudes about land use may be greatly shaped by the social and economic positions in society that one holds, and by one's source of employment. If one's livelihood depends upon harvesting and milling old-growth timber, one is probably less likely to hold the view that such timberlands ought to be protected or set aside in perpetuity. If one is employed by the oil industry, one is less likely to support additional wilderness protection of those areas known to possess oil and natural gas reserves. Of course, many of these positions might be described more appropriately as attitudes rather than values, but nevertheless employment and economic and social position clearly influence perceptions about what constitutes ethical land use.

Where you stand may also depend on where you pray. One's outlook on the world is heavily influenced by religious upbringing. The Judeo-Christian tradition, for instance, has been implicated in condoning and promoting exploitative attitudes toward nature. Genesis tells us that God made man in His own image and gave him dominion over all other plants and animals. It does appear that Christianity supports a sharp distinction between human beings and the rest of nature. In Lynn White's (1967, p. 1205) words: "Man named all the animals, thus establishing his dominance over them. God planned all of this explicitly for man's benefit and rule: no item in the physical creation had any purpose save to serve man's purposes . . . especially in its western form, Christianity is the most anthropocentric religion the world has seen." While in recent years there has been a trend toward focusing on the stewardship implied in Christian doctrine (see Berry, 1981; Denig, 1985; Nash, 1989; Cal DeWitt at the University of Wisconsin at Madison is also a leading proponent of this view), there is little doubt that, historically, Christian thinking has promoted a more exploitative view of land than eastern religions, such as Taoism, Shinto, and Zen Buddhism, which hold a more organic view of the world, without the sharp separation between human beings and nature. Eastern religions attach a sanctity and reverence for other forms of life and nature typically missing in the western view; there is greater emphasis on harmony. Amerindians have traditionally embraced a similar view, in which human beings are not separate from nature, but rather part of a larger unity of life. Consequently, they have had fundamentally different attitudes about land use, viewing land as something to be used temporarily and passed along to future inhabitants (at least until recently, when some tribes are split over conservation versus exploitation). Religious doctrine and religious upbringing, then, may significantly influence one's land-use values.

Where you stand may also depend upon where you live. In the United States there are clearly different spatial patterns of values and attitudes. Political scientists have often studied and described this phenomenon under the heading of *political culture*. Political culture is defined by Daniel Elazar (1972) as "the particular pattern of orientation to political action in which each political system is imbedded" (pp. 84–85). Elazar has identified three primary political cultures prevalent in the United States: the individualistic, moralistic, and traditionalistic. The *individualistic* political culture sees government primarily as a utilitarian mechanism through which it seeks to satisfy only those functions explicitly demanded by the people. This culture places importance on limiting intervention into the private sector. "In general, government action is to be restricted to those areas, primarily in the economic realm, which encourage private initiative and widespread access to the marketplace" (p. 94). The *moralistic* political culture, on the other hand, takes a collectivist view in which politics is seen as "a public activity centered on some notion of the public good and properly devoted to the advancement of the public interest. Good government, then, is measured by the degree to which it promotes the public good and in terms of the honesty, selflessness, and commitment to the public welfare of those who govern" (pp. 96–97). The well-being of the community or collective appears to take precedence over individualism. Finally, the *traditionalistic* political culture reflects a more elitist view of government in which one accepts and seeks to maintain the prevailing social order.

Elazar has used these three cultures, and different groups of cultural tendencies, to classify different states and regions. While the dominant political cultures in the South tend to be traditionalistic, the dominant view in New England states tends to be moralistic. While southern states such as Texas and Oklahoma tend to be traditionalistic/individualistic, western states such as Oregon and California are characterized as more moralistic and moralistic/individualistic. These differences in political culture, then, can be seen to create regional variations in the perception of ethical land use. It is clear that what might be perceived as appropriate and acceptable land use in one state may not be equally acceptable in other states. Geographical differences clearly have attitudinal and normative implications (see Zelinsky, 1973), although one must always be very careful in asserting such generalizations about states and regions.

Acknowledging the importance of these different influences on the formation of values and attitudes does not, however, lead us to the conclusion that land-use ethics is simply the task of tallying up different values and normative positions and then organizing land-use policy accordingly. It is my assumption that values and ethical positions about land use can change in response both to public dialogue and argument, and to private thought and reflection. I also assume that individuals are confronted with moral choices and judgments.

The Right and the Good in Land-Use Policy

An important way to look at values in land use is to distinguish between the *right* and the *good*—a distinction common in traditional moral philosophy (see Feinberg, 1973; Frankena, 1973; Moore, 1903; Ross, 1930). At an individual level, the good represents those things in life that a person desires and perceives as important—those things that constitute for the individual a productive and satisfying existence. They may include spiritual enlightenment, or a high-paying job, or more materialistic things such as the possession of a pink Cadillac, or a house on the beach with a pool and 4½ bathrooms. Land-use policies have largely to do with advancing various aspects and conceptions of the individual good, whether the protection of scenic resources, or personal mobility, or the promotion of a sense of neighborhood and belonging.

While traditional liberal theory views individual conceptions of the good as largely sacred (i.e., it is up to the individual to decide what a good life is), however, merely because one desires something does not ensure its moral correctness, or ensure that society should permit or encourage its pursuit. (By traditional liberal theory I refer broadly to those political philosophies that stress the interests and freedoms of the individual, and the need to refrain from collective interference with these.) One's conception of the personal good may entail the construction of a home or shopping center on marshland, as in our earlier example, yet collective

Table 2.1 Different Values in Land-Use Policy

Examples of the *Good*	Examples of the *Right*
Private: A comfortable home and satisfying family life	Keeping a promise to a neighboring landowner
Public: Aesthetically pleasing and efficient spatial patterns	Maximizing the welfare of worst-off members of society

conceptions of the right may constrain or prohibit the advancement of this value (for a host of possible reasons).

Thus there are public as well as private dimensions to this distinction. Public and collective bodies express moral beliefs and obligations about what is right, as do individuals. Important land-use values can be found in each of these categories (see table 2.1). For instance, the sort of house design a community finds attractive will obviously influence housing demand and the type of growth and land-use policies induced by this demand. If we extend notions of the good to a more collective level, we see that the community and its officials may express a priority for compact and contiguous forms of development, and perhaps a more concentrated and pedestrian-oriented downtown area. Values of the individual right are also clearly important. Does one landowner, for instance, owe to the public (however it is defined) an obligation to use his or her land in ways which are not wasteful or ugly? The final category, values of the collective or public right, entails fundamental questions of how and by which moral standards collective bodies mediate and decide between competing social claims exhibited in land-use policy debates.

Clearly these categories are interrelated and not amenable to sharp distinction. For example, an individual's desire for a certain standard and quality of housing (personal good) may as well constitute what the public feels is deserved by every individual (collective right). The distinction between the public and private good is particularly tenuous, as the former is largely an aggregation of the latter. There are some authors, however, who have suggested that the public good is somehow separate from or transcendent to the individual good (e.g., the organismic theory of the public interest; see Meyerson and Banfield, 1955). What follows deals largely with those different aspects or dimensions of the public right.

Teleological and Deontological Principles

We now come to an important distinction in moral philosophy between teleological and deontological principles. As Frankena notes:

A teleological theory says that the basic or ultimate criterion or standard of what is morally right, wrong, obligatory, etc., is the nonmoral value that is brought into being. The final appeal, directly or indirectly, must be to the comparative amount of good produced, or rather to the comparative balance of good over evil.

Thus an act is *right* if and only if it or the rule under which it falls produces, will probably produce, or is intended to produce *at least as great a balance of good over evil* as any available alternative; an act is *wrong* if and only if it does not do so. An act *ought to be done* if and only if it or the rule under which it falls produces, will probably produce, or is intended to produce *a greater balance of good over evil* than any available alternative. (Frankena, 1973, p. 14)

Thus, under a teleological theory (deriving from the Greek word *telos*, meaning *end* or *goal*), the correct land-use policy or action is the one that generates the greatest quantity of value. To reiterate, what is right is what will maximize what is good. But whose good is to be maximized? In philosophy two major forms of teleological theory have emerged: ethical egoism and utilitarianism (sometimes called ethical universalism). Ethical egoism holds that the morally correct action is the one that maximizes value for that particular individual. Utilitarianism applies this maximization of good to a collective or societal level. Much of our contemporary land-use policy is explicitly founded on utilitarian ethics (this theory and its assumptions are explored more fully in Chapter 3).

In contrast to teleological principles are those which are described as deontological. Derived from the Greek word *Deont*, which means "that which is duty or is binding," the deontologist rejects the assumption that the morally correct action or policy is necessarily the one that maximizes the good. "They assert that there are other considerations that may make an action or rule right or obligatory besides the goodness or badness of its consequences—certain features of the act itself other than the *value* it brings into existence, for example, the fact that it keeps a promise, is just, or is commanded by God or by the State" (Frankena, 1973, p. 15). One's specific moral standard may require a particular action or policy even where the consequence is a much lower amount or quantity of societal good or value. Many of the ethical theories and principles described in later chapters are deontological in nature (see fig. 2.1). Indeed, land-use policy has historically been inappropriately driven by a relatively narrow utilitarian/market failure theory of what is morally correct.

Disagreements over land-use policy have often been the result of clashes between teleological and deontological views, although the holders of these positions would not likely describe them in these terms. Let us consider an example to highlight the differences. Consider, for instance,

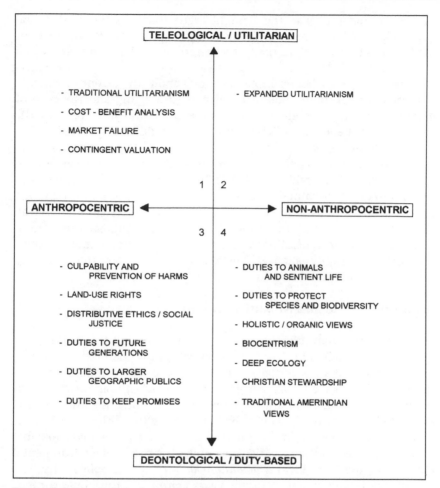

Figure 2.1 Moral theories and land-use positions.

a proposal to rezone a parcel of land located in a residential district, which would permit the operation of a small grocery store. The teleologist (utilitarian) would evaluate the ethical merits of this proposal by calculating the net benefits to the community of this new use. If such a change would generate more benefits than costs, that zoning change would be justified. On the other hand, assume that a neighboring homeowner, who would bear a disproportionately large portion of the negative effects of such a use (in the form of noise, light pollution, traffic, and vagrancy), feels betrayed by such a proposal. He recently bought his adjacent home with the understanding from the city (which, thankfully, he obtained in writing) that no such uses would ever be permitted in the future. The deontologist, then, might argue that it is the city's moral duty to keep its promise to the homeowner, regardless of the quantity of the benefits that would accrue to the neighborhood or community as a whole.

Consider as a further example questions about the extent to which a state or national forest should be opened to logging, and the type of harvesting permitted there. If clear-cut logging is shown to generate the greatest social benefits, the teleologist would argue that opening the forest for such uses is the morally correct result. But in this case as well there may be other moral standards of relevance. Perhaps we believe, for instance, that each individual ought to be given the right to experience such forests in their natural state, and that we have obligations to protect the many species of wildlife that depend on this ecosystem for survival. Perhaps we believe we have a moral obligation to protect this natural heritage for future generations and should thus mandate more sustainable forest harvesting practices. The teleological and deontological positions in this land-use dilemma would be quite different.

Anthropocentric and Nonanthropocentric Theories

Another important dimension upon which many of the ethical positions to be considered in later chapters will fall is the extent to which moral obligations are *anthropocentric*—that is, human or human-centered (sometimes also called *homocentric*). Conventional utilitarianism in general strongly assumes an anthropocentric view. The costs and benefits associated with particular land-use proposals are those that affect or accrue to human beings. On the other hand, there has been considerable theorizing in recent years, particularly under the rubric of environmental ethics, that there are various *nonanthropocentric* moral obligations. The animal rights movement in recent years epitomizes the nonanthropocentric view. Animals are owed obligations, not because they are necessarily the property of other humans, but rather because they have certain inherent rights. Some philosophers, notably Peter Singer, have argued that conventional utilitarianism ought to be expanded morally to consider the interests (e.g., the pleasure and pain) of sentient (feeling, conscious) animals in carrying out utility aggregations. To do otherwise, Singer argues, is to be morally arbitrary (see Singer, 1985).

Leopold's land ethic, espoused first in 1933 in the *Journal of Forestry* and later in his *Sand County Almanac* (1949), did much to promote the view that other nonhuman things and beings might be owed ethical obligations. Under Leopold's view a person is merely a "plain member," rather than a conqueror, of the larger biotic community. As members of this community we owe it certain moral obligations of respect. Other more contemporary environmental ethicists, such as Paul Taylor (1986), have expanded this notion considerably, arguing that all forms of life have a good of their own and thus have inherent worth regardless of whether humans place value on them.

Whether our moral obligations are anthropocentric or extend into the nonanthropocentric realm holds considerable implication for land-use policy. Do we owe obligations to other forms of life, and if so, to which ones? Do we owe obligations only to sentient (feeling) life-forms, or only to those life-forms with relatively high levels of intelligence? Instead of obligations to individual organisms, do we owe obligations to broader categories of life—perhaps species? Do we have ethical obligations, as some have argued, to the broader ecosystem or ecological community, again irrespective of the value it might hold for human beings? Who speaks for the land?

This issue can be restated in terms of what can be said to be of value in the world. Things in the world might be said to have three types of value: what I will call *instrumental* value, *intrinsic* value, and *inherent* worth (adapted from Hare, 1987). The first two values are anthropocentric, because they rely on people to express desires and preferences about something. A forest might be said to have both an instrumental value and an intrinsic value to humans. The instrumental value a forest holds might be found in the ability to harvest trees selectively (i.e., conservatively) and use them to satisfy a variety of human needs for building supplies, furniture, or firewood. The forest might also hold intrinsic value to humans— that is, it might have value to us as a forest, perhaps because we enjoy seeing and experiencing the forest, camping and hiking in it, and because seeing it provides us with some valued connection to nature. The notion of inherent worth argues that, irrespective of the value the forest might hold for humans (either instrumentally or intrinsically), it may have an inherent value—a value that is derived not from humans, but because the forest is a living organism, with a good of its own. (I am not taking on here the debate of tree plantations versus a forest.)

These two major ethical dimensions are combined in figure 2.1 to create a useful framework for categorizing the moral theories and positions about land use which will be discussed in subsequent chapters of this book. Anthropocentric-based theories, then, fall into quadrants 1 and 3; nonanthropocentric positions in quadrants 2 and 4. Teleological or utilitarian theories, on the other hand, fall into quadrants 1 and 2; deontological or duty-based theories in quadrants 3 and 4. While there are undoubtedly numerous other axes or moral dimensions against which ethical positions can be classified, these are two of the more important that are addressed in this book. For the purposes of illustration only, I place several specific moral theories and concepts in particular quadrants. The reader should note that I make no attempt to prioritize or rank these different ethical positions within each quadrant.

Neutrality and Reflective Equilibrium

While an understanding of how different social, economic, and other factors provides us with insight into the sources of land-use values and attitudes, these factors also suggest that, from a moral point of view, our judgments in making land-use decisions might at times be inappropriately biased, especially as a result of our specific personal circumstances. In the earlier example about how best to use a state or national forest, will individuals not be swayed in their judgment by the impact that decisions will likely have on their employment or livelihood? Setting forested areas aside to support recreational and wildlife values, or imposing selective harvest practices, for instance, may serve to reduce employment in the logging sector (at least in the short term). If one depends on the logging sector for employment, it is less likely that he or she will support such practices, despite their defensibility on other grounds (e.g., to protect endangered species, to protect the interests of future generations). Similarly, a person's judgment about the ethical merits of locating new low-income housing will tend to be influenced by the knowledge that such housing may be sited in their own neighborhood, or even next door. While individuals might otherwise believe strongly in the moral imperative of society providing affordable housing, knowledge of possible personal harm (e.g., peceived or actual reductions in property values) can serve to bias determinations of what ethical land use requires.

These types of personal factors might be seen as jeopardizing a person's ability to arrive at fair and impartial ethical judgments. While in a practical sense it is impossible to extract oneself from these personal circumstances, it is useful to keep in mind the potential bias created by such information. In the case of elected or nonelected land-use officials, such conflicts should require abstention from certain decisions (such as when an official has a direct financial interest in a project before him or her; see Chap. 14).

At a conceptual level it may be useful for individuals to imagine how their ethical judgments might be different if knowledge of such biasing factors are somehow suspended. How would the individual view proposals to preserve forestlands, for example, if he did not know that his own particular livelihood would in some way be affected? This concept has been called *neutrality* by some (e.g., Habermas, 1976). John Rawls (1971) has created the theoretical construct of the veil of ignorance, in which individuals would reach decisions about the principles of justice by which to govern society by being deprived of specific information about their own social and economic circumstances. While obviously a theoretical construct, the concept of neutrality implicit in it is important.

The issue of ethical neutrality also raises a broader question concerning the appropriateness of personal intuition in making ethical judgments about land use. It is self-evident to most that individuals come into a policy issue or question with certain existing moral perceptions or inclinations, and that when confronted with a tangible circumstance often have certain intuitive moral reactions. We might think, "This is simply wrong," and express indignation at a certain outcome that seems intuitively unfair to us. Furthermore, in confronting choices between different policy options, we may intuitively feel that one option is the more ethical or equitable, though we are perhaps unable to indicate why we feel this way.

I hold to the belief that moral intuition is an important ingredient in making ethical land-use policy. Our intuitions are important starting points for us in making moral judgments about land use. Our intuitions, however, need to be refined, checked, and balanced against what we feel are morally valid ethical principles and standards. In part this is because our intuitions may be biased for some of the reasons mentioned above. In making judgments about what is ethical land use, I find the concept of *reflective equilibrium* useful (see Rawls, 1971). It suggests that we may need to constantly equilibrate or balance our sense or intuitions about what is correct against what our broader ethical principles and standards tell us is the appropriate outcome.

The Appropriate Ethical Focus:
Individual Decisions or Larger Institutions?

A final issue to keep in mind throughout this book is whether the appropriate scale of moral consideration is at the level of the individual land-use decision, or at the level of broader land-use institutions. If we conclude, for instance, that ethical land use requires the adoption of a set of principles dealing with environmental preservation, do we look to implement or advance these principles in every specific land-use decision confronted, from a request for rezoning to a decision about the siting of a road? On the other hand, would not such ethical principles be advanced more efficiently by establishing broader land-use institutions to ensure that a myriad of individual land-use decisions serve these ends? Philosophers make a distinction between *rule* and *act*. Rule-utilitarianism, for example, seeks to establish broader social rules or institutions that serve to maximize overall social utility. Act-utilitarianism, on the other hand, evaluates the merits of each specific decision or act, taking that course of action which will serve to maximize utility in that particular circumstance.

As a practical matter, land-use decisions are made at both levels and such ethical principles will find application at each. Ethical obligations to protect the natural environment can serve to justify, for instance, the establishment of a state land-use plan and state land-use criteria that might require local jurisdictions to protect certain environmental resources (e.g., wetlands, forestlands) and qualities (e.g., scenic beauty). At the same time, however, individual localities will likely still be confronted with more specific decisions about how to manage these areas, in turn requiring reference to these ethical obligations. And, at an even more decentralized level, the local jurisdiction, even after establishing a comprehensive management framework (e.g., comprehensive plan, zoning, and other land-use controls) consistent with the state program, will likely still confront numerous individual permit requests and specific parcel or area decisions, again requiring reference to ethical principles. Thus the ethical issues discussed in this book apply at both institutional and individual decision levels.

Summary

In this chapter I have established some basic theoretical groundwork for the more substantive ethical discussions to follow. Land-use values and attitudes were defined and their origin briefly examined. A key point is that held-values about land use are not synonymous with land-use ethics. Ethical land use takes existing personal values as an input to making ethical judgments; land-use ethics is the broader concern of making moral choices, applying ethical standards and principles to specific land-use dilemmas, and defending these moral judgments. Special problems the reader should now consider are the extent to which his or her individual judgments will be biased by knowledge of personal circumstances or position (the question of neutrality), and the appropriate role of moral intuition in making land-use decisions.

An initial theoretical framework was presented for classifying and categorizing the different ethical theories and principles to follow. While there are certainly many different ways to do this, I find helpful the two-dimensional model presented in figure 2.1. Ethical theories or positions are classified according to the extent to which they are teleological (or deontological) and anthropocentric (or nonanthropocentric).

PART II

SETS OF LAND-USE
ETHICS AND OBLIGATIONS

3

UTILITARIAN AND MARKET PERSPECTIVES ON LAND USE

CONTEMPORARY land-use policy has been driven largely by a utilitarian ethic. Utilitarianism holds that the morally correct action is the one that will create the greatest aggregate level of social utility or benefits. Sometimes referred to as the principle of greatest happiness, utilitarianism holds that "actions are right in proportion as they tend to promote happiness, wrong as they tend to produce the reverse of happiness" (Mill, 1955, p. 8).

Considerable philosophical debate has centered on how social utility should be conceived of or defined; that is, what actually does the utilitarian seek to maximize? Is it to be defined exclusively in sensory terms —pleasure and pain—as the hedonists maintain, or in broader human developmental terms, such as personal growth and fulfillment, social and political participation. This again returns us to the earlier question of defining what the good is (see Smart and Williams, 1973).

While there is an active debate over how to define or conceive of utility or welfare, for many the question is easily resolved through reliance on private markets. Through market mechanisms it is up to each individual to determine his or her own preferences or life plans and to pursue them accordingly—that is, through one's "dollar votes." The market model is viewed, for reasons discussed in more detail below, as the most effective social mechanism by which to achieve the utilitarian ethic.

Land is viewed by the utilitarian as essentially a means to an end; as an economic commodity, to be used to satisfy human preferences (often narrowly defined) and optimize human welfare. The appropriate uses of land in this framework are those which generate the highest return for society, as determined by the pricing signals of a free market economy. The primary value of land is the economic value it holds—dollar-values can be attached to land in much the same way that they can be given to toasters, automobiles, or pieces of furniture.

Free Market Allocation as a Variant of Utilitarianism

While one need not support the free market allocation of land and land uses to support utilitarianism, the free market is commonly viewed, at least by economists and policymakers, as the most effective way to maximize social welfare. In theory, individuals and firms interact in the marketplace to reach mutually agreeable transactions that make all parties better off. But the market system clearly does not work well in allocating certain kinds of goods and services, notably land and environmental resources. These imperfections in the market have been acknowledged by economists and policymakers over the years, and these imperfections themselves have served as an important justification for governmental intervention. Commonly referred to as "market failure," government intervention is seen as essential to correct for these imperfections and to bring about production and land-use outcomes that would have resulted had the market been functioning perfectly.

The market perspective, then, views the allocation of the land and land uses as it would other productive inputs and consumption goods and services. Any economic system must find ways of answering several basic questions about the use of resources: What goods and services will be produced? How will they be produced? For whom shall they be produced? Land uses are both outputs of this economic process, as in the case of recreational housing, and inputs, as in the case of agriculture or forestry.

The Goal of Pareto Efficiency

What is important from the market perspective is that land be allocated to its most productive economic uses. This is essentially the criterion of allocative efficiency or, to put it in more formal economic terms, Pareto optimality. Pareto optimality is that condition in which, through mutually agreeable economic transactions, a point is reached at which no further transactions can be undertaken that would make at least one person better off without making anyone else worse off.

While Pareto optimality is, in theory, a useful concept, in a practical setting it is difficult if not impossible to attain. Consequently, the economic perspective modifies the Pareto standard in at least two ways. One contemporary modification is the stipulation of a theoretical or potential compensation to those who are harmed by a transaction by those who benefit from these transactions. Here the definition of the Pareto condition is one in which those who benefit do so to such an extent that, given costless transactions, they compensate those harmed by the outcome and still come out ahead themselves. This can be referred to as a compensatory or potential Pareto standard (also called the Kaldor-Hicks criterion). For instance, returning to our earlier marshland example, the shopping mall project could be justified from a Pareto efficiency standard because the economic benefits obtained from this use exceed the costs inflicted on others (e.g., reduced fish harvests, water pollution). In other words, the developers of the mall could conceivably compensate all those harmed by this use and still turn a profit. A second modification to Pareto optimality is to think of transactions as moving toward the optimum, rather than ever actually attaining it. This seems reasonable, and it replaces Pareto optimal transactions with those which are Pareto improvements.

Belief that free market arrangements will yield Pareto results is founded on certain other basic assumptions about how market systems work. Economic decisions about how land is used are, in theory, a function of the interplay of the forces of supply and demand. Demand is simply how much individuals are willing to buy of the goods and services generated by particular uses at given prices. Supply, on the other hand, is the amount that suppliers are willing to provide at different prices. In theory, the market system, through endless competition and exchange, will gravitate toward points of equilibrium at which the willingness of individuals and firms to pay for a good or service is just equal to the costs of production. Prices serve as the signals through which these transactions occur. The typically high prices of center-city land, for example, reflect the potential economic productivity of the uses this land can be put to, and consequently the economic demand for the use of such land.

Absolute changes in the quantity of demand and supply may also occur, serving to increase each for all levels of prices, and to shift demand and supply curves entirely. On the demand side, such shifting curves may be caused by changes in the income levels of consumers or changes in the prices of other goods. A growth in population would also, in the long run, affect the demand curve. On the supply side, sudden across-the-board resource price changes or new breakthroughs in technology might precipitate similar effects.

Assumptions of the Perfect Market Model

While the market system is acknowledged to contain certain limitations, it is typically justified and conceptualized in an idealized way. Support for an unfettered market system is based on the potential achievement of a "perfect" market model. Land-use policy interventions, however, are typically directed at correcting for one or more of the failings or limitations of the basic assumptions of this model. A brief outline of these assumptions of the perfect model will be helpful. Before we proceed, however, it is important to acknowledge two underlying value judgments of the market model: first, that the personal wants of individuals should guide the allocation of resources in society, and, second, that individuals are, in fact, the best judges of their wants and preferences. I will discuss these a priori assumptions in greater detail in Chapter 9 and suggest some alternative perspectives. For now, several of the more important assumptions of the perfect model are as follows:

- Competitive markets. Under this assumption, no producers or consumers are assumed to hold so large a share of the market that they can increase or decrease the price of a good by restricting the supply or output of a good. Essentially, all individuals and firms are assumed to be price-takers and not price-givers.

- Full information. All participants in market exchanges are assumed to be informed fully about the quality of the goods and services and the prices for their exchange.

- Self-interested actors. All actors in market transactions are generally assumed to be motivated by self-interest and personal economic gain and will behave in ways commensurate with this assumption. Individuals are thus assumed to be rational wealth-maximizers.

- Exclusivity of market goods and services. Goods and services sold in the marketplace are generally assumed to be "exclusive"—that is, they are assumed not to impose any "externalities" or "spillover effects" on other individuals or the community at large.

- Costless economic transactions. While it is disputable whether this is an explicit assumption under orthodox economics, it seems implicit in many discussions of the virtues and desirability of market transactions. As I suggest below, it is often quite costly for individuals and firms to engage in economic bargaining and transactions, and this represents a substantial impediment to the achievement of Pareto-superior market outcomes.

Having identified these assumptions, we can see that advocates of the market perspective on land use tend to fall into one of several camps. On the one hand, there are those supporters of the market who, while admitting the impossibility of satisfying all the assumptions, view the unfettered market as functioning well enough that we should not interfere in any substantial way. Another camp, in which many proponents of ethical land use and environmental planning fall, views the assumptions as inherently unattainable, and supports public interventions that seek to correct these limitations and to approximate the allocative outcomes that will result if such market "failures" do not exist (Brown, 1981).

The justifications for public land-use interventions to correct for market failures are strong and intuitively appealing. Each of the assumptions above can be questioned in one form or another, at one time or another. What follows is a brief overview of these different types of these market failures, their nature, magnitude, and implications for land-use planning and policy.

It is important to acknowledge before moving on that economic and market failure rationales can be and are frequently misused. Many public land and environmental allocation decisions are strongly influenced by certain economic interests (e.g., timber companies, oil companies, development), and are often justified on grounds of economic productivity. While public policy may favor certain economic interests, it is not necessarily true that such actions achieve or promote allocative efficiency. Indeed, decisions that favor particular industries or companies may, instead of correcting market failures, actually exacerbate them.

The Problem of Land-Use Externalities

Externalities, spillover effects, or neighborhood effects, as Friedman (1962) refers to them, are unintentional impacts or side effects of individual and collective activities; they represent costs and benefits that are incidental to other primary social and economic undertakings. These can be both positive and negative in nature. The use of land—and the activities that occur on and under it—is almost by definition "nonexclusive," in that numerous costs and benefits are generated which accrue to neighboring landholders and other individuals and groups in the community. Classic negative externalities that are generated by land-use activities are air and water and light pollution, noise, traffic, and visual blight.

Several important characteristics of spillover effects can be identified. First, typically these effects are unintentional or incidental to some more central or primary activity. Thus, since they are byproducts of some other economic activity, whether or not the producer is conscious of these effects, they are not generally considered in the economic decision-making calculus of these individuals and firms. As E. J. Mishan observes:

> The person or industrial concern engaged, say, in logging may, or may not, have any idea of the consequences on their profits or welfare of others. But it is certain that they do not enter into his calculations. The factory owners, whose plant produces smoke as well as other things, are concerned only to produce the other things that can be sold in the market. They have no interest in smoke, even though they may be fully aware of it. But so long as their own productivity does not suffer thereby, and they themselves are not penalized in any way, they will regard the smoke as an unfortunate by-product. (1975, p. 102)

This situation is, after all, consistent with the assumption of self-interest and rational wealth maximization on the part of market actors. If one individual externality-producer decides benevolently to reduce the amount of this externality produced, this action may place him at a competitive disadvantage, and he may soon be out of business as a result.

To better understand the economic impacts of externalities requires a brief explanation of the concepts of marginal benefits (MB) and marginal costs (MC). As the terminology implies, each represents that additional amount of gain or loss to accrue from each additional unit of production or consumption. We might illustrate these concepts by suggesting that a farmer, call him Rogers, is considering what levels of agricultural production (say, cotton) he should attempt to reach in the coming year. If we assume that the amount of benefit he receives from each additional unit of agricultural production is constant—Rogers is a price-taker—then it is economically logical for him to increase production to that point at which marginal benefits just exceed marginal costs. Under normal conditions, to exceed production point A in figure 3.1 (assuming curve MC_1) would not be economical for Rogers because his per-unit cost would exceed the benefits received and he would lose money.

For a number of reasons the marginal costs of production are typically rising. In the production process inputs and resources of the least cost and the highest quality are put to use first. As production levels increase, the quality of the inputs diminishes and their relative costs normally rise. For Rogers to increase production, for instance, would likely require him to bring into production cropland of lower productive quality, or to use existing land in ways that require more expensive inputs (e.g., more intensive use of fertilizers). Although marginal demand for the individual producer in a competitive market is constant, it should be noted that, at the market level, demand is usually declining. It is an economic axiom that the benefits and positive utility derived from additional units of any good or service are diminishing, as is the willingness of individuals and firms to purchase them.

This framework can now be applied to the problem of externalities. The logic of this framework suggests that an economic incentive exists for each firm or individual to undertake an activity until reaching a point of equilibrium—where the benefits of additional units of the activity no longer exceed the costs. However, when there are negative or positive spillover effects that are external to the decision-making calculus of the economic transaction, inefficient allocations from the point of view of society may occur. If we remain with the farming example, let us assume that Rogers's farming operation is such that it requires him to use large amounts of fertilizer on his fields and that these chemicals eventually make their way into local streams and aquifers and generally contaminate local water supplies. This contamination is a cost which his productive activity imposes on the surrounding community, but which he does not explicitly calculate when making decisions about annual levels of agricultural production. This phenomenon is often spoken of as a divergence between social and private costs (Turvey, 1963). If the true marginal costs are included in these public costs, as figure 3.1 illustrates, the marginal benefit–marginal cost relationship might be modified considerably. The cost of each unit of production would be substantially higher if these

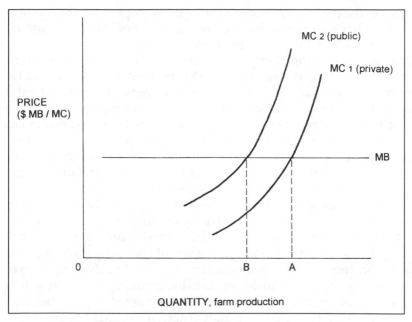

Figure 3.1 Marginal benefit and marginal cost curves for a hypothetical agricultural operation (Rogers).

social costs were considered. Negative externalities also serve to redistribute wealth because they permit a land user to force some of the costs of production on others without compensation (see Lee, 1981).

As a result of this divergence, production point *A* is too excessive and leads to the production of too many agricultural goods, while production point *B* represents the efficient production level when public or social costs are considered. Although Rogers may be quite cognizant of the potential ill-effects of his actions on the public water supply, there may be little he feels he can do if he is to survive economically. To stop this practice—that is, to adopt sophisticated and relatively expensive pollution control measures—would raise his production costs and thus in turn reduce his ability to sell his agricultural goods at a profit, given current market prices. Even if he is still able to make a profit, this represents considerable money out of his pocket, and he may think that this is unfair. Rogers may believe it is unfair, first of all, because none of his farmer-neighbors—his market competitors—would have to share in these sacrifices. After all, if we assume the same use of fertilizers and other environmental factors, they are just as much to blame for the pollution as he is. Moreover, he and his family have used these or similar farming practices for years, and no one has ever questioned his right to do so (or his right to use the streams that run through his property). If the community wishes to change these practices, he reasons, they should be required to compensate him for the economic losses he will incur.

The free market proponent might be hard-pressed to see a problem in the above situation, at least a priori. On the contrary, merely because there are economic activities that are "nonexclusive" in the usual sense does not mean that the market is incapable of bringing about economically efficient allocations of resources. To remain with the farming example, if the pollution created by the farmer imposes more costs on residents in the community than the benefits that accrue to the farmer from causing the pollution, then, in theory, the residents and the farmer ought to be able to negotiate a reduction that would make all parties better off. To simplify things, let us assume briefly that there are only two parties in this scenario—the farmer and a downstream landowner directly incurring the ill-effects of Rogers's agricultural runoff. Landowner number 2 we will refer to as Martines. Martines is generally unhappy about the level of pollution from Rogers's upstream farm because he relies on the river water for a variety of uses, including growing garlic organically as well as fishing and swimming. Figure 3.2 presents marginal benefit–marginal cost curves which indicate how a mutual agreement might be arrived at.

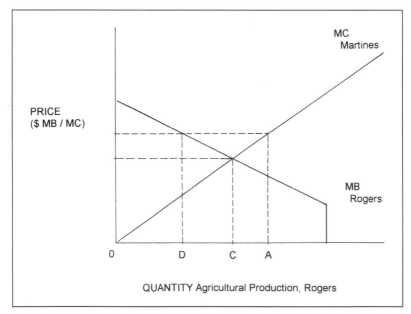

Figure 3.2 Allocative efficiency in a two-party world
(Rogers and Martines).

If Rogers is operating at production level A, an inefficiency is apparent as the costs imposed on Martines downstream exceed the benefits to Rogers. Thus if there are no impediments to negotiation, it is to Martines's advantage to make Rogers an offer to induce him to reduce his level of production, and thus the pollution generated from it (or to take certain steps to mitigate the negative side-effects of increased production). Furthermore, it is productive for Martines to continue to pay Rogers until reaching that point where the additional benefits to Rogers of his polluting activity just equal the costs imposed by this pollution on Martines. Consequently, the externality—in this case water pollution—does not a priori or by definition cause allocative inefficiency. The two parties in this case have economic incentives to transact and to reach a point of allocative efficiency.

An initial and obvious difficulty with this perspective is that it ignores the questions of equity. Although it may be possible for Martines to reach an agreement with Rogers, should Martines have to pay for the privilege of clean water—a resource he needs for many of the same reasons as Rogers? Should Rogers really expect to be compensated for no longer imposing harms on Martines? Furthermore, it is often quite difficult to determine who is, in fact, imposing costs on whom, and accordingly who should provide compensation and who should be compensated. These represent fundamental and important questions of fairness and equity and are essentially beyond the concerns of narrow market efficiency.

Determinations of liability in these land-use examples are, to market proponents under perfect market conditions, superfluous. Coase (1960) has developed a theorem which posits that, when the costs of transacting market agreements are low or nonexistent, decisions about liability will not affect the efficiency of the resource uses. For example, if we assume that Rogers has no a priori right to pollute the stream, but rather must purchase the right to do so from Martines, the level of agricultural production will gravitate to approximately the same point. For instance, if Rogers were currently permitted to produce only at level D, it would be economical for him to purchase the right to produce at greater levels from Martines, and it would be worth it to Martines to accept these offers. Such agreements would, again, be expected to continue until production approximates point C. Thus, the only thing that has been modified as a result of the change in liability is the distribution of wealth between Rogers and Martines (see Posner, 1972).

The assignment of liability is seen as important, however, in circumstances where the costs of transacting agreements, such as those between Rogers and Martines, are high. When the costs of such transactions are so high as to preclude such agreements, government and the courts can assign rights to those individuals and firms who would be willing and able to pay for them, were there not such impediments to transactions. Transaction costs represent a significant practical impediment to the achievement of allocative efficiency through the market system, and consequently they serve as a major rationale for many types of land-use policies.

The Problem of High Transaction Costs

In most cases, Coase's assumption of low or nonexistent transaction costs will not hold up. Transaction costs can be defined roughly as the costs of collecting, negotiating, and consummating an economic transaction in the marketplace. Because these costs represent, to a large degree, organizing costs, transactions involving few people entail typically lower levels of such costs, while economic activities involving large numbers of people entail higher transaction costs. Mishan (1975) divides these costs into three major components: (1) the initial costs leading to negotiation between groups and individuals, (2) the costs of maintaining and revising the agreement, if necessary, and (3) the capital expenditure, if any, necessary to effect the agreement. The major costs are likely to accrue in the first component, and Mishan further identifies its subcomponents: "(a) identifying the members of the groups, (b) persuading them to make, or accept, a joint offer, (c) reaching agreement within the group on all matters incidental to the negotiation with other groups, and (d) negotiating with the other group" (Mishan, 1975, p. 401).

Thus, market inefficiencies set in when transaction costs are significant. In large part, the problem of transaction costs is proportionate to the potential number of individuals and groups that are affected by an economic activity and that can ideally be involved in economic transactions. This is referred to as the problem of large numbers (Moore, 1978). Transaction costs are low only when a few individuals are affected—as in the case of Rogers and Martines—and higher when an entire community of individuals is impacted. Most land-use issues unfortunately fall into the latter category. Bergin (1978) provides an excellent example of the implications of transaction costs for the attainment of Pareto-efficient land-use allocations. In his scenario residents of a neighborhood are faced with the need to organize to prevent the location of a noxious development nearby:

> Assuming that there are 100 houses in the neighborhood, the trick is to get a large number of the owners, ideally 95 of them, to chip in to bid in fair proportion to their prospective losses. One of the 95 has got to take on the chore of organizing the soliciting of contributions to the bid. Since it is a chore, whoever does it is going to have to accept the fact that his benefit from the final trade, assuming he also chips in his propor-

tionate share to the bid, will be lower than many of his neighbors' benefits. . . . One can predict with fair certainty that the amount of time spent
on organizing will be substantial, for persons invited to solicit will be
well aware of the fact that their benefits will similarly be reduced by the
dollar values they put on the time they spend soliciting. . . . Recognizing
that fact, they will naturally tend to find perfectly good excuses for not
helping out. Remarkably enough, the entire deal can flounder right here;
for if the predicted time costs of organizing the soliciting threaten to
exceed the net benefits that any prospective organizer would get from a
successful deal, who will be noble enough to do it? (p. 84)

Land-use interventions in these instances are justified in order to approximate the market outcome that will result if such impediments to market
transactions do not exist.

Faulty or Imperfect Information

The perfect economic model assumes that economic actors have complete and accurate information about the alternative goods and services
available in the marketplace, and their quality. Unfortunately, information is costly to acquire, and the lack of such information offers a serious
impediment to free-market efficiency.

Much contemporary land-use policy is directed at correcting for the
imperfections resulting from information problems, and at approximat-
ing the efficient outcomes that will result if individuals and firms in fact
have all necessary information. Imperfect information also represents a
central reason why the market system cannot itself correct for the inefficiencies brought about by land-use externalities.

The presence of many land-use externalities goes undetected, and their
ultimate long-term effects are often uncertain. For instance, the practice
of allowing the filling in of coastal marshes, in our earlier example, may
over time result in significant water quality degradation, reduced commercial fish harvests, and long-term declines in wildlife populations,
among other impacts. While economic efficiency may suggest the need
to protect these resources and to curtail their destruction, information on
these long-term cumulative effects is typically inadequate. As a further
example, overcutting of forestlands may result in a host of similar long-
term effects (such as reduced fish life), as well as depriving individuals of
recreational access to valuable resources. Again the ecological impacts
may be gradual and uncertain, and the degradation may go unnoticed at
first by the public. While individuals in the community may value preservation of the forests, and indeed be willing to assemble bids to protect
them, inadequate information may prevent this from happening.

Land-use policies may be directed at correcting these imperfections in several ways. They may seek to enhance the quantity and quality of information available to parties engaging in land-use transactions. Recent efforts to ensure that the natural hazards present on building sites are apparent to housing and land consumers are an example of such policy-making (see Hildreth, 1980; Palm, 1981). Along the same lines, land-use policies may be designed to assist not merely in the transmission of information, but in the generation of new information and knowledge. Requirements that environmental impact statements be prepared for major land-use proposals are illustrative of this (see McEvoy and Dietz, 1977; Ortolano, 1984; Westman, 1985).

On the other hand, collective land-use policies may be designed to intervene directly to prevent inefficient land-use outcomes that would not result if complete information were available to economic participants. Take, for instance, the common example of the location of an unwanted land use in an exclusive residential neighborhood. It may be determined that the location of such a use—let us say a gas station—while bringing large profits to its owner, would wreak havoc on neighborhood property values. Faced with the choice of several alternative sites, the prospective gas station owner might be persuaded by a neighborhood group to avoid the site in question. The neighborhood group could assemble a compensatory bid which is sufficiently high to cover the added benefit the gas station owner might obtain from this particular site over an alternative one. Yet, under an unregulated land-use market (and perhaps under a regulated market as well), the required land could be purchased and construction of the gas station begun before neighbors are even made aware of this proposed activity through word of mouth or the newspaper. At that point the neighborhood organization would be unlikely to be able to afford to dissuade the gas station owner from further construction and an eventual move: the owner's investment is likely to be too high. Thus, an inefficient land-use allocation will result, even when transaction costs are low or nonexistent (assuming that an effective bid-collecting organization already exists, for instance). A regulatory or permitting system or an informed media might certainly serve to bring this proposed use to the attention of the neighborhood, thus enhancing the flow of information and perhaps providing sufficient time and opportunity to assemble and tender a successful bid. However, collective efforts to inform neighborhood residents of the use and its possible effects may be problematic or ineffectual, in turn justifying collective restrictions on the use of the land (e.g., to residential or some other use more consistent with the neighborhood environs).

Public Goods and the Free-Rider Problem

Another set of related problems, considered distinct from problems of information and transaction costs, are those founded on assumptions about individual incentives and their negative social consequences. The free-rider problem stems directly from the nonexclusive characteristics of land use and resource use, and from the perception of individuals that, regardless of whether or not they participate in an economic transaction, they will benefit from the results. In the previous farm pollution example, there are incentives, the argument goes, for impacted downstream residents to withhold their contribution to any organized bid to "bribe" the upstream farmer to curtail production levels (or to "drag their feet"), if they feel that other downstream residents will be able to amass a sufficient and successful bid without them. Each downstream resident expecting to reap the benefits of cleaner water anyway will only serve to reduce the level of benefits each will receive if he or she decides to contribute. The existence of the free-rider incentive structure—and individuals who behave in this predicted fashion—means that efficient allocations of land uses and activities that require the participation and contribution of large numbers of people will be thwarted.

The free-rider phenomenon represents a key theoretical underpinning for government interventions to create sufficient levels of "public goods" which would not otherwise be provided in the unfettered market. Public goods can be defined by two primary characteristics: They are goods or services that are (1) nonrivalrous—that is, one person's enjoyment of them will not diminish enjoyment or availability to other individuals—and (2) nonexclusive—that is, it is difficult or impossible to exclude individuals and the broader public from their enjoyment (Moore, 1978). The characteristics of public goods, in combination with the free-rider incentive, lead to underproduction of such goods in the free market. Public goods entail positive externalities—the inverse of negative externalities; these are benefits, such as the guiding beacons of a lighthouse, that are provided to the public at large, regardless of whether they have paid for them. Numerous land uses can be considered public goods: roads and streets, public squares and urban open spaces, greenways and protected landscapes, and flood control. Much land-use policy has to do with, and is justified by, the need to produce certain public goods. Pure examples of public goods are difficult to find, as most entail characteristics only approaching the pure case. For example, while a bridge is nonrivalrous to a certain degree, once its use reaches a certain level, absolute benefits decline.

Much contemporary land-use planning and policymaking has largely to do with ensuring that public goods are provided in the most socially efficient manner. Capital improvements programs, for example, are designed in part to coordinate decisions about the location and timing of public facilities so that public expenditures and investments made in one year are not undermined by subsequent decisions. It makes little economic sense to build a greenway at one point in time, and to tear it up a few years later to replace an aging public sewer line on the same site. Land-use planning often involves the organization and programming of these investments, which are usually interdependent in a functional, geographical, and temporal sense.

Land-use policies may be designed to affect spatial distributions in ways that minimize public expenditures for public goods. Promoting compact and contiguous forms of urban development has, in recent years, become a widely accepted objective among planners. Studies have indicated that by reducing scatter development, or leap-frogging, substantial savings in capital facility costs can be realized (e.g., see RERI, 1974). At a site planning level, the configuration of buildings and structures can serve to minimize the extent of public investments required. Land-use policies may be designed to utilize more efficiently existing public investments, such as schools, fire stations, and roads (many of which may not be public goods in the strict sense).

The Tragedy of the Commons and the Assurance Problem

The free-rider behavior described above can also be used to describe the degradation of certain common-pool resources. Examples of such resources, with clear implications for land-use policy, are federal and state public lands (e.g., national forests, grazing lands), common-pool ecosystems (bays, estuaries, local aquifers), air quality, and even the ambience of an established historic zone. Hardin (1968) describes this phenomenon as the "tragedy of the commons," in which an individual incentive structure leads to collective inefficiency and, eventually, ecological ruin. Hardin presents the classic example of the collective grazing pasture, or commons, in which each individual citizen has the right to utilize the resource to any extent he or she wishes. While the aggregate result of this incentive structure can be overgrazing and the destruction of the common resource, and a resultant decline in social benefits, for each individual livestock owner the benefits of adding additional livestock to the commons exceed his or her share of the reduction in social efficiency. The result, Hardin concludes, is a situation in which "freedom in the commons brings ruin to us all" (p. 1248).

The commons analogy can be applied with equal relevance to many land-use problems which do not at first sight appear to be resource-oriented. Take, for instance, the problem of neighborhood quality. It has

Table 3.1 Pay-off Matrix for Typical Prisoner's Dilemma

		Prisoner 2	
		Not confess	Confess
Prisoner 1	Not confess:	(0, 0)	(10, 1)
	Confess:	(1, 10)	(6, 6)

frequently been observed that, in neighborhoods undergoing negative change, there is often little incentive for individuals to engage in home and yard improvements, or even frequent maintenance and upkeep. If free-riding prevails, individual homeowners will see little reason to make these investments, as these will only serve to reduce the overall benefits obtained from the structure or lot. If others cannot be expected to provide similar upkeep, the total benefits obtained from their dwelling unit and land (or perhaps a business or some other use) will decline. If they all engage in such improvements, or at least in minimum maintenance activities, the benefits to everyone (the entire neighborhood) will rise (i.e., property values will rise as this area becomes a "good address").

The tragedy of the commons analogy highlights the fundamentally interdependent nature of private decisions about the use of land. A similar analogy is that of the "prisoner's dilemma," in which two suspected lawbreakers are held by police in isolation of each other. While the police will be unable to convict either suspect without the testimony of one of them, the one who agrees to turn state's evidence will receive a lighter sentence. Consequently, despite the fact that if the suspects acted collectively their benefits will be greatest, there is a natural incentive for each to rat on the other.

Consider the pay-off matrix in table 3.1. If the units in table 3.1 are years of prison, we can see that by agreeing not to tell on each other neither will receive a conviction or prison sentence. However, if each thinks the other will break down, it is to their individual advantage to confess, each seeking a lighter sentence by doing so. What is involved here is what is called the "assurance problem" (see Runge, 1984). If all parties can reach an agreement to refrain from selling out, the collective benefits will be maximized. Where such assurance does not exist, the tendency to sell out will be high.

A contemporary land-use example is found in the area of farmland preservation. For viable farming to continue in a region, the agricultural investment climate must be stable. When new uses, such as residential and commercial development, begin to encroach upon farming regions, they can serve to undermine substantially the perceived stability of the

Table 3.2 Pay-off Matrix for Two Farmers Subject to
the Impermanence Syndrome

		Farmer B	
		continues farming	packs up and leaves
	continues farming:	(20, 20)	(5, 10)
Farmer A			
	packs up and leaves:	(10, 5)	(5, 5)

Note: The impermanence syndrome is the disinvestment and fear by farmers that, largely because of development pressures, profitable farming will be difficult or impossible in the future.

region and the propensity of farmers to invest in the future. Urban development often brings with it traffic congestion, a loss of agricultural support industries, and new political constituencies anxious to control and regulate farm practices (e.g., the spreading of fertilizer and manure, and the operation of farm equipment in early hours of the morning). Extreme increases in property values also can accompany such development pressures, with an attendant incentive for farmers to sell out if they feel others will do the same. The pay-off matrix for two farmers, let us suggest, might look something like table 3.2.

Each farmer in this example would like to continue farming in the area, and would receive the greatest level of benefits from doing so—that is, if he or she could be assured that the agricultural climate would remain unchanged (or nearly so). If one farmer packs up and leaves, the benefits of staying are substantially lower for the other farmer. As a result of the uncertainty inherent in this situation, both will likely end up leaving (though in reality some farmers faced with these circumstances would certainly stay and hold out for higher land values). Certain land-use institutions, such as the voluntary agricultural and forestal districts programs in New York, Virginia, and other states, and the exclusive agricultural zones found in a number of states and localities, are designed to reduce this uncertainty. These are attempts to permit (often by the farmers themselves) a measure of control over the investment climate and to reach a sort of "mutual-assurance" that sellouts won't occur.

Benefit-Cost Analysis in Land-Use Decision-Making

The contemporary embodiment of the utilitarian ethic is the use of cost-benefit analysis in making governmental decisions about land and land resources. Cost-benefit, or benefit-cost analysis, holds that land-use actions or projects are desirable, first, if they are likely to yield benefits in excess of costs and, second, if they will maximize the ratio of benefits to costs (i.e., net aggregate utility). Cost-benefit analysis is typically used to evaluate the economics and justifiability of public projects such as flood control works, dams, or reservoirs. Indeed, many federal programs have mandatory cost-benefit analysis requirements. The U.S. Army Corps of Engineers, for instance, is required by law to undertake a benefit-cost analysis for any flood control project it proposes. In 1981, as a further example, President Reagan issued executive order #12291, which requires the Environmental Protection Agency (EPA) to undertake a cost-benefit analysis of any new proposed environmental regulation (see Smith, 1986). Moreover, the EPA must conclude that the benefits exceed the costs.

The conceptual and practical difficulties of undertaking cost-benefit analyses are numerous and well documented in the literature (see Feldman, 1991; Mishan, 1975; Thompson, 1980; Tribe, 1974). There are considerable methodological uncertainties about how to define and calculate benefits and costs, and which discount rates to use. Methodological techniques usually rely on estimating and predicting how the free market would have allocated a particular resource. Contemporary benefit-cost analysis, then, seeks to determine quantitatively the extent to which the market failure discussed above occurs; when the benefits of intervention exceed the costs, public policies become justified to correct for these market failures.

Any number of examples might be offered of land-use projects or proposals evaluated through the use of benefit-cost analysis, from highway projects to flood control to installation of public sewer and water systems. Agencies such as the U.S. Army Corps of Engineers and the Tennessee Valley Authority (TVA) have conducted benefit-cost analyses for dam and reservoir projects. The ethical dilemmas in using benefit-cost analyses to decide land-use decisions are illustrated well in one such case, the now-famous Tellico dam project. The Tellico dam was proposed by the TVA for the Little Tennessee River in the mid-1960s, and was intended to provide recreation, flood control, power generation, and other benefits. Although later benefit-cost estimates of the dam were less supportive, early benefit-cost studies prepared by the TVA suggested that the project was economically efficient, that the benefits exceeded the costs by a considerable margin (see Gramlich, 1981). This conclusion was based on estimating and tallying up the value of the various benefits (water supply, agriculture, and employment, in addition to flood control, recreation, and power generation) and the costs (construction costs) associated with the dam. While the Tellico dam illustrates the use of benefit-cost analysis in making such land-use decisions, it also illustrates the methodological disagreements on how to calculate benefits and costs (several different benefit-cost analyses were prepared with different results depending upon different assumptions).

Fundamentally, the Tellico dam example illustrates the ethical myopia of benefit-cost techniques. Although the narrow economic benefits might have been shown to exceed the costs (a conclusion seriously questioned in the later stages of the project's development), there were other ethical considerations present but not accounted for economically. For one, the dam was to flood the ancestral lands of the Cherokee Indians, and was strongly opposed locally for this reason. The dam, moreover, would have flooded natural flowing segments of the Little Tennessee River, an outcome that might be questioned on environmental conservation grounds. The Tellico dam project is famous to many now because of the discovery of the snail darter—a four-inch fish that was eventually placed on the federal endangered species list in 1975. The dam would have eliminated the species' only known habitat, a situation which led to a lawsuit challenging the dam on the grounds that it violated the Endangered Species Act. Eventually Congress approved the completion of the dam despite these concerns. Although the snail darter stopped the project for a period of time, the Tellico dam case illustrates the conflicts that frequently exist between economic and utilitarian factors on the one hand, and the broader set of moral considerations on the other hand (e.g., the immorality of causing the extinction of an animal species, or of destroying a river in its natural state).

Are there some benefits and costs which these techniques and methodological tools cannot calculate? Can we place dollar values on all benefits and costs associated with land-use proposals? Benefit-cost methodologies have been refined in recent years, with increasing use of such techniques as contingent valuation, and these are briefly reviewed below.

Benefit-cost analyses also raise serious ethical questions about the practice of discounting, or of evaluating all costs and benefits in their present value. The assumption here is that benefits derived today are worth more than those that accrue in the future. Critics of the practice argue that such techniques necessarily treat generations unequally and are biased in favor of current generations. (For a discussion of the practice of discounting and its environmental and land-use implications, see Pearce, Barbier, and Markandya, 1990.) We should note that differences between private and social discount rates are frequently argued to be another potential source of market failure. (For a variety of reasons, private discount rates will tend to be higher than the social rate, causing rapid and too early depletion of resources; see Solow, 1974.)

Surrogate Pricing and Contingent Valuation

In recent years economists and policy analysts have taken greater interest in finding ways to place economic or monetary prices or values on certain types of land and environmental good that are imperfectly traded in the free market. Frequently these figures are derived through the use of so-called contingent valuation techniques, in which individual consumers are queried, typically through a survey or questionnaire, on the extent to which they would be willing to pay to see a particular land-use or environmental outcome.

We can cite several recent examples of such efforts. For instance, in 1980 a research team from the University of Wyoming attempted to evaluate the potential economic benefits of preserving visibility in national parks in the Southwest. They asked a sample of over 600 households in four metropolitan areas what they would be willing to pay, in the form of higher electricity bills, to protect certain identified levels of visibility in the parks. (Some additional costs would be imposed on energy plants to undertake the necessary pollution control.) These visibility levels were depicted through a series of photographs presented to the respondents. Respondents were also asked to estimate their willingness to pay to prevent the visibility of a plume of pollution from entering the Grand Canyon, a situation which currently exists. Using these willingness-to-pay estimates, the researchers estimated the aggregate benefits to be derived from preserving visibility. (For a full explanation of this methodology, see Schulze et al., 1983.) As table 3.3 indicates, these predicted benefits are considerable and appear to reflect concerns about protecting the beauty, enjoyability, and ecological integrity of these parks. (Again, the benefits are aggregated from what individuals say they would be willing to pay to protect a certain level of visibility.) For residents of the southwest region, it is estimated that the aggregate benefit of preserving visibility in the Grand Canyon areas is some $466 million. If extrapolated to the nation as a whole, this amounts to some $3.5 billion in benefits. Estimating the costs associated with additional emission control necessary to protect park visibility, the authors conclude that the benefits will more than double these costs, thus strongly justifying pollution controls.

Another recent example involves efforts to place monetary values on the ecological, recreational, scenic, and other functions served by wetlands. Researchers at Louisiana State University and the University of Georgia have used a variety of techniques, including contingent valuation methods, to estimate these *true* market values (Gosselink, Odum, and Pope, 1974). These studies estimate the potential economic values of wetlands for commercial and sports fisheries, for aquaculture uses, and for waste treatment, concluding that the actual market value of wetlands grossly underestimates the true economic values served by these important natural areas. Their estimates indicate that the actual economic value of such areas exceeds $4,000 per acre per year (1974 figure). When income-capitalization is calculated (taking into account the stream of future ben-

Table 3.3 Benefits of Preserving Visibility in National Parks

(Annual Aggregate Benefits for the Southwest Region and the Nation)

Southwest Region Benefits for Preserving Visibility in the:	TOTAL ($ Millions)
Grand Canyon	466
Region—Grand Canyon, Mesa Verde, Zion national parks	889
Avoidance of plume blight	373
National Benefits for Preserving Visibility in the:	TOTAL ($ Millions)
Grand Canyon	3,520
Region—Grand Canyon, Mesa Verde, and Zion	6,180
Avoidance of plume over the Grand Canyon	2,170

Source: Schulze et al., 1983.

Note: Benefits are in terms of what individuals would be willing to pay to ensure a certain level of visibility.

efits), the per-acre value for these wetlands is more than $80,000. Many environmental advocates and ethicists argue against this type of economic analysis because it, again, has the potential for opening up tremendously valuable and important ecological areas to be sold to the "highest bidder." While an $80,000 per-acre value sounds high, it allows the loss of the wetlands if a developer comes along and is willing to pay $90,000 to build condominiums or a shopping mall on them (see Ehrenfeld, 1981, for a criticism of this methodology). Some environmentalists now argue, however, that this is a necessary and effective strategy by which to indicate the true human value of such resources (including scenic beauty), which are typically undervalued in the free market.

Summary

In this chapter we have examined in detail the utilitarian paradigm for guiding land-use decision-making, and the market failure model as a major variant. Although the utilitarian model has certain advantages, including the equalitarian nature by which it calculates net benefits, it is flawed and insufficient as an organizing moral paradigm for land use. In particular, land-use ethics, I argue, must contain important deontological components that act as restraints on utility maximization. The chapters to follow in Parts II and III elaborate upon these deontological components. Among the more important obligations are these: to prevent harm and to compensate for harms created; to acknowledge and protect certain land-use rights; to promote distributive justice; to protect and preserve the environment and other forms of life; to keep promises made; to permit individual choices concerning personal life-styles and life plans; to promote and protect the interests of future generations; to consider and minimize land-use impacts to jurisdictions and constituents beyond one's borders; and to ensure a fair system of political decision-making concerning land-use policy.

The moral importance of these deontological components does not necessarily preclude the application of a utilitarian ethic in land-use decisions. Utility maximization and Pareto improvements are to be preferred ethically, other things being equal. I do hold, however, that the deontological positions to follow must be seen as moral parameters that exist around utility maximization, and as such ought to receive priority in moral judgments about land use.

4

CULPABILITY AND THE
PREVENTION OF LAND-USE HARMS

Many land uses or land-use activities, if unrestricted, would create significant environmental and social harms. For instance, certain industrial and manufacturing uses may impose severe air, noise, and water pollution or other negative impacts on adjacent neighbors. Certain uses, such as shopping centers, often create severe traffic, water runoff, or air quality problems. Unregulated housing construction often generates substantial soil erosion and sedimentation harms, not only harming ecosystems but inducing damage to adjacent landowners. Erosion and sedimentation controls (e.g., sediment basins, filter fences, phased development) are restrictions placed on individual actions to prevent these types of harms. Failure to consider long-term storm-water runoff generated by a development is another example. Without government restrictions requiring minimum storm-water management provisions (e.g., restrictions on the extent of impervious surfaces, or infiltration trenches), development would create drainage and flooding problems for others and the public at large. As a further example, localities are increasingly preventing the location of development in floodplains, at least in part because of similar harms created. Once development locates in these areas, floodwaters are displaced onto areas not normally flooded, creating property damage, injury, and sometimes loss of life that would not otherwise occur.

The Principle of Preventing Harm

The occurrence of public harms has been viewed by many philosophers as a necessary condition for governmental intervention and the placement of social constraints on private actions. (For a more extensive discussion of this, see Beatley, 1985.) Nineteenth-century philosopher John Stuart Mill has influenced our views considerably about the appropriate role of government in a free society. His views are most succinctly expressed in his classic, *On Liberty* (1859). Mill viewed the freedom of individuals to pursue their own personal tastes and interests as essential, and only when those pursuits conflict with the freedom of others should the government be involved:

The only purpose for which power can be rightfully exercised over any member of a civilized community, against his will, *is to prevent harm to others*. His own good, either physical or moral, is not a sufficient warrant. He cannot rightfully be compelled to do or forbear because it will be better for him to do so, because it will make him happier, because, in the opinions of others, to do so would be wise or even right. . . . The only part of the conduct of anyone for which he is amenable to society is that which concerns others. (Mill, 1978 [1859], p. 9)

Many types of land-use restrictions can be seen as constraints on private liberties necessary to prevent the imposition of harms on other individuals and the public at large. Indeed, the placement of constraints on the liberties of private landholders is somewhat analogous to the constraints placed by criminal law on the behavior and actions of individuals—say, restrictions on pointing and shooting a gun. Just as we have enacted laws to preclude individuals from harming other individuals, by shooting or killing them, we also prevent land-use activities that inflict harm on others.

Mill and other philosophers saw the primary justification for the prevention of these types of harms in terms of utilitarianism: such governmental restrictions on private liberties result in greater net social benefits or welfare. Prevention of harm as an ethical imperative for land-use policy, however, need not have such an explicitly utilitarian basis. Prevention of harm may be viewed as an ethical requirement that exists regardless of what the social utility calculation might suggest. Few will accept the premise that allowing someone to shoot someone else is acceptable merely because it leads to a utilitarian or optimal outcome. If we return to the example of farmer Rogers polluting the river, we can see that many people would consider allowance of this pollution to be, on its face value, unethical, even if it were the socially optimal action. Something strikes an intuitive chord which tells us that, other things being equal, such harms ought to be avoided. Of course, restrictions on the imposition of such harms might be justified based on the argument that they (the restrictions) serve to protect the rights of those who would be harmed. Farmer Rogers ought not to be allowed to pollute the river because such harms violate the rights of downstream residents to access and use clean water. (The concept of land-use rights is described in greater detail in Chapter 5.) Although the notion of rights may be a defense of public restrictions on liberty, again the curtailment of public harms may be seen as ethically imperative even in those instances in which no clear public right exists.

What is suggested here, then, is a principle of preventing harms, land-use harms, in particular. Such a principle suggests that, other things being equal, there is a moral and ethical imperative on the part of land-use policymakers to avoid or minimize land-use harms. There is a moral duty to take appropriate actions to protect against or minimize the creation of public harms. The principle would also appear to have great application at the level of the individual landowner. Landowners and land users, ceteris paribus, have an ethical obligation to minimize the extent to which they impose harms on others and the community at large. It may suggest, for instance, that Farmer Rogers has an ethical obligation to operate his farm in a way that does not pollute the river and thus harm Martines downstream.

The ethical imperative of preventing or avoiding harm has been advocated frequently and embraced in traditional moral philosophy and environmental ethics. It is a generally acknowledged ethical principle that individuals must avoid causing pain or inflicting injury onto others (see Gert, 1988). Furthermore, a principle of preventing or reducing harm can be seen in the background and underpinnings of nuisance law and in the traditional use of zoning in this country. Nuisance law derives from English common law and protects one property owner from the harmful actions of another property owner "when the activity substantially and unnecessarily interferes with the use and enjoyment of his or her land" (Woodbury, 1987, p. 977). In John Cribbett's words: "The law of nuisance is summed up in an old Latin maxim, *sic utere tuo ut alienum non laedas,* use your own property in such a manner as not to injure that of another" (1975, p. 362). A majority of nuisance actions involve harms such as noise, odor, dust, or threats to safety. Most of these cases are decided by the courts on an individual basis, "with the court trying to decide how much inconvenience and disturbance a landowner must endure as an incident of modern life" (ibid., p. 363). If a court determines that a nuisance does, in fact, exist, it can then either enjoin the activity (issue an order requiring the owner to cease the activity) or award damages for the damages caused.

In many ways the practice of zoning and other land-use controls has emerged in response to the problem of land-use harms and the need to minimize their impacts. Reliance on the courts to take care of land-use harms through nuisance doctrine is costly, time consuming, and uncertain in outcome. Many of the early advocates of land-use controls saw such controls as a natural extension of nuisance abatement and a way to overcome these judicial limitations.

Types and Severity of Land-Use Harms

The types of potential harms created by land-use activities differ in their severity and seriousness and this may influence the ethical justification and importance of undertaking preventive or mitigative actions. For instance, some harms are clearly direct threats to public health and safety. The Hercules Rocket manufacturing plant near Salt Lake City, Utah, represents a clear and immediate threat to the lives of adjacent residents and strongly justifies the need for an "explosion buffer zone" around the plant (which does, in fact, exist). Other harms may be serious but not life-threatening. Severe traffic congestion generated by a particular use, say, a shopping center, may represent some safety problems, but the primary harm created is probably one of inconvenience.

The question of how to define harm arises in cases when a land user is clearly destroying something but there is no immediately recognizable external harm or effect generated by these actions. Can it be said, for instance, that a harm is created when a developer destroys, in the process of land development, some unique environmental feature—say, by destroying a natural waterfall? If the developer does not interrupt the natural hydrological conditions and functions of the site (i.e., does not affect anyone beyond that particular parcel of land), can destruction of the waterfall indeed be called a harm in the usual sense? The waterfall is not a publicly owned or used resource, and when it is in private hands the landowner can legitimately preclude anyone from visiting it and enjoying its beauty. Nevertheless, many citizens, upon learning of the waterfall's destruction, indeed feel harm in a significant way. Another example might be the practice of private logging companies in the western United States of clear-cutting thousand-year-old redwood trees. In pursuit of quick profits, these companies have adopted harvesting practices which almost ensure that redwood trees (at least outside the large national parks such as Sequoia and Redwood) will not be around in the future. Whether or not the harvesting of these trees creates any form of conventional negative externality (e.g., creating water quality problems in the streams or erosion problems in high slope areas), these actions can create real and emotional harms to many.

Ambiguity also exists about whether or not one can be said to be harmed aesthetically. It is one thing to contend that a paper mill or cement factory is creating a harm—the visual and environmental impact is clear and the health risks are empirically documented. What if, on the other hand, the impacts are more emotional and subjective—say, the visual harms created by the accumulation of old cars, unkept lawns, and various assorted junk that might be displayed in one's front yard? Can this type of circumstance be considered a public harm? Not because it creates a health hazard from water pollution or toxic substance that might be emitted from such "junk," but rather simply because it is unsightly to neighbors and other citizens who drive by the home on a daily basis.

Although the courts have generally been unwilling to consider such aesthetic effects as nuisances, this may be changing (see Woodbury, 1987). The Colorado Court of Appeals decision in *Allison v. Smith* (695 P.2d 791, Colo. Ct. App. 1984) indicates a changing attitude on the part of the courts concerning aesthetic harms. In this case, the owner of a resort cottage in the Rockies filed suit against an adjacent landowner on the grounds that the stockpile of old cars, scrap metal, and other "obnoxious debris" constituted a nuisance. The court found in favor of the plaintiff, concluding that the accumulation of junk and debris did substantially interfere with the use and enjoyment of the cottage owner's property. But not all use eyesores can, in the court's opinion, be viewed as nuisances:

> We note, however, that not all challenged activities found to be un-sightly eyesores, as here, constitute an actionable private nuisance. To constitute a nuisance, it is not enough that a thing such as accumulated debris and rubbish be unsightly or that it offend one's aesthetic sense. . . . The unreasonable and substantial interference tests . . . necessarily include a consideration whether the questioned activity is reasonable under all the surrounding circumstances. . . . Thus, legitimate but unsightly activity such as the accumulation of debris on land or the operation of a junkyard or auto salvage business may become a private nuisance if it is unreasonably operated so as to be unduly offensive to its neighbors, particularly when it is located in a residential district. (695 P.2d 791 [Colo. Ct. App. 1984])

Location and spatial circumstances are important in determining whether such visual or aesthetic harms have been created. Many localities are now regulating building and development in an effort to create and support a certain aesthetic character for a community (e.g., through architectural standards and design review boards). Can a modern building design be considered a harm when it is proposed for a traditional or historic neighborhood? (The question of community character is examined in more detail in Chapter 12.)

Reciprocal or Conflicting Harms

One problem with the principle of preventing harms is that many land-use dilemmas involve reciprocal or conflicting harms. For instance, two adjacent land uses might conflict or be inconsistent with each other, but it may not be evident which use is actually imposing the harm on the other. Perhaps the classic example is the proverbial conflict between farming (old land use) and suburban residential development (new land use). Each user group can legitimately claim that the other is imposing harms on it. The agricultural practices often create negative externalities by the nature of their operations, including noxious smells and fumes from the spreading of manure and fertilizer and the early morning noise of tractors and farm equipment. From the farmer's point of view, however, the entrance of new residential development into the community means certain harms and impediments to his or her normal farming practices, including increased difficulty in using the local road and street system, vandalism to crops and farm machinery, and the direct loss of the resource base (e.g., difficulty in finding additional land to rent as it is increasingly gobbled up by urban development) (Coughlin et al., 1981). Which users create the harms, and which are the recipients of harms is, in such cases, often difficult to determine beyond the obvious fact that suburbanites are the newcomers. But the occurrence of such harms continues to suggest and justify land-use actions that can reduce or minimize these incompatibilities (e.g., perhaps by directing new development into growth centers, or allowing the creation, as many states have done, of exclusive agricultural districts that serve to insulate farming from incompatible urban uses and vice versa).

This problem of conflicting harms sometimes is resolved through reference to some form of temporal standard. If we return to the farming/development example, we see that these conflicts have often been resolved by passing so-called nuisance laws, which severely restrict farming practices, like spreading manure and fertilizer and the early morning operation of farm equipment, and which often make it very difficult to continue normal farming operations. This strikes some as an unfair outcome, because the urban development uses that such ordinances are designed to protect are relatively new ones, while local farms may have been in operation in the area for centuries. Such a resolution of reciprocal harm might be justified by some on utilitarian grounds. A concept of "first in time, first in right" might be used, however, to respond to the fact that the farmer was there first and thus ought not be forced to curtail his operations for a relatively recent set of users. Indeed, some states have responded to this sense of equity by enacting right-to-farm laws that essentially prevent the adoption of these types of local nuisance ordinances (see Coughlin et al., 1981).

The Special Case of NIMBYs

The issue of land-use harms is particularly relevant to the problems of siting facilities or uses popularly called "NIMBYs" or "not in my backyard." These activities are commonly "public" in some dimension—for instance airports, power plants, public housing projects, hospitals, jails, and group homes are common examples of NIMBYs. (These are also sometimes referred to as "LULUs" or "locally unwanted land uses.") The harms they create may be real or imaginary, but they are nevertheless the source of substantial and often vocal opposition by homeowners and residents of the neighborhoods or areas in which they are to be located.

While such uses may indeed cause harms, they often are so essential to achieving certain basic individual rights, or elements of distributive justice, that the harms might be viewed as socially acceptable (i.e., a necessary evil). Moreover, for most people, these uses are likely to create harms no matter where they are located. While new airports can certainly be sited to minimize overall harm, the placement of a large airport is likely to create significant harms on some constituency no matter where it is sited. The same is true, for instance, of prisons. Short of a major restructuring of our society, it is hard to imagine doing without either prisons or airports, but to place an airport in the Everglades is certainly an unethical choice. Examples of NIMBYs which strike us as necessary to respond to the basic human rights or distributive justice include the following: group homes for the mentally or physically handicapped, public or subsidized housing projects, various medical or health care facilities, and shelters for the homeless (see Chapters 5 and 6).

Many communities have intentionally imposed land-use restrictions in order to discourage these types of uses and to make it as difficult as possible to site them locally. Some jurisdictions enforce zoning ordinances that make conditional a variety of such uses (e.g., from nursing homes to multifamily housing), allowing them only when certain criteria are satisfied. In the past, many communities have established criteria so onerous, or have interpreted these criteria in such a stringent fashion, that location of such undesirable uses has been difficult.

One approach to resolve this ethical dilemma is to agree on some fair distribution of these types of harms—the notion that, for such socially necessary NIMBYs, each city, community, or neighborhood ought to be willing to incur its fair share of the burden. This is not necessarily to say that each neighborhood ought to be willing to accept a group home, a hospital, a police station, or a public housing project; rather, one neighborhood might be asked to accommodate a group home for mentally retarded individuals, another a hospital, and the fairness of these locational decisions ought to be decided by considering the overall burden or overall sacrifice made by a community or neighborhood. It is common, of course, for the burden to be distributed unfairly, with certain areas and neighborhoods, often those which are less affluent, bearing an inequitably high burden of NIMBYs. (Consider hazardous waste facilities; see Bullard, 1990.) Who decides these types of siting cases is always a major issue, and we will return to this question in a later chapter.

And, of course, the occurrence of a public NIMBY does not necessarily negate the concept of culpability, described below, and various forms of compensation or reparation may be appropriate. Furthermore, the principle of preventing harm will demand that all appropriate actions be taken to minimize the harms created by NIMBYs.

It can also be argued that society has an ethical obligation to take all appropriate actions to reduce or eliminate the need for certain NIMBYs in the first place. Although most NIMBYs represent uses and activities that it would be difficult to imagine ever doing without, some NIMBYs certainly derive from broader wasteful social habits and life-styles. It is increasingly difficult, for instance, to site new community landfills. One approach to the moral obligation to prevent or minimize potential harms created by such a NIMBY is to take all reasonable actions to reduce the need for new landfills. The harms created by such uses seem to suggest an ethical obligation on the part of states and localities to adopt voluntary or even mandatory recycling programs and to encourage their residents to change their patterns of consumption. Similar logic could be applied to the location and siting of waste incinerators, an issue that has led to fierce local battles between different community factions. Similarly, such obligations might apply to the siting of low-level waste disposal facilities or new power generating plants. A major point here is that many types of harmful public uses are clearly the result of certain life-styles and patterns of consumption, the need for which might be reduced or eliminated in the long run (and often in the short run) through various local, state, and federal actions.

The Principle of Culpability

The principle of culpability holds that those who cause some harm or harmful condition ought to be held responsible for it. The principle comes into play in land-use policy in at least two ways: to address harms that might have been unknown or unsuspected, and to address cases of land-use harms that are indeed permitted but only in exchange for certain reparation or compensation.

Concerning the potential environmental effects of land development, certain activities are sometimes permitted in exchange for mitigation. Such mitigation requirements are increasingly common, for instance, in the protection of wetlands. Under federal and state wetlands provisions, developers are frequently permitted to fill or otherwise destroy natural wetlands if they mitigate—that is, if they are willing to restore an equal acreage of existing degraded wetlands, or create entirely new wetlands to replace those destroyed. If the shopping mall in our earlier example is permitted, and wetlands are filled in the process, it only seems fair that the developer be required to replace them or otherwise compensate for the damage. From an ethical view this seems required by culpability. To allow the destruction of natural wetlands is to allow the creation of serious and substantial public harms, and as such some form of compensation is equitable.

The science and technology of creating wetlands, however, is crude at best and many experts question whether such forms of mitigation can really amount to a true reparation or compensation (see Kusler and Kentula, 1989; Race, 1985). It is also not clear whether through such a practice a functioning system of wetlands can be maintained. When these uncertainties are taken into account, it is not uncommon for the required mitigation ratio to exceed 1:1 (one acre restored or created for each acre destroyed) and may be set at 3:1 or even 5:1 (five acres of restored or new wetlands required for each acre of natural wetlands destroyed; some states impose even higher mitigation ratios).

As a further example, many states and localities impose conditions on development which require developers to restore or otherwise compensate for the loss of environmental features, such as trees. For instance, it is increasingly common for localities and states to mandate the replacement of trees that may be cleared or destroyed during the development process. The state of Maryland, for example, is currently considering a statewide law that would require developers clearing an acre or more of forestland either to plant trees elsewhere to compensate for this loss, or pay $5,000 per acre cleared (1990 dollars), money which goes directly into a state reforestation fund (Schneider, 1990).

The national movement toward increased use of impact fees and other forms of development exactions is also a response to ethical culpability. (For extensive reviews of the use of exactions in the United States, see Alterman, 1988; Nelson, 1988; Snyder and Stegman, 1986). Development exactions, then, can be seen as just and fair because they address problems caused by a development or proposed development. It is fair to require developers to make certain road improvements because the development creates the need for these additional services. It is fair to require linkage fees for affordable housing if the proposed development generates a need for adequate nearby housing for future workers. New downtown office projects might legitimately be required to pay linkage fees for public transit improvements, because the projects will result in increased usage of, and demand for, a city's transit system.

Of course, some exactions can be justified not so much in terms of culpability (i.e., because of new demands created) but again in terms of advancing and protecting certain "rights" which society feels such projects should support. For instance, San Francisco and other cities impose day care requirements on new downtown projects, certainly another version of exaction. While the case can be made that these requirements are needed because of the increased demand placed on existing day care facilities, it appears that often the underlying rationale is different— namely, that employers have obligations to provide for, or contribute to, the provision of this service, because all workers are entitled to such a service.

Exactions might also be morally founded less on culpability and more on a kind of quid pro quo theory. According to this position, many forms of exactions can be seen as ethically justifiable because they are the result of an exchange or bargain between the public authority and the developer. The developer is given the chance to provide certain things—perhaps linkage payments for transportation or affordable housing—in exchange for the government's approval to build (for a further discussion of this, see Beatley, 1988). Such exactions in many communities amount to sizeable sums of money which, depending upon local market conditions, may in large part be passed along to housing consumers in the form of higher housing costs (see Snyder and Stegman, 1986). Exactions may thus create barriers to the entrance of certain income classes into a community and thus limit equal opportunity.

Interjurisdictional Harms

It should be obvious that the harms discussed in this chapter do not necessarily respect jurisdictional boundaries. The filling of wetlands to build homes or shopping malls will create harms that may directly affect residents in several states and indeed serve to degrade environmental systems of regional and national significance (e.g., Chesapeake Bay). There is often a tendency on the part of local officials to take actions to prevent harms within their own boundaries and to be less concerned with regional or extralocal harms. It is my position that the principle of preventing land-use harms applies with equal moral force when the effects are primarily outside the boundaries of one's political jurisdiction. Equally true, the principle of culpability may require local actions that seek to compensate or counterbalance the regional or extralocal harms created. Act locally, think globally; think locally, act globally.

Summary

In this chapter, I have presented the concepts of harm and culpability as important theoretical components of any set of land-use policies. Many land-use practices and activities create harms, and as such support a legitimate public role in minimizing and curtailing such harms. Moreover, there are situations in which, either because they are unavoidable or because society deems them acceptable, various harms are created and ethical land-use policy calls for the application of the principle of culpability in these cases (and requisite compensation and reparation).

The minimum ethical standard, ceteris paribus, can be stated as follows: Ethical land-use policy prevents or minimizes the imposition of harms wherever and whenever possible; the principle of culpability holds those who cause land-use harms accountable for them.

5

LAND-USE RIGHTS

STRICT UTILITARIANS would support any land-use action or project that served to create the greatest aggregate utility or good, regardless of the impacts on specific individuals. An alternative view is the rights-based approach. In the United States a variety of rights have been created and institutionalized through federal and state constitutions and through legislative and judicial actions. The constitutional rights guaranteed to all individuals, regardless of what a bureaucrat or legislative body might view as expedient or necessary to maximize social benefits, include the rights to free speech, assembly, freedom of thought, and freedom of religion. In other words, rights are viewed as inviolable; that is, they are not superseded or overruled by other, albeit important, public objectives. They are generally not to be traded off against other social desires or goals (though rights are usually not absolute).

In this chapter the reader is introduced to the central idea that there may well be *land-use rights* which are held by individuals and which may act in a similar way as constraints on the land-use actions undertaken both by private and public actors. Several of the rights introduced in this chapter are discussed in greater detail in subsequent chapters.

Types of Land-Use Rights

Rights can be thought of as legitimate claims that individuals have against other individuals or the state, claims that express entitlements to have something or to be free of something. For one to have a right "is to be empowered to press rights *claims,* which ordinarily 'trump' utility, social policy, and other moral or political grounds for action" (Donnelly, 1989).

Many of the rights we are concerned with here might be categorized as legal or constitutional; that is, they may be expressed or ratified in the form of specific legislation or constitutions. For example, the U.S. Constitution establishes certain rights, including the rights to free speech and religious freedom, as well as the right to compensation should the government take a person's land, rights which have clear implications for ethical land use. Court opinions have also established certain rights (e.g., common law principles and standards established through precedent).

Other claims, frequently described as moral rights, can be made based on what individuals or groups feel they are entitled to (Feinberg, 1973). These rights are established through political and social discourse, and indeed they are expressed in everyday conversation. I might make the statement, "I have the right to walk here," or "I have the right to know what's going on." While I am expressing the idea of a right, there is no belief on my part that there is a legal or constitutional basis for my "right." I am expressing the claim that I am entitled to something. A number of potential land-use rights fall under the heading of "moral rights" rather than being legal or constitutional in their derivation. The right to affordable housing and the right to a safe and liveable neighborhood are related land-use rights that most would acknowledge, yet they are not usually found specifically in most state or federal constitutions. I may believe that I should not have to be subjected to the extremely high crime rate in the neighborhood in which I live (e.g., with the attendant risks of being burglarized, mugged, or shot), but I am not likely to be able to force my city to spend more funds to reduce crime based on a specific legal or constitutional right. However, I may be able to convince my elected representative to make such expenditures based on the argument that all individuals are entitled to a certain level of personal safety (i.e., that there is a moral right to a certain level of personal security). Many of these types of rights can be considered moral rights, in that they may not be specifically codified through a constitutional or legislative action.

Another way to distinguish different land-use rights is between "negative" and "positive" rights. A negative right is essentially the right to be free from certain negative consequences or results. In land-use matters, this means to be free from trespass, or to be free from certain damaging activities (e.g., one might argue that one is entitled to be free from a certain level of noise or traffic). Positive rights, on the other hand, are rights that individuals claim they have to certain things. Possible positive rights that have relevance to land-use policy include the following: rights to shelter and housing; rights to health care; rights to transportation and mobility; and rights to certain environmental resources and amenities such as beaches and coastlines, mountains, rivers, and other scenic landscapes. Many of these positive rights find expression in documents such as the United Nations Declaration of Human Rights. Acknowledging the existence of such positive rights creates ethical imperatives in land-use decision-making.

Justifying Land-Use Rights

The rights of individuals have found justification through different political and legal theories. For many it is sufficient to be able to point to a legal document or a constitution, or a statement such as the U.N. Declaration of Human Rights, as the source of such rights without further justification. Others argue that all human beings have certain natural entitlements or natural rights (see Sumner, 1987).

Human and moral rights might also be justified based on the physical and emotional needs of human beings, thus incorporating an empirical dimension. Obviously human beings require food to survive; thus, adequate food and nutritional sustenance would seem to be a basic human right. Many land-use rights might be argued from a similar needs-based approach. Human beings clearly require adequate shelter to survive and thus this irrefutable empirical need might be argued to be the basis of a land-use right to minimum shelter. Similarly, humans need air and water that are reasonably clean and free of toxins for survival, thus suggesting a land-use right to a certain minimum level of environmental quality.

Such a needs-based argument can extend beyond mere biological or physiological needs to encompass such basic psychological needs as feelings of dignity and self-worth. As Jack Donnelly notes:

> The source of human rights is man's *moral* nature, which is only loosely linked to the "human nature" defined by scientifically ascertainable needs. Human rights are "needed" not for life but for a life of dignity; as the International Human Rights Covenants put it, human rights arise from "the inherent dignity of the human person." Violations of human rights deny one's *humanity;* they do not necessarily keep one from satisfying one's needs. We have human rights not to the requisites for health but to those things "needed" for a life of dignity, for a life *worthy* of a human being, a life that cannot be enjoyed without those rights. (1989, p. 17)

Rights are also derived and justified from a social contract view—the notion that individuals gain certain basic assurances and protections as a condition of giving up their freedom to a collective government. The idea of a social contract can be useful in hypothesizing what rational individuals *would* be willing to give up in exchange for agreeing to accede to the structure and infringements of organized society. John Rawls in his classic *A Theory of Justice* (1971) created a theoretical construct—the original position for hypothesizing about what conditions are acceptable to rational individuals, and what principles of justice are agreed upon in this decision-making setting. Under a veil of ignorance (i.e., without specific information about their own specific skills, social position, or life circumstances) rational individuals would, Rawls believes, choose to be risk-aversive, selecting the "Two Principles of Justice" as the basis for structuring social cooperation. The First Principle of Justice states that each person is to have "an equal right to the most extensive total system of equal basic liberties compatible with a similar system of liberty for all" (1971, p. 302). Rawls has in mind the usual set of liberties: "The basic liberties of citizens are, roughly speaking, political liberty (the right to vote and to be eligible for public office) together with freedom of speech and assembly; liberty of conscience and freedom of thought; freedom of the person along with the right to hold (personal) property; and freedom from arbitrary arrest and seizure as defined by the concept of the rule of law" (p. 61). These are basic freedoms which all rational individuals would seek to ensure for themselves under any circumstance. The priority given to Rawls's first principle means that "a departure from the institution of equal liberty . . . cannot be justified by, or compensated for, by greater social and economic advantages" (ibid.). While Rawls's specific list of basic rights (he calls them liberties) can be questioned as being limited, he does illustrate the major argument that individuals, in some original position, seek first to protect certain fundamental things that cannot be traded away or balanced against by increases in social utility or other social objectives.

Land-Use Rights as Trumps on Utility Maximization

An example may be helpful to illustrate the practical distinction between land-use decisions made on the basis of certain rights and those made on the basis of utility maximization. Let us construct a cost-benefit scenario much like the Tellico dam/snail darter case. Let us assume, for argument's sake, that a proposal has been made to build a major industrial complex in the town of Harpers Ferry, West Virginia, along the Potomac River. The chosen site of the complex is a parcel adjacent to the river, and indeed the river would be utilized extensively by the industry for waste disposal. The industrial proposal is supported heavily by the Chamber of Commerce and is perceived by the business community as a major economic boon that is needed badly in the locality. It would create needed jobs, would generate substantial secondary economic benefits for local businesses, and would add substantially to the local tax base. Despite the general support for the project expressed by a majority of residents, a vocal minority has expressed concern about the project, having obtained evidence that suggests that the manufacturing processes will generate significant risks in the form of water and air pollutants, even after all state and federal emission standards are satisfied. Evidence indicates that although risk to the average citizen may be relatively small, the elderly and youth populations will be subject to substantial health risks.

An independent consultant is hired by the town to prepare a cost-benefit analysis, to ensure that permitting the industry to locate there will be an economically justifiable action. Indeed, the consultant concludes, even after considering the economic effects of the health risks associated with the plant, that the benefits of the industry to the town and its constituents far exceed these costs. What should the city council do in such a case? Clearly one position is to deny the industry the necessary permits on the basis that each individual in the community has the moral right to be protected from serious health threats, such as those which would be created by this particular industry. Perhaps there are other options which might protect these rights without turning away the industry, such as requiring the installation of much stronger pollution control technology, but nevertheless the moral rights of individuals, acknowledged by local officials, can serve to trump utilitarian maximization. Often, however, city councils take the quick dollar and pass the buck.

Are Land-Use Rights Universal and Absolute?

An important question to consider is, will such rights be universal? That is, do the same rights apply to all individuals regardless of the culture or governmental jurisdiction to which they belong? The United Nations Declaration of Human Rights appears to assume, in a significant way, that such rights apply with equal force to all individuals regardless of their cultural, social, or governmental circumstances. The human rights owed to an individual in China are the same rights owed to an individual in India, Peru, and the United Kingdom. The actual differences between the rights of individuals in different countries are significant, of course. It appears that in many developing countries government officials deem it acceptable, for instance, to expose individuals to much higher levels of environmental risk in order to increase economic activity. The Bhopal disaster in India is illustrative of the lower levels of protection that individuals in developing countries are believed to be owed. As another example, while most developed countries acknowledge that individuals have certain rights to minimum social goods, such as housing and health care, these would not be characterized as rights in many developing nations. Equally true, even in First World countries such as the United States there is considerable variation between regions and states concerning what rights individuals are actually owed by society. It might be argued, for example, that in the state of Oregon the extent of environmental rights owed to, and expected by, individuals is much greater than in Louisiana. Oregon has a number of environmental laws and programs intended to bolster the environmental conditions of individuals and to enhance the number and extent of environmental resources individuals have access to (e.g., public beaches, state parks). On the other hand, as a result of years of development by the chemical industry, residents of Louisiana are exposed to high levels of toxic substances, and it can be argued that the environmental rights of individuals are less extensive there.

The question of universality is difficult to resolve. When rights are established through a constitution or through constitutional interpretation, as in the United States, these rights become universal at least throughout the nation (i.e., Oregon and Louisiana must respect and enforce the same rights to free speech). It is not my purpose to delineate a definitive and universal list of land-use rights; rather, my objective is to survey the landscape, to identify the primary potential components of such a set of rights. While I am not prepared here to delineate a specific list of these rights, I wish to argue that individuals generally have certain minimum rights—that is, individuals are entitled to minimum levels of protection from harms—and that these entitlements can and must serve as constraints on public policies which seek to maximize social welfare.

A related matter is the extent to which rights, once established, are absolute; that is, must society respect and uphold the right in all circumstances, regardless of the social costs or consequences? While rights are generally described as being inviolable, there often are certain situations in which society may need to overrule an individual's established right. There may well be limits to rights. An individual's right to free speech does not extend, to use the classic example, to yelling "Fire!" in a crowded theater. Limitations to some rights may be essential when they conflict with other rights. We will consider the issue of conflicting rights in subsequent sections.

A Variety of Potential Land-Use Rights

What follows is a tentative listing of the major types of land-use rights —rights that either have been established legislatively or judicially, or have been argued for in the past. In some cases these rights attach to landowners, in other cases to the general public. I begin by reviewing some of the more established land-use rights that are derived from constitutional provisions.

Federal and state constitutions delineate a number of rights, many of which have direct relevance to public land-use policy and decision-making. While not always immediately obvious, challenges to land-use practices and decisions are made frequently on the grounds of constitutional rights. The challenges made most frequently are those by developers and landowners who are adversely impacted by certain public land-use controls or decisions. Often it is argued that an ordinance or action is unconstitutional because it violates the due process provisions of the Fourteenth Amendment, or the requirement of just compensation when government takes private property, as mandated under the Fifth Amendment. The "takings" clause has become a major issue in the land-use policy area, and is discussed in much greater detail in Chapter 11. Other constitutional-based land-use rights discussed below include the rights to equal protection and due process, the rights to free speech and freedom of religion, and the rights to privacy. Following this review, we identify and discuss those potential land-use rights which are less constitutionally or legally based, and which tend to fall into the category of moral rights. Specifically, these include the rights to minimum levels of housing and shelter, health care, education, transportation, and environmental resources, and the rights to be free of certain environmental "bads."

Rights to Due Process and Equal Protection

Federal and state constitutions contain due process clauses, which establish both procedural and substantive requirements. The federal due process clause (in the Fifth Amendment and applied to the states through the Fourteenth Amendment) states that citizens shall not be deprived of life, liberty, or property "without due process of law."

Procedural due process seeks to ensure that all citizens are treated fairly in public decision-making processes and are given adequate opportunities to express their views in a fair and impartial tribunal (Godschalk et al., 1979). Procedural due process embodies a basic ethical intuition that laws and policies which affect citizens should be adopted and implemented through a fair process. Due process rights might be violated, for instance, if a locality approves a zoning change without first notifying adjacent landowners who might be affected by the proposed use; or procedural due process rights might be violated if a locality seeks to adopt a comprehensive land-use plan without providing sufficient public hearings and opportunities for public input. In certain quasijudicial land-use matters (e.g., the issuance of a special use permit) procedural due process may be violated when the impartiality of those making decisions (e.g., a hearings officer) is undermined (through ex parte communication, for instance).

Substantive due process holds that government actions, including land-use programs and policies, must be directed toward reasonable ends and the means to accomplish these must be reasonable as well. One might claim that a law or ordinance violates substantive due process because it seeks to regulate an activity that is beyond legitimate government ends. Even in instances where the ends are seen by the courts as legitimate, the strategy or program aimed at accomplishing the ends may be seen as arbitrary and capricious and with no rational basis. While the concept of substantive due process also reflects certain intuitions about ethical land use, the courts usually determine violations on a case-by-case basis, considering the specific circumstances of each. As a *right* it is largely vacuous without reference to other more substantive concepts and standards, many of which are examined in this book. It can be said, however, that citizens and property owners have the right to expect that public policies and regulations are adopted for good reasons and that the specific tools, techniques, and programs adopted are reasonably suited to achieving these goals.

Under the Fourteenth Amendment of the U.S. Constitution, states cannot deny their citizens the "equal protection of the laws." This standard generally requires that classifications under government laws be reasonable and that similarly situated individuals be treated similarly under the law. Equal protection requirements, as with due process, also embody certain intuitive concepts about ethical land use. If a land-use program involves a classification system (as they usually do)—by placing special restrictions on land in floodplains, for example—these restrictions should apply equally to all floodplain landowners. To do otherwise would be unfair. Some land-use classifications may also be illegal or unreasonable, such as classifications based on race. To use land-use controls to separate the community by race is discriminatory and a clear violation of equal protection.

Rights to Free Speech

Constitutional guarantees to free speech have been applied in recent years to land-use cases. The First Amendment states that "Congress shall make no law abridging the freedom of speech." It is a conventional and basic thesis that free speech is essential for the maintenance of a healthy democracy. Because the use of land and the operation of different land-use activities represent forms of expression or communication, these free speech requirements act as constraints on permissible land-use policy. One of the areas where the First Amendment free speech rights has been heavily debated is the regulation of adult entertainment establishments (see Pearlman, 1984). Increasingly, communities are enacting tough restrictions on where such activities as adult theaters and book stores may be located, often preventing them from operating within a certain specified distance of residential areas, schools, churches, or day care centers. These types of restrictions have been challenged on the grounds that they violate First Amendment rights (consider the case *Renton et al. v. Playtime Theatres,* discussed in Chapter 12).

First Amendment free speech violations have also arisen over efforts by cities and states to control billboards. Owners of billboards and the billboard industry have argued that such restrictions severely constrain the flow of commercial and noncommercial information, and thus ought to be considered unconstitutional. While a number of factors are typically considered by the courts in deciding these cases, it is often important for the court to determine that the ordinance or restriction is "content-neutral"—that is, the ordinance is not intended to prevent the expression of a particular point of view or "message," but rather seeks only to regulate the "time, place, or manner" of such expressions. Billboard restrictions may be found unconstitutional, for instance, if they affect only a certain kind of billboard that carries a particular message. (Billboards as visual blight may themselves violate the moral right to a visually pleasing environment; see below.)

Rights to Freedom of Religion

The U.S. and state constitutions also affirm rights to freedom of religion, raising significant questions about the validity of local land-use restrictions which severely restrict the siting or location of churches in a community. The U.S. Constitution states, again in the First Amendment, that "Congress shall make no law . . . prohibiting the free exercise of [religion]." While one may have the right to freely exercise or practice one's chosen religion, to what extent does the public interfere with this right by preventing the location of a church in an exclusive residential neighborhood, or, perhaps, by banning such uses entirely in the community? The functions of churches have clearly expanded in recent years, so that they are no longer simply places to worship each week. Moreover, even as conventional worship sites, churches, particularly those with large congregations, create clear and immediate impacts on adjacent uses, notably creating problems of noise, traffic congestion, and associated safety concerns. People also sometimes object to the location of churches because of the effects they may have on reducing property values.

But can one argue that, because their community bans the location of churches within their jurisdiction, rights to freedom of religion are being violated? What about zoning and land-use controls which restrict the location of churches—say, to certain higher-density residential or commercial zones—or which require churches to meet certain criteria or conditions before special use permits are issued? A majority of state courts appear to hold that outright exclusion of churches is invalid, and though these decisions are often partly based on due process analysis, it is clear that concerns about religious freedom are important in the thinking of courts (Cordes, 1989). A majority of states appear to find acceptable the imposition of reasonable site restrictions such as sideyard setbacks and other requirements designed to minimize the impacts of churches.

Rights to Privacy

While there is no specific provision for the right to privacy provision in the federal Constitution, the courts have implied the existence of such a right. Moreover, regardless of the constitutional basis, individuals might be said to have such a moral right. The basic concept here is that while society and government may have the authority to constrain individual choices and behavior in areas which affect other individuals and the broader public, there are certain limits to social interferences. In theory, individuals have the right to conduct those individual and private aspects of their lives in private and without interference. Just as the right to privacy has been used as a defense against government prohibitions on abortion, there are similar land-use regulations which may be forbidden because they infringe on personal privacy.

Some communities, for instance, have attempted to promote family values by enacting what are sometimes called "living-in-sin" laws. These laws restrict the number of unrelated individuals who may occupy housing units. Until recently, the city of Denver had such restrictions, prohibiting the occupancy of single-family homes in much of the city by two or more unrelated individuals. While this law has been defended by some as protecting property values and promoting "traditional family values," critics argued it blatantly discriminated against a certain personal lifestyle choice (i.e., heterosexual and homosexual couples wishing to live together). Such regulations, it can be argued, amount to infringements on personal rights to privacy, an issue that is discussed in greater detail in Chapter 12.

The Right to Decent Shelter and Housing

Housing (or shelter, as it is sometimes referred to) is one of the most basic human needs. While not usually a constitutional right, it is a moral claim frequently at the heart of many disputes about land-use policy. The U.N. Declaration of Human Rights (Article 25[1]), for example, lists housing as an important component of "a standard of living adequate for . . . health and well-being." In the United States many housing advocates point to the strong declaration in the 1949 Housing Act as the basis for the right. It states:

The Congress hereby declares that the general welfare and security of the nation and the health and living standards of its people require housing production and related community development sufficient to remedy the serious housing shortage, the elimination of substandard and other inadequate housing through the clearance of slums and blighted areas, *and the realization as soon as feasible of the goal of a decent home and a suitable living environment for every American family,* thus contributing to the development and redevelopment of communities and to the advancement of the growth, wealth, and security of the nation. (Emphasis my own.)

While most will agree in concept that a right to housing is a moral, if not a legal, right, the actual obligation can be defined in different ways. The right might be construed to be simply a right of shelter, regardless of its quality or condition. The person holding this position might argue that the primary debt to individuals is an assurance that they "have a roof over their heads." This can imply that the right is fulfilled even when individuals and families live in degraded and badly deteriorated housing, or when at least the public has provided alternatives to homelessness (through shelters and other forms of emergency housing).

Many believe, however, that the right to housing is more encompassing and inclusive than this, that what is required is housing of a minimum quality and condition. Indeed, in implementing housing programs and documenting housing needs in the past, we have established certain standards of decent housing. For instance, housing which does not have indoor plumbing, while perhaps acceptable one hundred years ago, is no longer considered acceptable by modern standards (even though many people in this country still occupy such homes). We have for years employed standards for overcrowding—for instance, the criterion that overcrowded housing conditions exist where residency exceeds one person per room. Obviously, then, the right to housing implies that housing ought to be liveable by current standards and ought to meet certain basic conditions.

The right to decent housing also implies affordability. It is obviously inaccurate to state that families of modest means have access to housing when the housing which is available is extremely expensive and beyond practical affordability. Most will agree, then, that effecting a right to housing implies the provision of affordable housing. From a land-use policy view, affirmation of the right to decent and affordable housing may imply, among other things, that communities reduce the impediments, financial or regulatory, to the construction of affordable housing, and that positive steps be taken to ensure that such construction occurs (e.g., through the use of density bonuses, low and moderate income set-aside programs, housing linkage requirements, and provision of adequate land).

Rights to Health Care and Education

Land-use policy can influence access to health care facilities in a variety of ways. Local governments make decisions concerning the location of new public hospitals and clinics, and take actions which influence the location of private facilities as well, especially through zoning.

The notion of a right to health care is not particularly new, but it is embodied, at least in the developed world, in the establishment of national health care systems. While the United States has no such nationalized system, many believe that all individuals have the right to certain medical treatment and facilities, regardless of personal income or ability to pay. Article 25 of the U.N. Declaration of Human Rights, for instance, establishes access to adequate medical care as a human right.

Access to education and educational facilities is often seen as an essential prerequisite for a productive society and economy, and as essential to the functioning of a democracy. Furthermore, education is clearly connected to personal opportunity—the abilities of individuals to advance themselves economically and socially through education and hard work. As such, access to education is viewed as an important right owed to all individuals.

Because educational facilities are spatially distributed, as are health care and other facilities, they raise questions of location, siting, and access. Land-use policy can, again, influence the location of educational facilities, both public and private, and in turn the access of particular neighborhoods and groups to these facilities.

Further defining the right to education raises a number of questions. At the primary and secondary education levels, what comprises minimum educational services? (The definition must include such elements as classroom facilities, minimum per-student dollar expenditures, teacher-student ratios, and the availability of special programs for the gifted or for those requiring remedial attention.) Furthermore, what does minimum "access" imply? To fully effect this right, should everyone have access in their neighborhood, or in close proximity, to high quality schools? Or is extensive busing acceptable, as has been employed in a number of localities around the country to overcome racial and economic segregation? Is there a particular travel time which becomes excessive and thus unacceptable?

In recent years there has been considerable discussion about, and litigation over, basic inequalities between different school districts, and there are concerns about the great disparities between economic and tax base resources available to different districts.

The Right to Productive Employment

The availability of productive and meaningful employment can be seen as an essential element of a meaningful life. Without it, individuals often lack the financial capabilities to achieve desired living conditions, and to achieve a happy and fulfilling existence. The quality and extent to which the employment is rewarding, in addition to its financial remuneration, is also important. Land-use policies and decisions can influence access to employment in a number of ways, especially the location of industrial and commercial activities. Land-use patterns sometimes arise in which employment opportunities are restricted to locations that are at great distance from where those who desperately need them live. Acknowledging the right to productive employment might suggest the need to facilitate or encourage the movement of such opportunities to sites that are closer to those populations in need of employment. Local governments are frequently confronted with evaluating proposals to build residential-commercial complexes, and the importance of promoting local employment opportunities is frequently a significant point of discussion.

Acknowledging this right might also question local land-use policies which seek to keep out industrial or commercial uses. Should specific towns or communities be able to restrict local land uses to residential uses, when significant numbers of its residents need jobs? Of course, other opportunities probably exist in nearby communities or regionally, and so individuals must decide if commuting or relocating is worth it. Is it morally acceptable for a community to prevent the entrance into the community of new industrial and commercial enterprises when it knows that a number of its residents have to commute long distances each day? Also, if there is a right to employment, what type of employment must be provided? Is it sufficient that such employment yield a certain liveable level of income (i.e., something beyond minimum wage), and that this employment be stimulating and fulfilling in important ways (e.g., personally satisfying to the employee)?

The Right to Physical Access

There has been considerable concern in recent years with the mobility of the physically handicapped and with overcoming barriers to this mobility. Federal, state, and local regulations now commonly require that new public buildings, businesses, and multifamily housing be designed, and existing buildings retrofitted, so that they are accessible to the physically handicapped (e.g., providing wheelchair ramps and minimum doorway and hallway dimensions, as mandated by legislation such as the Americans with Disabilities Act).

Physical accessibility to buildings, then, is viewed, at least in the United States, as a right for all individuals. Critics of such requirements, especially the retrofitting of existing structures, frequently point to the high cost of such improvements and renovations. Again, if we apply the utilitarian methodology, it might be hard to justify these societal investments—the costs are considerable and the benefits extend to only a few people. Advocates for the handicapped typically retort that, while these investments may only benefit a small minority, it is in everyone's self-interest because anyone can become disabled in the future. If for no other reason, supporting these types of provisions is a kind of insurance policy—if one were to become disabled, one would not want to live in a world where buildings, parks, and other places are inaccessible.

Rights to Environmental Goods and a Liveable Environment

The idea that all individuals have certain basic environmental rights is not particularly new. William Blackstone has argued eloquently, as have others, that a right to a liveable environment is indeed a human right: "Each person has this right qua being human and because a liveable environment is essential for one to fulfill his human capacities. And given the danger to our environment today and hence the danger to the very possibility of human existence, access to a liveable environment must be conceived as a right which imposes upon everyone a correlative moral obligation to respect" (1974, p. 32).

While no provisions exist in the U.S. Constitution, a number of states have sought to enact amendments to their constitutions guaranteeing an individual's right to a liveable or decent environment. The first of these environmental rights amendments was passed in Michigan in 1963, and, as of this writing, at least ten other states have enacted similar provisions (Banner, 1976; Roberts, 1970). Of these, however, only a few express these guarantees in the conventional wording of rights. Pennsylvania has perhaps the stongest wording: "The people have a *right to* clean air, pure water, and to the preservation of the natural, scenic, historic and esthetic values of the environment. Pennsylvania's public natural resources are the *common property of all people,* including generations yet to come. As trustee for these resources, the Commonwealth shall conserve and maintain them for the benefit of all the people" (Pa. Constitution, Art. I, Sec. 27; my own emphasis).

Such provisions are ostensibly intended to prevent state legislatures from enacting laws which harm the environment, or state agency projects or actions that have similar effects. The vague wording of these provisions undermines their utility, and it appears that rarely have state actions been curtailed as a consequence. The courts, moreover, are reluctant to contradict legislative interpretations of constitutional rights and impose a substantial burden of proof on those challenging legislative actions on these grounds (Banner, 1976, p. 244). Such declarations have, however, led some courts to conclude that state agencies have an obligation to consider the environmental effects of state actions, although a majority of states now have specific environmental impact requirements mandating this anyway (see Ortolano, 1984). At the very least, such provisions make important moral statements about the existence of environmental rights and their universality.

One of the most notable examples of an attempt to apply such a state constitutional provision is the case of *Commonwealth v. National Gettysburg Battlefield Tower, Inc.* (8 Pa. Commonwealth 231, 1973), in which Pennsylvania's attorney general sought to use the environmental rights provisions as the basis for enjoining the construction of a 307–foot observation tower adjacent to Gettysburg National Battlefield Park. The planned tower was to be located only 400 feet from the park and only 1,200 feet from the location where President Lincoln delivered the Gettysburg Address. The Attorney General and a variety of expert witnesses, including noted architect Louis Kahn, argued that the tower would represent a major visual intrusion on the "pastoral serenity of the battlefield scene" and would be "out-of-scale with its surroundings" (302 Atlantic Reporter, 2d series, p. 889). The state claimed that such an environmental intrusion would explicitly violate the state's constitutional provision establishing the public's "right to clean air, pure water, and to the preservation of the natural, scenic, historic and esthetic values of the environment." While the Pennsylvania courts did not foreclose the possibility that this constitutional provision could be used to prevent certain proposed land uses, they found that the facts of the tower case failed to support the conclusion that substantial damage to the environment and harm to the public's right would occur.

It can also be argued that the notion of environmental rights means that all individuals ought to be entitled to access to and use of certain types of environmental resources, such as lakes. This notion is perhaps most clearly expressed in the common law "public trust doctrine" derived from ancient Roman law (see Maleski, 1985; Sax, 1971a; Steiner, 1991). The public trust doctrine holds that there are certain lands held in common trust by the public and from which the public cannot be excluded through private property rights.

The common law of most states embraces the public trust doctrine in one way or another. It applies most consistently to tidal areas and navigable waterways. In most states, the public trust waters extend at least landward to the mean high-water line. While private property boundaries may extend into these areas, the public retains rights to use and access which cannot be obstructed by private landowners. The practical implication of this doctrine in coastal areas is that it preserves and protects the wet beach for the public and prohibits private shorefront landowners from fencing off or otherwise preventing public access to, or movement along, these beach areas.

The public trust doctrine is also employed to justify significant shoreline land-use restrictions intended to protect the quality of public surface waters. The most notable case of this sort, in which the public trust doctrine was strongly upheld by the courts, was *Just v. Marinette*. This case involved a challenge of Marinette County's (Wisconsin) shoreline zoning restrictions which the Justs (landowners) claimed deprived them of all economic use of their property and thus comprised a government "taking" requiring just compensation. The county adopted its shoreline zoning ordinance pursuant to state requirements, and classified shorefront land into several categories. The Justs originally purchased some thirty-six acres of land adjacent to Lake Noquebay, eventually subdividing and selling five of the six lots, keeping one lot for themselves. The one lot the Justs retained was zoned as wetlands conservation, allowing only limited uses by right (e.g., wild crop harvesting, sustained yield forestry), but allowing other uses conditionally (e.g., farming and the construction of piers, docks, and boathouses). The Justs failed to apply for a conditional permit but simply began filling in the wetlands. They were then sued by the county, and they countersued, claiming an unconstitutional taking had occurred, among other things (see Hunter, 1988). Eventually the case made its way to the Wisconsin Supreme Court, where a strong opinion was issued in support of the county's restrictions. The court found the county's regulations entirely acceptable and based its opinion in large part on the public trust doctrine—specifically, that preserving the integrity of the wetlands is essential to protecting the quality of public waters. The court's opinion strongly questioned the inherent right of landowners to modify the natural functions and characteristics of such land:

> An owner of land has no absolute and unlimited right to change the essential natural character of his land so as to use it for a purpose for which it was unsuited in its natural state and which impairs the rights of others. The exercise of the police power in zoning must be reasonable and we think it was not an unreasonable exercise of that power to pre-

vent harm to public rights by limiting the use of private property to its natural uses. (56 Wis 2nd at 11, 201 N.W.2d)

In this particular case, the court saw the important role of wetlands in cleaning and purifying waters—waters protected under the public trust. Few state courts have taken the public trust doctrine this far, but the underlying notion of public rights in environmental resources is increasingly being acknowledged. Joseph L. Sax has been one of the most vocal in arguing that the public trust doctrine could and should be applied to a variety of other types of environmental resources, from clean air to fisheries to coastal beaches.

> Long ago there developed in the law of the Roman Empire a legal theory known as the "doctrine of the public trust." It was founded upon the very sensible idea that certain common properties, such as rivers, the seashore, and the air, were held by government in trusteeship for the free and unimpeded use of the general public. Our contemporary concerns about "the environment" bear a very close conceptual relationship to the venerable legal doctrine. (Sax, 1971a, pp. 163–64)

These types of environmental rights can be established through other common law doctrines. For instance, in Oregon and Texas the public-owned beaches extend not merely to the mean high-water line, but to the first line of vegetation, expanding the public rights considerably. In both states the doctrine of customary use is applied to secure this public right. This doctrine holds essentially that the public has access rights to these areas because it has for centuries used these areas. (This doctrine is similar to the concept of adverse possession, by which one private party can secure title to another party's land as a result of continuous and known occupations.) State legislation such as the Texas Open Beaches Act (1959) serves to ratify this common law principle and creates a mechanism by which private individuals can act to protect these rights.

A major conflict between these public beach rights and private landowners rights occurred in Texas following the landfall of Hurricane Alicia in 1983 (see Godschalk, Brower, and Beatley, 1989). Because the point of demarcation between the public and private beach is the first line of vegetation, and because over time this line changes, the public beach represents a kind of rolling easement. When Hurricane Alicia struck the west beach on Galveston Island, it substantially moved landward this line of vegetation. Many private structures which were landward of the line prior to the storm were seaward of the line following Alicia, thus placing them on the new public beach (see fig. 5.1).

The state attorney general's office quickly issued the opinion that, if structures were damaged beyond 50 percent, and located seaward of the

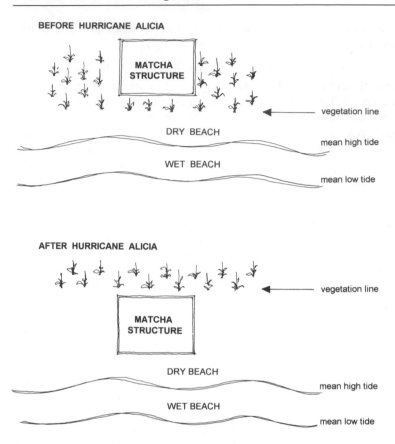

Figure 5.1 On Galveston Island following Hurricane Alicia (1983). *Source:* Mattox et al., 1985.

new line of vegetation, they were now on the public beach and thus could not be rebuilt. To allow reconstruction would be to allow private land-owners to violate a clear public right. These restrictions eventually led to a series of lawsuits by affected landowners (one of them by the Matcha family, as illustrated in fig. 5.1), lawsuits which were decided in favor of the state, reinforcing the customary use doctrine.

Many other similar environmental rights might be acknowledged and seen to motivate local and state land-use regulations. It can be argued that citizens and landowners have rights to solar access, leading to solar envelope zoning and solar access protection ordinances (see Osofsky, 1983). To prevent shading of public beaches, some coastal communities have enacted setback and height restrictions to prevent the casting of shadows. It can also be argued that the public has certain rights to basic recreational goods, such as bike and pedestrian trails, urban parks and greenways.

There is considerable disagreement about public environmental rights with respect to aesthetic or visual resources as already evidenced by the Gettysburg battlefield case. Long-time residents of visually impressive lands, whether the beautiful color contrasts of a volcanic Caribbean island or the rugged Rocky Mountains skyline, are often dismayed and disappointed when new growth and development diminishes this scenic beauty. Such concerns often lead to proposals to restrict the location or configuration of development to protect these aesthetic resources. Residents (as well as visitors) of western North Carolina were duly indignant when a 10–story high-rise condominium was constructed on the top of Little Sugartop Mountain in Avery County, in the heart of that state's scenic Blue Ridge Mountains. This visual "scar" can be seen for many miles and from many directions, and to many it is an affront to the rights of the public to enjoy the landscape as they had done for centuries. So much concern was generated by this project that it led to the enactment of the North Carolina Mountain Ridge Protection Act (1983), which now prohibits tall buildings in ridge zones (see Heath, 1984). It can be argued, then, that the public does hold, in addition to more biologically required environmental rights such as clean air and clean water, certain basic rights to visually pleasing landscapes. A number of localities have acknowledged similar public obligations. The city of Denver, for instance, has adopted building height restrictions in designated view corridors to protect views of the Rocky Mountains from public parks (see Beatley, Brower, and Brower, 1988).

The Right to Be Free from Environmental Harms

Certain land-use rights can be thought of as negative rights—that is, not rights *to* things necessarily, but rather rights to be free *from* certain things. These include the right to be free of certain excessive technological risks (e.g., from air and water pollution, exposure to toxic waters) or natural hazards (e.g., hurricanes, floods, earthquakes, landslides).

Land-use policies have particular bearing on the type and extent of pollutants—air, water, noise, light—that people are subject to. As noted earlier, development, agriculture, silviculture, and other land uses can have substantial impacts on water quality (surface and groundwater) through the generation of sediment, toxic runoff, pesticides, and fertilizers, among other pollutants. While control of "point" sources has met with considerable success during the last several decades, these nonpoint sources have become major aspects of the water quality problem. Similarly, many of the most serious urban air pollution problems are a direct result of nonpoint sources, notably the automobile (witness the situation in cities such as Los Angeles and Denver), and inefficient and sprawling land-use patterns (with the vast separation of work and home and the need for long commutes). Land-use decisions also clearly influence the siting and location of major point sources of pollution, such as municipal sewage treatment plants and industrial smokestacks. In making these types of land-use decisions—those which have bearing on the extent and distribution of these environmental harms, for instance—do we have a moral obligation to acknowledge and seek to protect certain minimum rights of individuals to be free of these pollutants?

Because a risk-free world is unrealistic, and probably unachievable, the question often becomes, What risk level is acceptable? What minimum levels of public safety are owed to all individuals as individuals, again irrespective of what might perhaps generate the greatest level of social benefits? These types of rights to minimum safety are at the heart of the justification for a host of occupational safety and public health standards. While it may make sense in terms of maximizing social utility to prohibit employers from exposing workers to unsafe workplace conditions (because of lost work days, lost social productivity, social drain caused by medical expenses), this is not principally why we enact such restrictions. We impose them because we feel that human beings are entitled to work in reasonably safe environments—they're entitled to this as human beings.

Deciding on the actual risk reduction levels that individuals are entitled to is often difficult, however. Federal and state environmental regulatory agencies have for many years grappled with the question of what constitutes "acceptable risk." In the case of clean air, under the federal Clean Air Act, the Environmental Protection Agency (EPA) establishes national ambient air quality standards for conventional air pollutants (the "criteria" pollutants), which states and localities must then work to achieve. These standards, in a real sense, identify thresholds of exposure beyond which no individuals should have to endure, no matter what their economic condition, no matter where they live. Compliance under the Clean Air Act has been less than stellar with numerous regions and localities, from which one might surmise that these ambient standards do not represent *real* rights, in that they are often superseded or ignored for economic reasons.

The Rights of Nature and Other Life-Forms

Long before the recent notoriety of animal rights groups in this country, there was considerable support for the notion that certain obligations are owed to other forms of life. This was expressed clearly in the environmental area through the passage of such federal legislation as the Endangered Species Act (1973) and the Marine Mammal Protection Act

(1974). Moreover, human land use frequently conflicts with and bumps up against the habitat needs of other species, some of which are threatened with extinction. Whether it is resort development in the Florida Keys threatening the remaining population of the Key deer, or urban expansion in Las Vegas jeopardizing the desert tortoise, such conflicts abound and are clearly on the rise. Increasingly it is argued that nature, broadly conceived, has certain rights which are generally inviolable in the pursuit of human welfare (see Nash, 1989; Taylor, 1986). These different ethical points of view are described and analyzed in considerable detail in Chapter 7, and so do not warrant extensive discussion here. The rights of nature and of other life-forms does constitute another category of moral, and sometimes legal, rights, which land-use ethics must consider.

The Problem of Conflicting Land-Use Rights

A major category of moral dilemmas which I raise here, but which are necessarily difficult to resolve, is the problem of what to do when certain land-use rights conflict with each other. Let's assume, for instance, that you embrace both the notion of the rights of other species to exist and the rights of individuals to affordable and decent housing. These two imperatives are coming into increasing conflict around the country (Beatley, 1989a, 1990a). Take the case of the threatened Stephens's kangaroo rat. Placed on the federal Endangered Species Act list in the fall of 1989, much of the species' remaining habitat is located in eastern Riverside County, California—also one of the few remaining sites for affordable housing in the Los Angeles metropolitan area. To preserve the species, large blocks of habitat will likely need to be protected and set aside, reducing the supply of developable land, and already a development fee has been imposed to fund the acquisition ($1,950 per acre interim fee), as well as preparation, of the necessary habitat conservation plan. These fees, it is argued, are then passed along to the housing consumer in the form of higher housing prices, in turn squeezing some people out of that housing market. As a public official contemplating this dilemma, what should you do? There seems to be a potentially serious conflict between these two land-use rights: to permit new housing to proceed without protecting an endangered species will violate the existence right of another form of life (and will likely violate the federal Endangered Species Act), but to undertake all the necessary protective actions, including setting aside sufficient habitat to ensure survival of the species, will substantially raise the cost of housing for new residents, in seeming contradiction to the rights of individuals to decent and affordable housing.

While this kind of moral balancing is best done with a complete understanding of the specific circumstances at hand, it is important to ensure that these conflicts are not framed or conceived of too inflexibly. An initial tack is to consider viable alternatives that might acknowledge and protect both rights. Among the alternatives might be a funding mechanism for habitat acquisition which spreads the costs over the broader community, thus reducing the price effects on new housing. Furthermore, the negative effects on affordable housing, perhaps to be brought about by the withdrawal of land for habitat conservation, might be counterbalanced through efforts to increase density or promote affordable housing in other locations. A complete consideration of land-use alternatives may ameliorate circumstances where land-use rights appear to conflict. Cooperation between all concerned parties is, of course, critical to successful resolution of such conflicts.

Summary

In this chapter I argued that individuals may be entitled to a variety of potential land-use rights; both rights to certain things, such as minimum health care and decent and affordable housing, and rights to be free from certain things, such as dangerous levels of pollution or environmental degradation. These rights may be legal and constitutional in their origin, or nonlegal or moral, deriving instead from the force of moral argument.

Land-use ethics should acknowledge that a variety of such rights may exist and that they may serve as constraints on, and trumps to, maximum utility. I avoided a detailed and specific specification of these rights, because it is best to leave the discourse and argumentation at local and state political levels (or federal, depending upon where these obligations are believed to reside). Determining what precise quality or level of housing is implied by a right to affordable housing, for example, is debatable and may depend on numerous local or regional factors, and is generally beyond the space limitations of this book. Important here is the key notion that individuals hold certain basic entitlements that cannot be violated by land-use policies which might be intended to maximize social welfare.

6

DISTRIBUTIVE OBLIGATIONS
IN LAND USE

ACCORDING TO philosopher John Rawls, social justice is the "first virtue of social institutions, as truth is of systems of thought" (1971, p. 3). It
is equally relevant to consider how *just* land-use institutions are and what
are the many discrete land-use decisions made by these social institutions. Because land-use policies and decisions have the potential to seriously influence the distribution of social costs and benefits, it is important to discuss alternative views of distributive justice as it is applied to
land-use policy. While many of the basic mechanisms for distribution of
social benefits—from government housing and welfare policy to the distribution of jobs and income—are largely outside the traditional domain
of land use, many are, in one way or another, reachable or influenceable
through land-use decisions. Land-use decisions and policies clearly and
undeniably influence the quality of people's lives and the distribution of
social and economic opportunities; they also affect, obviously, the quality and character of the land and its life-forms.

Concern about the distributive impacts of land-use policies and decisions can take several directions. On the one hand, there is the concern that through land-use policies we disrupt or interrupt an existing
pattern or distribution which is in some sense just or socially desirable.
More typically, we are concerned that land-use policies do not further
exacerbate existing social and economic inequities. Land-use policies
often fall hardest on the least-advantaged members of society. On the
other hand, it may be possible to use land-use policies to counteract or
counterbalance the inequities created by other social institutions—that
is, not simply to prevent certain groups and individuals from having their
economic and social position diminished, but using land-use policies
to advance and improve the position of certain individuals and
groups.

Let's consider a typical example of a land-use scenario that illustrates
how land-use policies and actions can significantly influence the distribution of social advantages. A state highway department has planned for
a new interstate highway that will connect two bustling metropolitan

areas. Both local and state officials agree on the urgency and necessity of the highway, and the large collective economic benefit which will result from the project. The highway department, after months of considering different routes, proposes a route which, it feels, will be the most efficient, least expensive, and least disruptive. The highway officials appear before those local governments which will be affected by the highway and seek their endorsement. Highway planners presenting the proposed route admit that no highway siting is free of physical and social disruption but assert that the selected route is the best alternative. Representatives from a low-income minority neighborhood, however, are extremely upset because the proposed route will split their neighborhood in half and wipe out a large portion of their community's business district. They contend that the proposed route is discriminatory and that either the highway should not be built at all or that its route should be changed to avoid their neighborhood. The highway planners respond by presenting a series of cost-benefit analyses which indicate that the proposed route will generate the greatest overall social benefits of any of the alternatives considered, including an alternative which would bypass that neighborhood altogether. Furthermore, they indicate that residents and businesses will be assisted in relocating to other parts of the city, and that fair compensation for damages will be provided. The local officials, after hearing these various presentations, endorse the proposed route and indicate that they believe the highway is desperately needed by their constituents.

In this example, the utilitarian alternative—the alternative which serves to maximize overall societal benefits—clearly imposes significant economic and social costs on a particular social group. Is such an outcome ethical? Will such a result violate our sense of distributive justice? Even with the compensatory actions proposed by the highway department, it is likely that residents of the impacted neighborhood will still be worse off than they were prior to the construction of the highway. In this case public land-use decisions not only fail to improve the condition of those at the lower end of the socioeconomic ladder but also actually worsen their position.

These types of impacts are certainly not unique. Just look at Boston, Los Angeles, or any major city impacted by an interstate. Land-use plans and policies can have considerable influence over the distribution of housing, jobs, health care, transportation, and recreational and other amenities. Because of these types of distributive impacts, any consideration of land-use ethics must necessarily consider explicitly the question of social justice. This chapter considers several alternative distributive goals and theories of distributive justice which land-use policy might promote or advance.

Promoting Equality and Equal Opportunity in Land Use

The ideal of equality has played a prominent role in political and popular discourse in this country, indeed from its early beginnings. The Declaration of Independence tells us that "all men are created equal." Despite the political and rhetorical support for the concept of equality, the reality of social and economic life in the United States and elsewhere is one of dramatic inequality—inequality among different social and racial groups and between sexes, inequality among regions of the country. Statistics suggest, for instance, that a small percentage of the population of this country controls a disproportionately large percentage of the wealth. A recent report by the Center on Budget and Policy Priorities indicates that the schism between rich and poor grew significantly during the 1980s:

> An analysis of recently released data on income trends in the 1980s shows that income disparities between wealthy and other Americans have widened significantly. The most affluent Americans reaped exceptionally large income gains during that decade, while middle income Americans gained little and low income Americans fell further behind.
>
> As a result of these trends, the richest one percent of all Americans now receive nearly as much income after taxes as the bottom 40 percent of Americans combined. Stated another way, the richest 2.5 million people now have nearly as much income as 100 million Americans with the lowest incomes. (Greenstein and Barancik, 1990, p. 1)

From a land-use perspective, these differences in income and wealth and the qualities of the life experienced by different groups are often quite apparent "on the ground." The contrast between such areas in Los Angeles as Beverly Hills and Watts is symbolic of this gulf. Many other aspects of this inequality are more subtle, including differences in the resources and quality of school districts, medical care, and park and transportation systems.

The ethical goal of equality in the context of land-use policy might be defined in several ways. Very often in this country we are more accustomed to thinking of political equalities when using the term, rather than economic or social equalities—that is, protecting basic opportunities for political participation and expression, such as freedom of speech and assemblage and equality of suffrage. This concern is consistent with the country's historic emphasis on free enterprise and personal initiative. The concept of political equality and its various potential meanings are discussed in detail in Chapter 14.

Another possible perspective is to define equality from an "equal shares" view: that is, we may have moral obligations to ensure that when allocating social and community resources, all social groups and all neighborhoods be given equal shares. If there is a limited pool of funds to be used for infrastructure improvements or recreational facilities, this position holds that the community has an obligation to ensure that these funds be allocated on an equal basis. Fairness means equality of allocation. Of course, from a practical point of view it is often difficult to determine the appropriate social and political "units" across which equal shares can be distributed (block versus the neighborhood versus the sector versus the community versus the city versus the region).

An equal shares point of view can be considered deficient because, on face value, it neither examines the history of allocations nor takes into account the starting points of different groups. Another possible position, one I refer to as the "distributive equalitarian," is concerned less with the size of shares being allocated and more with the resulting parity among groups. If only two primary social groups, or two distinct geographical neighborhoods, are identified, and one has abundant resources (schools, transportation, parks and recreation facilities, and medical care facilities) and the other has a paucity of these same resources, an equal shares strategy at that point in time does little more than reinforce existing social and economic inequalities. The distributive equalitarian deems as requisite those allocations which serve to reduce or minimize, albeit perhaps over some period of time, the basic inequalities between these groups. Such a distributive standard indeed requires unequal shares, at least in the short term.

Historically, a major criticism of this distributive equalitarian approach is the draconian nature of the outcome—and the socially unappealing image of the resulting world. Will it be that, under such a standard, all neighborhoods will look alike? Does distributive equality necessarily imply a Levittown kind of uniformity? Supporters would deny that. Although such land-use and resource allocations are based on the need to overcome inequalities in the *overall* quality of life, different social groups and neighborhoods need not expend these resources in precisely the same ways. One neighborhood may choose to support much greater access to child care or medical facilities, in turn choosing to support reduced improvements to its road and transportation system. Another neighborhood might place greater emphasis on improvements to its park and recreational system, with less emphasis on improvements in health care or child care, undoubtedly in part a response to the particular circumstances or necessities of the community. A standard of spatial equality, the distributive equalitarian argues, permits and encourages a diverse mosaic of different life-styles and community conditions.

Another way to define the ideal of equality is the "equal opportunity" concept. Here the emphasis shifts from assessing the results of social, economic, and political mechanisms (i.e., whether, and to what extent, major disparities exist between different groups or communities) to assessing the conditions under which these social resources and benefits are allocated. At a community or neighborhood level, has there been equal opportunity to solicit and compete for, say, government projects, prospective businesses, or the allocation of other goods and services? On an individual level, have there been sufficient opportunities to ensure that one has the chance to develop and utilize his or her talents fully?

To ensure an equality of opportunity, it may be unnecessary to achieve total equality among all income groups or neighborhoods (e.g., roughly equal levels of income, facilities, and public services), but instead to provide a certain minimum level of these things—that is, individuals should have access to a reasonably high quality educational system; reasonably adequate housing, parks, and medical care; and a reasonably efficient transportation system. If individuals and groups choose not to avail themselves of these facilities and opportunities, that is fine, as long as they have been given sufficient opportunities to decide. Emphasizing such minimum levels of opportunity or access is quite similar to the rights-based views discussed in Chapter 5. Access to minimum educational facilities, argued for on the basis of equality of opportunity, can also be seen as a basic right to education that all individuals should have.

Concerns about equal opportunity find considerable support among the land professions, especially urban and regional planning. This is often described in terms of the goal of expanding choice (see Davidoff, 1975). Indeed, recall that both the AICP code of ethics and APA ethical principles contain extensive reference to expanding choice.

Cleveland, Ohio, represents one of the best examples of a city that sought to implement such an ethic of expanding choice in the late 1960s and 1970s (see Krumholz, 1982). Its 1975 Cleveland Policy Planning Report states clearly the city's overall goal of providing a "wider range of choices for those Cleveland residents who have few, if any, choices" (Cleveland City Planning Commission, 1975, as quoted in Krumholz, 1982, p. 163). At that time, city planners undertook a variety of actions in pursuit of this goal, including ensuring availability of low-cost transit service, placing conditions on new development (e.g., to guarantee a certain number of local jobs), seeking to ensure low electricity rates, and establishing a new state park on the waterfront.

From a moral point of view, certain land-use actions or decisions can also be defended on the basis of "compensatory equality." This concept suggests that special benefits or considerations ought to be given to make up for inequitable past allocations. If it can be argued that a particular neighborhood or community faction has been discriminated against in the past, that group may require special treatment now in order to compensate for such past unequal treatment. In a practical sense the outcome of compensatory equality will likely resemble that of distributive equality; that is, compensatory equality views existing inequalities in resources and opportunities as the result of previous actions—largely, if not absolutely, explaining such inequalities—and thus provides additional moral weight for land-use actions intended to equalize such resources.

A Rawlsian Theory of Land Use

John Rawls offers yet another perspective on distributive obligations, found most essentially in his *A Theory of Justice* (1971). Rawls follows in the footsteps of the social contract theorists and seeks to construct a hypothetical "original position," to which discussants of social justice can revert in search of collective principles to govern social institutions. Rawls hypothesizes that, because individuals are inherently risk-averse in the absence of specific knowledge of their own talents and circumstances (under the "veil of ignorance"), they will naturally choose that set of principles which constitutes the maximin position (the best among the worst possible outcomes; see Beatley, 1984; Berry and Steiker, 1974). Rawls suggests that his Two Principles of Justice will be selected as the maximin solution from a short list of major alternative principles of justice (including utilitarianism). Specifically, the two principles to be chosen are these:

> Principle 1. Each person is to have an equal right to the most extensive total system of equal basic liberties compatible with a similar system of liberty for all.
> Principle 2. Social and economic inequalities are to be arranged so that they are both (a) to the greatest benefit of the least advantaged, consistent with the just savings principle, and (b) attached to offices and positions open to all under conditions of fair equality of opportunity. (1971, p. 302)

We have already discussed Rawls's First Principle, which establishes fairly conventional liberties. These two principles, it should be remembered, are ordered lexically or lexicographically; that is, the conditions of the first principle must be satisfied fully before moving on to the second.

The most interesting feature of these principles from a distributive land-use view is the so-called Difference Principle (DP), which permits social and economic inequalities only when they act "to the greatest benefit of the least advantaged" (ibid.). Note the difference between the DP and the distributive equalitarian position discussed above. While resulting inequalities are not acceptable under the latter, they are acceptable, and even desirable, under the former if they serve to advance the interests of the least advantaged.

Rawls presents a moral interpretation of the workings of society that is vastly different from that of many conservative philosophers. Rawls views life's distribution of benefits and burdens as largely arbitrary from a moral point of view; the result of talents, inheritances of resources and wealth, and personal circumstances, which the individual has done little to earn or create. This assumption is coupled with a strong view of society not as a collection of independent actors, but as a mutual and shared endeavor, in which everyone benefits from the cooperative actions of each:

> The intuitive idea is that since everyone's well-being depends upon a scheme of cooperation without which no one could have a satisfactory life, the division of advantages should be such as to draw forth the willing cooperation of everyone taking part in it, including those less well situated. Yet this can be expected only if reasonable terms are proposed. The two principles . . . seem to be a fair agreement on the basis of which those better endowed, or more fortunate in their social position, neither of which we can be said to deserve, could expect the willing cooperation of others when some workable scheme is a necessary condition of the welfare of all. Once we decide to look for a conception of justice that nullifies the accidents of natural endowment and the contingencies of social circumstance as counters in quest for political and economic advantage, we are led to these principles. They express the result of leaving aside those aspects of the social world that seem abitrary from a moral point of view. (Ibid., p. 15)

The DP shifts the orientation of public concern away from hidden-hand justice and a priori legitimacy of unrestricted transactions, so central to conservative Nozick (1974), to a morally compelling argument for a substantial redistributive function. Under the Rawlsian paradigm, land-use policy seeks to reduce social and economic inequalities (spatial and otherwise) unless those inequalities serve to maximize the conditions and benefits of members of the worst-off group. It suggests that land-use programs and policies—as with any other set of economic and social institutions—should be constituted so that the net benefits which flow from them are maximized for members of the community on the lowest economic and social rung. The Rawlsian position would not view as legitimate, for example, the highway siting in the earlier scenario, despite the large social or collective benefits that might be generated by such a project.

Under the Rawlsian distributive framework, once the welfare of members of the worst-off groups in the community is maximized, the lexical difference principle takes over and demands that, ceteris paribus, the welfare of the next worst-off group in the community be maximized. This hierarchical process occurs until the demands of those groups at the top of the community's social and economic pyramid are satisfied. Then, the Rawlsian framework becomes largely utilitarian (with, of course, the protection of certain basic rights outlined under the first principle). For instance, if a public official must choose between two competing land-use schemes or policies, which equally maximize benefits to all other social classes save one, the decision criterion then becomes that of maximizing total benefits within that group (assuming these are the only two options available). In these circumstances, other typical land-use objectives, such as the production of public goods and the correction of market failures, become more relevant.

Applying this Rawlsian model to land-use policymaking presents several major obstacles, however. First, there is the inherent difficulty of identifying distinct community groups and aggregations and placing each on some sort of relative community welfare scale (see Nozick, 1974, pp. 183–231). While at a level of political rhetoric it is relatively easy to speak of social and economic classes, in practical land-use decision-making contexts it may be quite complicated to delineate, distinguish, and operationalize these concepts. Nozick observes that there are numerous social groupings or configurations that can be employed to make this community ranking. Moreover, public officials, and the institutional and administrative contexts in which they operate, are faced with, and must respond to, various combinations of individuals (e.g., a single homeowner), community groups (e.g., taxpayer alliances, environmental advocates, neighborhood associations), and broad class interests (e.g., businesses, workers); attempting to organize and make sense of this in a Rawlsian framework may be quite difficult, but these practical difficulties are not insurmountable.

Rawls seeks to simplify the procedure through the notion of a representative or average member of a social class or position which can serve as a general proxy for the well-being of larger socioeconomic groups. Rawls suggests that "the class of least-advantaged persons may be taken to include everyone whose income is no greater than the average income of persons on the lowest relevant social position (or alternatively everyone with less than half the median income and wealth in the society)" (Scanlon, 1974, p. 193). Such grouping of income and wealth seems to be a logical and practical focus for land-use officials implementing the Rawlsian framework. But they must remember that, while the position of such average or representative members may rise, the conditions of specific individuals in this group may plummet.

Rawls's reliance on the concept of expected benefits also presents a serious ethical ambiguity for land-use officials. Rawls is fundamentally concerned with establishing social and economic institutions that will maximize the long-term expectations of those in the worst-off group; that is, decisions to institute land-use policies that will maximize the welfare of these groups in the short term (with a high degree of certainty) may conflict with those programs, policies, and institutions that may in the long run advance their positions to an even greater extent. For instance, is it wise to redistribute wealth in the short term (thus maximizing the welfare of these groups) when these funds can be funneled into private investments that will eventually provide jobs (and even greater benefits) for members of this group? At least two reasons might be suggested in defense of the more immediate maximizing by land-use policies: (1) the empirical claims that longer-term policies will yield greater benefits for the worst-off groups generally involve a higher degree of uncertainty than more discrete decisions made in the shorter term, and (2) even if these longer-range benefits exceed those in the short term, it is unclear whether individuals and groups will be in positions that will allow them to weather short-term deprivations in acceptable ways.

Although Rawls has suggested tangible income and wealth as measures for assessing and monitoring the condition of worst-off groups, the focus of the difference principle is actually on what he calls, "primary goods"— "things which every rational man is presumed to want . . . whatever a person's rational plan of life" (1971, p. 62). Chief among them are "rights and liberties, powers and opportunities, income and wealth" (ibid.). This suggests that determining the relative well-being of groups in the community may at times be a more complicated activity than simply assessing tangible levels of income and wealth. For instance, two individuals of equal income and wealth may possess different levels of primary goods, because one has certain social rights and opportunities that the other does not have (e.g., because of race).

It is of considerable importance that Rawls includes personal self-respect among the primary goods. This may limit the magnitude of the relative differences in the material welfare of different social groups. In other words, vast inequalities in wealth may not be tolerated if they cause substantial reductions in the personal self-respect of members of the worst-off groups (see Sennett and Cobb, 1972). While the tangible wealth and resources of these groups may rise (e.g., better housing, more aesthetically pleasing neighborhoods), the true value of this wealth and the self-respect it ensures may plummet. Consequently, the public official may forego those land-use programs and policies which maximize tangible income and goods for the worst-off, but create large and visible inequalities among social groups, for a more egalitarian distribution which minimizes harm to self-esteem. An alternative perspective, and one intimated surprisingly by Rawls, is to limit this reduction in self-esteem (which

Rawls calls the problem of envy) by isolating upper and lower income groups:

> Although in theory the difference principle permits indefinitely large inequalities in return for small gains to the less favored, the spread of income and wealth should not be excessive in practice, given the requisite background institutions. Moreover the plurality of associations in a well-ordered society, each with its secure internal life, tends to reduce the visibility, or at least the painful visibility, of variations in men's prospects. For we tend to compare our circumstances with others in the same or in a similar group as ourselves, or in positions that we regard as relevant to our aspirations. The various associations in society tend to divide it into so many non-comparing groups, the discrepancies between the divisions not attracting the kinds of attention which unsettles the lives of those less well placed. (1971, p. 537)

This might suggest that perhaps the best way to satisfy the DP is through land-use policies that reduce contact and interaction among different social and economic groups, thus reducing comparative envy and the possibility of diminishing one's sense of comparative well-being. Such a strategy, however, is ethically questionable in its focus on the manipulation of the social exposure and experiences of the worst-off and its possible use in rationalizing inegalitarian spatial and social patterns in a community.

Another operational limitation to the Rawlsian perspective is the practical difficulty of working one's way up this economic pyramid in any rational or systematic way. It may be infeasible to attempt, first, to maximize benefits completely for the worst-off, and second, to maximize benefits for the next worst-off social groups in sequential order. Practically speaking, it may be necessary for land-use policymakers to move back and forth, returning to lower positions whenever possible, and thus more opportunistically maximizing benefits to members of the worst-off groups and social positions. It is often impossible to order and organize the consideration of land-use policies and programs in such a way that decision-makers can select the optimal Rawlsian package. This observation may only suggest, however, the need in many situations to consider the Rawlsian perspective as a satisficing, and thus nonoptimizing, decision norm in actual land-use policymaking situations.

A final difficulty emerges in communities where focusing distributional decisions on a social hierarchy is infeasible because such a hierarchy does not exist. If, for instance, the community in question is largely homogeneous in its socioeconomic composition, does the Rawlsian perspective become invalid? Rawlsian analysis and the land-use imperatives which flow from it will generally remain useful for several reasons:

(1) while homogeneity may be the general tendency, there may still be considerable welfare variation, as well as the existence of individuals and groups falling on the fringes of what might be represented by a sort of bell-shaped local welfare curve, and (2) land-use obligations may be owed to communities and groups outside a jurisdiction's boundaries. The latter point again raises the question, How do public officials define the moral community (i.e., the focus of their moral responsibilities)?

The "Leaky Bucket" Issue

One objection sometimes raised in efforts to use land-use policies to accomplish distributive and redistributive objectives is that society may have more effective and efficient ways to do this (e.g., through a negative income tax). Using land-use policies to modify or redistribute broader patterns of societal wealth or income can be likened to the problem of the leaky bucket—while the goal is to transport some water (i.e., to accomplish distributive objectives), is more water lost in the process than the amount delivered (Okun, 1975, pp. 91–106)?

There are several potential replies to the leaky bucket quandary. One reply holds that what is morally desirable cannot be separated from what is practically feasible; that is, substantial redistributive schemes are politically unlikely in any foreseeable future (at any government level), while land-use policies and programs can and do serve this function. More important, however, the dynamics of the social and spatial environments, and processes of local development and change, are constantly redistributing wealth (broadly defined). Take, for instance, our highway project example. Let us assume that the highway constitutes the highest and best economic use for the land. If no impediments to market transactions exist (e.g., transaction costs are low or nonexistent), the builders or proponents of the road can easily outbid the residents of the adjacent impacted neighborhood. Yet, in numerous ways the lives of these residents are made worse off. Thus, such changes serve continually to disrupt and reallocate resources and wealth, even once a "satisfactory" distribution has been achieved (e.g., through other redistributive means). Moreover, the introduction of market imperfections may also have substantial redistributive effects. For example, lower income groups in the community may tend to be less able to organize and collect economic bids, say, to buy out a noxious adjacent use. Even if sufficient wealth is redistributed through other means, existing market imperfections may prevent effective application of this wealth, with these effects in turn falling disproportionately on certain groups in the community.

Regardless of how extensive or effective a system might be in place at federal or state levels to accomplish distributive objectives, land-use decisions will clearly impact people's lives in a variety of important ways. Even if one believes that land-use policies should not be used in any way, shape, or form for redistributive purposes, there remains the obligation to ensure that such policies and projects do not diminish or reduce the plight of the least-advantaged. Land-use policies and projects should, at the least, prevent the widening of income and social inequalities, unless they meet the conditions of the difference principle (DP).

Balancing Distributive and Environmental Obligations

Before closing this chapter, I will examine the relationship between the potential distributive obligations in land-use policy and the various environmental obligations to be discussed in Chapter 7. Quite often these obligations are viewed as contradictory, or at least working in different directions, and this may represent to the reader a substantial ethical quandary. Many questions of distributive ethics in land-use policy may, of course, simply lack any direct environmental dimension or connection. In other circumstances environmental conditions are clearly a major aspect or component of existing inequities in land use, for instance when low-income or minority communities are forced to endure especially high levels of air or water pollution. Environmental control strategies here can serve to *promote* distributive ethics.

Often there are times, however, when environmental land-use controls and policy have undesirable economic effects that may serve to exacerbate existing local inequities. Land-use and environmental restrictions are often criticized because they are believed to result in raising the average cost of housing in a community, and therefore in making affordable housing less available. Recent controversy over a proposal to limit development in environmentally sensitive areas in Howard County, Maryland, is illustrative. Here opposition to such a proposal was vociferous, with the primary charge being that such additional regulations would raise the cost of housing in the county. The proposed regulations were to limit development near streams and wetlands, to prohibit development on slopes of greater than 25 percent, and to require greater amounts of open space, among other provisions (Jennings and Shen, 1988). Not unexpectedly, the proposed regulations were strongly opposed by local builders and realtors, who claimed that the restrictions would add an additional $5,000 to the cost of new homes. (The average price of a home in Howard County at that time was $156,150.)

It is quite common to hear these kinds of criticisms of environmental regulations and controls on land use. If the protection of wetlands is increased, then the available land for development will decrease, thus pushing up the cost of housing. If restrictions are imposed on development in endangered species habitat or in other sensitive areas, then the cost of housing will likewise increase. If additional storm-water management requirements or restrictions on the extent of impervious surfaces are enacted, the actions will have price effects. Will each additional environmental control put affordable housing that much farther out of reach for many Americans and make their communities that much more exclusive? The logical extension of these concerns is to suggest that, in the name of promoting distributive obligations, society ought to minimize the extent of such environmental regulations. I cannot accept these conclusions, and I believe there are more useful ways to frame the ethical question.

The impacts on the price of housing and the market effects of environmental regulations ought clearly to concern us and might indeed work at cross-purposes to social equity and distributive ethics. The conclusion, however, is not, in my mind, to give up on such environmental safeguards, and I hold this view for at least two reasons. First, there are empirical questions. It is not at all clear that such restrictions will always translate into higher housing prices for consumers. Depending on the elasticity of demand for housing in an area, additional environmental requirements may be capitalized into the price of raw land—that is, the impacts are experienced by owners of vacant land who may now receive somewhat less for their parcels. Whether this is an ethical result is debatable, of course, but, considering the typical speculative profits earned by landowners in urbanizing areas (see Chapter 12 for a discussion of land profits), the impact is not altogether a bad one. Second, there are many contemporary causes for increases in the cost of housing (e.g., inflating attorney fees, broker fees, closing costs, cost of building materials, interest, and profit margins) and it is unfair to place too heavy a blame on land-use regulations.

Furthermore, the developmental pressures that are today being placed on wetlands, sensitive habitat, open space, and air and water resources are often generated not by affordable housing, but by second homes and resort projects. Because such uses do not satisfy essential housing functions and are indeed an expression of social affluence, price effects here raise few distributive issues. If environmental regulations raise the cost of a beachfront second home by several thousand dollars, for example, this does not, it seems to me, have significant distributive impacts (see Rolston, 1988a, pp. 281–82, for a discussion of similar points about destruction of forestlands and wilderness areas in order to maintain local jobs).

Even if we can assume that price effects occur, ethical land use will not support, in my mind, the idea of giving up on significant environmental protection. Protection of wetlands, biodiversity, open space, and water and air quality involves taking steps necessary to sustain the earth's basic environmental and biological functions. Most of these environmental processes and functions are irreplaceable and are, in their cumulative sense, essential to the long-term survival and flourishing of *Homo sapiens* and all other life-forms. Significant destruction of the environment, even on a small scale, is folly and threatens the well-being of generations to come. Although in this book I attempt to establish few moral priorities or hierarchies, it does strike me that the principle of maintaining and protecting the natural environment should take priority over distributive obligations where they are in direct conflict.

These ethical imperatives need not, however, *be* in direct conflict. First, many land-use actions directed at conserving or protecting the natural environment may also serve to promote distributive ethics. As mentioned previously, low-income neighborhoods and communities have, in the past, been forced to endure disproportionately high levels of environmental risk and pollution. Second, promoting distributive ethics need not occur at the expense of environmental protection. Even acknowledging the price effects that may occur from certain environmental land-use regulations, localities may implement many other types of land-use actions that will advance the interests of the least-advantaged. Hand in hand with environmental regulations must go local land-use actions which allow and promote multifamily and other forms of affordable housing, and which otherwise seek to promote the interests of the least-advantaged in society. Furthermore, it is unlikely that distributive obligations would be satisfied with even the complete elimination of all environmental programs and regulations. Indeed, the high cost of housing, as an example, is clearly the result of many factors, of which environmental land-use regulations are but a relatively small part. The challenge, then, becomes one of finding ways to promote distributive justice in land-use policy, while simultaneously protecting the natural environment upon which present and future generations will rely.

Summary

Land-use ethics must acknowledge the principle that land-use programs, policies, and projects, ranging from the enactment of an impact fee to the siting of a highway, will have clear distributive results. Some people's circumstances improve, while others worsen. Public land-use decisions must explicitly consider the question of obligations to distributive justice. Utilitarian results are frequently repugnant because they fail to adequately consider distributive results. We have examined several major positions in this chapter, including equalitarian and Rawlsian views of what constitutes a socially just land-use distribution.

At the very least, ethical land use demands that the social, economic, and physical conditions of those living at the lower end of the socio-economic continuum not be undermined or diminished by public land-use policies and actions. Furthermore, there is much to recommend in the Rawlsian position. Land-use policy can and should be evaluated by the extent to which it *improves* the conditions of the least-advantaged members of our society. Ethical land use, then, is not merely *neutral* from the perspective of distributive justice, but seeks to promote and advance it.

7

ETHICAL DUTIES TO
THE ENVIRONMENT

THE ENVIRONMENTAL impacts of land-use actions are substantial, and contemporary land-use practices threaten, in a variety of ways, the ecological integrity of our planet. Land-use practices and patterns can create and induce serious air and water pollution problems. Without significant safeguards, for example, site grading and land development can generate tremendous erosion and sedimentation problems. Urbanization, which usually results in the replacement of natural vegetation with pavement and other impervious surfaces, can create serious storm-water runoff problems as well as modifications to the microclimate. Other land-use practices, such as heavy reliance on septic tanks, lead directly to the degradation of water quality. Sprawling land-use patterns, which encourage the use of automobiles, contribute to urban air quality problems. Numerous metropolitan areas, for example, are in violation of minimum EPA ambient standards for ozone and carbon monoxide pollution.

As population growth and land consumption continue over time, there are fewer and fewer natural areas, areas largely untouched by human hands, and fewer opportunities to connect them through greenways and other green systems. A recent global analysis of existing wilderness areas undertaken by the Sierra Club found that there are, not surprisingly, relatively few places which do not bear human scars (McCloskey and Spalding, 1987). Wilderness and natural areas are increasingly lost to the human pressures to build and develop as if the frontier still exists in perpetuity. Globally, the planet is in the midst of an unprecedented period of species extinction and loss of biodiversity, and the chief cause is habitat loss (see Ehrlich and Ehrlich, 1981; Wilson, 1988). In many developing countries a primary cause of the loss of rainforests and natural areas is human settlement policy—and land tenure policies that encourage the settlement of rural areas and the decentralization of urban population (e.g., Gradwohl and Greenberg, 1988; Repetto, 1988). Loss of forestlands and other forms of vegetation in turn contributes to current global warming. (It is estimated that deforestation results in the emission of between one and two billion tons of carbon into the atmosphere each year; see Flaven, 1989.)

Justifications for land-use interventions to protect the environment have, in the past, relied heavily upon anthropocentric reasoning. Wetlands are preserved because they provide necessary functions beneficial to human beings—for instance, in the form of flood control, biological spawning grounds for commercially important fish, and important recreational uses. Restrictions are placed on the extent to which individuals and businesses are allowed to pollute, not primarily because such pollution is a priori immoral, but usually because such actions are allocatively inefficient: that is, if the free market could take such externalities into account, then pollution levels would tend to be much lower. The costs of unrestricted pollution, it is believed, when added up over the entire society, far exceed the benefits. In previous chapters we also explored nonutilitarian rationales; for instance, placing restrictions on the extent to which an individual is allowed to pollute surface waters not because such an outcome is inefficient, but rather because we believe it is wrong that an individual should be allowed to impose these kinds of harms on others and the general public.

Is it conceivable that certain ethical obligations may exist relative to the environment *itself*, rather than as instrumental to human beings who use or enjoy the environment? In this chapter we address this critical question, or what might be broadly described as the nonanthropocentric view. We will not disassociate ourselves completely from instrumental, anthropocentric views, but will find that certain types of environmental obligations may effectively advance both anthropocentric and nonanthropocentric moral obligations.

Before we address the matter of nonanthropocentric obligations, we shall briefly examine several special questions of environmental duty not previously taken up but which may figure prominently into any comprehensive treatment of land-use ethics. Specifically, we need to define the fundamental role of nature and the natural environment in human lives —not from a biological or ecological perspective, but from a psychological and emotional view.

The Role of Nature and Natural Areas in a Modern World

Very often land-use conflicts center around proposals to destroy or consume natural areas—whether a wild area or an urban park—and to put in their place human-made structures. This process raises a host of questions relating to equity and to expectations (e.g., citizens frequently feel shocked and surprised upon learning that a special patch of land they have come to appreciate and value will no longer be available to them); in addition, there is a broader question about the role and importance of such areas in human existence. As population growth continues to escalate and human pressures to build and develop continue to rise, it becomes increasingly difficult to preserve and protect these natural areas.

Do human beings really need to see and experience mountains, deserts, streams, and wildlife? Obviously we require certain environmental goods to survive, notably clean air, clean water, and productive soil. But is it not the case that most human beings can survive quite nicely—can live full and productive lives—without hiking in a forest, without watching a peregrine falcon fly, without walking along a seashore? Indeed, depending upon where one lives, few of these opportunities may currently be available.

Moreover, should our concern about the loss of nature, and natural areas, be lessened somewhat because of our ability to find replacements for nature? There is considerable evidence that, when we contemplate contemporary landscape architectural designs such as zoos, we increasingly see the replacement or substitution of pseudo-nature or natural artifacts in place of the real thing. And, if such artifacts can satisfy many of the same psychological and aesthetic needs as the real thing, why should we be concerned about the loss of nature? Several years ago Laurence Tribe fueled this debate by writing an article, "Ways Not to Think about Plastic Trees" (1974), in which he lambasts the increasing tendency to replace the real natural environment with fake substitutes, and the belief on the part of some (e.g., Krieger, 1973) that society can manipulate environments with such artifacts to create or simulate the experience of nature. Tribe argues that such trends are symptomatic of a narrowly utilitarian and anthropocentric view of nature. Even from a narrow anthropocentric view, it is apparent that plastic trees simply cannot replace the aesthetic and ecological functions of natural trees, but, to be sure, they "survive" the environs of smog-infested cities.

Incorporating pseudo-nature into modern architecture and landscape architecture is perhaps most dramatically illustrated in the new USAir terminal in the Los Angeles Airport (LAX). The terminal includes several pockets of natural landscape, including trees and vegetation, supported apparently with fluorescent lights and other artificial human sustenance. While it is admirable that efforts are made to at least bring a natural element to an otherwise conventionally nonnatural setting, one has to wonder whether this is indicative of what's to come in the future—when the human exposure to nature is obtained from such artificial pockets, momentarily enjoyed on one's way from the gate to the baggage claim area.

It can be argued that human beings require natural areas, that they must be exposed to *real* nature, above and beyond the biological and ecological functions they provide, for psychological well-being. Whether we have ethical obligations to preserve natural areas is at the center of many land-use disputes. Should we save wilderness areas? Do they serve important human functions that artificial nature and recreation in civilized environs simply cannot provide? Do we have obligations to preserve natural wonders, such as virgin prairie or Mt. St. Helens, or landscapes of special visual and aesthetic importance, such as the Virginia Piedmont, or coastal shorelines such as Cape Cod?

Many have argued that such landscapes and natural areas are important for stimulating the human contemplative faculty. Joseph Sax, for instance, argues convincingly for the important role played by national parks in this regard. Such areas are especially suited to promoting contemplative and reflective forms of recreation, increasingly important in a technologically dominated society and landscape. In Sax's words,

> While nature is not a uniquely suitable setting, it seems to have a peculiar power to stimulate us to reflectiveness by its awesomeness and grandeur, its complexity, the unfamiliarity of untrammeled ecosystems to urban residents, and the absence of distractions. The special additional claim for nature as a setting is that it not only promotes self-understanding, but also an understanding of the world in which we live. Our initial response to nature is often awe and wonderment: trees that have survived for millennia; a profusion of flowers in the seeming sterility of the desert; predator and prey living in equilibrium. These marvels are intriguing, but their appeal is not merely aesthetic. Nature is also a successful model of many things that human communities seek: continuity, stability and sustenance, adaptation, sustained productivity, diversity and evolutionary change. (Sax, 1980, p. 46)

The natural world and natural landscapes promote wonder and fascination, and there is a genuineness about them which seems to heighten this wonder. Frederick Law Olmsted, the famous landscape architect, spoke of this well over a century ago.

It does seem that as human beings we require "other things" in our lives for psychological balance and well-being. Ernest Partridge refers to this as "self-transcending" and argues that for human beings to achieve personal fulfillment, and to prevent us from becoming alienated and narcissistic, we require things in our lives which are independent and external to us: "our personal and moral life is enriched to the degree that it is 'extended outward' in self-transcending enjoyment, cherishing and contemplating things, places and ideals that are remote in space and time—ever, in a sense *timeless*" (Partridge, 1984, p. 126). Through this self-transcendence humans are able to "identify with, and seek to further, the well-being, preservation, and endurance of communities, locations, causes, artifacts, institutions, ideals, etc., which are outside themselves and which they hope will flourish beyond their own lifetimes" (ibid.,

p. 188). Thus, under such a theory nature and natural objects—mountains, trees, wildlife—may serve an important psychological function. If we are unable to preserve and conserve such resources, opportunities for self-transcendence will be difficult. Of course it can be argued that other opportunities outside of nature exist for self-transcendence. But can this basic need for cherishing and contemplating other things be directed toward aspects of the built environment—for instance, historic buildings or major public monuments (such as the Cliff Palace at Mesa Verde, the San Francisco Golden Gate Bridge, or the Vietnam Memorial)? Will the lives of people who reside in urban areas be substantially diminished by the loss of natural opportunities? How does one explain the intense popularity of Gateway National Recreation Area in New York City? Certainly by something other than human census data.

The Possibilities of a Nonanthropocentric Land-Use Ethic

Contemporary western attitudes about the environment have been heavily criticized for being overly anthropocentric—that is, attributing value to nature and the natural environment based exclusively on their utility to human beings. Considerable literary attention and debate have occurred, particularly within the environmental ethics community, about the possibilities of a different paradigm—one which recognizes that nature may have intrinsic value; that is, it may be seen to have value and worth in and of itself, irrespective of what human value might be given to it.

Economists have an especially difficult time accepting such a moral theory, since all decisions under their paradigm are based on assigning human value and expressing this value in the form of dollar votes and economic demand. If a wetland has value, we know this by referring to what people are willing to pay to buy it, or see it, or visit it, or hunt on it. One of the more vehement critics of the nonanthropocentric view of moral obligations to the environment is William Baxter. His now classic *People or Penguins: The Case for Optimal Pollution* (1974) presents the archetypal case for a system of human-centered valuation. Baxter has difficulty imagining how any ethical obligations to the environment might be acknowledged which do not relate to human needs and valuations. Baxter states his position succinctly in the following frequently cited quotation:

> My criteria are oriented to people, not penguins. Damage to penguins, or sugar pines, or geological marvels is, without more, simply irrelevant. One must go further by my criteria, and say: Penguins are important because people enjoy seeing them walk about rocks; and furthermore, the well-being of people would be less impaired by halting use of DDT

than by giving up penguins. In short, my observations about environmental problems will be people-oriented, as are my criteria. I have no interest in preserving penguins for their own sake. (Baxter, 1974, p. 5)

Arguing that there are moral and ethical obligations that derive from, and extend beyond, human interests immediately raises a host of difficult questions, perhaps most obviously, How inclusive should our conception of the moral community be? If certain things *other than human beings* have value in and of themselves, which *things* do? Do ethical obligations extend just to certain forms of intelligent life (say to primates or cetaceans)? Do they extend to all sentient creatures? Do these obligations extend to all other species of life (from plants to elephants)? Do ethical obligations extend as well to protecting the larger ecosystems upon which these other life-forms rely? A variety of positions can be taken, which we will survey.

We should remember that preservation and management of the natural environment can be, and often is, defended on utilitarian grounds. Many of the earliest proponents of conservation in the United States, including Gifford Pinchot, saw such efforts as essential to maximizing the benefits of such resources as forests, watersheds, and fisheries. Many supporters of the concept of stewardship follow a similar logic, arguing for moral responsibilities to manage carefully the natural environment so as to protect its long-term productivity, including scenic beauty. Recently there has been substantial interest in a Judeo-Christian notion of stewardship, which holds that similar obligations exist, primarily stemming from the fact that ultimate ownership resides with God (stewardship is further discussed in Chapter 8).

Expanding the Moral Community

It is an empirical truth that, over the last several decades, citizens and elected officials have expanded the moral horizons to include "other" considerations besides narrow anthropocentric concerns. Laws have been passed to protect the welfare of animals used in research and the treatment of animals in society generally. Many wildlife conservation laws, including the federal Endangered Species Act (1973), have been enacted to protect other forms of life from the abuses and overexploitation of human beings. To be sure, much of the motivation behind these laws is indeed anthropocentric and utilitarian, but a significant degree of motivation has gone beyond this. Expanding the moral community to include other forms of life is seen by some as the result of a natural historical expansion of moral considerateness. Roderick Nash likens this expansion to a modern-day form of abolitionism. Expanding the moral community

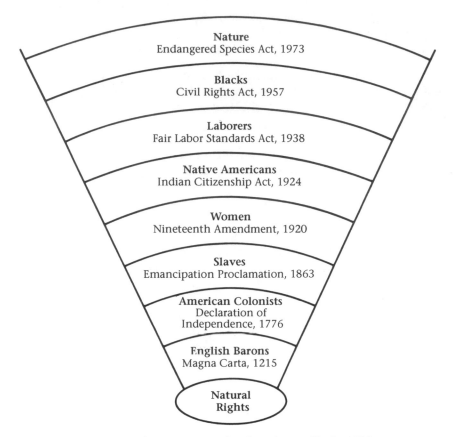

Figure 7.1 The expanding concept of rights. *Source:* Nash, 1989.

is entirely consistent, he argues, with the spirit and ideas of the American Revolution. This expansion of the moral community "fits quite squarely into the most traditional of all American ideals; the defense of minority rights and the liberation of exploited groups. Perhaps the gospel of ecology should not be seen so much as a revolt against American traditions as an extension and new application of them—as just another rounding out of the American Revolution" (Nash, 1985, p. 179). This incremental expansion of moral and legal rights is illustrated by Nash in figure 7.1, extending most recently to other forms of life, as expressed by the federal Endangered Species Act. In Nash's view it is natural that our moral journey begins with personal self-interest, and that gradually over time our moral community expands, considering family, tribe, nation, and ultimately nature and the larger environment.

Obligations to Organisms

It has been more than a century and a half since the first animal cruelty laws were enacted in the 1820s. And, indeed, for many years there has been a general societal consensus that some other forms of life— particularly those closest to humans—ought to be given a degree of moral consideration, and specifically ought not to be treated cruelly or subjected to unnecessary pain. In the last several decades, however, scholarly interest in the obligations owed to nonhuman organisms has expanded considerably. There is now a tremendous body of literature which examines this question, particularly in the areas of philosophy and environmental ethics (e.g., Clark, 1977; Fox, 1980; Midgley, 1983; Morris and Fox, 1978; Regan, 1982, 1983; Regan and Singer, 1976; Rodman, 1977, 1980; Singer, 1985).

The historic tendency to place human beings at the top of any moral hierarchy of life has been criticized by many as being indefensible from a rational view. To place humans at the top and to place other creatures in morally subservient positions is a function of the criteria one selects to determine relative value. Certainly human beings will prove to be superior if our criteria are based on certain skills at which humans excel (such as abstract thought and mathematical computation). But if the criteria chosen are different and less human-centered, other forms of life might rank above humans. Cheetahs run faster, for instance, and porpoises swim faster, butterflies excel in their beauty, while osprey have keener eyesight. "It is true that a human may be a better mathematician than a monkey, but the monkey may be a better tree climber" (Taylor, 1986, p. 131).

Much of the academic literature and debate in recent years has examined the theoretical and philosophical foundations for expanding the moral community to include animals and other forms of life. Some theorists have taken a kind of Golden Rule approach to such potential obligations. As R. M. Hare argues: "We have to ask what we wish should be done to us, were we in the position of the victim of a certain action" (1987, p. 7). Because only sentient life can be assigned such a morally relevant interest, these are, in his view, the only organisms humans have any obligations to. This modified Golden Rule does not work for creatures who have no sentience or desires.

Several theorists and philosophers have played a particularly important role in expanding the moral community to include other life-forms. Peter Singer, an Australian philosopher, presented one of the first comprehensive ethical arguments, and in many ways he is considered the founder of the modern animal rights movement. Interestingly, Singer's arguments are based on an extension of utilitarianism. It seems to him that if utilitarianism is morally defensible for humans, its methodology must consider as well the degree of pleasure and pain to other nonhuman forms of life. Singer presents his arguments most succinctly in his now classic *Animal Liberation* (1975). If the fundamental moral basis of utilitarianism is the equal consideration of pleasure and pain, interests and welfare, regardless of one's social position or station in life, is it not equally requisite to consider the experiences of other sentient life? In Singer's words: "If a being suffers, there can be no moral justification for refusing to take that suffering into consideration, and indeed, to count it equally with the like suffering . . . of any other being" (1986, p. 37). Notice that, under Singer's theory, for an organism to be given moral consideration it must be sentient; that is, it must be able to feel such things as pleasure and pain. Under this view, a developer or landowner may have some obligation to consider the effects of a proposed project on sentient life but not on other, nonsentient forms of life. Thus, moral consideration is given to deer but not to chestnut trees, to manatees but not to mangroves. (Of course, there may well be a moral requirement to protect nonsentient life, even under a theory such as Singer's, because to destroy such things might directly affect the interests of sentient life; e.g., harming the forest will harm the black bear and other sentient life living there.)

Just as utilitarian ethics has been criticized when applied exclusively to the human realm, there are those who have been equally critical of its application to the broader category of sentient life. The utilitarian result may often not be very appealing ethically; it might be acceptable, for instance, under such a theoretical framework to maim or injure an animal for its fur if one can merely show that the benefits in the form of enjoyment to humans exceed the pain endured by the animal. Further, it might be argued that land development which involves the destruction of habitat and certain populations of sentient animals is acceptable because the benefits (jobs, an improved tax base, housing opportunities, and so on) again exceed the negative effects on such nonhuman life-forms.

In contrast to this utilitarian foundation, other scholars have argued that all sentient creatures have certain rights that cannot be violated regardless of the amount of human utility that is generated from such actions. The most detailed and carefully argued of these positions is the rights-based approach of Tom Regan. Regan's position is well presented in his book *The Case for Animal Rights* (1983), which has now become, along with Singer's *Animal Liberation,* a major underpinning of the animal rights movement. Regan argues that because nonhuman animals experience pain and exhibit similar types of feelings and sentience, it is morally arbitrary to distinguish between them and human beings. Just as we believe that all humans have certain inherent worth, so also do sentient creatures: "we are each of us the experiencing subject of a life, each of us a conscious creature having an individual welfare that has importance to us whatever our usefulness to others. We want and prefer things; believe and feel things; recall and expect things" (1986, p. 37). Moreover, using criteria such as intelligence to determine moral worth is inappropriate. As a society we believe that even severely mentally retarded human beings hold inherent worth and have the right to life, liberty, and the pursuit of happiness.

Other theorists and philosophers have sought to reach more intermediate positions between what some might see as the extremist views of Regan, and others in the animal rights movement, and those who believe humans have no moral obligations whatsoever to other creatures. Donald Van DeVeer, for instance, has developed what he calls "two-factor equalitarianism" (TFE) as a way to deal with conflicts between human and nonhuman interests. For Van DeVeer such conflicts are resolved through consideration of two different factors: (1) the types of interests involved and (2) the extent of the relative level of psychological capabilities of the different creatures involved. The primary types of interests are either basic or peripheral. Basic interests are essentially survival interests (e.g., food, water, shelter, oxygen), while peripheral interests are secondary and unnecessary for survival (e.g., comfort, convenience, material goods). Serious interests, which occupy a sort of middle ground, are things individuals can live without, but "it is difficult or costly to do so. Hence it may be in the serious interest of a lonely child to have a pet or in the serious interest of an eagle to be able to fly" (Van DeVeer, 1986a, p. 56).

In interspecies conflicts, then, the ethical decision concerning which species should prevail is determined by assessing the types of interests and the psychological capabilities of the creatures involved. For creatures of similar psychological capabilities, the one with a basic interest would morally prevail over another creature's peripheral interest. Because of the complex psychological capacities of human beings, it is ethical under Van DeVeer's framework to violate even a basic interest of a creature of lesser capacities for a similar or serious interest of a human. It is unacceptable, however, to sacrifice the basic interest of a creature of lesser psychological capacities to satisfy only a peripheral interest of human beings: "On TFE killing oysters or (most kinds of) fish for food for human survival would be permissible; killing them only for the human pleasure of doing so would not be. On this view certain forms of hunting (recreational killing) would seem to be immoral. Similarly certain rodeo activities and bull-fighting would not be justified. The killing of seals for food by an Eskimo would be justified; the killing (and radical deprivation and suffering) of veal calves by people in agriculturally affluent areas may be wrong" (ibid.).

It can be argued that Van DeVeer is stacking the deck in favor of *Homo sapiens* by attaching such importance to psychological capacities. Sentient creatures do exhibit different levels of psychological capability, but clearly in Van DeVeer's eyes human beings have greater psychological complexity and this ought to be taken into account in resolving conflicts:

> In general, is there a justification for weighing human interests more heavily than comparable or like interests of animals in cases of conflicts of interests and, thus, justifying the extension of differential treatment toward animals in certain cases where it would not be justified if extended to (most) other humans? . . . The basis for doing so is *not* simply that human interests are, after all, *human* interests and necessarily deserving of more weight than comparable or like interests of animals. The ground is rather that the interests of beings with more complex psychological capacities deserve greater weight than those of lesser capacities, up to a point. . . . It might be proposed that humans are typically subject to certain kinds of suffering that animals are not. For example, humans are typically capable of suffering from the dread of impending disaster . . . in a way that animals are not. (1986a, p. 60)

There appear to be moral obligations to other forms of life, particularly sentient creatures, who are capable of feeling pain. Land-use patterns and practices, and the activity of land development, should be respectful of other life-forms. The blatant disregard for other forms of life has been illustrated in Boulder, Colorado, where an entire colony of prairie dogs was gassed with aluminum phosphide tablets by a developer preparing land for a new housing project (see Zales, 1988). The gassing took place one day before a planned relocation of the prairie dogs was to occur by a rescue group and the Boulder County Humane Society. The latter had planned to flush the animals from their underground burrows with soap and water and relocate them to another site, a practice that had succeeded for several other colonies in the past. Loss of life, when completely unnecessary and when imposed on fellow sentient and intelligent life-forms, is particularly inexcusable.

Numerous other examples of land development conflicts involving questions of the rights of animals and other forms of life can be cited. Consider the case of the beach park proposed for Surfside Beach, South Carolina. The park, Ocean Expo Marine Park, would include shows (similar to Sea World) involving dolphins and other marine mammals. Opposition to the park has developed for many reasons, but much of it is founded on objections concerning the capturing and keeping in captivity of highly intelligent mammal sea-life. In an effort to stop the park, Representative Alex Harvin has proposed a bill in the South Carolina legislature that would prohibit the capture and captivity of dolphins or whales in that state. Those found in violation of the act would be fined $1,000 or given six months in jail. Supporters of the legislation argue that dolphins and whales are not properly cared for in captivity and do not live very long compared to their natural life expectancies (most die after five years, compared to a normal life expectancy of some forty-five years in the wild). Others see these proposals as ridiculous. In the words of one legislator: "I think we're going overboard in trying to protect everything in this world except human beings" (Fretwell, 1990, p. A1). Other legislators have echoed the traditional view of animals relative to humans: "My understanding was the Good Lord put animals here and gave man dominion over them. . . . Now it looks like we're trying to put animals in a special place and not for the benefit of man" (ibid.).

Rights for Natural Objects

It is one thing, some would argue, to support expanding the moral community to include sentient creatures, but something else entirely to assign intrinsic moral value to the nonsentient elements of the natural world: mountains, rocks, rivers, trees, and the like. Those philosophers and environmental ethicists who support extending the moral community to these objects often do so on the basis that, again, they are essential to the survival of sentient creatures who might be said to have rights. A river is not valuable in itself, but because it serves as a habitat for many sentient life-forms.

Some ethicists have sought to extend the community to all life-forms, not simply those which are sentient. The deep ecology movement, which is discussed in greater detail below, holds that all life in the biosphere has an equal right to exist and flourish (Devall and Sessions, 1985, p. 67). Paul Taylor, in his influential book *Respect for Nature* (1986), argues for a similar bioequality, derived from what he refers to as the biocentric outlook. A key belief in this outlook (among four primary beliefs) is that "humans are not superior to other living things" (1986, p. 100). Taylor argues that we can rationally determine that other forms of life have inherent worth by taking their standpoint, or assuming their perspective, and realizing that they have a good of their own. Taylor's philosophical conclusions hold tremendous implications for policy, and because of the importance of Taylor's theory, I review and critique it in much greater detail in a subsequent section.

Christopher Stone made one of the earliest attempts to explore the idea that natural objects should be given not only moral consideration but also legal rights. His idea of legal rights for natural objects was initially outlined in an oft-cited article in a University of Southern California law review, later published as a book, entitled *Should Trees Have Stand-*

ing? Toward Legal Rights for Natural Objects (1974). In it Stone strongly criticized the conventional treatment of the natural environment in the prevailing legal system. Under traditional legal theory, damage to ecosystems and the natural environment is only relevant when human beings are actually impacted in some way—and only those people directly affected by the degradation can bring legal proceedings. Thus, in the case of an individual or a factory which has polluted a river, damage to the river itself would not normally be legally relevant, but rather harms that such pollution might cause to *people*. Furthermore, when courts issue awards, these run to the *people harmed* by these actions and not to the river itself (i.e., to restore or repair the river from the damages). Stone argues that damage to the environment ought to be considered in and of itself and that damages ought to run to the environment, not to people. Moreover, it ought to be possible somehow for legal actions to be initiated *by the environment* against those who damage the environment, and not have to rely on affected individuals to take action. Again, who speaks for the land?

Stone's solution was the possibility of assigning legal rights to natural objects, such as the river in our example above. If other inanimate objects and institutions can be given legal rights, for instance corporations and universities, it ought to be possible to assign similar rights to rivers. Stone argues that, for an entity to qualify as a rights holder, it must meet three basic criteria: (1) the thing can institute legal action at its behest; (2) in granting legal relief the court must take injury of it into account; and (3) relief must run to be benefit of it (Stone, 1974, p. 11). Stone believes that these criteria could be satisfied for the natural environment; he envisioned the establishment of "guardianships." Under such a system it would be possible for the courts (or someone) to appoint "guardians" for certain natural objects or systems (e.g., the river), who would then be able to initiate legal actions against those who degrade or harm the natural or object system. The guardian would also oversee the restoration or rehabilitation of the damaged object or system.

Stone's ideas have had considerable impact within the legal and environmental communities, and there is evidence of these concepts making their way into contemporary environmental planning and policy. The movement of the courts in recent years toward a more flexible interpretation of requirements for "standing" is one example. This has allowed environmental groups such as the Sierra Club Legal Defense Fund and the Natural Resources Defense Council to initiate legal actions against polluters and other violators of environmental laws without the necessity of showing that specific individuals have or will be impacted. Furthermore, most environmental laws enacted in recent years have specifically included citizen suit provisions that facilitate the initiation of legal action by citizens and others. Oregon and other states have similar liberal standing requirements as part of their state and local land-use systems.

The guardianship notion, then, finds some expression in liberal standing requirements which, in effect, allow members of the public to stand up for natural objects and systems. These ideas are also reflected in recent efforts to establish environmental trust funds which collect funds from damage awards or user fees and which ensure that monies benefit the natural system. While not a perfect example because impacts on people tend to be the primary concern, the federal superfund program (administered by EPA) does reflect this thinking, in that it seeks to pay for the cleanup of hazardous waste sites by assessing the costs to those responsible for the damages.

But to many moral philosophers the assignment of obligations to natural objects is faulty in its reasoning. R. M. Hare, you may recall, argues that sentient creatures are the only component of nature which are directly owed ethical obligations, because it is possible for us to imagine how we would want to be treated should we be in their position. Under Hare's position, assigning ethical duties to nonsentient or even inanimate objects in nature (e.g., rocks, rivers, cacti, mountains) requires an additional argument: "It is up to the conservationists, and not so difficult as some people think, to show that these inanimate things, though they themselves have no morally relevant interests, ought to be conserved in the interests of beings that do have such interests. Wise conservationists try to show this, instead of taking the short cut of assuming illegitimately that all kinds of things have morally relevant interests, and thus have rights, which could not have them" (Hare, 1987, p. 8).

Hare suspects that humans often project their own values and importance on such inanimate objects and then seek to justify their preservation based on inherent worth. Whether Hare is correct or not, it does not appear difficult to argue that preservation of mountains, rivers, rocks, and trees is essential to the preservation of living creatures, indeed sentient creatures, to which we do owe ethical obligations. While sentience is the deciding criterion for theorists such as Hare, for others like Paul Taylor it is the existence of biological life that is important. While Hare would not agree that plants have value "in themselves" (i.e., because they are nonsentient), Taylor and others argue that because of their biological existence they do have inherent worth. We return to these matters below.

Obligations to Protect Species and Biodiversity

While some people would dispute whether ethical obligations exist to protect or prevent harm of individual organisms, many more are willing to acknowledge that it is morally wrong to jeopardize the continued existence of an entire species. This has become a particularly central issue in public land-use policy, as urban development and habitat loss have increasingly become major causes of species extinction, both in this country and abroad. In the United States severe conflicts are arising between demands for housing and development, and the habitat needs of endangered or threatened species. Examples of species-development conflicts are numerous (see Beatley, 1989a). A recent proposal to build a shopping center in Austin, Texas, threatens the survival of several cave-dwelling invertebrates found nowhere else in the world (a spider, two types of beetles, a pseudo-scorpion, and a cave-adapted daddy-longlegs). New housing projects in western Riverside County, California, threaten habitat of the endangered Stephens's kangaroo rat. Second-home development on Big Pine Key, Florida, threatens the existence of the dwindling population of the Key deer, which, among other things, has fallen victim to road-kills as a result of the dramatic increases in automobile traffic accompanying new development. Endangered sea turtles all along the Atlantic and Gulf coasts have difficulty nesting because of the explosive shoreline development and the bright lights typically associated with it. The least Bell's vireo, a western songbird, is threatened in the San Diego area as a result of development in, and destruction of, its riparian habitats. A recent study by the Center for Plant Conservation indicates that urban development is threatening hundreds of native American plants (Shabecoff, 1988). Neither land-use theory nor practice have adequately taken this issue into consideration.

Globally, species extinction and loss of biodiversity is perhaps the single most disturbing environmental trend of our time, with estimates that as much as one-quarter of all species on the earth will become extinct by the next century (see Reid and Miller, 1990). Some scientists estimate that we may already be losing more than 17,000 species per year.

Much of the reasoning used to justify concern about loss of endangered species in recent years has clearly been anthropocentric and largely utilitarian in nature. There are many important reasons for protecting endangered plant and animal species. They represent a tremendous biological storehouse, the loss of which may deprive us of substantial medical, scientific, and commercial benefits. It is estimated that the total number of species in the world ranges from ten to one hundred million (of this there is even considerable uncertainty; see Wilson, 1988; 1992). We are now in the position of losing many species we have yet to discover or even catalog or understand fully. A large portion of commercial pharmaceutical products are derived directly from wild plants and animals, and potential scientific and medical benefits are tremendous (see Myers, 1979). Protecting species diversity may also hold out the potential of discovering new disease-resistant crops, or crops better adjusted to changing climatic conditions (e.g., the Buffalo gourd).

Endangered and threatened species are also important indicators of how healthy and sustainable our planet really is. The loss of the least Bell's vireo, or other songbird species, may hold little direct impact to most people, yet it may be indicative of the broader environmental degradation occurring—a harbinger of worse environmental calamities to come. Biologists Paul and Anne Ehrlich use a vivid analogy for species extinction: they liken it to the rivets popping out of the wing of an airliner (see Ehrlich and Ehrlich, 1981). With each popped rivet (extinction), the structural integrity of the airliner (earth) is further undermined, until the plane will no longer fly: "unfortunately all of us are passengers on a very large spacecraft, one on which we have no option but to fly" (ibid., p. xii). Endangered species and their habitats can also provide substantial recreational, aesthetic, and other benefits for humans.

Nonanthropocentric arguments have also been offered. Similar to the positions embraced by animal rights supporters, the protection of species diversity is sometimes defended on the grounds that species have an inherent right to existence, regardless of the utility or value such species might hold for humans. Ehrenfeld, one of the more frequently cited authors, argues for such a right in his classic, *The Arrogance of Humanism* (1981). There he puts forth what he terms the "Noah Principle":

> This non-humanistic value of communities and species is the simplest of all to state: *they should be conserved because they exist and because this existence is itself but the present expression of a continuing historical process of immense antiquity and majesty.* Long-standing existence in Nature is deemed to carry with it the unimpeachable right to continued existence. Existence is the only criterion of the value of the parts of Nature, and diminution of the number of existing things is the best measure of decrease of what we ought to value. (Pp. 207–8)

Concerns about the anthropogenic extinction of species are sometimes countered by those who argue that such outcomes are simply part of the natural scheme of things. Indeed, human propagation and domination of the earth can be the epitome of Darwin's survival of the fittest. Is not the human species simply doing what many other creatures have done for centuries—outcompeting other forms of life which eventually die out? Moreover, why should special concern be expressed about this human-induced extinction when we would perhaps not be very concerned about other natural causes of extinction. If we knew that the slow extinction of such species as the California condor or black-footed ferret were entirely the result of natural factors (which, of course, is not the case), many would object to any human intervention to prevent this from happening. Such an outcome, while perhaps not pleasing to those who enjoy watching or contemplating such species, is natural, it can be argued, and thus ought to be respected.

Others argue that, while at one time humans assumed a position in the ecosystem which was more modest and "natural," the magnitude of today's human destruction is clearly unnatural. This magnitude is unprecedented in the history of the earth. Moreover, it can be argued that human beings have certain moral and ethical obligations that derive from the explicit choices which *Homo sapiens* has that other creatures do not. Humans clearly have the technical and planning capability to develop, grow, and live in harmony with nature and to protect, to a large extent, the existence and diversity of species.

The willingness of *Homo sapiens* to acknowledge the existence rights of other forms of life is not uniform, however, but is biased in favor of certain types of species. Certain endangered species are clearly put at a marked disadvantage because they are not cute, cuddly, or otherwise visually attractive or appealing to the public. This explains why people express a disproportionately high level of concern and affection for bears but not bats, lions but not lizards, tigers but not tiger salamanders. The bias seems particularly evident in favor of large terrestrial mammals, especially those that are in some way anthropomorphic.

Stephen Kellert has done extensive surveys of public attitudes about such wildlife issues. Not surprisingly, people consistently attach a much greater importance on preserving and protecting the larger, more attractive animal species. Of substantially less importance are snakes, insects, and plants. Kellert gave respondents a list of different animal and plant species and asked which would they favor protecting if it would result in higher energy costs. While 89 percent favored protecting the bald eagle, only 43 percent favored protecting the Eastern Indigo snake and an even smaller 34 percent favored protecting the Kauai wolf spider (see Kellert, 1979). The psychological importance attributed to, or connected with, certain species in turn translates into a willingness to make greater sacrifices (monetary and otherwise) to preserve and protect them. These kinds of bias are troubling because the attractiveness of a species does not necessarily correlate to its ecological importance. More fundamentally, no species should have to rely on its visual attractiveness to humans as a measure of its worth or right to exist.

Biocentric Approaches and Obligations to Ecosystems

Perhaps our ethical obligations extend not to individual organisms or natural objects or to endangered species, but rather to a broader ecological plane. Can it be argued that in the use of land the primary moral obligation is to protect and sustain entire ecological systems rather than to single out any one or a few components of this system? The emergence of the field of ecology during the twentieth century, and especially the last thirty years, has done much to promote these types of ethical viewpoints. During this period there has been a growing recognition that the natural environment is an incredibly complex and interwoven system, and that modifications to any part of the system may impact other elements of the system, often (if not usually) in ways which are not understood fully in advance. Different biocentric or ecosystem positions have emerged in recent years, and I will briefly review the more central of these below and speculate on their implications for land-use policy. I begin with Aldo Leopold's land ethic, outlined over sixty years ago, which also serves as a foundation for many of the more contemporary theories.

Leopold's Land Ethic

In many ways an eco-centric ethic of land use was first developed and argued by Aldo Leopold, in an article first published in the *Journal of Forestry* (1933) that later appeared in his now classic *A Sand County Almanac* (1949). This book has, perhaps more than any other, crystallized, at least for those in the land-use and environmental professions, the notion that there are fundamental ethical issues involved in how we use, allocate, and appreciate land. Moreover, it is an ethic based on an ecological premise; Leopold saw the need to protect the integrity of the ecosystem as a whole. Indeed, Leopold views human beings as part of this ecosystem with certain ethical obligations deriving from this relationship. Equally, it is an ethic based on an aesthetic premise; Leopold saw the need to consider beauty in land-use decisions (see Little, 1992).

Leopold is particularly harsh to economists and those who hold that the appropriate ethical posture toward the land is essentially economic. Recall his oft-quoted passage that admonishes us to acknowledge other noneconomic factors: "quit thinking about decent land-use as solely an economic problem. Examine each question in terms of what is ethically and esthetically right, as well as what is economically expedient. A thing is right when it tends to preserve the integrity, stability and beauty of the biotic community. It is wrong when it tends otherwise" (1949, pp. 224–35).

Leopold is equally critical of our contemporary notions of progress. He questions whether, as a society and culture, we are indeed moving forward, given the types of choices we make in the process. Is it progress to forsake a marsh for a highway or a shopping center? Is it progress for people to recreate in automobiles at high speeds, failing to comprehend the beauty and wonder of the natural environment—an appreciation only available at a slower, more contemplative pace? Is it progress to permit the extinction of an animal species, or the destruction of wild lands, for the sake of material goods? Leopold raises the possibility that, rather than being in a period of *progress,* perhaps our current situation can better be described as *regress.* Here are three passages which, when linked together, form the core of his sermon:

> Our grandfathers were less well-housed, well-fed, well-clothed than we are. The strivings by which they bettered their lot are also those which deprived us of pigeons [referring to passenger pigeons]. Perhaps we now grieve because we are not sure, in our hearts, that we have gained by the exchange. The gadgets of industry bring us more comforts than the pigeons did, but do they add as much to the glory of the spring? (P. 109)
>
> Man always kills the thing he loves, and so we the pioneers have killed our wilderness. Some say we had to. Be that as it may, I am glad I shall never be young without wild country to be young in. Of what avail are forty freedoms without a blank spot on the map? (P. 149)
>
> In short, a land ethic changes the role of *Homo sapiens* from conqueror of the land-community to plain member and citizen of it. It implies respect for his fellow-members, and also respect for the community as such. (P. 204)

Primary to the development of Leopold's land ethic is the concept of community. He analogizes from the human community to the natural community. In a human community there are certain obligations that derive from the mutual interdependence of individuals. Individuals in the community benefit from the community as a whole, and thus in turn they have obligations to the community. Equally true, just as a person is a member of human communities, she or he is also a part of a larger biological community and as such has obligations to that community as well. "The land ethic simply enlarges the boundaries of the community to include soils, water, plants, and animals, or collectively: the land" (ibid.). The notion of people as "plain citizens" of earth, rather than its conquerors— plain members of an ecological community—is a powerful one with substantial implications for land-use policy. While Leopold offered few specifics concerning what such an ethical orientation requires, it is clear that major disruptions of the ecological community are unethical. It is also clear that, to Leopold, there is an ethical obligation to act as "stewards" of the land and not to waste its fruits or undermine its ecological integrity.

Holistic and Organic Ethics

In more recent years a number of environmental ethicists have further expanded and developed the Leopold land ethic. Some have argued that ethical obligations are owed to ecosystems qua ecosystems—not necessarily because ecosystems hold value to humans, or because they support other forms of life, but because of their complexity and uniqueness and thus their intrinsic value. Rolston (1988a) speaks of this in terms of "systemic value" and of the need to protect the larger ecological systems and processes that support all life: "When humans awaken to their presence in such a biosphere, finding themselves to be products of this process— whatever they make of their cultures and anthropocentric preferences, their duties to other humans or to individual animals and plants—*they owe something to this beauty, integrity and persistence in the biotic community. Ethics is not complete until extended to the land"* (p. 188, emphasis added).

There are, of course, practical difficulties in operationalizing an ethic based on obligations to ecosystems. Perhaps the most obvious difficulty is determining how ecosystems are to be defined. In reality the natural environment is comprised of a series of nested ecosystems—each smaller ecosystem is part of a larger one. On one level, a small five-acre wetland is clearly an ecosystem, and filling it in or otherwise destroying it might be considered immoral under an organic or holistic ethic. Such a wetland, however, is itself but one of many other similar eco-units which comprise and make up a larger ecosystem—an estuary, or a regional watershed, or ultimately a continental ecosystem. In the view of organic/holistic ethicists, which of these ecosystems are we obligated to protect? All levels? While the loss of the five-acre wetland may have certain localized repercussions, such an action, by and of itself, is unlikely to have major discernible impacts on the functioning of the larger eco-units, but any loss can be significant to a hydrological system. Can it be argued, then, that the organic view represents an ethical obligation to ensure the integrity of larger ecosystems with less concern for impacts on those of a smaller scale?

There are several problems with this interpretation, of course. One is that the same eco-dynamics and natural conditions which give rise to the ethical obligation at larger scales are present in the five-acre wetland case. On what grounds does the larger ecosystem have *intrinsic* value, while the smaller one does not? Furthermore, from an empirical point of view, destruction of the smaller ecosystem may have major impacts on the integrity of the larger ecosystem, when the cumulative effects of such practices are considered. (Indeed this has been a major shortcoming of our current regulatory approach to wetlands management—we fail to consider adequately the long-term cumulative effects of the continual loss of a few acres at a time.)

The organic/holistic view appears to give greater ethical importance to preserving the integrity of the larger ecosystem but also questions land-use practices that jeopardize the natural functioning of smaller ecosystems. But having concluded this, the skeptic might wonder, How can it be possible to satisfy the organic/holistic ethic while permitting any significant use of the land? First, land development can occur in ways which respect and sustain ecosystems; as we have already discussed at numerous points in this book, land use and land development are not uniform in their environmental effects. Land development can occur in ways which minimize disruption to hydrological, geological, and biological systems. (Consider Ian McHarg's famous book *Design with Nature* [1969] and the land planning techniques argued for therein.) Second, implementing the organic view provides additional moral weight to avoidance and protection of certain lands and natural processes especially critical for ecosystem maintenance (e.g., wetlands, estuaries, riverine systems). Third, while some degree of ecosystem disruption may be required to accomplish certain necessary societal land-use objectives (e.g., provision of new housing), the organic/holistic ethic emphasizes the moral imperative of *minimizing* the extent of this alteration. This ethic would seem to strengthen the criteria found in some existing environmental laws and regulations that prevent environmental destruction when there are *practicable alternatives* (e.g., section 404 of the federal Clean Water Act, which restricts placement of dredge and fill materials on wetlands; for explanation, see Salvesen, 1990). It also lends further weight to the conclusions of some courts, as in the classic *Just v. Marinette County* (1974) case, which ruled that landowners have no inherent right to modify the basic natural dynamics of a parcel of land.

Taylor's Respect for Nature

While organicists such as Callicott and Rolston argue that it is the natural ecosystem to which environmental obligations are owed, Taylor has taken an interesting and different theoretical approach in developing his theory, "Respect for Nature" (1986). In his book of the same title, Taylor argues that it is not the ecosystem per se which we have obligations to protect and sustain, but rather other forms of life (see also Taylor, 1981, 1983, 1984). All living creatures in Taylor's framework have inherent worth, regardless of whether they are sentient or nonsentient, plant or animal, endangered or nonendangered. Taylor argues that this respect for nature flows directly from a "biocentric outlook on nature." While this biocentric outlook cannot itself be further justified or derived—one simply has to accept it or not—once the outlook is embraced the attitude of respect is the only consistent ethical posture. Four beliefs make up the biocentric outlook:

1. The belief that humans are members of the Earth's Community of Life in the same sense and on the same terms in which other living things are members of that community.

2. The belief that the human species, along with all other species, are integral elements in a system of interdependence such that the survival of each living thing . . . is determined not only by the physical conditions of its environment but also by its relations to other living things.

3. The belief that all organisms are teleological centers of life in the sense that each is a unique individual pursuing its own good in its own way.

4. The belief that humans are not inherently superior to other living things. (Pp. 99–100)

What Taylor argues for is a kind of bioegalitarianism, where all forms of life have inherent worth and must be considered equally in any decision-making about land or environment. Taylor argues, interestingly, that the proposition that all organisms are teleological centers of life can be demonstrated by mentally assuming the posture of such organisms. Only by appreciating the entirety of their lives (a "wholeness of vision") can we see this. Note the similarity here between Taylor's views and those of animal rights activists such as Tom Regan.

Taylor does not simply argue that all forms of life have inherent moral worth, however. In *Respect for Nature* Taylor goes much further, laying out an extremely detailed framework for how the human world can implement these ethical obligations. He presents a detailed set of moral standards and rules of conduct which he believes flow directly from the biocentric outlook. Among the basic rules are these:

- The rule of nonmaleficence: the duty not to harm creatures in the natural environment, particularly those that do not harm human beings.
- The rule of noninterference: the duty to refrain from denying freedom to organisms and a general hands-off stance for ecosystems and organisms.
- The rule of fidelity: restrictions to deceiving or betraying wild creatures.
- The rule of restitutive justice: requirements to restore or compensate for previous injustices done to organisms and ecosystems. (My summary, see pp. 169–92)

Situations will undoubtedly occur in which satisfying one of these rules might violate another, and Taylor provides certain priority rules to deal with these circumstances. To effect the rule of restitutive justice, for instance, it may be necessary to violate the rule of fidelity (e.g., capturing the last California condors in order to ultimately save the species).

Whether one is willing to accept the assumptions of the biocentric outlook, these rules of conduct appear quite reasonable and directly applicable to land-use decision-making. Whether founded on Taylor's bio-egalitarianism or Regan's notion of inherent worth, it is reasonable to argue that there is a duty, ceteris paribus, not to harm wild creatures, as expressed by the Rule of Nonmaleficence (theorists such as Regan would, of course, not restrict the obligation to wild creatures, and would be concerned primarily with sentient life). The Rule of Restitutive Justice also seems reasonable, and indeed already finds expression in some of the environmental compensatory requirements discussed earlier (e.g., requirements to *mitigate* the loss of wetlands or endangered species habitat).

Problems arise when the desires and interests of humans conflict with those of other forms of life. What do we do when, as in an earlier example, the desires of certain peoples to construct a shopping center on a wetland conflict with the interests of other life-forms that depend on this habitat for survival? If other life-forms have the same inherent moral worth as humans, how can such proposals be permissible under Taylor's scheme? To address problems of competing moral claims, Taylor devises a set of five additional principles:

- The principle of self defense. (Individuals can protect themselves against dangerous or harmful organisms by destroying them.)
- The principle of proportionality. (In conflicts between humans and other species, nonbasic human interests cannot justify overriding a basic interest of other species.)
- The principle of minimum wrong. (People must choose alternatives which do the least damage to the natural world and harm or destroy the fewest number of organisms.)
- The principle of distributive justice. (Where conflicting interests are all basic, fair shares are equal shares, and certain adjustments are required to ensure all species are treated fairly.)
- The principle of restitutive justice. (Compensation is required for injustices done in the past; the greater the harm done, the greater is the compensation required; my summary, see pp. 256–313.)

While these principles are not so precise as to yield "neat solutions" in every case of conflict, they provide some direction. In applying the principles, Taylor employs the distinction between *basic* and *nonbasic* interests frequently discussed in environmental ethics (e.g., recall Van DeVeer's version in his two-factor egalitarianism). Taylor's principle of proportionality, for instance, applies to those situations in which the basic interests of nonhuman life conflict with the nonbasic interests of humans. Under the principles, and in these situations, nonbasic human interests cannot take precedence over the basic interests of other creatures. The nonbasic human interest of wearing a fur coat cannot override the basic survival interest of that creature.

Taylor's framework allows for circumstances in which humans can harm other forms of life. Clearly, humans can protect themselves from dangerous organisms and violate the basic interests of other forms of life when their own survival is at stake. Under the minimum wrong principle, Taylor also allows for certain circumstances in which the nonbasic interests of humans can overrule basic interests of other life, when these human interests are of a certain special importance: "What is the basis for this special importance? The answer lies, first, in the role such interests play in the overall view of civilized life that rational and informed people tend to adopt autonomously as part of their total world outlook. Secondly, the special value given to these interests stems from the central place they occupy in people's rational conception of their own true good" (1986, p. 281).

While such harms are permitted under Taylor's theory, the principle of minimum wrong requires that alternatives be chosen which keep this harm to a minimum:

> In order for humans to pursue valued ends that are fundamental to their cultural ideals of a high-level civilization and to their individual conceptions of their own true good, it is necessary that some of the Earth's natural environment used by wild creatures as habitat be taken over for human purposes. Although this is unavoidable . . . they can make special efforts to avoid ruining complete ecosystems and to desist from annihilating whole communities of life. They can locate and construct their buildings, highways, airports, and harbors with the good of other species in mind . . . they can control their population growth, change their habits of consumption, and regulate their technology. . . . One way to minimize habitat destruction is to make use of areas that have already been used for human purposes. (1986, pp. 287–88)

It may be useful at this point to consider the practical differences, if any, between the biocentric theory of Taylor and the holistic/organic views discussed earlier. While there may well be circumstances in which the two theories result in conflicting policy conclusions, one is struck with how similar in fact the land-use policy conclusions are likely to be. Taylor even acknowledges that although under his ethical system obligations are owed to organisms and not to ecosystems, the latter clearly sustain the former and as such would require protection. Moreover, because the sustaining and protecting of ecosystems results in the protection of a great many organisms, it amounts to a very efficient strategy to satisfying biocentric obligations (as opposed to taking a species-by-species approach).

Of course, the holistic/organic view expresses relatively little concern for human impacts on single organisms as long as the ecosystem is protected (witness Leopold's support for hunting, which is largely impermissible in Taylor's theory). Taylor's biocentric theory has great concern, on the other hand, for such impacts. But given the importance to the biocentric theory in sustaining ecological systems, it appears that the biocentric theory further justifies the organic/ecosystems view. Indeed, many will argue that it provides a more rational basis for arguing the importance of protecting ecosystems: we are morally obligated to protect and sustain them, not for their intrinsic value, but because they are the habitat and repository for numerous forms of life that *do* have intrinsic value.

Deep Ecology, Eco-feminism, and Land Use

The term "deep ecology" was coined by Norwegian philosopher Arne Naess to describe a certain reorientation to the natural world seen as essential (see Naess, 1973, 1979). In contrast to "shallow" ecology, which seeks to effect only marginal changes in how we treat or relate to the environment, deep ecology argues for a fundamental reorientation—one in which we overcome the traditional separation between human beings and nature. The deep ecology movement has picked up steam in recent years and offers yet another biocentric or ecocentric view of our obligations to the environment.

While the methodology invoked in deep ecology is decidedly more spiritual and emotive than philosophical, the conclusions are, in many ways, similar to the biocentric and organic views discussed earlier. Central to deep ecology is the view that individuals must develop and nurture a greater ecological consciousness. The two ultimate goals of deep ecology frequently cited are self-realization and biocentric equality. The former is to be achieved through a "meditative deep questioning process" in which individuals begin to understand themselves not as entities isolated from humans and other creatures, but rather as part of a greater whole. The idea of biocentric equality is obviously similar to Taylor's basic assumption of the equal inherent worth of all life-forms. For Naess and the deep ecologists this is a basic intuition, rather than something that can be philosophically derived. More specifically deep ecology holds that "all things in the biosphere have an equal right to live and blossom and to reach their own individual forms of unfolding and self-realization within the larger self-realization. This basic intuition is that all organisms and entities in the ecosphere, as parts of the interrelated whole, are equal in intrinsic worth" (Devall and Sessions, 1985, p. 67).

Deep ecology draws heavily from eastern religious thought (specifically Taoism and Buddhism), from feminism, from some elements of Christianity, from utopian thought and philosophy, and from the American literary traditions of naturalism and pastoralism. Ultimately, the focus of deep ecology is to foster a greater connection and association with nature, and to promote life-styles and behavioral patterns consistent with such a relationship (Tobias, 1985). Beyond these orientations, there have been few attempts to develop more specific rules of conduct or ethical principles which might give further meaning or direction to the deep ecology ideal. While it is not entirely clear what the practical policy or land-use implications of deep ecology are, it appears that considerable support exists for appropriate and alternative technologies, eco-utopian life-styles, policies of population control, wilderness preservation, and green politics.

Recently efforts have been made to join Taylor's biocentrism and deep ecology views. Devall, in *Simple in Means, Rich in Ends: Practicing Deep Ecology* (1988), embraces and applies Taylor's principles (and the views of others) in the planning of "mixed communities"—communities in which humans and other life-forms can live and coexist. Devall takes each of Taylor's principles and illustrates how they can be useful in resolving conflicts in mixed communities. Taylor's principles of self-defense, while allowing for the destruction of other forms of life in cases where human life is at risk, does not allow similar actions just to preserve economic interests. Devall uses the example of western ranchers killing wild animals to protect their livestock: "Economic self-defense is not a valid principle under the general principle of self-defense. For example, many ranchers in the American west claim (with scant, objective, scientific justification in some cases) that lambs or calves were killed by eagles, coyotes and bears, and that their own economic well-being is threatened. Coyotes, of course, are killing to fulfill a vital need—food. . . . The rancher's life is not threatened by an eagle or coyote or bear" (1988, pp. 178–79).

The principle of minimum wrong, as a further example, has clear and tangible implications for how human settlements grow and develop, requiring humans to minimize the impacts of recreational and other developments: "Humans can reduce their impact on habitat of wild species by withdrawing their activities from wildlands. They can designate huge areas as 'off limits' to future roads, dams, grazing, logging and mining. They can recycle areas which have already been polluted by human activities—such as large industrial areas in major cities—for other purposes. If some destruction of habitat is unavoidable, it can still be done with minimum impact" (ibid., p. 180).

Beyond illustrating and applying some of Taylor's principles, Devall does not present a clear or integrated picture of what a city or community founded on deep ecology concepts looks like. Clearly they are communities which tread lightly on the natural environment, and which respect the rights and interests of other forms of life and the larger ecological community. And he endorses a number of specific policy directions, including the need to designate as "off limits" large wilderness areas, to restore and rehabilitate damaged ecosystems, to promote more sustainable agricultural systems, and to contain the expansion of cities. Devall admits that there are few model communities to draw from and he issues a plea for greater attention to this. "Environmental groups have been very active in public debates on such issues . . . but we need more urban planners who are dedicated to the principles of deep ecology. . . . I cannot point to any model city which has developed on deep ecology principles" (ibid., p. 190).

In recent years considerable attention has been paid to eco-feminism, or ecological feminism, whose tenets closely relate to deep ecology. Eco-feminism holds, among other things, that women have special and different ways of relating to the natural world, and that such different ways of "seeing and living" may represent important alternatives to the present exploitation and domination of nature (see Booth and Jacobs, forthcoming).

While the causes may be psychological or biological (and there is considerable debate on this), eco-feminists see masculine values and patriarchal society as resulting in isolation and separation from nature, which in turn promote manipulation and domination. Feminine ways of viewing the world are more relational and acknowledge deep connections to nature (see Warren, 1987). The practical implications are again similar to deep ecology: there is the need to develop more harmonious and interconnected relationships to nature, drawing from feminine feelings and consciousness (for a discussion of the differences between deep ecology and eco-feminism, see, e.g., Kheel, 1991).

It is apparent, then, that deep ecology and eco-feminism, although perhaps more adamant in their demands and more emotional in their appeal than other ethical views toward the environment, have much in common with Leopold, Taylor, and others who advocate biocentric outlooks. They share the concept that *Homo sapiens* should assume a more modest position in the world, and then acknowledge that we are but a member of a larger biological community, and that other life-forms have inherent worth and value and must, to the extent possible, be respected in making decisions about land and the environment.

A Hierarchical System of Environmental Land Duties?

The ethical obligations to protect natural environments and their constituent parts are extensive and compelling. Land-use activities and patterns have had, and continue to have, a tremendous impact on the environment, and they represent a major policy area in which these ethical duties come into play. Protecting the natural environment can certainly be defended on the grounds of human self-interest; it seems clear to me that the very survival of the human race depends on a fundamentally different ethical orientation to natural resources, one which degrades and consumes these resources only sparingly and only when other alternatives are first exhausted.

But irrespective of the benefits of the natural environment to humans, I find convincing the arguments that nature has certain inherent worth that demands respect, to use Taylor's terms. This derives in my view from the existence of life, both sentient and nonsentient. This life can be seen to have a good of its own, can be seen to have inherent worth. Inanimate objects in nature—rivers, rocks, mountains—have no inherent worth in themselves in my view, but demand our protection and conservation because they sustain and provide habitat for living creatures. Unlike Taylor, I find the distinction between sentient and nonsentient life-forms to be a morally relevant one. When one develops land there is a difference, in my view, between the felling of a tree and, say, the killing of a black bear or a golden eagle. Greater moral obligations and duties are owed to the latter than the former because of their sentience.

Similarly, I believe our moral obligations to larger categories of organisms—that is, to species or communities of organisms—are greater than to single organisms. The right of an entire species to exist must outweigh the rights of a single creature. We are sometimes faced with difficult choices between the interests of endangered and nonendangered species where such a prioritizing may be necessary. For instance, the endangered desert tortoise (particularly its young) have, in recent years, been heavily preyed upon by ravens (a nonendangered species). The killing of some ravens may be essential to ensure the very survival of the tortoise as a species. As figure 7.2 indicates, moral priority must also be given to protecting the larger ecosystems which sustain species and organisms. If confronted with a choice between preserving an endangered species and the larger ecosystem which sustains multiple species (many of which may be endangered), the duty to preserve the ecosystem, in my view, takes precedence.

At every biological level, ethical land use requires that all efforts be made to minimize the extent of damage and destruction to the natural environment, and such impacts are permissible only for *important* social purposes. "Important" is, of course, open to substantial interpretation, but we must recognize that some degree of use and consumption of the natural commons is necessary. The strictest interpretation of "important" is to hold to the belief that destruction is only justified to promote the basic survival needs of human beings (e.g., to grow food, to build shelter

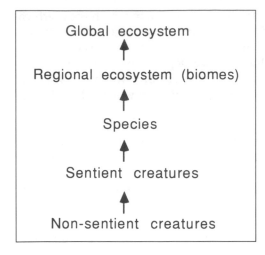

Figure 7.2 A hierarchy of environmental land obligations.

and housing). I, like Taylor, however, recognize that for human existence to have value may require *other* land uses which extend beyond mere survival, and which promote such things as cultural values (e.g., from art museums to opera houses) and recreational values (e.g., from tennis courts to jogging trails). Beyond this, what is *necessary* or *essential* to human society is necessarily left to individual moral judgments.

Ethical land use requires, as well, serious efforts of good faith to discover and promote alternatives to environmental destruction and degradation. Different land-use configurations and plans may have dramatically different impacts on the natural environment. Satisfying the basic housing needs of our society, for example, need not be so land intensive. Land, moreover, is not uniform in its environmental features and characteristics, and development of certain areas (e.g., wetlands, shorelines, floodplains, and riverine areas) are particularly damaging from an ecological point of view. The availability of alternative sites for destructive or damaging land uses must be considered.

A special comment is also appropriate concerning the concepts of environmental *restoration* and *mitigation*. Ethical land use acknowledges that people have caused destruction to the natural environment for centuries, and with the development of technologies to restore (at least partially) degraded landscapes arises the moral obligation to restore the natural environment wherever possible. Ethical land use supports efforts to promote the recovery and reestablishment of populations of species, such as the red wolf, which have historically been eradicated over much of their original habitat. Ethical land use demands efforts to restore larger ecosystems, such as the hydrologic systems of the Florida Everglades and the Lower Mississippi Valley, to their natural conditions. Such actions seem consistent with our earlier notions of culpability and seem to be dictated even where the financial costs are high. Such restoration activities provide us with the opportunity to pass along a world and a common habitat which is in better condition than when it was inherited.

On the other hand, we should be realistic in recognizing the inherent limitations of human technology in this area. We should admit the great difficulties and uncertainties that exist in attempting to approximate the "natural" result. This issue is perhaps most clearly illustrated in the area of wetlands mitigation. It is a common practice today (at both federal and state levels) to permit the filling or degradation of *natural* wetlands in exchange for certain mitigation actions—either the restoration of degraded wetlands of an equal or greater acreage elsewhere, or the creation of new wetlands. The evidence is fairly convincing that, while it may be possible to restore or create certain functions of natural wetlands (e.g., their flood retention capacities), it is nearly impossible to replicate their full natural workings, especially their biological productivity (see Kusler and Kentula, 1989). If such natural systems are permitted to be damaged or degraded, some form of adequate compensation should be mandated, but ethical land use demands that all efforts be made to prevent the destruction in the first place. Mitigation and restoration cannot be used as an excuse to permit the destruction of such areas.

These environmental obligations, then, hold substantial implication for contemporary land-use policy and planning. A reverence for, and serious moral consideration of, the interests of other forms of life and the habitats upon and in which they rely, implies a new sense of caution about how natural lands are used. It implies the need to minimize the extent of the human "footprint." It implies, perhaps, a vision of a shared planet and an obligation not to squander the limited common habitat (see Beatley, 1989a). Among the specific land-use and planning policies that seem required by such an ethic are these: higher urban and suburban densities and more compact and contiguous development patterns; the redirection of growth back into existing urban centers and the revitalization of declining areas; in filling and utilizing already degraded and committed lands for new developments before encroaching on environmentally sensitive habitat areas; the creation of regional networks of green spaces connecting existing parks and open spaces, and protecting hydrological and other important elements of the ecosystem; and restricting the extent to which resorts, second homes, and other less essential forms of development are subsidized or permitted at all.

The vision of a shared planet may call for other changes in life-style that extend beyond simply the amount of land we directly consume for development. A number of contemporary threats to species in this country involve, for example, water projects (e.g., dams, reservoirs, diversion

---

Environmental Ethics

As a member of the world community I understand that:

Every person has a right to a safe and healthy environment in which to live. Plants and animals, too, share that right.

Our air, water, and atmosphere are replenished and maintained by the diverse natural communities of the world. We, too, share in that upkeep.

All life on earth—human, plant, and animal—is joined in one world community. This is our natural heritage.

As a member of the world community I pledge:

To show respect for the world's natural heritage by taking care not to harm or degrade it through ignorance, carelessness, or misuse.

To continue to increase my understanding about the diversity of life and to share that knowledge with others.

To express my opinion on issues of concern that affect our natural heritage and to actively support its protection.

_____   _____
Date   Name

Figure 7.3 This environmental ethics pledge was prepared by the Carlsbad Caverns Guadalupe Mountains Association and the Guadalupe Mountains National Park. It is made available at the Guadalupe Mountains National Park's gift shop and museum, for public consumption and, it is hoped, application.

systems). The vision of a shared planet may necessitate sharply curtailing the extent to which we wastefully consume a scarce resource such as water (particularly for agricultural use in the arid West). The same can be said about energy consumption, when as a consequence we severely and irreparably damage the habitat of endangered and nonendangered species (e.g., the destruction of a riparian ecosystem as a result of a hydroelectric project, or the creation of acid deposition as a result of coal-burning power plants, the tremendous damage done by the Exxon Valdez tanker in the recent Alaska oilspill). There are many ways in which being a plain citizen may require rethinking basic life-style and consumption patterns, many of which play themselves out in the land-use arena. And, perhaps most fundamentally, the notion of sharing the planet with fellow human beings and all life-forms will require serious efforts on a global scale to control population growth. Such strategies as higher densities, urban infilling, and energy conservation can do only so much to reduce the human impact when the quantity of people, their activities, and resource demands are expanding at exponential rates. The pressure on all environmental systems increases in relation to human demands for survival.

Summary

Ethical land use includes major duties to protect the natural environment. Ethical land-use policy acknowledges both the instrumental values served by and the inherent worth of the natural environment. Land-use ethics must acknowledge that humans are but plain citizens on the earth and have no right to use land and natural resources in a wasteful manner. Land-use ethics requires a basic respect for all forms of life, and a concerted and serious effort to minimize the impacts of human actions on the other members of the biotic community. These obligations extend to individual organisms, species, and the larger ecosystems which sustain them. While some degree of human intrusion on the natural environment is inevitable, there is an ethical obligation to ensure that the human footprint is a small one.

8

LAND-USE OBLIGATIONS
TO FUTURE GENERATIONS

WE FREQUENTLY hear the plea that a certain land-use policy or a certain decision about land resources ought to be made because it is *owed* to future generations. Whether the issue concerns saving a historic Spanish church in New Mexico from demolition, or preventing a coastal wetland in Connecticut from being filled, the impacts of land-use actions and decisions on future peoples and societies are clearly relevant. In this chapter I examine the arguments typically made about future generations and review the contemporary theories and positions which may have relevance for land-use policy and planning.

One only needs to consult the preambles of land-use legislation or the transcripts of land-use debates to be convinced of at least the rhetorical relevance of arguments about future generations. The National Environmental Policy Act (NEPA) of 1969, the cornerstone of environmental policy in the United States, talks prominently of the obligations of the current generation to those in the future. The act states that it is the continuing responsibility of the federal government to "use whatever practicable means . . . to improve and coordinate federal plans, functions, programs, and resources to the end that the Nation may . . . fulfill the *responsibilities of each generation as trustee of the environment for succeeding generations*" (see 42 U.S.C. sections 4321–47; emphasis added). Almost every federal environmental law speaks of similar obligations. Moreover, it is common in political debates about various environmental and other legislative proposals to defend initiatives based on the need to protect and promote the interests of future generations.

The Impacts of Land-Use Policy on the Future

There is little doubt that land-use actions and policies affect the future in many ways and have considerable impact on the quality of life for future citizens. Land-use decisions can change the physical landscape in fundamental ways—for instance, by destroying valuable elements of the natural environment, such as wetlands, forests, scenic vistas, beaches, and wild areas. Land-use actions today can create serious future risks to public health and safety, such as permitting the disposal of hazardous wastes, or creating serious air and water pollution problems, or encouraging development to occur in areas subject to natural disasters such as floods and earthquakes.

Land-use actions and policies can influence, as well, the quality of the built environment. Land-use actions, such as the demolition of historic buildings, can diminish the possibilities for cultural and historic enrichment in the future. Land-use policies today can lead to undesirable urban living conditions in the future—for instance, by allowing economic and racial segregation or by permitting the proliferation of visually stifling architecture. In fundamental ways the world we live in today has been shaped by extensive and innumerable land-use decisions made in the past, a situation which raises a basic ethical quandary: Although the natural tendency in making land-use decisions is to consider the needs of current citizens, do we have an ethical obligation to consider the needs of future residents and future generations in making such decisions? In Joel Feinberg's words:

> We have it in our power to make the world a much less pleasant place for our descendants than the world we inherited from our ancestors. We can continue to proliferate in ever greater numbers, using up fertile soil at an ever greater rate, dumping our waste into rivers, lakes and oceans and cutting down our forests, polluting the atmosphere with noxious gases. All thoughtful people agree that we ought not to do these things, meaning not merely that conservation is morally required (as opposed to merely desirable), something to be done for their sakes. *Surely we owe it to future generations to pass on a world that is not a used up garbage heap. Our remote descendants are not present to claim a liveable world as their right, but there are plenty of proxies to speak now in their behalf.* These spokesmen, far from being mere custodians, are genuine representatives of future interest. (1980, pp. 180–81, emphasis added)

It is clear, as well, that in land-use and other public policy areas decisions are frequently made about the future and about the imposition of costs and benefits on future residents, but those who make policy decisions often fail to recognize them as such. Conventional economic investment practices—those in both the public and private sectors—treat the future in a particular moral way, through the practice of "discounting" (i.e., converting benefits and costs to present value through the use of a discount rate which roughly reflects the opportunity costs of using these investment resources in other ways). The assumption behind the practice of discounting is that benefits and costs occurring in the future are not as valuable or relevant as those which occur today. There is, then, the natural tendency to favor projects and investments which produce benefits in the near term and which perhaps impose costs in the distant future.

Arguments against Obligations to Future Generations

There has been a vigorous debate in many philosophical circles about whether obligations to future generations even exist. A considerable body of literature on the issue has developed over the years (two excellent anthologies are Partridge, 1981, and Sikora and Barry, 1978) and a variety of positions on this question have been taken. Let's briefly review these different points of view, beginning with those which might be grouped into the "negative camp"—those which for a variety of reasons hold that such obligations do not exist or are of little moral weight.

A number of philosophers and theorists have taken the position that it is nonsensical to base specific policy decisions on concerns about future generations. Martin Golding, for instance, has argued that no such obligations exist because future generations cannot be said to be part of our "moral community." For a moral community to exist requires either an explicit social contract or arrangement in which parties are mutually benefitted, or altruistic or sympathetic impulses. In Golding's mind it is impossible to achieve a social contract or any degree of reciprocity between the current generation and populations yet to exist. Achieving the conditions of a moral community under the second alternative is equally unlikely. To express altruism or sympathy for future generations requires us to develop some notion of what will or could be *good* for future generations. Because of the inherent difficulty in doing this, we cannot conclude that future people are really part of our moral community. In Golding's words: "They comprise the community of the future, a community with which we cannot expect to share a common life. It appears to me that the more remote the members of this community are, the more problematic our obligations to them become. That they are members of our moral community is highly doubtful, for we probably do not know what to desire for them" (1972, p. 69).

Golding's concern about knowing what is *good* for future generations is a commonly heard argument against such obligations. It is difficult enough for a society to determine what the present generation needs or wants, and even harder to hypothesize about the requirements and desires of distant populations. This concern is, not surprisingly, most vehemently expressed when it comes to discussions about *distant* generations. While we might be able to speculate with some degree of accuracy about the needs and wants of the next generation, it becomes impossible to speak with any degree of accuracy about the needs and wants of people, say, 500 or 1,000 years from now.

It is the position of some philosophers that it makes no sense to speak of the *rights* of future generations, because to assign rights requires the identification of specific individuals. And because these individuals will be born in the future, we cannot specifically identify them now. Therefore the assignment of rights is inconceivable. Furthermore, the specific actions and policies we adopt today will actually influence who these individuals are in the future. Under strict policies of population control, for instance, many individuals may simply not be born in the future—again adding to the indeterminacy of future populations. This phenomenon is sometimes described as Parfit's Paradox, after the work of philosopher Derek Parfit (Parfit, 1984; 1981–82).

Irrespective of the moral implications, it is clear that the lack of knowledge about specific individuals does contribute to what Care (1982) calls the "motivation problem." Is there not a natural human tendency to be more concerned with the conditions and needs of people who exist now and whose faces and names are real and not hypothetical?

Other scholars have argued against obligations to future generations on the grounds that future populations will tend to be better off than current populations. They will be more prosperous, the argument goes, and will have the benefits of numerous scientific and technological advances presently unavailable. The use of discounting in cost-benefit analyses, for instance, is often justified on the grounds of increasing prosperity. Moreover, postponing solutions to basic environmental problems until the future is often defended on the grounds that, given expected scientific and technological advancements, future generations will be better able to deal with such problems (see Goodin, 1980).

There is another position—that we should not be terribly concerned about the world we leave to future generations because they will have no appreciation for what has been lost. If present generations have little concern for protecting wilderness areas, or national parks, or 1,000–year-old redwoods, then future residents will not feel harmed by their loss because they will not have known them or experienced them. This position is summed up by the common expression, "What you don't know won't hurt you." Future generations living in California, for example, will not feel harmed or pained by the gradual loss of open spaces because they will be born into a heavily developed landscape. Moreover, dealing with a host of environmental calamities (from toxic waste dumps, to polluted air and water, to loss of visually stimulating landscapes) may, to future generations, simply be part of their normal lives—again, because they don't know any differently.

Some philosophers have sought to ameliorate concerns about future generations by hypothesizing that, no matter how degraded and spoiled the planet becomes, if given the choice future populations would still rather be born than not.

While some scholars acknowledge that we might know in a general way what the needs and interests of future generations will be, they still argue that it is extremely difficult to make specific public policy decisions based on future generations. First, unlike the present population, future generations cannot be consulted about their opinions on specific land and resource issues. They cannot express their views through voting, letter writing, and other democratic means. It is difficult to know, for instance, whether future generations will prefer, if given a choice, to establish a new national park along a seashore, or in a pristine mountain region, or in the north woods, or perhaps not at all.

Furthermore, when dealing with nonrenewable resources, including land, policy decisions based on concerns for future generations involve complex questions of how to slice and distribute a limited pie. To distribute fair slices of this pie among different generations requires knowledge of how many generations are to be considered. But the number of generations are potentially infinite. Thus, the present generation's share is either indeterminable or infinitesimal—neither of which is very helpful to policymakers.

Finally, some scholars have expressed reservations about obligations to future generations based on the belief that there are too many problems faced by the present generation which must be addressed first. If we have spare or slack resources, the argument goes, we should be concerned first with improving the lot of those who presently exist.

Arguments in Support of Obligations to Future Generations

Despite the criticisms expressed by many in the philosophical community about the defensibility of obligations to future generations, others have found greater merit in such concepts. A number of philosophers have argued that, from a moral point of view, future populations ought to be assigned equal moral weight as compared with current generations. As Robin Attfield notes: "Future people count, to speak morally, as much as present ones. . . . Our obligations to people are not lessened at all by the mere fact of their futurity" (1983, p. 95).

Contradicting the concerns expressed by some about the "knowability" of the needs and wants of future generations, many philosophers have argued that it is not a great mystery what these needs and wants will be. Certain human needs and interests will not change much. We can be fairly certain, for instance, that human beings in the future will demand

and require the basic conditions for a healthy life, including clean air and clean water, a balanced diet, decent and affordable shelter, and an environment free from hazardous substances. While it may be impossible to assign rights to specific individuals, there is absolutely no doubt that future individuals will exist (short of a nuclear holocaust or a large asteroid) and will consequently have such basic biological and social needs.

A number of moral methodologies have been employed to argue in support of obligations to the future. Rawls extends his contractarian approach to incorporate the futurity issue. Recall that under Rawls's *Justice as Fairness,* the principles for a just society are derived by reverting to an "original position," in which rational individuals make decisions under a "veil of ignorance," devoid of information about their specific talents or circumstances (see Beatley, 1984a; Rawls, 1971). While under the Rawlsian original position all contracting parties are assumed to be contemporaneous (that is, from the same generation), he believes that individuals will be motivated to express concern about their immediate descendants. This concern will lead, Rawls believes, to the adoption of what he refers to as the Just Savings Principle. The Just Savings Principle requires present generations to adopt a reasonable rate of investment and savings to ensure that just institutions are protected in the future.

This savings by the current generation must include "not only factories and machines, and so on, but also knowledge and culture, as well as the techniques and skills, that make possible just institutions and the fair value of liberty" (Rawls, 1971, p. 288). Beyond this Rawls is unclear about what must actually be saved or protected. The basic sentiment is that rational individuals, when deciding on the basic principles of justice to govern them, will not condone a myopic present-generation focus. It will be unacceptable to consume and pillage, leaving nothing for one's descendants.

Other philosophers have modified and extended the basic Rawlsian contract (e.g., Hubbard, 1977; Manning, 1981; Routley and Routley, 1978). Routley and Routley, for instance, have sought to extend the conditions of the original position to include not just contemporaries, as Rawls assumes, but also representatives from each and every generation.

Kavka has argued for obligations to future generations based on Lockean theory. He argues that the present generation has an obligation when making decisions about land and resources to leave "as much and as good for others." Kavka elaborates on these requirements: "Accordingly, we say that a generation may use the earth's resources provided that it (i) does not waste them (i.e., uses them to satisfy human interests) and (ii) leaves 'enough and as good' for future generations. In the spirit of the justification Locke offers for his second condition, I interpret it to mean that, in this context, the generation in question leaves the next generation at least as well off, with respect to usable resources, as it was left by its ancestors" (Kavka, 1978, p. 120).

Consequently, under this Lockean interpretation constraints are placed on the extent to which present generations can consume land and resources. Specifically, land and resources must not be wasted, and use cannot exceed that point at which "enough and as good" remains for future generations. But given that any use of land and environmental resources diminishes the absolute quantity available in the future, Kavka relies on certain assumptions about science and technology. If, for instance, a certain quantity of farmland is needed currently to produce sufficient food to feed people, it is permissible under Kavka's framework to pass along a smaller farmland resource base to future generations only if advancements in agricultural production can yield similar production levels with less land or eroded land of lower quality: "It might first appear impossible that any generation live up to the Lockean standard. . . . How could a generation use *any* resources at all and leave an equal number of descendants with as many resources as they themselves inherited? The question is readily answered by noting that some physical resources are renewable or reusable, and that knowledge—especially scientific and technological knowledge— is a usable resource that grows without being depleted and enables us to increase the output of the earth's physical resources" (ibid.).

While Kavka's logic might work with respect to certain types of land and land uses, it does not generally work well with respect to unique and irreplaceable resources. Wilderness areas, old-growth forests, coastal marshes, and other natural areas are essentially irreplaceable and non-renewable, and under a strict interpretation of Lockean principle these areas would have to be retained exactly as they are.

Utilitarianism has also been employed as a philosophical methodology for support of obligations to future generations (see Surber, 1977). It can be argued that the present generation has an ethical obligation to conserve land and resources and to reduce waste and consumption, in order to maximize utility across generations. Attfield (1983) argues, as a variation of this, that the basic needs of all individuals—both present and future generations—must be satisfied because this will, in the long run, serve to maximize social welfare. Such a utilitarian view raises an interesting dilemma concerning population growth. Under classical utilitarianism it is the absolute utility produced which is important, not the average utility. Embracing this common version of utilitarianism might argue for allowing or even promoting unlimited population growth, despite the fact that the quality of life may decline over time—the more people living, the greater the absolute welfare or utility generated, assuming that, on balance, people are glad to be alive (see also Narveson, 1967, 1987; Parfit, 1981–82, 1984; Sikora, 1975).

Reverence for the future can also be seen in the cultures of Amerindians. By and large, until the twentieth century, American Indian tribes and nations did not view land as being owned in the traditional western sense, but only to be used temporarily (see Chapter 11). There was, then, a much greater importance given to respecting the future and the need to protect the earth and its bounty for those who come later. Native American cultures, moreover, have had a much greater sense of the moral connection and continuity between past, present, and future. The Iroquois Tribe provides perhaps the best known example of this perspective in their seventh generation principle. The Iroquois tribal council opened each meeting with the following invocation: "In our every deliberation we must consider the impact of our decisions on the next seven generations" (as quoted in Nollman, 1990, p. 58). Explicit consideration in the decisions of the council, then, was given to those who would live some 200 or more years later.

Specific Types of Obligations Owed

Despite the legitimate criticisms of some scholars that it is difficult to determine precisely what the obligations to the future are, there seems little doubt that the actions of the current generation can have potentially serious, even grave, impacts on the future, and that possibility alone creates certain moral obligations of care. But what does this level of care imply and can we be more specific about the implications for land-use policy and planning?

There has been considerable speculation in the literature about what exactly is owed to future generations. One of the more frequently cited obligations is to keep options open and to avoid making irreversible decisions concerning land and resources. As already mentioned, many decisions about land use and resources involve the consumption of essentially a nonrenewable resource. While preserving a wilderness area may be viewed as less important to the needs of the present generation, obligations to future generations might argue for the need to maintain the option of protecting it. If the next generation decides that such lands are indeed extremely important to them, they will then have the option of acting upon these desires. If wilderness lands are destroyed, the option is closed, essentially forever. The extinction of species is perhaps the clearest and most dramatic case of an irreversible action. Once the black-footed ferret or Florida panther or golden lion tamarin are lost, they are lost forever. If these species end up being more valuable in later generations than they are today, there is no way by which to bring them back. That future generations will value such resources as wilderness lands, old-growth forests, greenways, and endangered wildlife more than current generations do is not inconceivable, given the sort of changes in attitudes in the United States we have witnessed in just the last 100 years. It was not until 1872 that the first national park in the world was created (Yellowstone), and it was only in 1964 when the first serious legislation designed to designate and protect wilderness areas in this country was enacted. It was only in 1973 when the federal Endangered Species Act was enacted—the first comprehensive effort to protect threatened and endangered flora and fauna in the United States. Thus, considerable changes in human values and priorities can occur within a relatively short period of time.

But a keeping-the-options-open ethic need not mean that as a society we are frozen from making decisions. As Goodin observes: "Having chosen one path, it will always be costly to shift over to some other; but, while costly, the shift is at least possible. . . . Thus we may, consistent with that rule, pursue certain options provided our policy is *reversible*—provided we can backtrack if necessary" (1983, p. 7).

Rolston argues that different types of land use and environmental degradation will have different levels of irreversibility: "a decade for forage, a century for timber regeneration, 100,000 years for soil loss, forever for extinction" (1988a, p. 267). These different levels of irreversibility in turn imply different levels of caution in land-use decision-making. Greater care and caution should be exercised in taking actions which are completely irreversible, such as the extinction of a species, while the requisite level of caution may not be as great in the case of a forest, which can be regenerated to a large extent, albeit over a long period of time.

Of course, the notion of keeping options open does imply that, at some point in the future, society will be permitted to make a decision about the resource in question. For the sake of argument, suppose there is an eighteenth-century courthouse currently in jeopardy of being torn down to make room for more intense downtown development. A small group of local historians are presently interested in saving the building. They argue that even if the current residents of the community do not value the structure sufficiently to support its preservation, the city council ought to preserve it for posterity. The razing of the courthouse would be irreversible and the city council, they claim, should at least keep the option open to save it at some point in the future. But, if the city council takes the advice of these historians and saves the building—essentially retaining the decision about whether to preserve it for future generations, how long should this *option* be kept open? Say the next generation of residents feels no stronger about the building than the current generation does. At that point the historians (perhaps a different group of individuals by that time) might make the same plea to keep the options open. But what if the generation after that one again feels equally unconcerned? Without some concept of "expiration," the argument of keeping the options open strikes many as highly circular. It seems reasonable to establish, say, a 20-year, 50-year, or 100-year period, in which certain land-use options are kept open to preserve a community's cultural and natural resources. If attitudes do not change over the said period of time, then it might be seen as morally acceptable to allow an irreversible land-use decision (demolish the courthouse) to be made. Some irreversible actions, however, such as the extinction of species, should not be permitted under any circumstances, as a result of other ethical standards outlined in this book.

I have come to believe that human beings in the future *will* rely upon and require the same basic biological prerequisites for survival as the current generation, and so obligations must exist to protect these conditions. The most dramatic threat to these basic survival conditions may well be those global-level alterations to the environment, most notably global climate change and ozone depletion (though there remains considerable disagreement about the reality and rate of the former). In each case the actions and policies of the current generation (compounded by those of past generations) threaten to destroy or undermine severely the basic conditions for the existence of future generations. Important, as well, are the innumerable alterations of the environment on local or regional scales, including air and water pollution, loss of wetlands and open space, and hydrological alterations, deforestation, and desertification. As noted earlier, while it is difficult to know whether and at what point these alterations and degradations will be so extensive that life as we know it may be difficult, clearly the cumulative result is a much less hospitable planet for future generations.

Sustainability and Stewardship

Obligations to future generations and concepts of sustainability are closely linked. In recent years there has been considerable interest in, and support for, the concept of "sustainable development." Sustainable development was strongly advocated by the World Commission on Environment and Development (the Brundtland Commission) and is a centerpiece of their seminal report, *Our Common Future*. Sustainable development is defined there as development that meets the needs of the present "without compromising the ability of future generations to meet their own needs" (World Commission on Environment and Development, 1987, p. 43). (Many believe the term *sustainable development* to be an oxymoron, and I prefer to use the term *sustainability*.) Such sustainability implies respecting the physical limits and natural carrying capacities of the earth, and understanding and living within its finiteness and regenerative capabilities; it requires "society to live on the 'interest' of our ecological endowment, while maintaining and protecting the ecological 'capital'" (Rees, 1990, p. 18). True concern about sustainability has tremendous implications for land-use policy and suggests, among other things, substantial changes in forest production and management practices (consider, e.g., the impressive sustainable forestry practices of the Menominee Indian tribe of Wisconsin; see Landis, 1992); reductions in the degree to which water, soil, and other natural resources are exploited; and the strong need to further develop renewable energy sources (e.g., solar).

In recent years there have been considerable discussions in the planning and design professions about the need for "sustainable communities"—or the need to incorporate principles of sustainability in the design and operation of cities, towns, and communities (e.g., see Van Der Ryn and Calthorpe, 1990; Walter, Arkin, and Crenshaw, 1992). Sustainable communities are communities that strive to reduce resource consumption (e.g., energy, water) and the generation of wastes (e.g., air pollution, solid waste) and seek to promote, as well, greater liveability and social equity. The concept of sustainable communities lends support for a number of specific urban and regional policies and programs, including these: promoting more efficient compact and contiguous development patterns; reducing dependence on the automobile and promoting greater use of mass transit and other alternative modes of transportation; and promoting mixed-use development and infill growth. The interests of future generations, then, require that land-use practices are, to the extent practicable, founded on principles of sustainability.

A similar set of values is found in the notion of "stewardship." Here the basic idea is that the present generation is only temporarily using the land, and the fact that it must be passed along to those in the future implies an element of care. This notion further reinforces the moral necessity of considering the needs and interests of future populations—indeed, the concept takes away the presumption that current generations can do whatever they would like with land and resources. While the stewardship concept has clearly found secular support, some of its more adamant advocates draw heavily from religious thought to defend the concept. Wendell Berry is one of the more prolific and eloquent defenders of stewardship, drawing from the biblical story of the promised land. He argues that such biblical passages establish that land is a gift—"not a free or deserved gift, but a gift given upon certain rigorous conditions" (1981, p. 270). The gift is a temporary one, so landholders have certain responsibilities to care for and nurture the land and to pass it along to future generations in a similar or improved condition. "You may eat the harvest, but you must save the seed, and you must preserve the fertility of the fields" (1981, p. 273). While this is a powerful mandate,

Berry and others who advocate stewardship are often vague about what it actually demands of property owners and society. The moral admonitions of Berry and others are most specific when it comes to agricultural uses—where landowners are strongly encouraged to practice small-scale, low-energy, soil-conserving modes of production (see Barbour, 1980; Dubos, 1972; Jackson, Berry, and Coleman, 1984). The notion of land as a commodity, that is held temporarily and in trust for future generations, is an extremely appealing ethical concept. It helps to establish the sometimes foreign idea that the use and ownership rights of *future* generations may create legitimate moral constraints on the use and ownership rights of the *current* generation.

Edith Brown Weiss argues similarly that the human community must be viewed as a "partnership" among generations, in turn demanding that principles of "intergenerational equity" be followed:

> The purpose of the partnership is to protect the welfare of every generation. To do so, each generation must recognize that it is part of the natural system with special responsibilities as well as rights. . . . No generation knows in advance when along the spectrum of time it will become the living generation. But every generation wants to inherit the common patrimony of the planet in as good condition as it has been for previous generations and to have as much access to it as did previous generations. The theory of intergenerational equity thus calls for equality among generations and among members of a generation, with the understanding that all are entitled to a certain level of quality and access. (1990, p. 9)

To promote this intergenerational equity, Weiss proposes three principles: (1) each generation must protect the diversity of the natural and cultural resource base (the "conservation of options" principle); (2) each generation must pass along the planet in no worse condition and each generation is entitled to an equal level of environmental quality (the "conservation of equality" principle); and (3) each generation must ensure all members equitable access to the planetary legacy (the "conservation of access" principle). To implement these principles, Weiss proposes some interesting legal and institutional changes, including the formulation of a declaration of intergenerational rights, the appointment of ombudsmen for future generations, and the establishment of planetary trust funds and user fees. Fees would be imposed on those who utilize and degrade the environment, with the proceeds going to pay for cleanups or protection efforts. To Weiss such a framework ultimately requires a new planetary land ethic: "Intergenerational equity requires a new planetary ethos in which each generation views itself both in relation to past and future generations of the human species and as an integral part of the natural system. Each generation has a right to use the natural system for its own benefit but also an obligation to care for it so that future generations will inherit a robust planet in no worse condition than previous generations received it. Only by adhering to such principles will each generation treat future generations fairly" (1990, p. 31).

These types of obligations to future generations seem to reinforce the moral duties to the environment identified in earlier chapters. They further establish the moral necessity to protect, preserve, and conserve ecosystems and the species and organisms which rely upon them. But this moral basis (future generations, that is) is explicitly anthropocentric, and as such requires the preservation and protection of other *things* which may affect, in a significant way, the quality and integrity of the lives of future generations. As we have seen, this may include the protection of historic and cultural resources (e.g., historic buildings and landmarks, battlefields, and archaeological sites) and visual and scenic resources (e.g., irreplaceable resources such as the Grand Canyon, the Columbia River Gorge, the Adirondacks, and the Outer Banks of North Carolina). Land-use obligations to future generations also imply consideration of the ways in which many discrete short-term decisions cumulatively influence multigenerational land-use patterns. Ethical land use requires that the long-term view be taken, that the traditional short-sightedness of public land-use policies and decisions must be overcome.

Land-use obligations to future generations also seem to imply that there are ethical limits which must be placed on the extent to which land and resources can be consumed in the present generation. There is considerable intuitive logic to the notion that the present generation ought not to consume more than its fair share. Granted, it is difficult to determine what the "fair share" is. Leaving "as much and as good" for future generations, at least when it comes to land, is difficult, if not impossible (even assuming substantial scientific and technological advancements). The undeniable facts are that the planet has a finite land and resource base and, in a remarkably short period of time in our planet's history, the human population has grown by incredible leaps and bounds. Although earth's population was only about one billion in 1900, its current population is estimated at nearly at 5.4 billion and growing. Projections by the United Nations indicate that world population will rise to an amazing 8.5 billion by the year 2025 (United Nations, 1991). Accompanying this population growth has been the rapid exploitation and consumption of land and environmental resources. A global land-use survey undertaken by the Sierra Club in 1987 found that a relatively small percentage—34 percent—of the planet earth's surface can still be considered to be wilderness—that is, largely untouched by human hands (see table 8.1).

Table 8.1 Amount of Wilderness Remaining Worldwide

	Amount of Wilderness (in Square Kilometers)	Percentage of Continent That Is Wild	Number of Wilderness Areas
Antarctica	13,209,000	100	2*
Asia	11,864,000	27	306
Africa	9,177,700	30	437
North America	9,006,700	36	89
South America	4,222,700	24	91
Oceania and Australia	2,666,300	30	94
Europe	741,000	7	31
	50,887,400	34**	1,050

Source: McCloskey and Spalding, 1987.

*This figure represents one continuous block of land that is divided in two for the purpose of biogeographical classification.

**This figure is derived by dividing the total amount of wilderness for the world (50,887,400 sq. km.) by the total size of the world's land mass (149,664,000 sq. km.).

If Antarctica and Greenland are subtracted, the percentage is even smaller (McCloskey and Spalding, 1987). While I am hesitant to proffer what might be a fair land and resource consumption rate for each generation, it is clear that recent generations have consumed, destroyed, and degraded land at a rate unprecedented in human history and well beyond any conceivable generational "fair share." Adopting a more reasonable fair share would reinforce many of the types of policies already discussed in this book, including efforts to reduce wasteful consumption of land, to promote more compact and contiguous development patterns, to protect more of the remaining undeveloped land, and to infill and reuse degraded lands. As McCloskey and Spalding note, "The remaining wildland is the patrimony of the world—of all living things, and all generations to come" (1987, p. 2).

Ultimately, of course, because many of our more serious land-use pressures are a consequence of population growth, ethical land use would support efforts to manage population. While such policies are not typically thought of as land-use policies, it is clear that in many countries and regions, protecting the interests of future generations will be difficult without addressing the explosive population growth occurring now.

Ethical land use which acknowledges obligations to future generations also suggests the need to correct, whenever and wherever possible, the degradation and overexploitation brought about by current and recent generations. If current and recent generations have utilized or exhausted an unfair proportion of the planetary stock—whether through excessive soil erosion, or hazardous waste disposal, or loss of open space and wetlands, or whatever—perhaps there is an obligation not simply to restrain ourselves from continuing such actions but also to seek to restore, repair, or otherwise correct for such previous degradation. While it is impossible to replace an extinct species such as the dusky seaside sparrow *(Ammaspiza nigrescens)* or to recreate an ancient forest or Ice Age bog, it may be possible to take actions which, at least partially, put things back the way they were. It is, for instance, possible to restore and reclaim, at least partially, mined lands (see Hunt, 1989).

Recent Land-Use Conflicts

Given the rate and magnitude of the impacts of the human species on land and the environment, it is not surprising that many of our major land-use conflicts involve the issue of future generations. In this section we will explore several dilemmas in more detail and examine what the implications of concern about the future might be for their resolution.

One of the most contentious land-use conflicts in recent years involves the management and utilization of old-growth forests in the United States. As figure 8.1 indicates, few old-growth forests remain in the United States, as the gradual development of the country has turned such areas into farms, silviculture operations, and housing developments, among other uses. Most of these remaining unharvested areas are located in the Pacific Northwest, but even in Oregon and Washington only relatively small amounts of old-growth timber remain, on the order of 10 percent. At current rates of harvesting, these forests, and the jobs affiliated with them, may no longer exist in another thirty years. These old-growth forests are irreplaceable; many of the trees are between 500 and 1,000 years old. Moreover, the forest ecosystem sustaining these trees has taken thousands of years to develop and evolve (see Norse, 1990). These forests are as biologically rich and complex as any in the continent and their functioning is poorly understood by forest ecologists even today. Most of the remaining old-growth forests are located in national forests, and a debate over the extent to which, and whether or not, these trees should be harvested has been ongoing for decades. The issue has come to a head in the media and in public debates as a result of the federal listing in 1990 of the northern spotted owl as a threatened species under the federal Endangered Species Act. The owl makes its home in these old-growth forests, and many environmentalists view the owl as one strategy for protecting the remaining old-forest ecosystem.

This contentious land-use question has pitted environmentalists against logging and development interests, and in many ways this conflict effec-

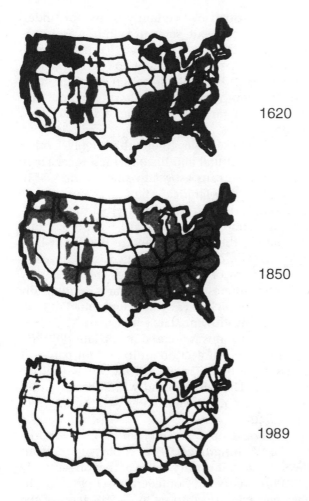

1620

1850

1989

Figure 8.1 Extent of virgin forests in the United
States over time.

tively illustrates the differences in values at work here. To many people,
these last remaining forests should be preserved forever, while others
believe the jobs and tax revenues associated with the forest products
industry, which can be obtained in the short term, are more important? A
recent federal study concluded that, in order to preserve the owl, some 3
million acres of old-growth forest require protection, at a potential cost
of 20,000 timber-related jobs.

In my view, consideration of the interests of future generations is a
highly relevant moral factor in these types of land-use decisions. These

forests *are* irreplaceable, as the spotted owl certainly is. As our understanding of, and sense of importance about, such areas improves, future generations will likely feel that the quality of their lives has been diminished significantly by the loss of such areas. Current and recent generations have clearly and vastly exceeded any fair allocation of this resource throughout time. The benefits from harvesting are short-term and temporary, and harvesting this kind of rare forest is, from a societal view, nonessential, as clear alternatives exist.

Let's shift our emphasis in land-use issues to one that involves not a natural habitat or resource, but a cultural and historical resource. There has been much concern among Americans, especially since World War II, over the increasing loss of historically significant buildings and historic and cultural landscapes. Typically, such lands are converted to low-density housing developments and shopping centers. The issue of cultural resource preservation has come to the fore especially in the East, where many Civil War battlefield sites are coming under increasing development pressures. It is ironic that many of these battlefields are in jeopardy at precisely the time when public interest in the Civil War is dramatically on the rise (witness the now-famous PBS series by Ken Burns aired in 1990 about the war). In Virginia, a rapidly growing state where many Civil War battles were fought, national attention was focused in the late 1980s on plans to construct a shopping center project on an important parcel of land adjacent to the Manassas National Battlefield Park, where the two battles of Bull Run were waged. Though the land was eventually purchased by the federal government, this case illustrates well the extent of these potential land-use conflicts.

More recently a conflict has developed in Culpeper County, Virginia (about 100 miles southwest of Washington, D.C.), over plans to build an industrial park on the site of the largest cavalry battle of the war—Brandy Station. Here more than 20,000 Union and Confederate troops fought in June 1863. While the developer has agreed to set aside 248 acres of the 1,445-acre site, local preservationists argue that this acreage is relatively unimportant and that the areas where the greatest fighting occurred will be destroyed under this proposal (Masters, 1990). Local opinion appeared to be split on the issue, with advocates of battlefield protection arguing against the proposed rezoning (along with those concerned about the impacts on the Rappahannock River and the rural character of the county) and others arguing that the tax base and jobs to be created by the project outweighed the loss of the battlefield. Supporters of the rezoning also point out that a large segment of the battlefield was already lost when the Culpeper airport was built, and that the area had been designated for a number of years for industrial use. The Culpeper County Board of Supervisors approved the rezoning request and the project appears free to proceed. Hurrah for progress.

Events such as these raise serious questions about our land-use obligations to posterity. Just as it is impossible to bring back to life an extinct species or to recreate an old-growth forest once it is felled, it is equally impossible to retrieve a historic landscape. And it is hard to imagine that Brandy Station will be no more, that the historical integrity of this landscape will be lost forever. Do we have ethical obligations to preserve this heritage? Is it sufficient to preserve a few remnants of the Civil War landscape, such as Gettysburg, while permitting other historic sites, perhaps the majority of them, to be lost to development? While it is certainly a matter of practical ethical judgment as to how much land and history we can save—that is, balancing these objections against other worthy social needs—ethical land use demands that all practicable efforts be undertaken to save such landscapes. Whether a Civil War battlefield or an Indian ceremonial site or a historic building, this land-use heritage is important in helping current generations understand who they are and where they came from, and these sites will serve the same important function only if they are protected and preserved for future generations. And, we know, there is considerable money to be made through tourism when such landscapes are saved for future generations.

These battlefield/development conflicts illustrate the kinds of impacts that public land-use decisions can have on cultural and historic resources. Just as harvesting the last remaining old-growth forests would deprive future generations of the immeasurable enjoyment of these natural areas, and the natural heritage of which they are a central part, so also can land-use actions reduce or eliminate historical resources and cultural heritage. When such areas are lost, the quality and richness of future existence is diminished. It is easy to cite examples where such historical resources will be lost as a result of land-use actions. In the U.S. Virgin Islands, for instance, conflict has arisen over proposals to develop a salt pond, the first landing site of Christopher Columbus. In the Middle East, a Turkish dam threatens to flood the unexcavated ruins of the ancient village of Hasankeyf. That historic and cultural resources are threatened by land-use decisions remains too common an occurence in an era of supposedly human enlightenment.

Summary

There is little doubt that land-use actions and policies, individually and cumulatively, significantly affect the future. Land policies today can diminish or enhance the quality of life for future generations in numerous ways. Traditionally, future generations are rarely considered seriously in land-use decision methodologies such as benefit-cost, where impacts in the future are explicitly discounted to the present.

Although many philosophers and theorists question whether it is meaningful to speak of the interests and welfare of future generations, ethical land use acknowledges such obligations. At the minimum, land-use decisions must seek to ensure the basic ability of future generations to achieve a reasonably high quality of life. While we may be unable to predict precisely what the land-use preferences or desires of residents of our planet will be 100 or 500 years from now, we can be fairly certain that they will need food, clean air and water, shelter, open space for recreation, and natural beauty for sustenance and meaning in their lives. Many current land-use policies and practices, if continued, would seem to jeopardize achievement of these basic conditions in the near and distant future. Moreover, ethical land use acknowledges that we have special obligations to protect landscapes and natural and cultural resources which may tremendously enrich the lives of future generations.

PART III

ETHICS AND
INDIVIDUAL LIBERTIES

9

PATERNALISM AND VOLUNTARY RISK-TAKING

JOHN STUART MILL, in his classic treatise *On Liberty* (1859), presents a convincing and compelling defense of the sanctity of personal "tastes and pursuits" and the importance of limiting public interferences with them. Personal freedom to pursue one's preferences and chosen life-style are essential, Mill felt, and public or collective interference with personal freedoms is justified only to protect the liberties and freedoms of other individuals or the collective as a whole. To interfere with an individual's liberty merely to protect him or her *from* themselves (i.e., when their actions do not appreciably harm others or the public) amounts to paternalism, which is unacceptable in a free society.

Gerald Dworkin defines paternalism as the "interference with a person's liberty of action justified by reasons referring exclusively to the welfare of good, happiness, needs, interests, or values of the person being coerced" (1971, p. 108). In this chapter we consider the extent to which certain land-use policies and actions can be considered paternalistic and the moral validity of such policies (see Kleining, 1988; Van DeVeer, 1986b). Clearly many land-use policies involve placing restrictions on individual actions and individual decisions about acceptable risk levels. As in most aspects of society, land-use regulations often place severe restrictions on what individuals are permitted to do. Do restrictions on personal liberties amount to paternalism? If they do, are there theories or ethical principles which might serve to defend such government interventions?

We begin with a specific land-use example that illustrates many of the issues we are concerned with here. Consider the following scenario: A property owner owns a fifty-acre parcel of riverfront land and wishes to construct a new family home just a few feet from the banks of the river. While large floods are rare on this river, the proposed house site falls within the established 100-year flood zone. Upon requesting a building permit from the county planning office, the property owner is told that she will not be permitted to locate the structure in the flood zone. Although the property owner has sufficient land lying outside of the flood zone on which to construct the house, she very much desires the riverfront location because of the view and other recreational amenities offered by the site. In appealing the denial of her building permit, the property owner argues that she and her family understand the risks of living in the floodplain and that the government has no right to prevent her from taking such risks. In short, she accuses the county of being paternalistic, in overruling the personal risk-taking judgments of individuals.

Constraining Liberty to Protect Liberty?

In this case, is the county in fact acting paternalistically? One compelling reply on the county's part is that such floodplain restrictions are not intended primarily to protect the property owner and her family *from* herself, but rather to prevent the impacts of her actions on other individuals and the larger public. Construction in floodplains clearly has larger public consequences. It serves to displace floodwaters onto other properties and to change the basic hydrological characteristics of the river. Moreover, when flooding occurs, there may be considerable public expense involved in emergency actions needed to protect the lives and property of the family (e.g., sending a National Guard helicopter to snatch the family off its roof, or sandbagging and other property protection actions) and in post-disaster emergency relief. In the United States, a fairly extensive system of financial disaster relief—flowing to both families and communities—has developed, and such post-disaster aid amounts to millions of dollars each year, as was the case with hurricanes Hugo and Andrew.

Consequently, a key initial question is the extent to which proposed land-use actions have external impacts—that is, are interferences with private risk-taking decisions necessary to prevent such effects on other individuals and the public at large? In the case above, it appears that restrictions to develop in the floodplain are not paternalistic, but satisfy Mill's test concerning legitimate government intervention. One way to characterize this is the need to constrain liberty to protect liberty—that is, under Mill's theory, restrictions to individual freedoms are justified when the unfettered exercise of these freedoms conflicts with other freedoms. Your freedom to drive your car at extremely fast speeds is necessarily limited in order that other broader public freedoms might be ensured—for example, the freedom to safely utilize the street and road system to get from one place to another, or the freedom to safely walk across a street. Without constraints on your freedom to drive fast, other freedoms are without value.

Elsewhere (Beatley, 1985) I made the distinction between the direct and indirect effects of such individual land-use decisions. Building in the floodplain clearly has direct hydrological and other effects on the natural riverine system. There may also be more indirect effects—such as several already mentioned, including the subsequent provision of disaster relief and emergency assistance. One can conceive of even more indirect effects that might also need to be considered. If we were to allow the family to construct the home where they wish, and a subsequent flood destroys the home, killing the family, are there other long-term effects that ought to be considered? As a society, do we have the right, and perhaps the obligation, to consider the lost income and productivity these fatalities represent? If the building in question were a business rather than a residence, should we consider the lost income and economic activity that the business would have produced? If, as a public policy, we allow *any structure* to locate in floodplains, would not periodic floods represent tremendous cumulative economic and social losses? Indeed, riverine flooding in the United States amounts to millions in damages each year. Are such longer-term effects, albeit more diffuse and indirect, a legitimate basis on which to justify government interference with individual risk-taking decisions? These questions are not unique to land-use policy; they have been debated extensively in other areas of public health and safety (witness the fierce debates over mandatory seatbelt and motorcycle helmet laws, and restrictions on smoking in public places).

The conclusion here to some is that there is no such thing as an *individual* decision or action—that is, one which does not affect others and the larger public in some way or another. On these grounds, it can be argued, government has a right to intervene whenever it deems appropriate; that is, whenever it views the social impacts of private behavior to be excessive. But such an unconstrained view of government seems too permissive and seems contrary to the benefits and virtues of personal liberty and choice. Generally, most will agree that, wherever possible, decisions about life-style ought to be left to individuals. And, indeed, for many individuals taking certain risks is an important part of a productive and gratifying life. When one enjoys piloting a plane, or scuba diving, or skydiving, or living in a dangerous floodplain, certain risks may accompany those activities, avocations, and elements of life-styles that make life worthwhile.

Is there, then, a line to be drawn between government restrictions to individual actions to prevent major, directly external effects, and restrictions to preclude or minimize effects of a more indirect and uncertain nature? After all, in the normal course of life we are affected or influenced by the actions of innumerable individuals and institutions, in both positive and negative ways, and we certainly do not expect government to interfere to prevent or correct for these innumerable impacts. Is it fair to restrict the ability of an individual to take a certain risk on the grounds that, should the individual be killed, society would lose his or her productive contribution? Various societal events could lead to the same results, and it can be argued that the benefits, and the importance of preserving personal choice-making, outweigh these potential societal effects.

Cases of Pure Paternalism?

It seems reasonable to hold to the tenet that where private land-use decisions impact others and the larger public in substantial ways, such as to locate a residence in a high-risk flood zone, government restrictions are not paternalistic. However, are there cases in which government is justified in constraining individual actions even when there are few, or no, apparent "external" effects? Can government obstruction of private risk-taking be legitimate even when potential external effects have been compensated for in advance (e.g., perhaps the property owner in the example above signs a document releasing the government from any obligation to rescue the family or to provide financial assistance after a flood)? In other words, are there additional theoretical or ethical grounds which might allow, or even require, the government to restrict such risky behavior?

Let's consider an additional example: A developer proposes to locate a condominium complex on a barrier island. County commissioners are concerned about the proposal because they fear that future residents of this proposed development will be unable to evacuate in time should a hurricane or major coastal storm threaten the island. As a result, they demand that the developer supplement the existing evacuation capacity by constructing an additional bridge to the mainland and by providing storm-proof hurricane shelters sufficient to accommodate a major portion of the residents who could not evacuate. The developer objects to these demands, and argues that these are questions of individual risk, best left to individual housing consumers. "If they feel it's too risky to live here, they will purchase units somewhere else." While admitting that other residents of the county will not be affected significantly by this decision (e.g., their ability to evacuate will not be reduced significantly), the commissioners, citing the safety of future residents, refuse to grant permits for this development unless these improvements are agreed to.

Thus, in this case the impacts of this risky land-use action are largely restricted to the residents of this barrier island. If we further assume that the island is a designated undeveloped barrier unit under the federal Coastal Barrier Resources Act of 1982, the development will not qualify for federally subsidized flood insurance or federal disaster relief, and will thus have few of these types of external societal effects. Given these assumptions, does government have the moral right to impose such safety standards? Is it not the case, as the developer argues, that it is a matter of individual risk judgment—that is, if living on a barrier island with low ability to evacuate from a hurricane is an acceptable level of risk for each individual, then how can government land-use bodies legitimately interfere with such decisions? Of course, one could revert to the indirect social costs argument again—for example, that the potential loss of life in the event of a hurricane will have larger societal impacts. But again, these types of indirect effects seem remote and clearly can be used to justify intervention in almost *any* circumstance.

One position might be to revert back to J. S. Mill's framework and consider the special obligations government has to protect children. Recall that Mill held that government interference with individual liberties is unacceptable when these actions are "self-regarding"—that is, do not harm others. In Mill's view this standard of liberty did not apply to children: "It is perhaps hardly necessary to say that this doctrine is meant to apply to human beings in the maturity of their faculties. We are not speaking of children or of young persons below the age which the law may fix as that of manhood or womanhood. Those who are still in a state to require being taken care of by others must be protected against their own actions as well as against external injury" (Mill, 1978, p. 9).

It is perhaps morally acceptable to allow *adults* to choose risky places in which to live and work, but minors usually have little say in determining whether such risks are acceptable. Under this position it is appropriate, indeed essential, that government continually evaluate whether the risk levels that children are subjected to are too high. Just as this has required government to enact a variety of child protection laws (e.g., child labor laws, child auto restraint laws), it might also require government to veto a decision about risk made by an adult if, as a consequence, it subjects a child or children to risk levels which society feels are too high.

Another approach might be to attempt to determine what is acceptable risk-taking by hypothesizing from what might be thought to be the social norm. That is, we conventionally define what is irrational in this manner, so why not determine what are inappropriate land-use decisions in a similar way? For example, if we find an individual casually walking back and forth on a ledge of a building forty stories in the air, we would tend to define such actions as irrational and we would likely take actions to stop such behavior, regardless of how enjoyable or stimulating the individual claims it to be. We take such actions because we know that the *average person* will not assume such great risks. (We could also argue, of course, that the individual ought to be constrained because, if she or he fell, they would possibly harm others.) Equally true, it might be argued that because the *average person* does not think it is rational to live on a barrier island without having a hasty retreat possible in the event of an oncoming hurricane, we might prevent individuals from taking such a risk. Yet, this seems a largely arbitrary and indefensible position, and it appears to justify public prohibitions of many personally risky activities, such as skydiving, which provide tremendous personal satisfaction to many people. While the average person views skydiving as too dangerous, we do not generally think of skydivers as irrational or crazy. Similarly, while most people might be uncomfortable with the idea of living on an isolated barrier island, we do not generally consider as crazy those who revel in such a thought.

Problems of Incomplete Information and Faulty Judgment

Government restrictions on personal freedoms are also frequently defended on the grounds that there exist certain imperfections in the process and circumstances by which individuals make risk judgments. There are several variants to this position. One variant holds that government must restrain certain personal decisions because individuals do not have access to *all*, or to *accurate*, information needed to make an informed judgment. We might refer to this theory as the "standard of complete information," which suggests that the decisions and preferences of individuals are quite different if they have a full and complete understanding of the potential outcomes of their actions. Will individual housing consumers really choose to purchase units in the barrier island case if they have full and accurate information about the risks of living there? Recent studies indicate, for instance, that residents of barrier islands often lack an accurate understanding of the hazards of living in such locations. For example, most underestimate the number of hours it actually takes to evacuate (see Ruch and Christensen, 1981).

The problems of inadequate information about land-use risks have, in recent years, led many states and localities to enact real estate disclosure provisions. In California, for instance, under the Alquist-Priolo Act of 1972, real estate agents are required to inform prospective purchasers of property when land and property lie within a known earthquake fault zone. Under a number of state coastal programs, property owners are required to be informed of erosion rates and location in high-risk coastal zones. At a local level, Salt Lake County, Utah, has recently enacted provisions that require the preparation of a special engineering study for development proposed in certain high risk-locations (e.g., areas of high liquefaction potential, surface faults, and avalanches). In addition to requiring the project design to mitigate, to the extent possible, any hazard present, the ordinance also requires that "the type and severity of the hazard shall be recorded as a deed covenant running with the land" (Salt Lake County, 1989, p. 5; see Berke and Beatley, 1992). In Palo Alto, California, under that city's voluntary seismic retrofit program, owners of seismically vulnerable structures are required to undertake a detailed engineering analysis to identify structural deficiencies. Once this engineering report is prepared, it must be placed on file with the city, and all tenants in these buildings must be notified of its existence. Thus, while the ordinance does not specifically require that building owners undertake improvements, it does mandate that tenants be informed about the risks which may exist (see Berke and Beatley, 1992).

Such disclosure provisions have serious flaws, however. The California Alquist-Priolo disclosure requirements, for instance, suffer from serious imperfections, including the fact that real estate agents are not required to use the words "earthquake" or "seismic" when making the disclosure—the prospective buyer must only be informed that the property lies in a "special studies zone." Many agents wait until fairly late in the sales process to make the disclosure and tend to downplay its significance (see Palm, 1981, 1989). More fundamentally, it appears that, even when disclosures are conducted in a good faith manner, people tend to ignore these factors and focus on other considerations more immediately important to them (e.g., the amenities of a particular home, salability, schools, proximity to parks, and the like).

Several other variants of the complete information theory can be identified. The "reflective rationality" variant, for instance, suggests that it is not simply the existence or absence of information per se, but the time and ability of individuals to understand and integrate this knowledge into their decision-making process. There are simply too few hours in the day for individuals to digest and incorporate fully into their actions all the data and information on environmental hazards, and other benefits and costs of building a home in a particular location or in a particular way. This is especially true when data require specialized skills and background. For example, detailed information on the specific materials, construction practices, and engineering design for a particular building may be available to a potential homebuyer, but such information is largely useless without a specialized background in engineering or architecture. This fact accounts for much of the justification for public building code regulations. Clearly much of the consumer protection legislation in recent years is justified on the grounds of faulty or inadequate information about risks, as well.

There is also considerable evidence to show that individuals process information about risks in ways which *bias* their decisions and judgments. Specifically, human beings have been shown to use certain simplifying "heuristics" to process information about risks (see Tversky and Kahneman, 1974). Several different heuristics have been identified, each resulting in particular decision-making biases. Perhaps the most widely known is the heuristic of the gambler's fallacy. Here, individuals will tend to judge the probability of a disaster-event according to when the last such disaster occurred. After a hurricane strikes, for instance, the tendency is to believe that, if the storm was a 100-year event, another similar event will not occur for another 100 years—despite the fact that the same magnitude event can occur the following year, or the following month. Availability is another documented heuristic. Here, individuals evaluate the likelihood of an event such as a hurricane according to their ability to visualize or bring to mind such an event. Individuals who have not had any direct experience with hurricanes in the past, or who are living in areas where a hurricane has not occurred for a number of years, may underestimate the actual risk of such an event. Public education and information dissemination programs may help to overcome this bias, but another heuristic—anchoring—suggests that, no matter how compelling new information or evidence is, individuals naturally resist too dramatic a shift from their preexisting view: their current perceptions tend to anchor them.

While an individual might understand the risks involved at an intellectual level, there is a natural tendency for people to believe that "it can never happen to them." If a hurricane strikes, the natural tendency is to think that, although *others* might be killed or harmed, they will be able to escape unscathed. Empirical studies support the observation that individuals hold unrealistically optimistic views about their own lives, which conflict with more objective, probabilistic facts. A study by Weinstein (1980), for instance, found that college students exhibit much greater optimism that more *good* things (e.g., good jobs and salary) and fewer *bad* things (e.g., heart attacks) will happen to them than to the average person. (Perhaps this accounts for the bumper sticker: "Hire college students while they know it all.")

Another variant of this position argues that, for individuals to make valid decisions about risks, they must understand the implications of these risks in an *experiential* manner. It is one thing to understand in an intellectual manner the probability and potential effects of a hurricane, but it is another thing entirely to experience such an event. Seeing and feeling the fury and force of such an event will create, the theory holds, a different understanding of these risks than would a simple reading of a factual and probabilistic account of the storm. Moreover, if individuals had this fuller, more emotionally genuine understanding of the risks, their decisions about them would be greatly different. Dworkin illustrates this point by discussing why he and others typically fail to fasten their seatbelts when riding in an automobile: "I, also, neglect to fasten my seat-belt and I concede such behavior is not rational but not because I weigh the inconvenience differently from those who fasten the belts. It is just that having made (roughly) the same calculation as everybody else I ignore it in my actions. . . . A plausible explanation for this deplorable habit is that although I know in some intellectual sense what the probabilities and risks are I do not fully appreciate them in an emotionally genuine manner" (1971, p. 121).

This "experiential understanding" variant again might serve as justification for government interference with individual choices. It might also argue for the need for mechanisms for disseminating knowledge about risks in perhaps a more experiential manner. Perhaps it should be a mandatory requirement that any future resident of the barrier island community in the above scenario must first watch a hurricane video— one that graphically illustrates the force and deadly potential of such natural phenomena. Camille, Hugo, Andrew—these are storms one never forgets. This is not so dissimilar than the films typically shown in high school driver's education classes, which impress upon students the *real* impacts of accidents and the need for safety.

Retrospective Rationality

Another theoretical position one might embrace as a justification for interfering with individual decisions about risk is what Goodin (1976) has called "retrospective rationality." This theory justifies collective intervention in cases when it can be reasonably assumed that the individuals being restrained will ratify or agree with these restraints after the fact— that is, they will *in retrospect* be glad the government prevented them from taking certain actions. J. S. Mill discusses one such situation, frequently repeated in the philosophical literature, in which an individual is about to walk across a bridge that no longer exists. A friend sees that the individual is about to fall to his death and takes action to restrain the individual. Clearly the friend is interfering with the liberty of choice of the individual about to walk across the bridge. On the other hand, after the circumstances of the bridge are explained, the individual whose liberty has been restrained thanks his friend—he is glad *in retrospect* that such restrictions were placed on his freedom.

Can such a theory be used to justify constraining the choices of prospective homeowners who wish to live on an isolated barrier island? While residents may *now* be willing to assume the risks of living without adequate means of shelter or evacuation, it is conceivable, even likely, that should a large hurricane threaten the island they will be thankful that government land-use bodies mandated the construction of the hurricane shelter and bridge.

It is interesting that this retrospective reasoning is used often by elected officials when justifying a variety of land-use decisions that may be unpopular with constituents. They reason that later in time constituents will come to support the decision (e.g., once they see the project or results of the decisions).

Collective Contract and Deferred Authority

A broader moral basis for justifying government restrictions to personal liberty, one which can also encompass some of what I discussed above, is found in the notions of deferred authority and collective contract. Deferred authority holds that there are a number of situations in life in which we consent to, defer, or give away some of our decision-making authority for our own good. A common example is when individuals accept the advice of doctors and dentists. They have the medical knowledge, experience, and expertise to make determinations concerning what is best for *our* health.

It can be argued that many land-use restrictions which might be considered paternalistic derive from this deferred authority. It can be further held that such deference and consent stem from the fundamental notion of the collective contract (discussed in earlier chapters). We are willing, and indeed desirous, of deferring certain decision-making responsibilities to the collective because it offers a level of protection we would not otherwise be able to provide for ourselves. Most individuals, for instance, have insufficient background and expertise in engineering to determine whether a building is structurally sound enough to withstand certain physical forces (such as an earthquake or gale force winds, or even an overloaded attic). It is more feasible and efficient for the collective to undertake such functions, and so we enact building codes and employ building inspectors to perform such services. Equally true, no single individual is in a position to make determinations of whether consumption of foods and prescription drugs is dangerous or not. We have neither the scientific expertise nor the time to undertake such assessments, so we gladly defer such responsibilities to the broader collective. In exchange for the benefits of deferred authority we must, of course, be willing to abide by the resulting restrictions on individual freedom. When the Food and Drug Administration bans a particular substance because it is found to be carcinogenic, we are restricted in our choices—we can no longer purchase this substance even if we wish to. When we establish a system of construction standards and building regulations, as individuals we again lose certain freedoms—certain choice options, such as buying and living in a substandard housing unit are no longer available to us.

One important question is, How do we determine which aspects of individual freedom and decision-making are deferred and which are not? One could agree that she or he is willing to defer authority on building standards, but not on the issue of whether it is safe to construct a home in a floodplain. One response is that decisions about risk and risk management are made within a representative democratic context. The collective, in a sense, is always in the process of defining and redefining the "contract." If constituents feel that government has overstepped its bounds and has taken away certain authorities which are more properly left to individuals, there are clear and available political means to express such concerns. In a representative democracy, public officials are elected and programs are created with the implicit or explicit consent of constituents. Constituents have consented to society's taking over certain risk-analysis and risk-reduction functions. George Will, an unlikely supporter of this position, argues that this is indeed the measure of social progress. He talks specifically in terms of what he calls the "take-for-granted quotient" or TFGQ. A modern society is one where this quotient is expanding. Modern life is increasingly too complex for individuals to cope with by themselves:

> We must take much on trust. If we took time to understand everything, we would never get the lawn mower sharpened or the screen door repaired.
>
> A flourishing economy, indeed a functioning society, depends on the mass of men and women not thinking about a large and growing number of things they depend on in daily life. One measure of the modernity of the modern world is the TFGQ—the take-for-granted quotient. A crucial task—crucial, although often mundane—of modern government is to enlarge the TFGQ.
>
> It does this by inspecting restaurants, so customers need not calculate the risk before deciding to trust an unfamiliar kitchen. It certifies the safety of elevators so we never need to make a prudential calculation before inserting ourselves in a box hauled aloft by (I am guessing) pulleys and cables and things.
>
> Of course, government, as is its wont, often gets carried away and tries to reduce to zero life's risks. Nevertheless, to keep modern society flowing, government must act in many small ways to take large amounts of hesitancy out of life. It does this, for example, when it provides insurance for deposits in thrift institutions. Such insurance removes the drag of anxiety from a crucial social activity—saving. (Will, 1985, p. 5A)

Another important point is that, whether or not one feels it is government's legitimate role to assume such risk management functions, individuals often *assume* that this is the case. If government (federal, state, local) is in the business of reviewing and approving or denying development proposals, regardless of the ultimate objectives of such a review, citizens and housing consumers *assume* that government has ensured that the building and location are safe. "If it were dangerous to live here," the prospective resident of the barrier island might theorize, "then government would never have issued the necessary permits." Thus, a sense of security (perhaps false security) is generated by the mere fact of land-use bodies placing their regulatory stamp of approval on a project. There is an expectation, then, that government has judged a project or site to be safe, and individuals will, in turn, tend to base their own personal decisions upon this (e.g., whether or not to buy a home in a particular location). Perhaps 100 years ago when government health and safety regulations were not as extensive as they are today, the assumption of caveat emptor may have prevailed in the minds of most citizens—citizens today expect a certain level of protection from a variety of potentially harmful activities and technologies. This *implied* safety has been increasingly validated in liability cases in state courts (see Kusler, 1985). Courts are increasingly willing to embrace the notion that the issuance of a government permit has an implied warranty attached to it.

Balancing Safety against Other Goals

Public decision-makers, elected and nonelected, are still left with the questions, how much risk is acceptable and how much risk-reduction is desirable? As Will (1985) notes, there may be a desire on the part of public officials and government bodies to reduce risks to zero. It is important to acknowledge here that reducing or minimizing social risks is not costless. Rather, there may be significant monetary and nonmonetary costs associated with the prevention of risk-taking. Building codes that mandate certain minimum structural requirements undoubtedly raise the cost of construction. Housing codes that mandate certain minimum conditions which existing housing must satisfy (in contrast to building codes that apply to construction of new homes) can displace many people if applied stringently in a locality. Here the dilemma becomes one of balancing the need for minimum public health and safety standards with the need to ensure that all citizens have opportunities for minimum housing.

This dilemma is illustrated particularly well in communities and states which have sought to impose seismic retrofit requirements on existing structures, primarily older unreinforced masonry buildings. A number of communities have enacted mandatory retrofit ordinances which, in order to protect residents from being killed during an earthquake, require that certain structural improvements (e.g., bracing) are undertaken by certain deadlines. If the improvements are not made, the building can be condemned or demolished. Los Angeles has enacted such a mandatory program and has encountered serious implications for low- and moderate-income residents. Seismically deficient structures, not surprisingly, tend to house those on the lower end of the city's socioeconomic ladder.

The city has not been aggressive in condemning those properties when deadlines have not been met, because to do so would displace individuals and families who have few other housing options (see Comerio, 1989). Rental structures which have undertaken required seismic improvements are permitted under the city's rent control ordinance to raise their rents in order to recoup the costs of the improvements, in turn displacing renters. Thus, there is a natural conflict between society's desire to ensure that all citizens are protected from disasters such as earthquakes and the need for available and affordable housing.

Again we confront the issue of personal choice. If you are willing to live in a structure that may perform poorly in an earthquake—that is, you are willing to assume this risk voluntarily—in exchange for an affordable place to live, is this not a decision that you ought to be able to make? Of course, one reply is that this is not a fair or equitable choice. Most citizens believe that government is responsible for ensuring that people have access to affordable housing *and* that they are not exposed to extremely high seismic risks. The solution in some communities (and discussed in Los Angeles) is to find ways for the public sector to pay for or subsidize the seismic improvements.

The seismic example illustrates that government risk-reduction requirements may have significant costs and may conflict with other social goals or ethical demands. Even in the barrier island case, assuming the costs of the proposed safety improvements are borne by new residents in the form of housing costs, required safety improvements clearly involve a real trade-off with other things. This might be illustrated in the form of a personal trade-off matrix (table 9.1)—the greater the safety level, the higher the price of a home; the lower the safety level, the lower the home price (see Beatley, 1989c).

Should individuals determine the appropriate trade-off in this situation? Should they be permitted to accept a lower level of protection in exchange for a more affordable home? Of course, for many of the reasons already discussed in this chapter, we may answer in the negative; nevertheless, it is important to understand that government interferences with individual liberties often involve significant costs and trade-offs.

Table 9.1 Hypothetical Hurricane Risk/Housing Cost Trade-off Matrix

	Evacuation Time off Island	Housing Cost
Without mitigation improvements	48 hours	$70,000
With mitigation improvements	8 hours	$80,000

Source: Beatley, 1989c.

Other Factors of Moral Relevance

Other factors can be considered when land-use bodies contemplate restrictions to personal risk-taking behavior. The seriousness of the decision is clearly important. What are the potential implications of failing to restrict an individual's actions? Restricting an individual from locating his or her home in the middle of an avalanche zone is a question with serious implications—the consequences of allowing this personal freedom can be severe, for example, death and property destruction. And the consequences of such a choice are irreversible—one is likely to have few opportunities to modify or reverse the decision later. On the other hand, actions to restrict the color of one's home seem less morally justified because the potential consequences of such a choice are less serious, though perhaps less beautiful. Moreover, such a decision is reversible.

It is important to consider the extent to which these types of government restrictions significantly obstruct or interrupt major choices about one's life plan. As already stated, democratic and free societies demand that one leave as much freedom to individuals as possible. Individuals know best what their own preferences and aspirations are. To what extent are land-use regulations likely to prevent the achievement of important aspirations or life plans? This raises the matter of the range of alternatives available to those whose liberties are constrained. In the example of the barrier island, is it the case that preventing construction on the island without the requisite safety improvements will severely or fundamentally interfere with the achievement of personal life plans? First, the requirements imposed by the county do not preclude development, but merely establish certain minimum safety conditions. Second, even if development on the island is precluded entirely, this does not represent, it seems to me, a major curtailing of individual choice. There are many alternative locations in which people can reside and work which provide similar amenities and enjoyments. Alternatives to the barrier island appear to be extensive.

Whether collective constraints on individual risk-taking decisions are reasonable should be considered in the context of a healthy representative democracy. Individuals who have been restrained in their decisions do have political recourse, and there usually are opportunities to argue for or against such restrictions in public forums. The stronger the democratic context in which such restrictions are imposed, the greater is their moral defensibility.

Summary

In this chapter we examined the extent to which land-use bodies have the right and obligation to place restrictions on individual decisions concerning risk. Land use can involve a variety of risks, from exposure to natural events such as hurricanes, floods, and earthquakes, to exposure to technological and humanmade hazards, such as nuclear power plants, power transmission lines, and hazardous waste facilities. Central questions are these: To what extent should individuals be allowed to place themselves at risk to such hazards? And to what extent should public land-use regulations that curtail individual risk-taking be legitimately characterized as being paternalistic?

Ethical land use acknowledges that, to the extent practicable, decisions about land-use risks ought to be left to individuals—well-informed individuals know best what their own life plans are and how best to achieve them. Land-use ethics recognize, however, that there is a morally legitimate role to be played by the collective in moderating and regulating such individual risk-taking behavior. Many land-use restrictions that are sometimes characterized by critics as being paternalistic clearly are not, because they are necessary to prevent or minimize impacts on *other* individuals and the public at large. Ethical land use recognizes also that legitimate moral grounds may exist for individual constraints even when external impacts are absent or insignificant. Collective interventions that seek to inform individuals about land-use risks, however, are preferred (e.g., hazard disclosure provisions), if they can be shown to be effective.

10

EXPECTATIONS AND PROMISES IN LAND-USE POLICY

LAND-USE DECISIONS are linked closely to the notion of expectations, and land-use disputes often revolve around disagreements between the expectations of different groups and factions in a community (see Beatley, 1989b). Expectations can be thought of as those beliefs held by individuals that concern the future actions of others and the conditions and circumstances that, they believe, will prevail in the future. Our personal (and public) actions are, in large degree, structured by the expectations that we have about the future. In many ways life can be characterized as a continual process of forming, modifying, and acting upon expectations. Expectations represent the equivalent of understanding the rules of a game. Expectations can be created through different ways, including explicit promises made by public officials, tacit promises, and general economic and social trends. In this chapter we examine the sources of land-use expectations, the role played by expectations in land-use conflicts, and their implications for the conduct of ethical land-use policy and planning.

In sharp contrast to our dependence upon expectations is the dynamic nature of the world in which we live. Personal relationships change, political offices change hands, and natural and humanmade environments evolve, often quite dramatically (e.g., in the case of a devastating earthquake, or the demolition or destruction of an important visual landmark). Our expectations about the future may or may not be accurate. We are sometimes benefitted and sometimes harmed when our expectations are inconsistent with reality. We are benefitted, for instance, when a trip to the dentist for a root canal does not result in the excruciating pain we think it will, or when the cost of a meal at a restaurant is not as high as we expect it to be. We are harmed by expectations when the reverse is the case, for instance when we expect a good friend to visit but find that, because of unforeseen circumstances, she cannot.

People are similarly harmed and benefitted when their expectations about the future uses of land are inaccurate. To illustrate the importance of expectations in land-use disputes, consider the following hypothetical case: the Lake Ridge neighborhood in the (fictitious) city of North Orange, Florida, has for fifty years been a quiet, slow-paced residential community. It consists primarily of large single-family structures, situated on large wooded lots. The Parkers, looking for a safe, quiet, and relatively isolated place in which to raise their children, bought a home here five years ago. Several months ago, however, a development company sought and received an amendment to the zoning ordinance which will permit it to construct a commercial/office complex on land that adjoins the Parkers' property. Concerned about the prospect of such activities disrupting their otherwise tranquil residential surroundings, the Parkers protest the change before the North Orange city council, claiming they would not have moved to that particular neighborhood if they had known such a use would be likely, or even permissible, in the future. To the contrary, they had been led to believe that the area would remain exclusively a single-family residential neighborhood in perpetuity.

This scenario is fairly common in land-use disputes across the United States. How should the issue be resolved? Is there any moral weight to the claim that, because the Parkers took certain actions and made certain investments based on their expectations about the area remaining exclusively residential, their demand should be met? Does the local government have any ethical obligation to uphold these expectations? How much weight should be given to the Parkers' claims? In determining the weight of the Parkers' claims, what factors are morally relevant? Let's consider further the possible sources of expectations and whether the nature of these sources makes any substantial moral difference.

Different Sources of Land-Use Expectations

When one evaluates the moral relevance of expectations in public land-use decision-making, one must ask initial questions. What is the source of one's expectations? How did they come about? How were they shaped? What factors served to influence them? In the Parker case a number of factors might have contributed to the impression that the neighborhood would always remain in single-family use, among them the following: the apparent physical nature and visible stability of the neighborhood; comments about the neighborhood by real estate agents and other property-owners; the past actions of the city council with respect to similar zoning amendment proposals; and perhaps even the city's comprehensive plan, which may explicitly state that the area is to remain permanently in single-family residential use.

But do these different potential sources of the Parkers' expectations about their neighborhood have equal moral weight? It is my position that the *source* of expectations is quite important from an ethical point of view, and that certain sources create greater moral legitimacy than do others. A primary question in the Parker case is, Can it be said that, by approving the proposed zoning amendment, the North Orange city council is in some sense breaking an explicit promise made to the Parkers? Critical to answering this question is knowing whether private expectations are formed on the basis of explicit or nearly explicit promises made.

As illustrated by the Parker case, it can be claimed that explicit public land-use promises were issued through a number of means, including these: resolutions and proclamations adopted by public bodies; the enactment of laws and ordinances; the comprehensive plan and other officially adopted plans and policy documents; and the public statements made by elected or appointed officials. Such explicit promises might arise not only through local actions, but also from the actions of public and collective bodies at higher jurisdictional levels. For instance, it might be argued that state and federal constitutions contain a number of fairly clear and explicit promises concerning land-use expectations (many of which were described in earlier chapters). Indeed, the establishment of constitutional rights can be viewed as a form of social contract in which government or society *promises* to protect and defend certain individual entitlements. The Fifth Amendment of the United States Constitution, for instance, establishes a governmental promise, it can be argued, that government will not expropriate private property for public purposes— such as taking land to build a highway—without providing the owner with fair compensation, the so-called "takings" clause (see Bosselman, Callies, and Banta, 1976; Mandelker, 1982).

Promises As the Basis for Land-Use Expectations

An individual may feel rightfully wronged when another individual fails to perform a task or duty that she or he has agreed to perform, in an explicit and forthright fashion. If I promise to meet you at an appointed time, you are rightfully indignant when I arrive an hour late without an excuse. The promise I make to you represents a clear obligation, which ethically I should be expected to keep, other things being equal. Had I not intended to keep the promise, I should not have made it in the first place.

But why should government land-use bodies be concerned with keeping the promises they or past administrations make? It is clear, first of all, that failure to keep promises may have substantial long-term social and economic consequences. If I do not keep my promise to meet you at the appointed time, it is likely that you will not trust me in the future. At a collective level it can be argued that the formation of expectations is essential to the smooth and efficient operation of our lives and society. If we must be skeptical of all promises made, inefficiencies will result and life will be made considerably more difficult for us. For instance, the Parkers may be skeptical about their ability to find a *stable* and relatively protected residential environment in North Orange in the future, and they may simply stop trying, despite their desires to the contrary. Perhaps more dramatically, they may even begin to consider as suspect all of their normally acquired expectations about the future, and they may adopt a relatively pessimistic view about their ability to control the environment in which they live anywhere.

A failure to acknowledge and respect promises may also jeopardize *reciprocity* and the trust it is based upon. If I do not keep my promise to you, then you may feel justified in breaking your promises to me (and to others). If the local city council makes an explicit promise to the Parkers to protect their residential community from other uses and then fails to do so, perhaps the Parkers (and others) will feel justified in failing to respect the numerous other promises they have made to the collective (e.g., respecting traffic laws, not littering, even voting). When public promises are repeatedly made and disregarded, an impression is created that public officials are not generally acting in good faith; it questions their motives and can be construed as lying (see Bok, 1978). The breaking of collective promises, then, can be seen as jeopardizing the individual collective trust upon which a community heavily relies.

But this sounds very utilitarian in nature and, as I have already argued, utilitarian and economic arguments are by themselves an insufficient moral foundation for land-use policy and planning. Indeed, in the case of land-use promises there is a more basic principle of fairness at work. We are usually worried about keeping promises not because of economic or other ramifications, but rather because to break a promise is unfair to those to whom we have made them and because it violates a moral and ethical standard of considerable importance to us. In short, breaking promises, without good reason, is morally wrong. We keep promises simply because we're *ethically obligated* to keep them and this is the quintessential deontological ethical standard. We keep promises because we think it the right thing to do, and because just as we would wish others to keep their promises to us we should keep our promises to them. This discussion suggests a basic principle that, other things being equal, governing bodies and their representatives (past and present) involved in land-use decisions ought to keep the promises they make.

Let us return to the Parker scenario. What if the North Orange city council adopted a resolution (prior to the Parkers buying their home) which made an explicit public promise to the residents and property owners of that neighborhood that it would be maintained exclusively for residential uses? Ceteris paribus, residents of the area would seem to have a legitimate reason to demand that public land-use bodies adhere to this commitment. To do otherwise would violate the basic moral obligation to keep one's promises. But what if the promise is expressed, perhaps no less explicitly, in the city's comprehensive plan? Or, what if the promise is not explicit, but made tacitly, through a long and consistent set of land-use decisions made by the city council in the past? A variety of factors must be considered when judging whether public land-use promises have, in fact, been made.

When and How Have Public Promises Been Made?

If public land-use bodies have ethical obligations to respect promises made, it becomes important to determine when and how such promises can be said to exist. While the Parkers may argue that the city of North Orange should not permit the construction of the commercial/office complex because it violates a promise issued in the past to prevent this type of action, public officials might respond that no such promise was explicitly made. Indeed, they might retort that, in the past, the only promise made was the promise that before approving such actions adequate studies of the impacts on adjoining neighborhoods would be prepared and public input from the neighborhood would be solicited. This, the officials could argue, is a far cry from promising that such uses would never be allowed in the neighborhood.

Another important matter is whether a particular statement is indeed a promise or rather just a statement of an *intention* to do something. Just because you may state orally that you intend to leave your land forever undeveloped, and although the expectations of others may be affected by these statements, you have not *promised* to keep it undeveloped. It can be argued (and lawyers do) that while the latter implies a moral obligation, the former does not. The Parkers may have construed general statements on the city's behalf (e.g., expressing their intention not to permit or provide for any additional commercial or office uses in the city) as promises that such uses would not be allowed in these residential neighborhoods. Prichard makes this point eloquently in examining the difference between an employer's resolve not to reduce wages and his explicit promise not to:

> The expectation, so far as it is produced, will in each case be based on quite different beliefs. In the one case it will based on the beliefs (1) that the employer was speaking truthfully, and (2) that he is not likely to change his mind on such a matter. In the other it will be based at least in part on the belief that the employer thinks he has bound himself simply by promising, whether he produces the expectation or not, together with

the belief that since he is a comparatively moral, i.e. conscientious, being he is likely to do whatever he thinks he is bound to do. (1949, p. 171)

It is difficult to see much practical difference between these circumstances, however. Both shape expectations and both serve to pattern the behavior of others. If a community states that it intends to build a highway in a particular location, and at some future date decides to build it in a different location, or perhaps not at all, individuals who have structured their actions and investments according to these previously stated intentions are harmed nonetheless. Many statements of future intentions (I intend . . . , I will . . . , We plan to . . . , etc.) can be seen to amount to a form of explicit promising, even when the word "promise" does not appear in the statement. Such public statements create, it seems to me, prima facie obligations to adhere to these intentions, recognizing that individuals and groups in the community are impacted by them. When the actions and expectations of a great many people are so fundamentally affected by the stated intentions of public land-use bodies, these intentions take on the solemnity and moral importance of promises. This suggests that public land-use bodies should exercise greater care in the issuance of statements of public intentions and the ways in which they are made.

Other factors in evaluating the legitimacy of private expectations based on public promissory statements are the reasonableness of the promises made and the capacity of the promiser to make the promise in the first place. Can someone really be indignant at the failure of another individual to keep a promise if the promise made is clearly beyond the control of the promiser—say, to make the sun rise at midnight? While the person (or collective body) issuing the promise may be considered no less morally culpable for failing to live up to the promise, should not the promisee have known that keeping the promise was impossible and adjusted his or her expectations accordingly? Many political promises can be placed in this category (see French, 1983). In the Parker example, although a local land-use board or city council may have issued a promise that a neighborhood would be preserved in its original character, is this a promise that any public land-use body (except the most totalitarian) could ever keep? Even the mere passage of time will leave its mark on the appearance of structures in a neighborhood and, thus, perhaps violate the expectations of residents that their neighborhood would not change in the least over time.

A related issue is whether expectations are legitimately formed based on the statements of political bodies which necessarily change in composition over time. If a mayor or city council promises that a neighborhood will be protected from the intrusion of other land uses, does it go without saying that the official or officials may not be in a position to effect the promise in the future? Should not the recipients of such promises understand this and adjust their expectations accordingly? One position is to consider all future-oriented promises made by elected officials in the same category as "making the sun rise at midnight." Yet, on the other hand, it seems reasonable that public officials could be held to their promises when opportunities exist to do so in the future (e.g., they are reelected or remain in office). Moreover, it is also reasonable to suggest that those collective land-use bodies that make promises at a particular point in time qua public bodies (e.g., planning commissions, city councils) should be held accountable for them even when all elected or appointed officials are replaced. While newly elected or appointed public land-use bodies should rightly have considerable flexibility in setting new agendas, they should also be bound to a certain considerable degree by explicit promises made by their predecessors. This position is closely analogous to the legal and contractual obligations which governmental units might incur over time. If the local government issues bonds to pay for the construction of, say, new roads or an aquarium or an airport, it is not relieved of the obligation to pay back these borrowed monies simply because voters may choose new individuals to represent them.

The Nature and Content of Land-Use Promises

The nature and content of the promises made are also morally relevant considerations. What were individuals actually promised? For instance, it may be important that a promise was made to attempt to do certain things, rather than a promise that certain things would come about. A public official might have indicated that she or he would do everything within their power to ensure that the Parkers' neighborhood would not change, but this is different than a promise that the neighborhood would not experience change. There is in this type of statement an implicit disclaimer that the official may be unable to guarantee that these changes will not occur. Such statements are, in a sense, a recognition that there are many types of influences—economic, demographic, political, social—which are essentially beyond the control of the public official.

Another way to view these types of promissory statements is to consider their similarities to conventional contracts. Indeed, this comparison is appropriate in that people tend intuitively to equate promises with contracts. Contracts, however, often include clauses or contingencies that modify or nullify certain promissory obligations (e.g., life insurance policies often include clauses that prevent payment if death results from certain specific exclusions, such as skydiving). Consequently, it might be argued that the promises issued by public officials or government land-use agencies often contain similar kinds of contingencies or exclusions. For instance, in the Parker case it might be argued that the city actually promised to protect and preserve the neighborhood from nonresidential uses as long as the city's economy and economic base were strong, or as long as unemployment was not a problem. If such conditions changed in the future, necessitating that the city promote or allow other forms of land use in the Parkers' neighborhood, such actions would not be violating the promises made to residents—but rather simply exercising an important contingency clause.

This introduces the idea of "conditional promises." Acknowledging that the promises issued by public officials and land-use agencies can be qualified by such explicit or implicit stipulations or conditions shifts the debate somewhat to a discussion of what these conditions actually are and whether or not the factual circumstances warrant invoking them. The Parkers might be willing to acknowledge that the promise issued to them by the city contained a stipulation that excluding such commercial and office uses from their neighborhood was conditional upon reasonably good economic conditions in their city—but they might dispute the contention that the city really was in a period of economic exigency. It might also be argued that for such clauses or conditional promises to have any moral validity, they must be understood fully by those to whom promises are issued (i.e., to those whose expectations are being affected by such promises). Did the Parkers or other members of the neighborhood really understand that promises to maintain the low-density residential character of the neighborhood were contingent upon favorable local economic conditions? Did homebuyers really believe when they purchased their homes that the city might permit these types of "incompatible" land uses merely because the local economy had not performed very well in recent months? It would seem reasonable to hold that for such *conditional* provisions to be invoked, they must be understood by all parties to the promise, not just the promisor.

Land-Use Plans As Promissory Documents

A particularly important ethical issue here is the extent to which a community's comprehensive land-use plan (sometimes called a general plan) can be considered a promissory document. It seems to be a particularly important and potentially significant document in terms of the shaping of people's expectations and behavior. It is my position that when a community plan is prepared and serves as the historical basis for guiding community and land-use decisions, it represents a potentially significant source of expectations and constitutes, ceteris paribus, the expression of public promises. Planners and elected officials, as a consequence, have a general duty to respect and implement the promises contained in the plan. The precise moral position of the plan depends on many factors, of course, including its language and content (e.g., what sort of qualifiers and conditional statements are contained within; its degree of explicitness) as well as the actual status and historical importance assumed by the plan in local decision-making (e.g., have the policies and statements of the plan been consistently upheld in the past; or, as is the case with many plans, does the plan simply collect dust on a shelf in city hall, having little historic connection to actual public decision-making about land use and community affairs?). Another important factor is the legal status of the plan. In states such as Oregon, Florida, and California, the local comprehensive (or general) plan is a legal document and consequently has a more direct and immediate impact on local land-use decisions. In Oregon, all local zoning and implementing ordinances must be consistent with the plan, providing additional legal weight to the moral requirement of following the plan. (For a review of the status of local plans in various states around the country, see DeGrove, 1984.)

But even if a local comprehensive plan carries the weight of law, as it does in Oregon, can it not be argued that few citizens are aware of its existence or importance in local decision-making? This we might refer to as the "problem of common knowledge," and it suggests that, for agreements or promises to have any moral weight, they must be understood by all or most parties involved. Can the city council in the Parkers' case simply deny that the promise to maintain the neighborhood in residential use must be kept because generally few citizens read or otherwise paid any attention to the plan in the first place? On the contrary, it seems morally sufficient to know that even just a few people knew of the plan—perhaps just the Parkers—and modified their behavior accordingly. Unless the city maintains that the plan was generally a "paper plan" (i.e., was not actively employed in making local decisions), or that certain specific clauses or conditions are contained in the plan, then the city would seem morally bound to satisfy the Parkers' claims, if at all possible.

This discussion suggests a number of important policy implications for local land-use planning processes. First, again it suggests that, ceteris paribus, the local plan should be viewed as a promissory document, and consequently citizens have legitimate moral objections when their public agencies and officials violate its substantive provisions. Second, it suggests the importance of crafting plans more carefully to adequately capture and incorporate those clauses or conditions which might be needed to deal with changing local circumstances over time. If it is generally agreed by elected officials that the plan should include an escape clause that allows more flexibility on siting commercial and office uses in times of economic exigency, then the plan should explicitly state these clauses or conditions. This allows citizens and homeowners to better anticipate such decisions. Third, because in most communities the plan represents a serious and important promissory document, localities should spend greater time and effort distributing and otherwise informing the public of its content. The more widely understood the plan is, the more beneficial it will be in allowing individuals to structure their expectations and behavior accordingly. It *puts people on notice* and minimizes the chances that officials later will have to consider hardship claims based on people's failure to fully understand the document.

An interesting example of one community's attempt to formally institutionalize this education of the public about the content of the plan is seen in an ordinance recently enacted by Montgomery County, Maryland. Under new amendments to the county's Master Plan Disclosure Law, homebuilders must ensure that prospective homebuyers are aware of what the county plan says. Specifically, all homebuilders must have copies of the county plan in their sales offices or model homes and must be able to provide the homebuyers with official maps showing the location of future highways, parks, and other public facilities or improvements in the area. Perhaps most significantly, all homebuyers must sign a disclosure statement in the sales contract which attests to the fact that they have either reviewed these local planning documents or have waived the right to do so. Increasingly, it seems, states and localities are enacting laws which require that prospective homebuyers or property owners are fully appraised of what planning and zoning requirements apply to them. As a further example, under South Carolina's Beachfront Management Act of 1990, all real estate transactions involving property seaward of the forty-year setback line must now contain a disclosure statement which indicates the relative location of regulatory lines as well as the latest local erosion rates. Such disclosure provisions serve to allow the formation of more accurate expectations about both the natural changes apparent on beaches and dunes and the regulatory and other planning restrictions to which property owners will be subject in the future (e.g., like being unable to reconstruct one's beachfront home should a hurricane destroy it in the future; see Beatley, 1990b).

Viewing land-use plans as promissory documents also suggests that localities (or public land-use agencies at any governmental or institutional level) think more carefully about the procedures and circumstances under which these plans are modified. Conceiving of comprehensive land-use plans in a promissory light does not mean, of course, that they are to be cast in stone and never changed or modified. It does suggest, however, that procedures be crafted carefully so that affected parties have a central role to play in updates or revisions and that the revisions process be widely acknowledged and understood, so that expectations about the plan can change accordingly. These concerns probably also suggest that revisions or updates to plans be undertaken on a regular cycle or time schedule (e.g., every three or five years) and that frequent ad hoc modifications to the plan be avoided if at all possible. Indeed, many state and local planning provisions mandate that such major amendments or updates occur only at predetermined intervals. Frequent modifications open the door for major inconsistencies between the promissory content of the plan and the expectations of individuals about what these plans say.

The Role of Tacit Promises in Land Use

In many land-use policy situations, it is not so much an explicit statement or plan element that creates expectation on the part of individuals, but rather more informal or more implicit actions or behavior. These types of promissory bases I broadly describe as "tacit promises." The idea of tacit promises is based in large degree on the premise that repetitive past actions or behavior can create certain legitimate expectations that these actions will be repeated in the future. If a local government has behaved in a certain way relative to a certain land-use issue for a very long period of time, it can be argued that if the government changes its behavior it is violating a tacitly issued promise. Ruben explains:

> I believe that one way to understand the root idea behind tacit promising . . . is to see it as an account of how a man's (otherwise morally neutral) past behavior can sometimes entitle others to expect the same sort of behavior from him in the future. Consider, for example, the following case. . . . Two friends are in the habit of meeting one another at 5:00 P.M. for a drink. The practice is well established and has continued without interruption over the course of a number of years. The friends may not have ever discussed the practice with one another, much less explicitly agreed to, or consented to, the practice.
>
> One day, one friend fails to appear at the appointed time. Now, what I want to claim here is that the second friend, who did appear, was morally entitled to expect the first friend, who failed to turn up. The first friend ought (prima facie) to have come, and I want to say that we say this without having to know some other morally relevant fact about the case, for example, that some harm will befall the second friend because the first friend failed to appear, or even that the second friend will necessarily suffer acute disappointment, or whatever. One way in which we might describe this situation is by saying that, because the friends had met regularly in the past, they had tacitly promised to meet at 5:00 P.M. in the future. Thus by not appearing, the first friend had broken a tacit promise he had made. (1972–73, p. 73)

From this example we can imagine a variety of land-use disputes that might involve tacit promising. Can a landowner or developer argue, for instance, that a governmental planning body has tacitly promised to permit a project to occur as a result of a pattern of past behavior? Let's consider an example. Assume that the Antonionis have been farming their land in Dare County, Wisconsin, for many years. Mr. Antonioni, however, is getting on in years and has been looking forward to retiring from the farm and perhaps moving to downtown Madison, where he and his wife can rely on public transportation and generally take life somewhat easier. To finance their retirement plans, the Antonionis had always counted on their ability to sell their land—its value having risen dramatically in recent years as a consequence of the considerable development pressures the county has been experiencing. The Antonionis have been approached by a number of developers over the years about selling their land, but they have never, until now, been interested in selling out. Now, finally, they would like to sell their land and move, thus enjoying the fruits of their many years of labor. But when Mr. Antonioni approaches several development companies about selling the farm, he learns that a newly elected County Board of Supervisors is considering a major rezoning action which would essentially prohibit all new nonfarm uses in their area, dramatically reducing the development potential of the Antonioni parcel. The Antonionis are upset and, appearing at a public hearing on the proposed rezoning plan, they express their outrage that the financial nest-egg they had counted on for their retirement might be taken away from them in one fell swoop. They argue to the county commissioners that it is unfair to change the rules at this point, and they remind the commissioners that for some twenty years or more their neighbors have always been able to develop *their* land if *they* so desired. The Antonionis believe it is unfair of the county to undertake such a rezoning after creating these expectations of development potential over these many years. They request that either the rezoning plan be rejected or that they be paid compensation by the county for this loss in development potential.

But how valid are the arguments of the Antonionis? Do they have a legitimate gripe with the county? Did the twenty or so years in which the county essentially allowed any development proposals in their area indeed create legitimate expectations on the part of the Antonionis that, when they were ready to sell, they, too, would reap these development gains? Did the pattern of county decision-making amount, in effect, to a kind of tacit promising?

A number of factors might be considered in evaluating the legitimacy and validity of the Antonionis' arguments. One consideration is the extent to which the county's actions and policies, upon which the Antonionis formed their expectations, occurred over a continuous and lengthy period of time, and the extent to which the county's actions can be described accurately as a coherent pattern of policy. Did the county engage consistently in the permitting of development proposals over a relatively long period of time, say, twenty or thirty years, as the Antonionis claim? The longer this period, ceteris paribus, the more understandable is the formation of expectations and the greater is the moral weight which the Antonionis claim would seem to hold. Furthermore, was the pattern of action consistent—that is, did the county uniformly and regularly issue permits over this period? If the true history of the county's actions or policies is that they were much more erratic, changing their land-use policies perhaps with every new elected board of commissioners, then claims that tacit promises have been made would have less validity. The extent of permitting activity over the years may also be an important factor to consider. While the county may have consistently allowed development in the area in the past, if the amount of permitting activity is relatively small, say on the order of one or two requests every five years or so, then the legitimacy of the expectations is more questionable than had the county been issuing numerous permits on a monthly basis.

It can also be argued that some land-use expectations are formed as a result of what might be called "passive validation"—that is, opportunities when public land-use agencies could have intervened in the past but chose not to. For instance, a major issue in many rapidly urbanizing rural areas is the extent to which local governments can legitimately place new restrictions on traditional farming practices, such as the spreading of manure or the operation of farm equipment (e.g., restricting its use in early morning hours). Farmers who are opposed to such restrictions might argue that the government's failure to enact them for so many years in the past amounts to a passive validation—an acceptance of the validity or permissibility of such practices by the *failure* to act.

It is common in such situations for public land-use bodies to attempt to lessen the economic and other effects of changing rules. The concept of "amortization," for example, employed heavily in land-use and zoning regulations, is usually justified on these grounds. Under typical amortization provisions, when land-use regulations change, a use or activity is allotted a certain period of time (e.g., five, ten, or twenty years) before it must cease. This period is usually intended to be long enough to allow affected property-owners sufficient time to recoup their economic investments. Thus, a new local ordinance prohibiting all billboards will usually incorporate an amortization provision allowing existing billboard owners a certain period of time before the billboards must be removed.

The concept of "nonconforming uses" in zoning is supported on similar grounds. Should a city council choose suddenly to change its zoning ordinance—say, to preclude certain commercial uses from residential districts (e.g., gas stations, small markets)—it would generally be viewed as grossly unfair to require the owner of such an establishment to change the use or raze the structure because of such zoning changes. Rather, the use becomes "nonconforming" and the new restrictions apply only when certain things happen in the future. Should the use cease for some period or if the building is destroyed by fire, then the new rules would apply. Under the original South Carolina Beachfront Management Act, already mentioned, no new buildings were permitted in the oceanfront no-construction zone (the "dead zone"). It would certainly be viewed as unfair (and politically and legally difficult) to require all existing structures in this zone to be removed. Consequently, under the act, the structures essentially became nonconforming uses and, if "destroyed beyond repair," could not be rebuilt (see Beatley, 1990b). This, again, was seen as equitable because it theoretically gave owners of existing structures use for a considerable period of time. However, most supporters of these provisions did not count on the occurrence of a large hurricane (Hugo) only a year after the law went into effect. When many homes in the dead zone could not be rebuilt because of the law, the sense of inequity was universal and later led (along with serious concern about the state's financial liability) to major modifications to the act (in particular to the elimination of the dead zone restrictions).

The circumstances of building in highly dynamic coastal areas raise the interesting question, How do existing natural conditions influence, or how ought they to influence, the formation of expectations about the use of land? Should a developer or landowner assume, in the absence of past restrictions, that it is entirely permissible to build in extremely sensitive natural areas—that is, when building there seems to interrupt basic natural processes, and places people and property at substantial risk? In arguing against taking challenges, for instance, attorneys for the South Carolina Coastal Council have maintained that prohibitions on building on the beach (again under the original South Carolina Beachfront Management Act) should not require compensation because there can be no "legitimate expectations" to construct things there in the first place.

> There can be no justified expectation to build on property unsuited in its natural state for construction of a home. Beachwood East subdivision is located on shifting sands and subject to ongoing serious threats of erosion. Given the fact that the property is unsuitable for building and that existing neighboring construction does not legitimize the Respondent's [Lucas] desire to build on the subject lots, he totally failed to show that he has been thwarted in this substantial, justified expectation concerning the property. . . . The highest and best use of the Respondent's property is to leave it in its nature state as well. . . . In this case, there is a

current unjustified expectation to build upon property unsuited for building, regardless of what the Respondent paid for the property. (Harness, 1990, pp. 25–26)

The classic opinion of the Wisconsin Supreme Court in *Just v. Marinette* makes a similar argument. Land ownership implies no inherent right to modify the fundamental natural characteristics of a parcel of land. Again in the court's words: "An owner of land has no absolute and unlimited right to change the essential natural character of his land so as to use it for a purpose for which it was unsuited in its natural state and which impairs the rights of others" (56 Wis 2nd at 11, 201 N.W.2d).

Thus, we should not be concerned that, when preventing development in wetlands or barrier beaches, we are thwarting expectations, because by definition there can be no legitimate expectations to build in such locations. The problem with this reasoning, however, is that historically land-use bodies (succumbing to real estate and development lobbies) *have* allowed construction in these areas and have allowed the formation of expectations that such practices are indeed permissible in the future (creating tacit promises). Clearly, construction in these areas *has* occurred in the past and is technologically feasible—therefore, landowners and developers argue that there is nothing intrinsic to these natural areas that automatically declares them off limits. Rather, it takes the actions and policies of land-use bodies over some period of time to establish that expectations of building in these areas are illegitimate.

Vesting Standards As Public Promises

An issue of considerable importance in recent years is the matter of when the right to develop "vests"—that is, at what point are a landowner's or developer's investments, and the public validation of these development intentions, sufficient enough to prevent the public from halting a project? While different courts (federal and state) have answered this question differently, most courts agree that the valid issuance of all required development permits (e.g., building permits) is one case when vesting has clearly occurred. Once a development permit is issued, public land-use agencies are generally prevented from stopping the development, unless the permit expires. There are circumstances where one type of approval or permit is issued, but not all permits have been obtained. For instance, a developer may receive approval of a preliminary plat but approval of the final plat, as well as perhaps several other permits, must still be obtained. Does having received a preliminary plat approval entitle the developer to legitimate expectations that final approval will be given? While there is undoubtedly considerable variation in the legal answer to this question, from an ethical view there is little reason to have subsequent permit reviews (e.g., approval of the final plat) if the proposal in question is already vested—that is, has the right to proceed regardless of the outcome of the subsequent permit reviews. And it would seem entirely reasonable for developers and landowners to temper any expectations of final project approval until all permits are received. On the other hand, fairness may prevent efforts by public land-use agencies or public officials to use certain permit requirements late in the process as a way to reverse earlier decisions about project approval. Final plat approval in most cases appears necessary to ensure that certain suggested changes are incorporated in a project or subdivision design, and not as an opportunity for the public body to reconsider the entire concept of the project. The developer in such a case would have a legitimate expectation that the project would receive final plat approval if the earlier stated conditions were satisfied. Evidence of the developer's good faith expense and investment in the project (i.e., evidence that the project is proceeding), may also be instrumental in preventing a public body from revoking development permission.

Such vesting rules can be viewed as appropriate safeguards for builders and developers who invest large amounts of time and energy in their projects—the standards in a sense amount to promises by the public that once certain thresholds in the development process are reached the public will not unfairly change its mind. They provide assurance to the development community that their investments and expectations will be respected.

The Relationship between Tacit and Explicit Promises

Different sources of expectations about land use are identified here, including explicit promises, tacit promises, and general economic and social trends. Clearly from a moral point of view the validity of land-use expectations depends upon these sources. I argue that a crude hierarchy of these different sources can be constructed, something similar to what is presented in figure 10.1 (from Beatley, 1989b). Generally, expectations formed on the basis of explicit promises carry the greatest moral weight. Explicitness is important because there is less uncertainty about what the public is promised or assured. Explicit land-use promises are placed on one end of the continuum (i.e., high legitimacy of claims) in figure 10.1 while social and economic trends are placed on the other end of the continuum (i.e., low legitimacy of claims). Again, there appears little moral validity to claims made by landowners or developers, that simply because prevailing economic conditions or development patterns suggest that a particular land use or activity would be profitable, their expectations of profits are legitimate expectations which must be satisfied. The

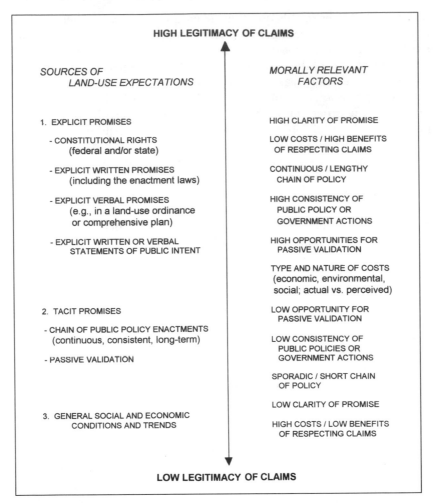

Figure 10.1 A hierarchy of sources of expectations about land use.
Source: Beatley, 1989b.

mere fact that these trends give rise to such expectations does not entitle individuals to assume that public land-use bodies will or should permit them.

Balancing Land-Use Promises against Other Ethical Obligations

We began this chapter by establishing the a priori moral weight which all promises should be afforded. Other things being equal, public officials and public land-use bodies have a moral and ethical obligation to keep the promises they make. But one can imagine a variety of circumstances in which keeping public promises, explicit or tacit in origin, will serve to violate or undermine some other important value or ethical obligation. In the earlier example of the tacit obligation of one friend to meet another friend for drinks, it would be an absurd moral outcome for one of the friends to deny life-saving assistance to a drowning man simply in order not to break the promise to the other friend. Saving the life of another human being clearly takes precedence over keeping the promise to imbibe. On the other hand, the friend is not justified in breaking the promise merely to satisfy some other personal whim (e.g., the individual feels more like swimming than meeting the friend as promised). Consequently, in considering the extent to which promises are binding, it becomes important and necessary to consider the seriousness and strength of the competing ethical demands.

It may be necessary to break public land-use promises to prevent substantial environmental calamities or to prevent the extinction of an endangered species, for example. It may be necessary to break promises to ensure that minimum land-use rights are achieved or maintained (e.g., rights to clean air and water, to open space, to a safe neighborhood), or that obligations to future generations are respected. It is beyond our task here to delineate and consider the various conflicting circumstances and their possible resolution. One might even have identical circumstances in Tuscaloosa, Alabama, and in Bozeman, Montana, yet reach different resolutions for each city. What is required, however, is a balancing of the seriousness or solemnity of the conflicting obligations and the strength and validity of the land-use promises in question. Overruling promises is more permissible when the strength and validity of the promise is low (e.g., perhaps a tacit promise, with little continuity, or consistency) and when the conflicting obligation is very strong.

There are any number of actual examples which can be cited to illustrate such conflicts, but conflicts over proposals to develop the habitat of endangered and threatened species have, in recent years, become increasingly vociferous. These situations may pose serious conflicts between obligations to keep explicit or tacit promises made to developers or landowners and strong ethical demands to ensure the existence and survival of other forms of life. While others might balance these conflicting obligations in different ways, I view the existence rights of other forms of life as extremely strong morally, usually taking precedence over previous promises to allow the development or other use of land. Of course, land-use promises, even in these circumstances, continue to hold considerable moral weight, and they may suggest the need for actions to mitigate the impacts of breaking the promises, such as in the form of full or partial monetary compensation.

This raises the broader question, To what extent should we consider the *impacts* of keeping or breaking promises? When balancing promises against other obligations, both the extent and the type of impacts ought to be taken into account. In terms of the extent, it is important to determine the magnitude of the impacts of breaking a public promise. It can be argued that, in the case of the Antonioni scenario, although the economic impacts were indeed real, there is a substantial value to the land remaining. Indeed, while the Antonionis may be unable to put their land to its highest market use, other economic uses remain, including its traditional use for farming. The economic impacts in other situations may be more severe. The range and distribution of impacts may also be important to consider. Are just a few individuals affected by a land-use body's actions, or are the impacts widespread? Allowing the conversion of a regional park to some other nonpublic use, disregarding promises made that this park would be retained and even expanded, would likely affect thousands of individuals. The types of impacts may also be important. In the event that a familiar landmark in one's community is lost (e.g., the razing of a historic church or the loss of an important vista), the impacts may be primarily psychological rather than economic. The impacts in the Parker and Antonioni scenarios, on the other hand, involve real and immediate economic costs. It may also be important to distinguish between those impacts or effects that are prospective and those that are manifest. While it is clear that the economic effects in the Antonioni scenario are real, they are more prospective and speculative—based on anticipated profits. A developer who has invested considerable funds in preparing a site for development (e.g., by installing streets, curbs, and gutters) stands to incur losses which are more manifest. In the balancing process, greater effort should be made to avoid breaking public land-use promises when the impacts are likely to be extensive and widespread, and when the costs are immediate and real.

It is also possible, of course, that land-use bodies will be confronted with conflicting promises—that is, where a choice must be made between keeping one promise and breaking another. A recent case in Charlottesville, Virginia, involved plans to construct an additional nine holes of golf in a prominent park (Pen Park), promised some ten years ago by the city. Recent plans by the city to finally build these additional holes, however, have been strongly opposed by residents of nearby neighborhoods and by local environmentalists who object to the additional loss of wetlands and other natural lands which they have enjoyed for many years. The conflict pits the explicit promises made by the city to the golfing community against the less-explicit promises made to neighborhood residents and the city in general that these natural lands would always be available. Indeed many citizens perceived these lands to already be protected because of their park status! This case illustrates that sometimes public officials may need to choose between or balance conflicting promises, judging their relative merit using many of the criteria identified in this chapter (e.g., content, explicitness, continuity).

Summary

In this chapter we examined the nature of land-use expectations and the role that public promises play in creating or nurturing such expectations. I argued that public officials and land-use agencies create legitimate land-use expectations through the issuance of explicit and tacit forms of promises. Ethical land use requires the acknowledgment of public land-use promises and the role they play in shaping private expectations. Furthermore, other things being equal, ethical land use requires that public land-use promises be kept over time. On the other hand, land-use expectations formed on the basis of economic or social trends (especially expectations to significant profits from land development) do not hold the moral weight of promises and thus do not require public land-use agencies to act to uphold them.

Land-use ethics must acknowledge that public land-use promises may result from both explicit and tacit actions. I emphasized, in particular, the importance of the comprehensive land-use plan as a promissory document, upon which many individuals and businesses rely in forming and acting upon their expectations about the community. Public land-use bodies and officials should acknowledge the moral importance of such public documents in shaping public expectations. Efforts should also be made to clarify, whenever possible, the intentions of public land-use bodies, and to reduce the extent to which individuals and the public at large may misinterpret certain actions or statements as promises. Public meetings and coverage through the media are two ways to achieve better understanding by the public of their community's land-use plan. Often, however, such plans are based more on economic considerations (i.e., development) than on environmental considerations. Nearly twenty-five years after the publication of Ian McHarg's seminal work, *Design with Nature* (1969), comprehensive land-use plans across the United States still generally fail to account for such critical environmental needs as the conservation of hydrological systems and the creation of community and regional networks of open space. As Cotton Mather, the renowned geographer, has said on numerous occasions, "America will be a great country once it is all paved."

11

PRIVATE PROPERTY, LAND-USE PROFITS, AND THE TAKINGS ISSUE

S⊤EWART U⊅ALL describes eloquently in his seminal work, *The Quiet Crisis* (1963), the fundamental clash between Native American views of land and those held by European settlers, especially the English. To Native American cultures land was so imbued with special collective meaning and importance that private dominion or control was inconceivable. "Here is affection for the land, but no notion of private ownership. The idea that land would be bought or sold was an alien concept to the Indians of America" (1963, p. 6). Environmental historian Donald Hughes offers a similar assessment:

> Land in the Indian view was not "owned" in the sense that word had in Western European societies; rather it was held in common. In the meaning, Indians felt that all living beings share the land, and that includes plants and animals as well as human beings. But in a more local sense, ownership was tribal and the land was considered to belong to the community even when it was used by families or individuals. Among Indians, cooperation and group interests predominated, particularly where ecological conditions meant subsistence living in a difficult environment. (Hughes, 1983, p. 61)

To Amerindian cultures the land was not something to be owned, but was to be used and treated with great respect because it belonged to everyone, other forms of life included. As a consequence, until the twentieth century these cultures managed to utilize and care for the land for centuries without major degradation. "The result of the Indian attitude toward land in the years before contact with the Europeans was the practicing of lifestyles that were not destructive. There were no great areas of depleted game, no major deforestations, and no noticeable pollution except for a few tree-covered trash piles" (ibid., p. 64). Native Americans did, of course, use and change the land in significant ways to satisfy their own survival needs, and it is arguable that much greater levels of environmental degradation would have occurred had their populations been greater.

The settling of the continent by Europeans certainly introduced, then, a concept of land ownership foreign to most of these indigenous cultures (Large, 1973). The common view of the European settlers, which largely prevailed following the fifteenth century, was that land is largely an economic commodity that one can own and exercise dominion over, much in the same way one treats personal property such as a chair or a piece of clothing. Like the chair, land is seen as a personal asset, an indication of personal wealth fully *possessable* by the owner. One can legally exclude others from the use of this property and can sell it or transfer it to someone else if desired. And one can generally use it as one pleases.

The view of land as something which can be *owned* and over which *dominion* can be exercised has many origins. Certainly in large degree these attitudes reflect European laws and customs (see Hargrove, 1980, 1989). The development of these attitudes in the United States has undoubtedly been encouraged by the sheer size and expansiveness of the nation. There was so much land available that the prospect of ownership was a reality for most Americans. Indeed, considerable efforts were made to promote and facilitate land ownership, and to promote the settlement of the ever-moving West, through such legislation as the Homestead Act of 1862 (see Benedict, 1953; Robbins, 1941). Furthermore, this nation's abundance of land and relatively modest population size at the time meant that the problems of waste and misuse of land and resources could be overlooked—one could despoil the environment with relatively few noticeable effects on one's neighbors or on the larger environment.

The Defense of Land as Private Property

There has been considerable thought and writing about the origins of private property in western culture. Is private property a natural right? Does it derive from a social contract? Is private property ultimately a creation of society and, as a result, does society have the legitimate authority to periodically retract or modify these rights?

In the western context, notions of private property in land are often attributed to John Locke. Locke argued for what he called a labor theory of property, notably in his 1690 *The Second Treatise of Government* (1952). The main idea behind this theory is that "people are entitled to hold, as property, whatever they produce by their own initiative, intelligence and industry" (Becker, 1977, p. 32). To Locke, property rights are "natural rights" in that all people in the pre-society state of nature are entitled to them. Locke held that because one's body, in the state of nature, is one's property, one also has property rights over the product of one's labor. When a person "mixes" his or her labor with the natural land (by tilling or farming, for instance) a person thereby makes this his or her property as well. Certain conditions, however, are placed on the extent to which property can be acquired in this manner. Namely, one must not take more than one can use, and one can only acquire property where there is "enough and as good left in common for others" (Locke, 1952, p. 17).

Locke's theory has played an important role in justifying property rights in the United States. The imagery of the labor theory seemed to match well the land and settlement conditions of eighteenth- and nineteenth-century America. There is a certain ethical appeal to the theory—if land is abundant and available for use, it ought to be each individual's right to utilize this land productively. Principles of fairness and desert seem to dictate that, by working and improving the land, ownership should be bestowed. This view is reflected in legislation such as the Homestead Act of 1862, which allowed individuals and families to secure land by settling and improving it over a five-year period.

Lockean theory has been heavily criticized, however, because it is in many ways unrealistic. Why, for instance, should the mixing of one's labor with land (whatever that actually means) entitle one to ownership of the land, and not simply to a fair *return* from one's labor? Perhaps more seriously, it is difficult to imagine how land can be acquired fairly under the standard of "leave as much as and as good for others." It is hard to imagine, even in a state of nature, how one can leave as much and as good for others while assuming property rights over land. Clearly in any system of private property in land there are losers—those who will not have access to landownership. "If a present or future shortage of land can be established, then any appropriations of land past or present under the procedure Locke recommends, enclosure from the common through labor, is an injustice to those who remain unpropertied" (Hargrove, 1980, p. 143; see also Scott, 1977). Also, Locke's requirement that one can only take as much land as one can use is difficult to interpret. Does this preclude speculative land ownership—for example, the frequent cases when land is not actively *used* but rather is held for years? Does use mean personal use, in the sense that each individual landowner must be actively *laboring* (i.e., what of nonresident landowners who earn profits from the land, in a variety of ways, but who have no direct hand in these activities)? Thus, while Locke's theory may be useful rhetorically for justifying a system of private landownership, today it seems flawed in a number of respects. Furthermore, Locke's attempt to pin these ideas to a pre-society state of nature seems unrealistic at best.

Lockean notions find considerable expression in the United States, however, especially in the views and writings of Thomas Jefferson. Jefferson is frequently cited as an early American who was important in bolstering the view of land as private property. Moreover, Jefferson provided additional justification for a system of private property in land by making the explicit connection to the freedoms and moral character of the citizenry. Jefferson saw landownership as a way to ensure the economics of personal freedom so essential to a democratic society. In his view, the ownership of land bestowed a level of independence that nonfreeholders simply do not have. In Scott's words: "Widespread ownership of land was central to Jefferson's idea of a good society. Landowning made a man economically and politically independent. With it an individual did not have to depend on another for his living or vote according to the demands of his employer" (1977, p. 57).

If one owns land, then one is not politically or economically beholden to others. Jefferson was an unabashed supporter of the small farmer and saw the farmer as the bastion of the nation's morality. Extensive land ownership was necessary to ensure the high moral character of a nation's citizenry. As Jefferson observes in an oft-quoted excerpt from his 1787 *Notes on the State of Virginia:*

> Corruption of morals in the mass of cultivators is a phenomenon of which no age nor nation has furnished an example. It is a mark set on those, who not looking up to heaven, to their own soil and industry, as does the husbandman, for their subsistence, depend for it on the casualties and caprice of customers. Dependence begets subservience and venality, suffocates the germ of virtue, and prepares fit tools for the designs of ambition. . . . While we have to labour then, let us never wish to see our citizens occupied at a work-bench, or twirling a distaff. (1955, p. 165)

These attitudes about land are reflected in the U.S. Constitution and in state constitutions. The Virginia Constitution, for instance, states that "all men are by nature equally free and independent and have certain inherent rights, of which, when they enter into a state of society, they cannot, by any compact, deprive or divest their posterity, namely, the enjoyment of life and liberty, with the means of acquiring and possessing property, and pursuing and obtaining happiness and safety" (Thorpe, 1909, p. 3873).

The 1784 New Hampshire Constitution includes similar language. It states that all men "have certain natural, essential, and inherent rights; among which are—the enjoying and defending life and liberty—acquiring, possessing, and protecting property—and in a word, of seeking and obtaining happiness" (ibid., p. 2453). Section 4 of Jefferson's draft of the 1776 Virginia Constitution even contained the provisions for a specific land entitlement for every person who did not already own land. It stated that "Every person of full age neither owning nor having owned (50) acres of land, shall be entitled to an appropriation of (50) acres or to as much as shall make up what he owns or has owned (50) acres in full and absolute dominion, and no other person shall be capable of taking an appropriation" (Peterson, 1975, p. 248). While this provision was later eliminated from the draft, it conveys importance given to landownership by leaders such as Jefferson.

Other arguments in defense of land as private property are explicitly economic and utilitarian. A market economy simply cannot function well, if at all, without a well-defined and enforceable system of property rights, extending to land as well as to other types of goods. "Property rights are an instrument of society . . . and help a man form expectations which he can reasonably hold in his dealings with others" (Demsetz, 1967, p. 348). Without ownership, one is not assured that she or he will be able to reap the benefits of one's labor and effort. There is consequently little incentive to undertake socially productive labor. A system of private property, then, establishes a set of expectations which facilitates economic investments and productivity.

In recent decades there has been considerable interest on the part of conservation and land planning advocates in emphasizing a different notion of private property in land—one that rejects the belief that property owners have any type of absolute dominion over land. Rather, there is much to suggest on legal and moral grounds that landownership entails privileges and responsibilities, not absolute rights.

Land Ownership as a Private Privilege Collectively Bestowed

Obviously, land-use conflicts frequently involve fundamentally different conceptions and understandings of what landownership allows and implies. Those who wish to develop their land are often infuriated by government regulations that impose collective restrictions on their actions. On the flip side are those who view land not as an absolute right, but rather as a privilege which society grants to individuals because it is *in society's interests* to do so (e.g., because some reasonable degree of reliance by property owners that they will benefit from personal investments is essential to a smooth-running market economy).

Supporters of the latter view frequently refer to the system of English property law inherited by the states in this country (all states except Louisiana eventually adopted English common law). English property law finds its roots in the feudal system, in which the monarch retained absolute control and ownership over land. In the American system the government or the *state* has replaced the monarch and is, it is argued, the ultimate owner of land. With the inheritance of English property law come certain operational provisions which further buttress the case that ownership is but a privilege. Central among these provisions are eminent domain, property taxation, and escheat. The power of eminent domain allows the state to take privately held property in order to advance public objectives, such as to construct a highway or build a dam. Usually, the state must pay the owner the fair market value of the land (this is discussed in greater detail below). If ownership were absolute, surely the government could not take property away from individuals against their will. Property taxation—the ability to extract periodic payments from landholders usually on an ad valorem basis—can be traced back to the payments made by feudal landholders, ultimately to the king. Property taxes, then, are analogous to rent—rent paid to the collective in exchange for the right to use the land for personal gain. Under the doctrine of escheat, when a landholder dies intestate (without a will) the land automatically reverts back to the collective if no heir can be identified— further proof that ultimate ownership is retained by the government or the state. In such situations the land is not simply "up for grabs," but reflects the government's underlying ownership.

Another dimension to this argument is the view that, ultimately and fundamentally, *property* is a socially created concept. Here an important distinction is made between property and *possession*. While an individual might possess something—a Pueblo ceramic, an Amish quilt, or a parcel of land—such a thing only becomes one's *property* when the collective acknowledges these rights (e.g., through a bill of sale) and is willing to enforce these rights by excluding others from its possession and use. Without a socially created system of land property rights (e.g., including a system of deeds and titles) and institutions by which to enforce them (e.g., a judicial system and police), property *would not exist.*

Others have pointed to the very characteristics of land, and the uses which can be made of it, as a defense of a more collective notion. These characteristics suggest a fundamental difference between land and other goods and objects over which one might have ownership rights.

The Changing Bundle of Rights

Even the staunchest supporters of the concept of private property rights in land (with perhaps the exception of libertarians) acknowledge today that certain collective constraints must be placed on the use of land. Indeed, collective restrictions are anything but new and are virtually as old as organized civilization. As Bosselman, Callies, and Banta note, significant regulation on land use and development existed even in medieval England:

> More detailed land-use regulations were found in urban areas. In 1189 neighbors were required to give 1½ feet of their land each and to construct thereon a stone party wall three feet thick and sixteen feet high. Other provisions of the same date protected views and access to light.

References to earlier wood construction and several Eleventh Century and Twelfth Century fires indicate clearly the reasons for these regulations. Again in 1297 it was additionally ordered that everyone must keep the front of his own house clean, that "low pentices" were to be removed and that pigsties were to be kept from the streets. By the middle of the Fourteenth Century detailed building regulations required roofs to be covered with stone, tiles or lead. (1976, p. 62)

There has, then, never actually been any such thing as absolute private property in land. Whether defended as a necessary facilitation of economic productivity or as a reflection of the underlying public ownership of land, few dispute the position that such restrictions are historically precedented. Ownership of land involves a certain mixture or composition of rights and one often refers to these rights as a "bundle of sticks."

Over time, as government restrictions and regulations on land use in western countries have increased, the number of sticks remaining in the private bundle has been reduced. In large degree this diminution of the bundle has accompanied changes in social and environmental circumstances. In the United States, for example, the wide, expansive nature of land and resources no longer exists as it did in 1930 when the population was half what it is today. The more crowded the nation becomes, the more necessary are restrictions on the freedoms of individual landholders. It is thus not surprising that, in European countries, where land is a much more limited and finite resource, government restrictions on land use have historically been greater than in the United States.

Environmental circumstances have also changed in fundamental ways. As population growth has continued, and the capability of people to fundamentally modify and despoil the natural environment has increased, the need for environmental education and greater land-use control has expanded. Moreover, especially since World War II our scientific understanding of the impacts and repercussions of many of our previously uncontrolled actions has expanded dramatically. Remarkably, it has been only thirty years since Rachel Carson wrote her ground-breaking book *Silent Spring* (1962). It is also the case that human sensibilities about, and appreciation for, the natural environment have grown. For example, although a few individuals mourned the extinction of the passenger pigeon in 1914, it was not until 1973 that the U.S. Congress enacted the Endangered Species Act, and although John Muir mourned the flooding of the Hetch Hetchy Valley, it was not until the 1960s and 1970s that legislation like the Wilderness Act and the Wild and Scenic Rivers Act was enacted. Much of this legislation was, of course, a direct result of the fact that there were increasingly fewer of such lands to protect, but it also partly reflects certain changes in societal priorities.

Land-Use Profits

Much of the contemporary conflict over land use and land-use regulations involves basic questions about the fairness of profits derived from land use. When a government takes actions which devalue land, such as through downzoning, developers and landowners frequently complain that something of *theirs* has been taken away. I discuss in more detail below the matter of unconstitutional takings, but here I briefly raise the concern about the ethics of taking profits from land-use activities. In response to the complaints of landowners in downzoning cases, planners and proponents of land-use regulations are quick to reply that there is nothing *deserved* about the land values which are taken away, so landowners should not feel indignant at losing something that was not theirs in the first place.

Let's explore the arguments on each side. Proponents of land-use controls often believe that the profits or increased land values resulting from development are speculative windfalls which developers and landowners have done little, if anything, to actually create. Indeed, this so-called unearned increment, if it belongs to anyone, belongs to the public. To a considerable degree, increases in land value are a direct function of public investments in roads, bridges, public transit, sewer and water facilities, and so on. A recent example of this phenomenon is seen in the rapid increase in land values occurring around the sites of Washington Metro stations (a regional subway system). Developers and landowners did nothing to bring about these improvements and certainly did not directly pay for them. The public paid for them and so it is the public that ought rightly to benefit from increases in land value. Furthermore, even if increases in land value are the result of larger social trends or movements, such as the shifting of populations and economic activities to suburbs, it is again not the direct result of any individual action on the part of developers/landowners.

Those developers and landowners experiencing these increases feel differently, of course. First, they will argue that, in many cases, these increases reflect certain actions or improvements undertaken directly by them (e.g., land assemblage, development planning). Certainly the development site contributes to profits from land development, but this site requires the right development, and the right concept plan to make the project work. More fundamentally, though, developers are taking certain financial risks—often major financial risks—in buying land and in making necessary plans, investments, and improvements. Neither government nor society as a whole takes these risks. Those who assume the risks, then, are entitled to the profits generated from them. (Of course, the recent and ongoing savings and loan bailout by U.S. taxpayers raises serious questions about who assumes these risks after all.) While developers *might* make large profits, it is also possible for them to *lose* money. Their arguments also relate back to the earlier theory about the economic role of private property—risk-taking, they contend, is a driving force behind any productive free market economy. Without such economic risk-taking, economic growth and ultimately quality of life will decline. And, without the expectation that profits can be seen from these activities, who would wish to take these risks in the first place?

It is also unfair, developers and landowners will argue, to say that they have not contributed to funding such improvements as Washington's Metro system. In the United States the ad valorem property tax system by definition bases taxes on the fair market value of property, even in the case of speculation. If the profits from land speculation and development are deemed by society as undeserved, then why are developers/landowners *taxed* on them? Being taxed for some period of time, even years, on these values is further evidence in support of the legitimacy of these profits.

Part of the problem in this debate, of course, is that we are dealing with developers and landowners who have entered the game at various points in time. Developer X may have paid relatively high prices for his or her land, and the target of anti-windfall arguments (i.e., the original landowner who gained from speculation) may already have left the market. Having paid such high prices in turn may justify maximizing the use of such lands and the need to generate high profits from the actual development of the land.

A number of proposals have surfaced over the years to address this issue. Hagman and Misczynski present one of the most comprehensive discussions of such proposals in their book, *Windfalls for Wipeouts* (1977). A basic theme is to find ways of taxing windfalls (e.g., perhaps a Metro transit tax district) and then to utilize these funds to compensate landowners whose property is devalued, as in the case of our downzoning above. The state of Oregon has adopted a provision which requires the refunding of property taxes where land is reduced in value due to downzonings. The concept of transferable development rights (TDR), which is in use in a number of jurisdictions around the country, works in a similar fashion. Under this land-use technique, individuals who experience downzonings are allowed to transfer or sell their unused development rights for use in other locations where additional density is permitted in exchange for them (see Costonis, 1973; Pizor, 1986; Stokes et al., 1989). As a land-use technique, TDR might be used to reduce conflict over the takings issue discussed below.

Ethical Aspects of the Takings Issue

A common objection made by developers, landowners, and others to public land-use restrictions is that such regulations amount to the public's *taking* of land without due compensation. The Fifth Amendment of the U.S. Constitution is the source of the takings provision. The takings clause states: "Nor shall private property be taken for public use without just compensation." In reply, planners and land regulators typically argue that such regulations represent a legitimate application of police power—that is, the public has the right to place legitimate restrictions on the use of land even when these result in a lowering of land values and a diminution of the profits to be made through the sale and development of land. Whether this is legitimate regulation or unconstitutional *taking* of land requiring compensation is at the heart of the takings issue. When are controls on land use so extensive and onerous that they amount to a government expropriation of land, similar to cases of the government taking land to build a highway, dam, or an airport? (Such a takings ruling is also known as inverse condemnation.) Any discussion of what constitutes ethical land-use policy must address, to some degree, the takings question. What follows here is intended more to identify and expose the broader philosophical and valuative dimensions of the takings debate; it is not intended to serve as an exhaustive legal analysis, as numerous legal treatises examine the legal history and case law on the issue in tremendous detail (see, e.g., Bosselman, Callies, and Banta, 1976; Costonis, 1975; Large, 1973; Michelman, 1967; Sax, 1971b, 1988; Siemon, 1990).

Alternative Takings Doctrine

Federal and state courts have approached the takings problem in a variety of ways. Different takings or inverse condemnation theories have been employed, each with a somewhat different view of what constitutes permissible government control of private property. One view, the "physical invasion doctrine," holds that a compensable taking occurs when government moves to occupy or trespass upon one's land—that is, to physically invade. Again, if the government chooses to use one's land for a legitimate public purpose, then fair compensation is certainly required.

Under the physical invasion doctrine, government need not necessarily *invade* one's property by foot or build something on it—government actions can create certain hazards or noises which invade as well. A classic example of this type of situation is found in the case of *United States v. Causby* (328 U.S. 256 [1946]) where noises from low-flying aircraft in Greensboro, North Carolina were found to prevent the practical use of the plaintiff's farm (the chickens would not lay eggs). The courts have also used the physical invasion doctrine to decide takings in cases where government actions were responsible for flooding land or discharging weapons over land. When, through government actions, one's land is *physically* altered or invaded in some fashion, the courts are likely to find that a taking has occurred. In most cases, however, we are concerned with the effects of public regulations on land use, such as a zoning ordinance that restricts permissible density, or an environmental standard that might prevent construction in a sensitive natural area. These cases do not usually involve a physical invasion.

A second theory that has been utilized by the courts places great importance on the distinction between regulations which seek to prevent a *harm* and those which seek to secure public *benefits*. Under this doctrine, government need not pay compensation when harms are being prevented but would be required to when it seeks to secure a public benefit. The most notable federal decision employing this distinction is the now-famous *Mugler v. Kansas* case (123 U.S. 623 [1887]). Here the government's shutting down of a brewery was upheld on the grounds that the actions were merely abating a public nuisance. No compensation was due, even if, as the owners of the brewery claimed, the building had no other use and thus the property was completely devalued. In the words of the court:

> A prohibition simply upon the use of property for purposes that are declared, by valid legislation, to be injurious to the health, morals, or safety of the community, cannot, in any just sense, be deemed a taking or an appropriation of property for the public benefit. Such legislation does not disturb the owner in the control or use of his property for lawful purposes, nor restrict his right to dispose of it, but is only a declaration by the State that its use by any one, for certain forbidden purposes, is prejudicial to the public interests. . . .
>
> The power which the States have of prohibiting such use by individuals of their property as will be prejudicial to the health, the morals, or the safety of the public, is not—and, consistently with the existence and safety of organized society, cannot be—burdened with the condition that the State must compensate such individual owners for pecuniary losses they may sustain, by reason of their not being permitted, by a noxious use of their property, to inflict injury on the community. The exercise of the police power by the destruction of property which is itself a public nuisance, or the prohibition of its use in a particular way, whereby its value becomes depreciated, is very different from taking property for public use, or from depriving a person of his property without due process of law. In the one case, a nuisance is only abated; in the other, unoffending property is taken away from an innocent owner. (123 U.S. 623, pp. 668–69)

Critics of this doctrine are quick to note the difficulty in determining whether a regulation on land-use policy is intended to prevent a harm or secure a benefit: "many regulations prohibiting a 'public harm' can just as easily be characterized as procuring a public benefit. For example, when the government prohibits dredging or filling of wetlands, this action can be viewed as either merely prohibiting a noxious use or as providing the public with the benefits of open marshes. Thus the unadorned harm/benefit distinction fails to illuminate the takings inquiry because of its inherent manipulability" (Hunter, 1988, p. 326).

There is little doubt that these distinctions are often difficult to make, and that, depending upon one's political and economic interests, the doctrine can be used to justify and rationalize one's particular view about a regulation in question. Consider land-use regulations, such as large lot zoning that is intended to protect open space in a community. Affected landowners and those in the development community would surely characterize such actions as an attempt on the part of government to obtain certain valuable benefits (open space in this case) for the public free of charge. On the other hand, advocates of the regulations might argue that they are perfectly valid, even if substantial economic devaluation occurs as a result of them, because they are intended to prevent the creation of a public *harm*—specifically the impacts of new homes and development on the visual attractiveness and aesthetic beauty of the landscape, not to mention potential loss of wildlife habitat.

Moreover, land-use regulations are frequently aimed at preventing land-use incompatibilities—and it may be difficult to determine what use or activity is, in fact, the harm. Nevertheless, one should consider the extent to which public harms might be created by land-use activities. There is little doubt in my mind that dredging or filling wetlands for any reason creates public harms, in a broad sense, and that the ecological and human impacts of such practices justify government restrictions even to the point of reducing the economic market value of such property. I return to this issue below.

Perhaps the most frequently used takings test, however, has been the "diminution of value" test. Here the primary consideration in determining whether a taking has occurred is the extent or degree to which the government regulations in question reduce or diminish the value of land or property. This economics-based doctrine finds its principal roots in the 1927 Supreme Court decision in *Pennsylvania Coal Co. v. Mahon* (260 U.S. 393 [1922]), in which the court found that a Pennsylvania law, prohibiting coal mining where the rights to the surface land were not owned, was an unconstitutional taking of property (in this case, taking the company's subsurface mining rights). While the court did not precisely identify when a regulation is a legitimate exercise of police power and when it is a compensable taking, Chief Justice Holmes, writing the majority opinion, is clear that such a demarcation point can and will be reached:

Government hardly could go on if to some extent values incident to property could not be diminished without paying for every such change in the general law. As long recognized, some values are enjoyed under an implied limitation and must yield to the police power. But obviously the implied limitation must have its limits. . . . One fact for consideration in determining such limits is the extent of the diminution. When it reaches a certain magnitude, in most if not all cases there must be an exercise of eminent domain and compensation to sustain the act. . . . *The general rule at least is, that while property may be regulated to a certain extent, if regulation goes too far it will be recognized as a taking.* (260 U.S. 393, pp. 393–415; emphasis my own)

While this economic test has not been applied uniformly, it is fair to characterize it as the dominant theory in use today in federal and state courts. The theory has, of course, been modified. One important modification, now frequently cited by courts, is the concept of reasonable "investment-backed expectations." This modification was introduced by the Supreme Court in its 1978 opinion in *Penn Central Transportation Co. v. City of New York* (438 U.S. 104). Here the Penn Central Company sued New York City and claimed that, because of the city's historic district regulations, which prevented the company from building a fifty-five-story building on top of Grand Central Station, the city had *taken* their property. Under this refinement of the diminution of value test, it is relevant to consider not only the extent of the reduction of value occurring as a result of land-use restrictions, but also the extent to which expectations of such uses are reasonable. It was important to the court that the restrictions in question did nothing to interrupt the existing uses of the property:

The New York City law does not interfere in any way with the present uses of the terminal. Its designation as a landmark not only permits but contemplates that appellants may continue to use the property precisely as it has been used for the past 65 years: as a railroad terminal containing office space and concessions. So the law does not interfere with what must be regarded as Penn Central's primary expectation concerning the use of the parcel. More importantly, on this record, we must regard the New York City law as permitting Penn Central not only to profit from the terminal but to obtain a "reasonable return" on its investment. (438 U.S. at 136)

In June 1992, the U.S. Supreme Court decided another major takings case in *Lucas v. South Carolina Coastal Council* (505 U.S. [1992]), further reinforcing the view that takings will occur when all development potential is denied. This case involved a coastal property owner (as discussed briefly in the previous chapter), David Lucas, who owned two small beachfront lots in the Wild Dunes resort on Isle of Palms, South Carolina.

Following the enactment of the S.C. Beachfront Management Act (BMA) in 1988, Lucas found that he would not be permitted to construct a beachfront home on either lot under the new law (both lots were seaward of the new setback line). Lucas took the Coastal Council to court claiming an unconstitutional taking. Winning at the trial court level, Lucas was awarded $1.2 million. The decision was overturned on appeal by the state supreme court, holding that the BMA merely sought to prevent the creation of a public harm (e.g., destruction of the public beach). On an appeal filed by Lucas, the U.S. Supreme Court reversed and remanded, issuing a majority opinion which reinforces the notion that when a regulation serves to preclude all reasonable economic use, a taking will likely have occurred.

The court held as well, however, that land regulations could deprive all economic use and still be constitutional when they merely sought to enforce preexisting common law restrictions (such as the doctrine of customary use discussed in Chapter 5). In the words of the majority opinion:

> Where the State seeks to sustain regulation that deprives land of all economically beneficial use, we think it may resist compensation only if the logically antecedent inquiry into the nature of the owner's estate shows that the proscribed use interests were not part of his title to begin with. . . . Any limitation so severe cannot be newly legislated or decreed (without compensation) but must inhere in the title itself, in the restrictions that background principles of the state's law of property and nuisance already place upon land ownership. A law of decree with such an effect must, in other words, do no more than duplicate the result that could have been achieved in the courts—by adjacent landowners (or other uniquely affected persons) under the state's laws of private nuisance, or by the state under its complementary power to abate nuisances that affect the public generally, or otherwise.

On remand, the South Carolina Supreme Court concluded Lucas had experienced a temporary taking for the period since 1988 (when the BMA was originally enacted). The court returned the case to the circuit court level to determine the actual extent (if any) of the monetary loss incurred, and eventually the state purchased the lots in question.

The dominance of these economic-oriented perspectives generally means that courts are likely to declare takings when a landowner is deprived of a reasonable economic use of his or her property because of land-use regulations. Any number of recent federal or state opinions can be cited as evidence of the importance of this economic thinking, and *Lucas* certainly reinforces this trend.

The Ethics of Current Judicial Theory

Which, if any, of these judicial takings tests is the more valid or ethically defensible? As noted early in this book, we are less concerned here with what the courts say and more with what strikes us as ethically and morally requisite. Indeed, takings legal challenges are themselves exercises in argument and philosophical discourse, with different parties (including friends of the courts) assuming different ethical postures.

What one feels about how far government can legitimately regulate land use reverts, in large degree, to fundamental conceptions of property. Is private property in land seen primarily in terms of personal freedom and as a largely inviolable right? Or, is private property to be viewed as a privilege, bestowed collectively and necessarily and legitimately subject to the conditions and stipulations laid down by the collective? How one views the institution of property necessarily influences the choice of a takings theory.

I find much to support in the view that private property in land is a *special* kind of property, imbued with such important public characteristics that its use must be seen ultimately as a privilege. Individuals who own property in land are subject to the conditions and standards of care established by the polity, even when these change over time. The changing of the land-use rules to which landowners are subject gives rise to ethical concerns, and suggests the possible need for actions and policies to reduce or minimize the impacts of these changes.

There is also no denying that, for property in land to serve important economic functions, there must be some legal assurance that government will not be allowed to squelch or extinguish ownership without fair compensation. For this reason, and out of basic concerns of equity, it seems to me clearly unethical to physically expropriate or invade (to use the terminology of the courts) private property without a legitimate and valid public purpose, and without payment of just compensation. This, most would agree, is the least that is required.

Such compensation also seems required in cases where, while government may not physically invade or trespass, government restrictions prevent a landowner from *personal access* and *use* of his or her property. If, for example, a law were enacted prohibiting a property owner from walking upon, or otherwise accessing, say, his or her wetland property, this would be similar in effect to physical appropriation. However, where access or use remain, compensation appears less justified. For example, while it is probably not the economic "highest and best use" as determined by the market system, preventing the alteration or filling of the wetlands will still provide personal benefits associated with the use of and access to these areas. The owner can physically occupy the property in this sense and is entitled to legal protection from trespasses. Moreover, the owner is not restricted from selling, transferring, or otherwise exercising control over ownership of the land. The fact that such underlying ownership rights remained in the *Lucas* case has led some commentators to conclude that this should not have been considered a taking.

Beyond these basic entitlements, property ownership must surely be subject to collectively determined rules about what constitutes *ethical* land use. In determining ethical land use, the various theories and positions and principles described and discussed in this book become relevant. Take, for instance, restrictions to building in endangered species habitat. Whether these restrictions are ethically valid does not, in my view, turn on whether the owner is able to attain a "reasonable economic use," but rather on ethical duties to preserve species. If by allowing development we bypass the takings problem but lose a species, then the outcome must surely be unethical. Furthermore, if restrictions to development are necessary to prevent the extinction of another form of life, then it is hard to accept that takings (requiring compensation) have indeed occurred. This is but one of many environmental and other ethical considerations that can and should be used in reaching decisions about land-use policy and planning.

This is not to suggest, however, that the diminution of value or thwarting of investment-backed expectations that may result from land-use regulations are not important moral and ethical considerations. They must be factored into the decision-making process and weighed against the many other ethical considerations that may be present. Clearly, severely downzoning a parcel of land, for instance, should not be undertaken frivolously. In this regard I find considerable usefulness in the concept of "preventing harms." It seems to me that severe diminution of value is more ethically acceptable when the regulation is necessary to prevent the creation of public harms. Complete prohibition of building on a parcel of land is, in my mind, much more justifiable if it is intended to prevent groundwater contamination or extinction of a species than if it is intended to preserve the last remaining piece of neighborhood open land, commonly used for a variety of public recreational purposes (e.g., touch football, hiking, and the like). In the latter case it would seem more appropriate for the public—that is, the government—to purchase this land from the owner if the intention is to preserve it in an undeveloped state as a sort of public park. However, even in the latter case there seems to be no moral presumption that compensation is required merely because a diminution of value has occurred—again, landownership and land development are more privileges than rights.

A similar approach is to give special importance to land regulations intended to protect health and safety. Many land-use restrictions are intended to prevent serious injury or loss of life to citizens and these objectives seem to hold greater moral weight than others. In the past this has been a judicially relevant factor in some takings decisions. This is illustrated by the 1989 decision of the California Court of Appeals in *First English Evangelical Lutheran Church of Glendale v. County of Los Angeles*, a case that involved county restrictions on rebuilding structures in a riverine floodplain. Specifically, the Lutheran church owned a twenty-one-acre retreat (campground) located in a canyon in the Angeles National Forest. A flood in 1978 destroyed the building and the county prohibited its reconstruction because it was located in a designated flood protection area. The church claimed that these land-use restrictions constituted a taking. The case eventually made it to the U.S. Supreme Court on the matter of whether compensation can be awarded for interim takings. The U.S. Supreme Court said nothing about whether this particular situation constituted a taking, deciding only that interim takings are possible and sending the case back to the California courts. The California appellate court found that certain uses—agriculture and recreation—still remained, but suggested that, even if *all* uses were precluded, restrictions such as these would still not amount to takings because of their importance in protecting public health and safety:

> If there is a hierarchy of interests the police power serves, and both logic and prior cases suggest there is, then the preservation of life must rank at the top. Zoning restrictions seldom serve public interests so far up on the scale. More often these laws guard against things like "premature urbanization" . . . or "preserve open spaces" . . . or contribute to orderly development and the mitigation of environmental impacts. . . . When land-use regulations seek to advance what are deemed lesser interests such as aesthetic values of the community they frequently are outweighed by constitutional property rights. . . .
>
> The zoning regulation challenged in the instant case involved this highest of public interests—the prevention of death and injury. Its enactment was prompted by the loss of life in an earlier flood. And its avowed purpose is to prevent the loss of lives in future floods. Moreover, the lives it seeks to save and the injuries it strives to prevent are not only those on other properties but on appellant's property as well. (258 California Reporter, p. 904)

Other important factors are the extent of environmental or ecological degradation that could result and the extent to which development cannot be undertaken without altering, in a major way, the natural features and characteristics of the land. This idea of a "natural use theory" of property is exemplified by the decision of the Wisconsin Supreme Court in *Just v. Marinette* (56 Wis. 2d 7, 201 N.W. 2d 761 [1972]). Under this view a taking cannot be found to occur if, through land-use regulations, government is only preventing a landowner from undertaking ecologically damaging land development. Hunter expands on this notion and advocates the development of an "ecologically sound and coherent theory of property":

> Such a theory would be based on an understanding that land plays a critical ecological role in shaping what type of environment we live in, the quality of our life and even what we become. It would also be founded on the notion that private land-use decisions, if predicated solely on a growth-oriented, economics-based view of land, will not lead to a stable environment or an acceptable quality of life. By turning to ecology, the courts would define private and public rights in land by examining the objective tenets of the environmental sciences. The Constitution, which must look somewhere to define these public and private rights, would (at least with respect to undeveloped land) look neither solely to the marketplace nor to changing public values, but rather to the laws of nature. (Hunter, 1988, p. 379)

In legal and constitutional parlance, my resolution to the takings dilemma would best be characterized as a reliance on due process. My answer to whether compensation should be paid is, "it all depends."

Summary

Many of our contemporary political and legal disagreements about land involve fundamentally different understandings of what property rights in land actually are. Some people perceive such rights to imply absolute dominion and control over land resources. Many landowners feel that, because they "own" the land, they have the right to do what they wish with it and consequently resent government actions such as zoning and land-use controls which place restrictions on this ability. Landownership, however, has never been absolute, but, as it should be, a collectively bestowed privilege. To be sure, a system of private property rights serves important economic and social objectives, but such rights must ultimately be subject to collective constraints. As population and land pressures become greater over time, and our understanding of the fragility and importance of environmental systems expands, collective constraints on certain private property rights may also be necessary.

The matter of unconstitutional takings due to land-use regulations has been decided by courts in the United States through the consideration of different theories and factors. The diminution of a property's value and the extent to which reasonable economic uses of the land remain have become dominant considerations in deciding takings cases. A somewhat different approach is argued for here, however. The ethics of a particular land-use policy or decision will depend on numerous factors, expounded in this and the other chapters of this book, including duties to protect the natural environment, to protect land-use rights, to prevent harms, and to protect the interests of future generations. These must be considered, along with the extent of devaluation incurred by a landowner and the thwarting of perhaps legitimately formed expectations, in determining the merits of particular restrictions. Basic fairness does suggest, at a minimum, that it is unethical for government to physically take or expropriate private land without just compensation. If use and access to one's land are permitted, however, I find no a priori claim to compensation as a result of land-use regulation.

PART IV

ETHICS, COMMUNITY,
AND POLITICS

12

DEFINING LIFE-STYLE AND
COMMUNITY CHARACTER

Cᴛᴛɪᴇs, ᴄᴏᴜɴᴛɪᴇs, and other local jurisdictions in the United States often enact land-use restrictions in an effort to create or preserve a certain type of community character, which may reflect certain local preferences about life-style. Should communities have the freedom to shape and design their communities with these considerations in mind? Do they have the right to restrict or even prohibit certain activities or life-styles which the community leaders feel are inconsistent with their community value system? This chapter examines these questions: To what extent can localities legitimately set and enforce restrictions based on community character or life-style issues? What parameters might exist for the setting of these community standards?

One common view which we should consider is that communities can and ought to shape themselves as they see fit—that there is considerable merit to promoting a system of physically and socially "distinctive" communities. Moreover, this can be seen as positive in that individuals are then free to select those communities and living environments that best suit them. This view is not without problems, however, and we will return to this issue at several points in this chapter. While in theory individuals and families can sort themselves out—that is, move into or out of communities they may like or dislike—there are clear practical limitations to doing this. One's desired life-style may involve living in a low-density, low-crime suburban community, but such a move may be precluded for financial reasons. Many individuals, for financial or other reasons, will simply not be as mobile as might be assumed. Thus, there may always be a sizable minority in any community who may be forced to live with what the majority feels the character and style of the community ought to be. Individual choice for these members of the community may be reduced rather than expanded.

Ethical land use must acknowledge and, whenever possible, facilitate the many different life-style choices individuals will make. While communities have the moral authority to establish physical, aesthetic, and other community standards, their actions are more questionable when they seek to influence or control individual behavior because it is viewed as immoral, rather than because such actions have significant effects on other individuals or the larger public. Ethical land-use policy should, to the extent possible, allow individuals to choose freely and pursue their own unique tastes and preferences. In Mill's eloquent words: "the principle requires liberty of tastes and pursuits, of framing the plan of our life to suit our own character, of doing as we like, subject to such consequences as may follow, without impediment from our fellow creatures, as long as what we do does not harm them, even though they think our conduct foolish, perverse, or wrong" (1978, p. 12).

Several categories of land-use actions usually associated with efforts to define and establish community character are discussed below, specifically these: regulation of adult establishments, such as pornographic theaters and bookstores; restrictions on density and use and the number of unrelated individuals allowed in a dwelling unit; and regulations to promote aesthetic and architectural character.

Land-Use Actions Affecting Life-Style and Community Character

Communities have historically undertaken a variety of land-use actions in an effort to define and protect a desired sense of community character. Communities often seek to control their character by restricting the density of uses; for instance, by restricting new development to detached single-family uses on large lots. Communities are increasingly placing restrictions, usually through zoning ordinances, on certain *undesirable* activities, such as the location of adult entertainment uses—often prohibiting these uses within a certain distance of residential uses, day care centers, schools, or places of worship (see Pearlman, 1984). Often these undesirable uses are restricted to industrial or commercial zoning districts.

Increasingly, there is concern about managing the visual landscape, notably through banning such visually intrusive uses as billboards and creating architectural review boards and appearance commissions, which regulate the exterior shape and design of new buildings. Moreover, some communities prohibit the entrance into the community of certain types of commercial uses which they deem inconsistent with desired community character. For example, the town of Cannon Beach, Oregon, has prohibited the operation of what it calls "formula food" restaurants. These are defined in its zoning ordinance as restaurants which are "required by contractual or other arrangements to offer standardized menus, ingredients, food preparation, interior or exterior design, or uniforms" (Beatley, Brower, and Brower, 1988, p. 6). The town of Hilton Head, South

Carolina, places extensive restrictions on the color and texture of buildings constructed there, prohibiting, for instance, McDonald's golden arches. The Red Roof Inn there is one of only a few in the nation without a red roof. The town of Breckenridge, Colorado, prohibits restaurants and other buildings in its historic downtown from having drive-through windows, because these are believed to be "out of character."

Some communities have imposed zoning regulations that are intended, either directly or indirectly, to prevent certain living arrangements which are seen by some citizens as immoral and thus which contribute to the diminution of neighborhood property values. Some communities, for instance Denver, Colorado, have sought to prevent occupancy of residential structures by more than two unrelated persons. While these types of restrictions are often justified on the grounds that they serve to protect property values for adjacent residents, it is clear that, in many cases, these restrictions reflect a direct expression of community moral standards.

On the face of this issue, it strikes one as entirely reasonable and legitimate that communities have the power and authority to influence their character and image. It is frequently argued that individuals, when they choose which community in which to reside or retire, evaluate these and a variety of other factors (local tax rate, quality of schools, proximity to a major airport, level of services provided) in making these locational decisions. Interjurisdictional homogeneity, from a social point of view, would seem undesirable. Some individuals clearly prefer to live in large, high-density urban places, while others prefer rural or exurban environments. These two types of communities obviously offer different advantages and different packages of amenities. The resident of Manhattan may value access to cultural amenities, public transit, and world-class restaurants. The resident of Hooper, Colorado, may be willing to forsake these types of amenities for others of greater personal importance, including fresh air, sunlight, green spaces, lower crime rates, and beautiful scenery. From an ethical view this heterogeneity of community types and character can be seen as a positive thing—it allows individuals and groups to "vote with their feet" and to select that local composition or mixture of amenities that best suits their preferences and life plans. Allowing communities to promote and influence their own distinctiveness, then, promotes a freedom of choice. This position can be labeled as the "distinctive communities ethic."

On the other hand, liberal democratic theory (or that political philosophy which emphasizes individual freedoms and welfare) leaves life-style, religion, and other personal choices essentially and fundamentally to the individual. If an individual desires to live in a home with other unrelated individuals, or to eat at fast-food restaurants, or to express himself or herself through billboards, or to live in a home of modern architectural design, or to frequent adult entertainment establishments, then are not these decisions best left to the individual? Recall that, under Mill's classic theory of government intervention, the public has no right to infringe on these types of individual choices unless they interfere with the rights of others. Thus, an initial ethical conclusion is that local interferences with individual life-style choices must be justified by good reasons. Prevention of serious land-use harms and protection of public health and safety are legitimate reasons we have identified in earlier chapters to justify significant restrictions on personal freedom. A primary issue relative to community character is whether these more subjective and personal issues are of such importance that they warrant and justify significant restraints on personal freedoms. Ultimately what appears necessary is a balancing between legitimate local pursuits of community character and the need to protect and preserve individual life-style choices. Communities, in an effort to promote and preserve a certain community character, must seek to maximize personal choices and liberties at every opportunity.

In Chapter 5 we examined in considerable detail the array of potential land-use rights which can be acknowledged. A locality's attempt to create and sustain a particular image and to establish certain moral standards must be constrained by individual rights. Much of the conflict over local attempts to regulate on the grounds of religious morality or aesthetics arises because such efforts may infringe upon constitutionally protected rights, such as First Amendment free speech rights. These conflicts are discussed below.

Aesthetic and Architectural Character

Many communities seek to manage their visual or aesthetic character in ways that reflect or define a certain perceived community character. The examples are numerous. Towns such as Hilton Head, South Carolina, for instance, have imposed severe restrictions on the color, architectural style, and other aesthetic features of dwellings and commercial buildings. Under this town's land management ordinance, proposed buildings and developments are subjected to a rigorous process of design review and stringent performance standards addressing aesthetic considerations. Off-premise signs are prohibited, and the size of signs is severely restricted. Performance standards protect trees and vegetation and require that certain visual buffers are provided along major roadways. The exterior colors of buildings are controlled so that structures blend in with the natural surroundings and are consistent with the Hilton Head "style." Hilton Head has sought to promote and maintain a certain aesthetic character.

Compare the aesthetic character of Hilton Head with that of Las Vegas.

In Las Vegas the architectural style and architectural standards are dramatically different. Almost anything goes here. Signs are large and visually intrusive; neon and flashing. On the main strip there is even a volcano which periodically erupts. The visual character of the community is completely different, and perhaps entirely appropriate to the nature and life of this city. Hilton Head and Las Vegas are different communities, with different self-images, and with different community standards of what is visually attractive and visually acceptable.

Should communities have the right to impose these types of land-use restrictions—to define and enforce certain community standards of aesthetics or visual integrity? The question pits the rights of individuals against a collectively imposed definition of "community." Perhaps an individual in Hilton Head wishes to construct a single-family residence which is *different* in color (a barn red) and style (colonial) from the Hilton Head image. Perhaps a business interest wishes to locate here. Is it fair or ethical for the town of Hilton Head to prevent the owners of a McDonald's franchise from erecting the usual golden arches?

Clearly part of the issue here is that people have different perceptions and tastes about what is ugly or beautiful (although empirical studies do suggest certain common visual likes and dislikes). Differences in aesthetic taste have been recently illustrated by the construction of Walt Disney Company's new corporate headquarters building in Burbank, California. To the dismay of some neighbors, the building's facade incorporates eighteen-foot statues of the Seven Dwarfs. The company describes the building as "entertainment architecture," and the distinctive building has elicited various reactions from residents. In the words of one neighbor who can see the building from her lawn: "It's a really classy looking building, so it doesn't destroy the neighborhood. . . . It's like you're in a small town with a little more in it. It's one of the fun ways of getting offices without making it look like a city office building. I like the colors. It's not garish" (Yan, 1990). However, another neighbor has completely opposite reactions to the building: "It stands out too much. You look down at the end of the street and all you see is a big, ugly building. I don't think it keeps within the atmosphere in a residential neighborhood. The color is awful. I wish they could tear it down" (ibid.).

There are numerous other contemporary examples of such aesthetic conflicts. Increasingly, for example, homeowners who wish to maintain a natural landscape around their homes clash with other neighbors who wish to maintain traditional manicured lawns. Should some homeowners be forced to maintain such traditional lawns in order to satisfy some collective image of what the neighborhood or community should look like? Similar disputes arise around the placement of outdoor ornaments. (Should homeowners have the right to install such things as pink flamingos, even though perhaps the majority of surrounding neighbors view such objects as "tacky"?)

It is common, then, to find such sharp disagreements about the aesthetic merits of building designs. Just as people's tastes and preferences about artwork are different, so also it is to be expected that their aesthetic inclinations about buildings and landscapes will be different as well. Does this subjective nature of aesthetics suggest that individuals ought to be able to choose for themselves which style or color home they prefer? Should businesses be able, then, to decide whether a neon sign or wooden sign is more to their aesthetic liking?

Of course, some aesthetic and visually oriented restrictions may be justified to prevent real threats to public health and safety. Excessive road signage can be a traffic hazard and may need to be curtailed for safety reasons. In coastal communities exterior lighting is increasingly being controlled in order to reduce its negative impacts on endangered sea turtles (sea turtle hatchings are disoriented by the lights). Signs, lights, and other similar exterior visual features, then, do create *real harms* which must be controlled. But in most cases, the primary rationale for such controls is an aesthetic one—a purely subjective preference expressed collectively for a particular visual style or character. Do communities have the moral right to establish such collective aesthetic standards and to impose them upon *all* residents?

As in other conflicts between attempts to define community character and individual desires, an important matter is the extent to which important moral or legal rights owed to individuals are being infringed upon. Do individuals have the moral or legal right to express themselves aesthetically—that is, by painting their homes in the color of their choice, or erecting golden arches or other similar signage, or not mowing their yards? One potential right is the right to free speech which might especially be affected by billboard restrictions. Billboard restrictions can be determined to be unconstitutional if they are aimed at controlling a certain kind of billboard with a certain kind of message. This question was a major factor, for instance, in the U.S. Supreme Court's decision in *Metromedia Inc. v. City of San Diego* (953 U.S. 490 [1981]). This city's ban on off-premise signs was invalidated by the court in large part because the court viewed the restrictions as applying only to noncommercial forms of expression. Most courts, however, appear to view billboard restrictions as legitimate regulations of the *medium* of communication and generally not aimed at controlling the content or substance of the message. As in other First Amendment cases, courts typically will consider the extent to which those restrictions serve an important public purpose and the extent to which other effective avenues of expression exist.

Free speech does not seem to be significantly affected by regulations on such things as house color, architectural design, or landscape design. It strikes me that these efforts of communities are more ethically legitimate and defensible. First, whether an individual can paint her house red rather than brown, or is required to have a wooded front yard (visual buffer) rather than a conventional grass one, does not seem to infringe on any basic or fundamental entitlement which must be protected. Furthermore, preventing communities from establishing and imposing certain aesthetic or visual standards precludes the ability of individuals to seek out and live in communities with particular aesthetic regimes. In the absence of strong individual rights or entitlements, communities ought to be allowed to collectively decide upon and establish such standards.

Regulating Adult Establishments

Let's consider in more detail several of these types of community character regulations. Many cities have become concerned in recent years about the proliferation of adult entertainment establishments and have either prohibited uses or severely restricted where and when such activities are acceptable. These local actions pit the desires of the broader community to shape and define itself—indeed to set moral standards that presumably reflect the feelings of the majority of residents—against the desires of individuals (both entrepreneurs and consumers) to pursue a certain kind of life-style and a certain form of livelihood or recreation.

One challenge sometimes made to these types of restrictions is that they infringe on the free speech guarantees of the First Amendment of the U.S. Constitution. Prohibiting the location of all adult establishments in a jurisdiction, it can be argued, infringes on personal expression, itself an element of one's choice about life-style and life plan (one's feelings about what one wants to accomplish in life, how and where one wants to live, and so on).

But even beyond the specific First Amendment challenge, is it fair that a certain type of life-style or one person's conception of a good and fulfilling life be so constrained? Do such restrictions (e.g., those imposed by the city of Detroit, which require that adult theaters be located no closer than 1,000 feet from other adult theaters or no closer than 500 feet from a residential area), really have the effect of preventing this type of life-style if one is determined to pursue it? Clearly such restrictions constrain somewhat the availability of these activities, but they may not prevent them or preclude them from occurring somewhere in the city. As Pearlman notes, the actual impacts on these establishments may depend on local economic and other circumstances: "Whether it [the Detroit ordinance] limited the access to a form of expression depends on what the ordinance did to the supply-and-demand characteristics of commercial pornography establishments. It may be that lack of concentration diminished the supply because it made access more difficult or because a number of such operations need to be close together to stimulate demand. On the other hand, if pornographic operations were separated, one could argue that demand would increase because patrons would feel safer not going into a combat zone" (1984, pp. 258–59).

But given our earlier discussions in Chapter 4, can it be argued that pornographic and other adult establishments do impose harms on others, consequently justifying the actions of local government to restrict them, perhaps even to prohibit them? Such uses often create crime and other social problems, particularly when they are concentrated in a particular area of a city.

On the other hand, is it not often the case that those who object to such uses are objecting to them more on moral grounds than because of any direct negative externalities or harms created by such uses? Many residents are simply offended by the existence or presence of such uses, by the mere knowledge that they exist in *their* community. Seeking to ban or severely regulate these uses is not, in their minds, primarily intended to reduce the direct effects of such uses.

The U.S. Supreme Court had the opportunity to rule on such a set of restrictions in *The City of Renton et al. v. Playtime Theatres Inc. et al.* (106 S.Ct. 925 [1986]). This case involved the passage of a zoning provision by Renton, Washington, substantially restricting where adult theaters could be operated in that community. More specifically, the city ordinance prohibited such theaters from locating within 1,000 feet of any residential zone, single-family or multi-family dwelling, church, park, or school. The owners of two theaters in downtown Renton (who had purchased the theaters *after* the enactment of the zoning provisions) filed a lawsuit against the city claiming that their rights under the First and Fourteenth Amendments of the U.S. Constitution had been violated, and sought declaratory and injunctive relief. The U.S. District Court ruled in favor of the city, while the U.S. Court of Appeals reversed the decision and remanded for reconsideration. The city appealed to the U.S. Supreme Court and won, with Chief Justice Rehnquist delivering the majority opinion.

The issues of this case raise important ethical questions, many left unresolved by the court. A primary issue in the court's mind was the extent to which the zoning ordinance is a "content-neutral" time, place, and manner regulation. Historically, regulations that seek to regulate free speech on the basis of its content are usually presumed on their face to violate the First Amendment. The court found that the ordinance was content-neutral because it was not designed to regulate the content of films, but rather their "secondary effects" on the surrounding community. In the court's words: "The ordinance by its terms is designed to prevent crime, protect the city's retail trade, maintain property values, and generally 'protec[t] and preserv[e] the quality of [the city's] neighborhoods, commercial districts and the quality of urban life,' not to suppress the expression of unpopular views" (p. 929).

The court concluded that such content-neutral regulations are permissible if they can be shown to serve a "substantial governmental interest" and do not unreasonably limit alternative avenues of communication. The court found that these conditions are satisfied by the Renton ordinance. As to proving a substantial governmental interest, it is sufficient to the court that the city was able to cite the experiences of other cities with the so-called secondary effects of adult theaters, especially the experiences of the city of Seattle. As to preserving reasonable alternative avenues for communication, the court determined that the 520 acres, or 5 percent of Renton's land area, where such uses *could* be located under the ordinance, were sufficient to provide ample opportunities for these activities. Moreover, the court strongly rejected the arguments of the theater owners that there were no "commercially viable" sites within this 520–acre area: "We disagree with both the reasoning and the conclusion of the Court of Appeals. That respondents must fend for themselves in the real estate market, on equal footing with other prospective purchasers and lessees, does not give rise to a First Amendment violation. And . . . we have never suggested that the First Amendment compels the government to ensure that adult theaters, or any other kind of speech-related businesses for that matter, will be able to obtain sites at bargain prices" (p. 932).

This decision raises key ethical issues that have implication for a variety of land-use regulations. Several of the more important are identified by Justices Brennan and Marshall who argue, in their dissenting opinion, that the Renton law is not content-neutral at all, in that it regulates the location of movie theaters *solely* on the basis of the content of the films shown in them. This is indicated by the fact that the regulations only apply to adult theaters, and do not address other adult activities, such as bars, massage parlors, and adult book stores, which can be expected to generate similar secondary effects. Moreover, they argue that the burden of making adequate findings of the existence of these secondary effects cannot be met simply by citing the experiences of other cities. Even assuming the ordinance is content-neutral, they argue that it has not been shown that a significant governmental interest has been served or that there are reasonable avenues of alternative communication. The minority opinion argues that the ordinance does, in fact, serve to restrict substantially the ability of this use to occur or exist in the city:

Respondents are not on equal footing with other prospective purchasers and lessees, but must conduct business under severe restrictions not imposed upon other establishments. The court also argues that the First Amendment does not compel the government to ensure that adult theaters, or any other kinds of speech-related businesses for that matter, will be able to obtain sites at bargain prices. However, respondents do not ask Renton to guarantee low price sites for their businesses, but seek only a reasonable opportunity to operate adult theaters in the city. By denying them the opportunity, Renton can effectively ban a form of protected speech from its borders. (p. 938)

Thus, to what extent do these types of uses generate serious negative externalities or secondary effects that can be quantified and objectively observed? Even if such effects are detected, is it always ethically legitimate to regulate severely such activities in response to them? What is the *extent* of the effect that can and cannot be tolerated? If one additional crime is proven to occur in some proximity to such theaters in the course of, say, a year's time, is this sufficient to justify such restrictions? Do other kinds of effects, such as devaluation of property, always and necessarily justify such controls? For instance, let us assume that the theater in question planned to show movies rated R, rather than X, and it could be proven that, in *this* particular locality, conservative sexual values are so strong that even this prospect is offensive—in turn leading to similar property value reductions (people are offended by the sight of a risqué marquee). Would regulation of this type of theater (i.e., one showing R-rated films) be as morally justified as the regulation of the X-rated theater?

There is, as well, the matter of the broader societal effects of such activities, and while a discussion of these seems somewhat removed from local land-use decisions, they are often brought up in debates about such ordinances. Some citizens have argued that the proliferation of adult theaters and pornographic activities creates broader, perhaps less directly quantifiable, impacts; for instance, encouraging violence against women, or contributing to a moral decline in the country. This raises the general question, To what extent should land-use policy be directed at mitigating such uncertain effects?

This case confronts, as well, the more fundamental concern of whether, and the extent to which, a community can legitimately regulate the personal activities and life-styles of its residents. One position is that basic fairness should permit people to choose freely and pursue their own life plans, when the pursuit of these life plans does not unreasonably harm other individuals or society as a whole. Furthermore, indications of the latter should be more than supposition and conjecture. It can also be argued that severely regulating or restricting certain, what appear to be minor, freedoms (such as the ability of an individual to attend an X-rated movie) threatens to jeopardize the broader system of personal liberties and freedoms that permit a society where individuals can effectively choose and pursue their own life plans.

What about cases where the clientele for certain activities such as adult theaters resides primarily in other jurisdictions? Does this modify in any important way a community's obligation to tolerate such life-styles? It can be argued that, while the community might have an ethical obligation to be tolerant of the diversity of life-style choices of *its* residents, it certainly has no obligation to be tolerant of citizens living in other jurisdictions. Ethical land use seems to imply that *their* communities should be more tolerant and should permit such activities there instead.

The Renton case raises a concern about the extent to which land-use controls, while not prohibiting certain activities explicitly, can serve to prohibit them in effect. This effective prohibition can result from restricting the extent of land zoned for a particular use to an impractical sliver (as in the Renton case), by requiring a special use permit with criteria that no applicant can ever meet, and so on. Land-use policymakers must be careful to prevent restrictions or regulations from becoming de facto prohibitions.

Protecting and Promoting Family Values

Some communities have sought to regulate the density and type of development in an explicit effort to create and maintain a family oriented environment. Permissible development may be restricted to single-family detached units on large lots, or promoting an atmosphere and physical conditions deemed to be safer and perhaps in some sense more wholesome than dense, urban environments. While such patterns of community development may be desirable to many people, are these kinds of efforts to define character and quality-of-life ethically legitimate and acceptable?

Several issues concern us here. As in the case of restrictions to adult establishments, one community's effort to protect "community character" may infringe or the basic *rights* of other individuals. Large-lot zoning schemes have often had the effect, intentional or not, of being exclusionary—keeping out certain "types" and classes of people. Should communities have the freedom to define their own physical and aesthetic character even if the result is to deprive one or more individuals of affordable housing and access to the community?

Local zoning ordinances also place restrictions on the number of unrelated individuals permitted to occupy residential units. The 1973 case *Village of Belle Terre et al. v. Boraas* (416 U.S. 1) is perhaps the most notable legal test of such land-use actions and illustrates well the ethical dilemmas associated with promoting community character. Belle Terre, a small village on New York's Long Island, adopted zoning provisions that restricted land uses to one-family dwellings. Under the ordinance no restrictions were placed on the number of *family* members that could occupy a dwelling (related by blood, adoption, or marriage), but no more than two unrelated individuals could live in the same unit. The conflict arose when the town brought action to stop the occupancy of a home by six college students (i.e., unrelated individuals). The case went all the way to the U.S. Supreme Court, with the majority siding with the village. Despite the claim of Boraas and the other lessees that these restrictions amounted to, among other things, a violation of their constitutionally protected right to privacy, the Court saw the restrictions as a valid exercise of police power. In the words of the majority:

> The regimes of boarding houses, fraternity houses, and the like present urban problems. More people occupy a given space; more cars rather continuously pass by; more cars are parked; noise travels with crowds.
>
> A quiet place where yards are wide, people few, and motor vehicles restricted are legitimate guidelines in a land-use project addressed to family needs. . . . It is ample to lay out zones where *family values, youth values, and the blessings of quiet seclusion and clean air make the area a sanctuary for people.* (p. 9, emphasis my own)

To the court, the village's restrictions on the number of unrelated residents were sufficiently justified by the need to keep down noise and traffic, and to maintain a certain family environment and quality of life. But could such restrictions, on the other hand, be intended primarily to keep out certain individuals whose life-styles are not to the liking of the community? Justice Marshall's dissent in Belle Terre raises many of these types of concerns, and he concludes that the village's restrictions appear to violate an individual's rights of association and privacy.

Choices concerning who to live with, and what type of household or living arrangement is most preferred or desirable to an individual, would seem beyond legitimate government control: "The choice of household companions—of whether a person's 'intellectual and emotional needs' are best met by living with family, friends, professional associates, or others—involves deeply personal considerations as to the kind and quality of intimate relationships within the ambit of the right to privacy protected by the Constitution" (p. 16).

Justice Marshall makes the valid observation that the village ordinance discriminates against a particular type of life-style choice. While restricting the number of unrelated individuals permitted in a household, it contains no restrictions on the number of family members or related individuals that are permitted in the same home: "Belle Terre imposes upon those who deviate from the community norm in their choice of living companions significantly greater restrictions than are applied to residential groups who are related by blood or marriage, and compose the established order within the community. The *village has, in effect, acted to fence out those individuals whose choice of lifestyle differs from that of its current residents"* (pp. 16–17, emphasis my own). If the primary objective of the restrictions is to keep down traffic, noise, and similar impacts, it would seem more defensible, as Marshall notes, to place restrictions on the number of cars, or the number of permissible occupants, regardless of family status.

Although the Belle Terre case arose in the early 1970s, the debate continues over the moral defensibility of these kinds of restrictions. Prince George's County, Maryland, has recently been sued over its zoning restrictions which require houses with three or more unrelated residents living there to provide one parking space as well as a minimum seventy-square-foot bedroom for each person. The ordinance is clearly aimed at University of Maryland students living in and around College Park (the main campus). In the words of one critic: "The whole intent of all this is to drive the students away from College Park, to satisfy a small group of people who absolutely abhor lifestyles that differ from their own" ("U-Md. Students," 1990, p. F9).

Similar restrictions imposed by the city of Denver resulted in a major political battle there. In certain areas, Denver's restrictions have prohibited the occupancy of a single-family house by two unrelated individuals since the 1950s. Opponents of these provisions refer to them as the city's "living in sin" law and argue that the city has no right to regulate such things, which in effect discriminate against homosexual and heterosexual couples wishing to live together. Supporters of the provisions argue that such restrictions help to maintain "traditional family values." In the words of one resident: "If you have children growing up in a cross-section of the population of Denver, it's not a healthy or appropriate atmosphere for bringing up children" (Kelleher, 1989, p. A12). Recently the city voted to eliminate these restrictions.

Other Morally Relevant Factors

Determining whether specific actions or ordinances intended to protect and advance a particular community character are ethical depends upon many considerations, as we have noted. Clearly, when such restrictions affect in significant ways the freedom of individuals to choose particular life-styles, the reasons for such restrictions should be good ones. Does a particular architectural standard indeed seem to protect a certain visual or aesthetic feeling in the community or is the need for such a standard questionable, merely adding to the cost of buildings and homes in a community? Is the complete prohibition of adult establishments really necessary to achieve certain community safeguards concerning pornography (e.g., to keep such land uses away from children and schools), or would restrictions on the location, number, and design of such facilities serve the purpose of protecting community standards while also respecting individual life-style choices? Is an ordinance restricting the number of unrelated individuals living in a single dwelling unit really essential to prevent traffic, parking, and other problems, or can other approaches be adopted that respect individual desires to pursue this particular life-style? The reasons for restrictions must be legitimate, and there must be no alternatives that can both protect and advance community character as well as protect individual liberties and life-style choices.

Furthermore, is it ethical for communities to restrict or ban a land use simply because they (presumably a majority of the residents) feel that the use or activity is morally wrong? I personally find such reasoning to be less defensible than circumstances where restrictions are imposed to prevent clear and tangible physical results of a negative sort, such as crime, traffic, or visual disorder. Again, ethical land use respects the rights of individuals to choose life-styles to their liking, especially when such life-styles do not in any direct or serious way affect others. Ethical land use exhibits tolerance of the many of what Mill calls "self-regarding" decisions which individuals make.

In an important way it can be argued that many of the community-character regulations discussed here, rather than squashing or thwarting a diversity of life-styles, actually *encourage* diversity. Indeed, such regulations, say of visual character or of adult establishments, are absolutely necessary for the achievement of some, perhaps many people's, chosen life plans—that is, one's chosen life plan may involve as a central component living in a community of homogeneous land use, where buildings are of a simple architectural style, or where no adult establishments can be seen to exist. Under this view an appropriate way to ensure that people will be able to achieve their individual life plans is to let them choose which type or kind of community they wish to live in—let them "vote with their feet," as Tiebout has argued.

When taking this view, an important consideration is the extent to which individuals *have* choices and freedoms in a broader geographical context. Even if communities place outright bans on certain activities on moral grounds alone (i.e., simply because the city leaders don't like the *idea* that such uses exist within their community), will such actions really impede the freedom of individuals seeking these activities in other perhaps adjoining localities or in the region as a whole? To achieve some life-style choices, an individual may actually have to move to another community, and how feasible are these types of adjustments?

The ethical legitimacy of efforts by a community to prohibit certain uses and activities, then, and to promote the development of a certain type of community character, may depend to some extent on the characteristics of *other* communities in the region. It can be argued that one community ought to be permitted to impose severe restrictions or prohibitions on activities deemed undesirable, because there are other localities in the region where these life-styles can be pursued and accommodated. Here one can advocate a pluralistic network of communities, with various combinations of life-styles and social perspectives, and in which people choose which combination best suits their personal life plans. Minority perspectives would not be trampled in that individuals always have the option to exit if the character or moral standards of the community were not completely to their liking.

While this type of perspective is intuitively appealing on its face, it suffers from certain limitations. First, individuals in our society are probably not as mobile as popular opinion would believe. The ability to *exit* may simply not exist for many individuals, particularly those in the community who are economically disadvantaged. Second, social intolerance permitted in one community may in time spread to others in the region, in essence foreclosing these other avenues for pursuing one's desired life-style.

In considering the ethics of community character–related land-use restrictions, several other factors must be considered. Obviously, such restrictions must be constrained by the land-use rights which individuals, no matter where they live, might be deemed to hold (i.e., legal or moral rights). Completely banning all adult establishments might violate individual First Amendment rights (and would seem to be contrary to a respect for personal life-style choices), and the courts appear to lean in this direction. Banning all signs in a community, including campaign signs, might violate free speech rights. The imposition of large-lot residential zoning, while intended to promote a certain desirable physical environment (i.e., low density, rural and small town character), might be exclusionary and as such violate constitutional rights to travel and equal protection to affordable housing, and other possible rights. The inability of a homeowner to design with nature by using native grasses and plants in his or her landscape design not only restricts artistic freedom but also hurts the environment (i.e., by *having* to have a lawn, one has to use gas for the mower, fertilizer, and lots of water). The ability of communities to establish and protect a certain community character must be constrained by, and balanced against, these types of land-use rights which all individuals may be seen to possess regardless of where they reside. The extent to which one sees community-character restrictions as ethical will turn on one's belief about what land-use rights individuals hold. Another way to look at this is to consider the extent to which community-character restrictions infringe on personal freedoms. Other things being equal, the less severe the infringement is the more ethically supportable it will tend to be. Aesthetic design control, while limiting the freedom of individuals to express themselves visually or architecturally, does not seem as onerous in its effort as restrictions on the number of unrelated individuals permitted in a single residential unit. Restrictions on the latter seem to represent a more fundamental infringement on life-style choice.

Summary

While ethical land-use policy seeks to minimize the imposition of harms created by certain activities or uses, it must be sensitive not to unduly thwart or restrict personal life-style choices. Ethical land-use policy respects a diversity of life-style choices and seeks to facilitate and encourage as much personal freedom as possible in the selection and pursuit of one's own unique tastes and interests. Communities must avoid land-use restrictions which are intended primarily to extinguish life-style choices seen as inappropriate or immoral but which do not result in significant public harms.

On the other hand, communities ought to have the moral authority to promote and protect, through democratic means, a particular community image or character to the liking of the majority of its residents without, of course, condoning "ethnic cleansing." In an important sense, this is itself a way of protecting certain life-style choices. A community's attempt to define and advance its particular image or character, however, must be sensitive to the diversity of other life-style views which exist, and must not, in pursuit of protecting a particular community character, overrule or thwart the legitimate land-use rights of all individuals.

13

DUTIES BEYOND BORDERS: INTER-JURISDICTIONAL LAND-USE ETHICS

LOCAL JURISDICTIONAL BOUNDARIES function poorly with respect to planning and land-use issues. This is perhaps most dramatically apparent in the case of environmental problems. The boundaries of ecosystems and natural environmental processes usually do not correspond very closely with local city or county limits. Rather, whether it's an estuary, a groundwater aquifer, or an airshed, these resources frequently span multiple jurisdictions. Many environmental problems, as we are increasingly coming to recognize, extend not only beyond local boundaries but also beyond state and even national boundaries, as in the case of acid rain. Concomitantly, the actions and choices of one jurisdiction will often affect the condition and quality of environmental resources experienced in another jurisdiction. If one locality chooses to pollute the air, other localities downwind will undoubtedly be forced to endure the consequences of this decision. If one locality chooses to undertake excessive extraction of groundwater from a regional aquifer, eventually other jurisdictions in the region will feel the results.

These cross-boundary or interjurisdictional effects are not restricted to environmental problems, but extend to other social and economic realms. One locality's decision to permit the location of a large regional shopping center may serve to create traffic and congestion problems which citizens in other localities must endure. Local decisions to restrict the building of multifamily and other forms of affordable housing will influence housing availability regionally and will contribute to the exacerbation of an extralocal or regional problem. One locality's growth management cap may serve to funnel growth into other localities in the region, and perhaps even to other regions, causing higher than normal growth pressures in places that may not be prepared to deal effectively with it.

The primary ethical matter considered in this chapter is whether, and the extent to which, local jurisdictions have an ethical obligation to consider these interjurisdictional impacts when making local land-use decisions. In short, to what extent do we have duties beyond borders? It is my position that extralocal obligations exist, although it may be difficult to arrive at precisely the extent of these obligations.

A common human tendency is to assign greatest importance to the welfare of one's own kind—to one's own clan or tribe, if you will—and, thus, it is not surprising that public officials are more concerned with the impacts of land-use actions on *their* residents and *their* constituents than on the residents of other jurisdictions who may also be affected. Local land-use policy is often very parochial in its outlook. From a political point of view it may be suicidal for an elected official to appear to be *too* concerned with the plight of one's neighbors. Moreover, meaningful consideration of the cross-boundary effects of local land-use actions may be costly. If, for instance, a jurisdiction is concerned about, say, its rapid extraction of a common regional groundwater aquifer, the alternatives to its heavy use may involve significant financial or other forms of sacrifice. It might require, for instance, the need for water conservation measures (not entirely popular with constituents) or the need to look elsewhere to supply a portion of the community's water supply (e.g., perhaps by using a river source, which may impose treatment costs that are not present with the groundwater source). Politicians may have difficulty getting reelected if they are perceived to be more concerned with the constituents in an adjoining jurisdiction than with their own. There is a natural and understandable tendency, then, to be geographically provincial in land-use matters, which contradicts the natural world and its requirements.

Against these tendencies, however, are some significant ethical and moral obligations. Just because an action creates harms which are, in a sense, exported does not necessarily reduce the ethical imperative of minimizing or eliminating these harms. Just because the citizenry of neighboring communities may have difficulty obtaining affordable housing (which is a land-use right, it can be argued) does not diminish the moral imperative of finding ways to uphold and satisfy this right.

One position is that these moral and ethical obligations grow directly out of the fact that localities are socially and economically interconnected in fundamental ways. Economic trade and interdependency, as well as common social ties, suggest that localities are not isolated moral islands. Furthermore, from a moral point of view it may seem irrelevant which locality or jurisdiction one is a resident of—each individual resident would seem to be entitled to the same level of moral respect and attention regardless of his or her particular mailing address.

Obligations to Minimize Regional Harm

At the very least, each individual jurisdiction should consider the extent to which its land-use decisions negatively impact upon adjoining or other jurisdictions, and that each has an obligation to minimize or, whenever possible, to eliminate such harms.

Let us return to the regional groundwater example. Let's imagine, for instance, that a number of localities in a region rely on an underground aquifer for their water supply. The town of Kearney, however, receives much of its municipal water supply from a nearby river. Kearney has within its jurisdictional boundaries much of the groundwater aquifer's recharge area—an area on the outskirts of town which has, until recently, been largely out of the path of intensive development. A proposal has recently been submitted to the Kearney City Council, however, for a very large housing project to be located in this recharge area. The project would virtually consume the recharge area and, because sewage disposal would be handled through individual on-site septic tanks, the other cities and towns in the region which rely on the aquifer are greatly concerned about the potential for contamination. The communities are so concerned about this potential that they send a delegation to talk with Kearney officials and request that the city require the developers to redesign the project so that the threat of groundwater contamination is minimized. Specifically, they request that either the development in the recharge area be restricted to low-density, large-lot residential uses, or that the developer be required to install a centralized sewage collection and treatment system. As might be expected, the developer vehemently objects to such proposals, arguing that either approach would jeopardize the financial feasibility of the entire project. Members of the city council who are concerned about losing the development, as well, emphasize the need to expand the city's tax base and the need for additional affordable housing.

This is a clear hypothetical example of how the land-use decisions of one jurisdiction may negatively affect others. What is the extent of the ethical obligations in this case? On the one hand, it can be argued that Kearney should first and foremost consider which option will best respond to the needs of its own constituents. If it truly needs the taxes, and the housing, then these should be the deciding factors, and the project should be allowed to proceed as planned. On the other hand, an ethic of concern for the cross-boundary impacts of such a decision would move us in a different direction. Such a high-density project, relying as it does on on-site sewage disposal, would clearly have the potential for severe impacts on the aquifer—imposing such harms on other localities strikes one as intuitively morally wrong. Another posture might argue that Kearney has an obligation to find a way to prevent any appreciable amount of development in the recharge area which might create even the threat of future contamination.

Perhaps an intermediate position is that while Kearney does have the obligation to consider fully and, indeed, minimize these potential impacts, the extent of this restraint must necessarily be balanced against the costs and level of sacrifice which *its* constituents must bear. The tax base and housing benefits of the development suggest that a compromise position might be found. It might be agreed that, while the density of the development will not be reduced to the extent desired by neighboring localities, it will be reduced substantially, to a level where most environmental and engineering experts feel the chances of contamination from septic tank leachate is minimal. Moreover, the city and the developer might agree to a long-term septic-tank testing and monitoring program, among other options, to be alert for contamination.

It is possible, of course, to assume a utilitarian perspective in this example. It can be argued that the community that values the groundwater resource in question to a greater extent ought to be willing to pay for it. If the surrounding cities and towns so value the use of the groundwater resource, they ought to be able to compensate Kearney (or the housing developer) in order to prevent these potentially damaging land-uses from occurring in the recharge zone. If they are unable to amass a bid sufficiently attractive to Kearney (or the developer), then the potentially polluting use could indeed be deemed the most efficient outcome. But again, such an outcome strikes us as intuitively unfair. Why should these activities be permitted if they serve to harm others?

Does it matter that several of the other localities have themselves been poor neighbors in the past? In determining one city's moral obligations to adjoining or neighboring locations, does it make any difference that in the past these same localities have by and large tended to think of their own communities first? Does the lack of reciprocity diminish regional moral obligations? Take, for instance, the neighboring community of Dawson. Just two years ago the Dawson City Council voted to allow a relatively large housing project to be built in the floodplain, upstream of Kearney and several other towns. Kearney strongly objected to the proposal because its environmental engineering staff concluded that such a project would displace flood water and would serve to exacerbate flooding downriver. Dawson approved the project over the strong objections of Kearney and seemed little concerned about the regional consequences of these actions. Does such behavior on the part of Dawson officials, in turn, relieve Kearney of moral responsibility in future potentially damaging policy decisions, such as allowing development in the recharge zone? It strikes me that it does not and that, regardless of the past moral sensibilities of the localities, Kearney still faces the possibility of creating harms and has obligations to minimize these harms.

Here again we also confront questions about what constitutes harm. For instance, there are certain land-use actions undertaken by a locality which affect only land within its own borders, but which are met with disappointment or indignation by residents and officials living in other jurisdictions. Such actions might include allowing certain open space lands to be developed which may have served a regional populace, or allowing pristine public beachfront to be developed that had been enjoyed by residents throughout the area.

The concepts of culpability and mitigation may find important application as well in an interjurisdictional context. If Kearney approved the recharge zone development in the above hypothetical case, thus causing eventual degradation of the resource, the principle of culpability would seem to suggest some form of compensation or mitigation to the users of the resource, perhaps in the form of impact fees used to establish a groundwater monitoring program, or an agreement to eventually contribute to a regional water treatment and distribution system, should groundwater contamination be significant in the future. As in earlier applications of the culpability standard, such compensation should not be invoked as a rationale or justification for degradation. The stronger ethical obligation in the groundwater example is to *prevent* the regional harm in the first place.

One of the most notable land cases involving a local project creating such regional environmental impacts is *Save a Valuable Environment v. City of Bothell* (89 Wn.2d 862, 576 P.2d 401, 1978). This case involved the city of Bothell, Washington, which rezoned farmland to permit the construction of a large shopping center. While the land in question was within the city's jurisdictional boundaries, it was abutted by two counties which had zoned their land in this area for agricultural and low-density residential uses. A nonprofit environmental group—"Save a Valuable Environment"—challenged the city's rezoning on the grounds that it amounted to spot zoning and would have negative effects on the environment and the economy of the region (see Zurvalec, 1979). Sustaining the lower court's opinion, the Washington Supreme Court decided in favor of the environmental group and concluded that the potential impacts of the project could be substantial and that the city must consider these effects on adjoining jurisdictions when making land-use decisions. In the Supreme Court's words:

> The crux of the problem is that construction of a major shopping center would have serious detrimental effects on areas outside Bothell's jurisdiction. Letters, from officials of Snohomish and King Counties, the Washington Department of Highways, and the Puget Sound Governmental Conference all indicate Bothell's environmental impact statement failed to address serious problems created by the shopping center proposal. First, agricultural and low density residential uses of land around the center could not be maintained. Pressures for secondary growth would be severe. Not only would desirable agricultural land be lost but inten-

sified commercial uses would require substantial investments in highways, sewers, and other services and utilities. The economic and aesthetic values of the essentially rural character of the valley would be lost. Second, highway construction requiring millions of dollars of local, state and federal funds would be necessary. Serious increased traffic congestion would create a potentially serious air pollution problem in the valley. It would also, of course, add substantially to the aesthetic loss. Third, new alignment of the North Creek to accommodate the shopping center, together with anticipated increases in runoff, might create a danger of flooding. Finally, the unstable peat soil on which the center is to be built may settle unevenly, with consequences which have not yet been investigated.

The Bothell shopping center, then, would create a host of regional and cross-jurisdictional impacts, from traffic to air pollution to flooding. While the city had considered only the impact within its boundaries, the Supreme Court clearly felt that the city had a moral obligation to consider a much broader geographical area.

Under these circumstances, Bothell may not act in disregard of the effects outside its boundaries. Where the potential exists that a zoning action will cause a serious environmental effect outside jurisdictional borders, the zoning body must serve the welfare of the entire affected community. If it does not do so it acts in an arbitrary and capricious manner. The precise boundaries of the affected community cannot be determined until the potential environmental effects are understood. It includes all areas where a serious impact on the environment would be caused by the proposed action. The impact must be direct. For example, areas which would experience an increased danger of flooding or air pollution, or areas which would experience pressure to alter the land-uses contemplated by their own comprehensive plans, would be part of the affected community. (Pp. 868–69)

The Washington Supreme Court in this case, then, lays down a strong mandate for localities to consider the regional impacts of their land-use actions. The court upheld the lower court's decision that the failure to consider regional welfare caused the rezoning action to be "spot zoning," and thus arbitrary and capricious. The court believes, however, that the shopping center need not necessarily be forbidden, if appropriate actions had been taken by the city. "If it is possible to substantially mitigate or avoid potential adverse environmental effects, and if Bothell takes the necessary steps to do so, responsible planning for the shopping center may be reasonable" (p. 870). These broader environmental impacts were not considered adequately, and mitigative actions not imposed, and so the rezoning, in the court's view, could not be reasonable.

While the court concluded that Bothell must consider regional environmental impacts, it did not require that the city, or other jurisdictions in the area, undertake any kind of regional or interjurisdictional planning. Moreover, the court did not specifically delineate a particular set of standards or principles which localities must satisfy. There has, however, been considerable commentary and speculation about what the language of the court's opinion implies. In the view of one commentator, the following is suggested:

> It is clear that at the very minimum the municipality must follow the basic requirements of due process and allow residents and property owners within the affected region the opportunity to be heard at a public meeting and to have their rights considered to the same extent as its own taxpayers. To effectuate these due process requirements, the municipality should hold open hearings when considering a zoning decision that will have a broad impact on the environment. To further demonstrate its good faith, the municipality's planning commission should conduct environmental impact studies that monitor the total effect of the proposed project on all affected areas and be able to demonstrate how they considered the total effect in their decisionmaking process. (Zurvalec, 1979, pp. 1272–73)

These types of regional environmental effects seem to imply an ethical imperative for establishing regional or interjurisdictional planning frameworks, and they illustrate the importance of environmental impact review procedures which would carefully analyze the broader impacts of a proposal such as a shopping center. Indeed, state environmental impact review requirements, for example, such as those mandated under California's Environmental Quality Act of 1970 (CEQA), can perhaps best be understood as an institutionalized procedure for documenting the regional and extralocal effects of projects, including private land development (see Renz, 1984).

What of the obligations to minimize the harms created by a locality when it is difficult or impossible to identify *who* is actually harmed? It is relatively easy to estimate or determine more precisely the environmental effects of allowing the construction of a specific shopping center or of extracting excessive amounts of groundwater, but it may be more difficult in other cases. Allowing or promoting the use of pesticides in farming operations may create health risks to consumers many states away through air and water pollution and pesticide residue on the crops. Allowing toxic wastes to be dumped into the Atlantic Ocean, while perhaps not causing any immediate harm to residents of shorefront communities in Long Island and New Jersey, may have serious long-term effects on people and marine life and tourism in the region. The problem, of course, is that these impacts are incurred by the "faceless"—people and lifeforms that are not familiar to us. We have a more difficult time visualizing these impacts. Again, we confront the problem of "out of sight, out of mind." Nevertheless, if we have reasonable factual, empirical, and scientific bases for believing that local actions will create such systemic or long-distance or long-term harms, then ethical obligations to prevent or minimize them would appear to exist.

Duties to Consult and Inform

Even if one questions whether there are clear substantive duties which one locality has to other localities—for example, to make a particular decision because it minimizes harms to other localities—perhaps there is, at a minimum, a duty to consult with and otherwise consider the view and concerns held by public officials and constituents in other jurisdictions.

An earlier case in the 1950s, *Borough of Cresskill v. Borough of Dumont* (15 N.J. 238, 247–48, 104 A.2d 441–48, 1954), illustrates these duties. Here, the borough of Dumont, New Jersey, rezoned a residential district to a business district. Several adjacent boroughs complained about this action and contested the action. Specifically, the adjacent boroughs of Cresskill and Haworth claimed that the rezoning would lead to traffic and safety problems, depreciate surrounding residential property, and be inconsistent with both their "comprehensive zoning plans" as well as that of Dumont. Eventually finding the action to constitute spot zoning, the New Jersey Supreme Court spoke strongly of the duty of one locality to allow the residents of other affected jurisdictions to have a say-so in the decision:

> The appellant [the borough of Dumont] spells out from the language of these constitutional and statutory provisions that the responsibility of a municipality for zoning halts at the municipal boundary lines without regard to the effect of its zoning ordinances on adjoining and nearby land outside the municipality. Such a view might prevail where there are large undeveloped areas at the borders of two contiguous towns, but it cannot be tolerated where, as here, the area is built up and one cannot tell when one is passing from one borough to another. Knickerbocker Road and Massachusetts Avenue are not Chinese walls separating Dumont from the adjoining boroughs. *At the very least Dumont owes a duty to hear any residents and taxpayers of adjoining municipalities who may be adversely affected by proposed zoning changes and to give as much consideration to their rights as they would to those of residents and taxpayers of Dumont.* To do less would be to make a fetish out of invisible municipal boundary lines and a mockery of the principles of zoning. (15 N.J. 247; emphasis my own)

The Assurance Problem

Recall from earlier discussions of the tragedy of the commons that a significant reason that individuals do not undertake unilateral resource conservation is that they have no assurance that other individuals will undertake similar restraints. Commonly referred to as the "assurance problem," it has considerable importance in interjurisdictional ethics. Should a jurisdiction be expected to "do the right thing" (to be ethical) if it is reasonably certain that other localities will not do the same? Does one locality have an extralocal moral obligation if other localities do not discern or are unwilling to abide by similar obligations?

The tendency for one locality (and the elected officials of that locality) to feel that their ethical responsibility not to pollute is negated by other localities which are clearly not going to exercise similar restraint is easy to understand. Why should one locality or a few localities make sacrifices if other localities will not? I argue that, while unilateral actions may not always be required, a locality's moral obligations neither evaporate nor diminish merely by the fact of inaction by other localities which ought to undertake similar actions. If on careful examination public officials in community A believe their actions will substantially reduce harms to citizens in communities C and D, or will respond to moral obligations to protect the ecosystem or endangered species, or will serve to protect the rights and interests of future generations, the fact of inaction by other localities will not necessarily negate these duties.

There is, of course, the matter of inefficaceous action. If, for instance, a locality is considering whether to impose certain land-use restrictions which may put the community at a competitive economic disadvantage when compared with similar jurisdictions in the region, and the objective is to protect the water quality of, say, San Francisco Bay, some serious questions about the likely effectiveness of this action could be raised. While the sacrifice by the community may be great, the actual efficacy of the action may be rather small. If no other localities are taking similar actions, the benefits of reduced non-point runoff will tend to be minuscule. Citizens, in this case, may have a legitimate complaint that their sacrifice is too great and is unjustified by the small, perhaps indiscernible, improvements in the water quality of the Bay. One can imagine circumstances, however, where the unilateral restraint of one jurisdiction might prevent significant and serious calamity to other jurisdictions. One locality's denial of, say, an oil refinery or toxic waste facility might, it can be argued, make a tremendous difference.

The assurance problem highlights the important role played by institutional and legal requirements for land-use planning imposed by extralocal bodies (i.e., regional and state planning agencies). Much of the activity in state land-use planning since the 1960s is partly a recognition of the fact that it is not fair (nor very likely) to expect local governments to undertake land-use measures which benefit regions or states (and have only marginal benefits locally) when doing so penalizes their relative standing among other localities.

Efforts in recent years to create regional and state level planning processes can be viewed as attempts to overcome these assurance problems. For instance, in Florida, as a result of the 1972 Florida Environmental Land and Water Management Act, "Developments of Regional Impact" must go through a special review and impact assessment procedure. Projects that exceed certain size thresholds (e.g., residential projects of a certain number of units or hospitals with a certain number of beds) must undergo a regional impact assessment and review (e.g., see DeGrove, 1984). This and similar types of regional review provide opportunities for consideration of cross-jurisdictional effects, and the chance for neighboring localities to express concerns; such review thus responds to ethical duties to inform and consult. Regions such as the Shenandoah Valley in Virginia could help conserve their sense of place—and their natural and cultural heritage—if communities would begin to work together in a regional context, rather than as unrelated independent communities.

Duties to Regional Welfare

While the distinction between preventing a harm and promoting a public good is problematic, there is at least a partial intuitive basis for it. Just as a locality can be said to have a duty to prevent or minimize regional harm, it can also be argued that localities have duties to contribute to the advancement of certain regional needs.

These obligations to regional needs have been most firmly established in the area of affordable housing. In a number of states there is clearly a legal, as well as a moral, obligation for localities to consider the impacts of planning and zoning actions on the availability of housing, and indeed obligations to affirmatively promote affordable housing. These regional housing obligations have been perhaps most aggressively mandated in New Jersey, as a result of a series of court cases challenging the exclusionary practices of certain townships. In the ground-breaking *Southern Burlington County NAACP v. Township of Mount Laurel* (67 N.J. 151, 336 A2d. 713, cert. denied 423 U.S. 808, 1975), the township's zoning ordinance was challenged on the grounds that it served to exclude the entrance of low- and moderate-income families into the community. Because of the ordinance's minimum lot size and minimum floor area requirements, as well as its limitations on the number of permissible bedrooms and school-age children for an area, it was argued that the practical result was to prevent the availability of affordable housing. The New Jersey Supreme Court decided in favor of this view and established a broad doctrine that localities must provide adequate housing for low- and moderate-income families, at least consistent with the community's "regional fair share": "every such municipality must, by its land-use regulations, presumptively make realistically possible an appropriate variety and choice of housing. More specifically, presumptively it cannot foreclose the opportunity of the classes of people mentioned for low and moderate income housing and in its regulations must affirmatively afford that opportunity, at least to the extent of the municipality's fair share of the present and prospective regional need therefore" (336 A.2d 713 N.J. 1975, p. 724; cited in Bagne, 1978, p. 285). Another promising approach to overcoming the inequities of assurance problems is seen in the imposition of statewide planning goals under Oregon's innovative growth management system. Oregon's housing goal similarly requires each local jurisdiction to provide for the housing needs of all income levels of Oregonians (see De-Grove, 1984).

Other examples of regional needs include improvements to transportation, waste management, and other public facilities. There might even be regional obligations to allow certain religious land uses, such as churches and congregational facilities. It can be argued that a locality, in deciding whether and where to permit such religious activities, should consider the spiritual needs of the region and should perhaps permit such uses even where the majority of a congregation lives in other communities. This is precisely how the Ohio Court of Appeals decided in *State ex rel. Anshe Chesed Congregation v. Bruggemeir* (97 Ohio App. 67, 115 N.E. 2d 65 [1953]), in which a conflict arose over a request for a special-use permit to build a church in a single-family residential district in the village of Beachwood, Ohio. The village denied the permit request, concluding that the use would injure neighboring properties and would not serve the public welfare. The village's latter conclusion was based in large part on the fact that the vast majority of the congregation of this proposed church would be from other jurisdictions (indeed, the congregation numbered about 5,000, while the entire population of the village at the time numbered but 1,800). In the view of the Ohio Court of Appeals this was insufficient reason to turn down the permit, and their denial of the church went against the regional obligations of the village:

> It must be observed that a village, which is contiguous to and a part of a great metropolitan area from which it derives its very existence, cannot arbitrarily refuse within reasonable limits to contribute its share to the general welfare of the community as a whole.

The membership of a religious institution is not confined within municipal boundaries. People seek out the church of their choice without concern as to the political subdivision in which it may be located. From the evidence as to the present facilities for religious services in the village, there can be no doubt that a great majority of the 1800 residents of Beachwood attend devotional services outside its physical boundaries. The ground for refusing the permit, that the great majority of . . . members live outside the village . . . is without substance in fact or law. (97 Ohio App. at 74)

In all of these cases of regional obligations, whether it involves regional fair share housing requirements, or obligations to protect the regional ecosystem, the merits of regional planning and cooperation are clear. Ethical land-use decisions and relationships between local jurisdictions strongly support the creation of such regional mechanisms for cooperation and planning.

Cross-Boundary Distributional Obligations

Obligations among communities may also entail more than simply reducing the *negative* impacts of their programs and policies (e.g., controlling the extent to which they pollute a common pool environmental resource), and more than satisfying certain minimum regional welfare requirements. Rather, interjurisdictional ethics may also require the undertaking of actions which bestow additional new benefits on adjoining and other communities. For example, such duties may prevent a locality from restricting or controlling growth to too great an extent because such growth can be expected to benefit a number of nearby localities. A community which is considering a limitation on the absolute quantity of growth may, for instance, hold certain regional economic and social advantages which serve to attract this growth—growth that, as a result of such an action, may shift to other regions (or perhaps other states and nations), with benefits in turn lost to adjoining communities. The extent to which this is a disadvantageous outcome from a moral point of view will, of course, depend on how officials perceive duties to other localities in the region and the types and magnitude of the predicted impacts.

Charles Beitz (1975, 1979) is a scholar specializing in the international relations area. He argues that Rawls's principles of justice, and specifically the difference principle, ought to extend beyond single nation-states and encompass the global community. This is so, in large degree, Beitz argues, because nations are not independent economic and social units; rather they constitute interdependent spheres of social cooperation in the same ways that individual states do. Acknowledgment of an "international difference principle" suggests an obligation to reduce inequalities among nations (i.e., redistribute wealth) unless these inequalities serve to maximize the welfare of those nations which are worst off. But, just as Beitz seeks to apply the principle in governing ethical relations between different nations, it might also be used to guide morally appropriate intercommunity considerations. For instance, the official concerned with a proposed set of local policies designed to attract new industry might make adjustments to these policies (or choose an entirely different set) in order to yield maximal (or greater) benefits for those neighboring localities which occupy the lowest positions on the region's economic affluence scale. Perhaps even more radically, it might suggest that the community should make actual or in-kind wealth transfers to neighboring communities (albeit an unlikely prospect) in an effort to reduce regional inequalities.

When economic and social relations are viewed through Rawls's conceptions of cooperation and mutual benefit, land-use policies and programs focus on reciprocity and shared enterprise. The social and economic advantages and wealth accruing in one community are acknowledged as determined in important ways by the actions and efforts of many communities and society as a whole. Furthermore, the determinants and influences of positive local development (such as the presence of certain natural features and resources; or characteristics of the built environment, such as the location of a college or an interstate highway) can be perceived as arbitrary from a moral point of view, in the same way that the natural talents and life opportunities of individuals are viewed by Rawls as arbitrary. Attempts to *share* tax base increases from commercial and industrial development illustrate this intuitive notion.

This position may be considerably undermined, of course, to the extent that local growth and prosperity in a community is *not* perceived as being morally arbitrary (e.g., a community may actively work to create the right business climate; may institute job training programs; or may provide substantial tax concessions, all things that might contribute to a sense that these benefits are *deserved*). On the other hand, it is debatable whether a community's economic growth is a direct result of any efforts or actions deserving reward, or merely the result of larger economic and social trends and determinants largely beyond the control of single local governmental units.

The Rawlsian position on inter-community relations in its extreme application is analogous to what has been called the *maximalist* posture in international relations (Hoffman 1981, p. 153). Under the maximalist perspective a public official essentially ignores jurisdictional boundaries and views with equal moral weight the interests and claims of individuals and groups inside and outside of one's official borders. However, the maximalist posture could require a community to expend its entire resources and energy in enhancing the welfare of non-residents before attending to the needs and interests of its own residents. This is an unreasonable expectation because, first, it ignores the strong moral relevance of community membership and affinity, and, second, it ignores the basic political inability of bringing about such outcomes. With respect to the former point, it seems entirely reasonable that public officials feel stronger moral ties and obligations to those whom they were elected to represent. This is both an empirical observation and a morally relevant fact. On the second point, it is often simply unrealistic to conceive of a substantial interjurisdictional redistributive function capable of being sustained in the local political process. Wouldn't local elected officials be voted out of office by local constituents if the electorate feels that they are being forced to make significant sacrifices for the benefit of residents who live elsewhere?

Summary

The general standard of interjurisdictional land-use ethics, then, ought to be that individual localities and discrete jurisdictions should consider the impacts of their land-use actions on individuals in other localities. Generally, an ethical obligation exists to minimize or, to the extent possible, eliminate the environmental and economic harms imposed on jurisdictions and peoples beyond its borders. Reasonable sacrifices to this end may be required, even when other localities fail to acknowledge similar obligations. Moreover, ideally, the sacrifices of local jurisdictions should be shared in a spirit of cooperation, and efforts should be made to overcome the assurance problem by establishing new institutions or legal frameworks which ensure that equal or fair sacrifices will be imposed on all localities. At a minimum, ethical land use requires localities to consult with and inform other adjoining or affected jurisdictions about their land-use actions and decisions when significant regional impacts are likely. As in so many decisions relating to life and ethical land use, the Golden Rule applies: Do unto others as you would have them do unto you. Abiding by such a rule would solve many environmental and socio-economic problems.

14

THE ETHICS OF
LAND-USE POLITICS

LAND-USE DECISIONS are inherently political decisions. They typically flow from the deliberations of a variety of governmental bodies, from local city councils to the U.S. Congress. The political aspects of land-use decisions reveal ethical and moral dilemmas, which are the focus of this chapter.

Democracy is ultimately seen as a just and fair system by which decisions are made about land and natural and cultural resources, but there are different ways in which democratic processes can function. Among the important questions to be considered are these: How do we define political equality in land-use deliberations, and how do we know we have achieved it? Who should have ultimate moral authority for making decisions about land use—elected representatives or average citizens? What political mechanisms best respond to (and implement) our ideals of political equality (referenda or local elections)? What standards of ethical behavior ought public officials who are involved in land-use decisions adopt and be held up against?

Political processes are frequently likened to market systems (see Downs, 1957; Hite, 1979; Mueller, 1979). Political votes are analogous to dollars in a market economy. Constituents vote for those candidates and support those legislative positions which best reflect their personal preferences. Individuals express their opinions and preferences to legislators in numerous ways in addition to voting, among them these: direct contacts, such as telephone calls and letters, newspaper editorials and letters to the editor, campaign contributions, and activity patterns (i.e., what individuals actually do and how they behave; as seen in traffic patterns, attendance at public events, extent to which city parks are used). In theory, legislators respond to these expressions by initiating legislative responses and by developing packages of community measures and programs which respond to these preferences. Individual legislators, in turn, accomplish these political objectives in numerous tactical ways, including logrolling and legislative compromises.

The Goal of Political Equality in Land-Use Decisions

The analogy between economic markets and political systems breaks down, however, when the ultimate objectives of each system are considered. The basic operational objective for the functioning of market systems is economic efficiency, or, more specifically, Pareto optimality. Economic inequalities are accepted as givens and, indeed, the perfect market model says nothing about the ethics involved with these inequalities. Similar inequalities are, however, unacceptable in the political realm (at least in theory) and, in fact, the primary operational constraint on political decision-making is political equality. From an ethical viewpoint it is clear that political equality, not market efficiency, should be the primary basis for making decisions about land use.

The concept of political equality can be defined and conceived of in a number of ways. Below I identify the more important conceptions and elaborate upon their implications for land-use policy. If the ethics of land-use politics are to be assessed according to the extent to which political equality is achieved, it is obvious that one must clarify what this ideal means.

Equality of Political Participation and Political Access

A conventional notion of what constitutes an equitable land-use decision is one in which all individuals and groups affected by a decision have an opportunity to have their voices and opinions heard. Citizen participation has long been an important value in the planning field and it is seen as a desirable part of any local land-use or comprehensive planning process. The "Ethical Principles in Planning," for example, explicitly states that planning process participants should "recognize the rights of citizens to participate in planning decisions" and should "strive to give citizens . . . full, clear, and accurate information on planning issues and the opportunity to have a meaningful role in the development of plans and programs" (APA, 1992, p. 1).

Theoretically, greater citizen involvement can improve land-use planning and policymaking. It increases the quality and extent of information about the advantages and disadvantages, and the positive and negative effects, of a contemplated land-use policy or action. When public officials make land-use decisions in the absence of citizen involvement, they lose not only important information about public preferences and values but also the practical insight and knowledge that citizens hold concerning important empirical and factual relationships. For example, citizen involvement in a decision about open space may reveal that while citizens place a high level of importance on parks and recreation, the particular parcel of land in question presents some practical limitations.

At the broader, societal level, the promotion of citizen participation is recommended because of its educational function and its ability to promote the development of a "public-spirited type of character" (Pateman, 1970, p. 29). To Mill, Rousseau, and other philosophers, participation is essential to democracy in that it forces individuals to break out of their narrow perspectives of self-interest and to consider the larger public good. Public participation in land-use affairs also seems to have this effect.

Processes of citizen involvement can also be important because they help to promote and facilitate interaction among otherwise conflicting individuals and groups in the community. Coming together, sharing and confronting alternative values and views of the community or the world, can do much to promote social harmony and a greater understanding and tolerance for different social life-styles and perspectives. At a community or local level, of course, this result depends on the existence of a socially or culturally diverse community. Extensive participation and interaction among a homogeneous community may result in few of these kinds of benefits.

More fundamentally, there is a logical assumption that participation in land-use policymaking actually makes a difference in land-use planning and policy decisions; that is, most citizens would not wish to participate in land-use decisions if they knew their input would have no discernible effect on the final outcome. This, then, highlights the major limitation when a definition of political equality rests exclusively or largely on equal political participation. Very often such participation does not translate into political power.

But the role of citizen participation in land-use decisions must also be placed in the context of a representative democracy. It can be argued that citizen participation *should not,* by definition, translate into political decisions for several reasons. It should not, first, because of the sporadic and incomplete nature of this participation. It is typical, for example, for public officials to make land-use decisions based exclusively on what the sentiment at a particular public hearing happens to be (and perhaps even a show of hands in the audience). Consider the case of a proposed public housing project. Neighbors of the proposed site turn out in large numbers to oppose the project and elected officials, citing and responding to this expression of public opposition, vote the proposal down. Yet, this may not be the ethically correct decision, largely because those individuals who need and deserve this housing are simply not in the room to counterbalance the neighborhood opposition.

Furthermore, it is unclear whether those who are active in the participatory processes, whether testifying at a public hearing or serving on a committee, are themselves necessarily representative of the larger populace. Not surprisingly it is often the more affluent, better-educated members of the community who are more actively involved in land-use affairs (for a general review of factors influencing participation, see Verba and Nie, 1972). A study by Beatley and Brower (1990) of a massive citizen-based planning program ("Austinplan") in Austin, Texas, found that the income and education levels of participants differed dramatically from those of the general population. In a survey of Austinplan participants, some 60 percent earned over $40,000 per year, and well over half held graduate degrees. The average Austinite earned substantially less income and had substantially less education. And while a comparison of the substantive attitudes of these participants with a random sample of the general population showed remarkable similarity on many issues, there remain serious questions about the representativeness of this group of actively involved citizens. Certain community interests will tend to be systematically overlooked if great weight is placed on who participates or shows up at public meetings. In the case of Austin, for instance, minority involvement in the planning process was virtually nonexistent, even though more than 30 percent of the city population is non-Caucasian (African-American and Hispanic). Many of the other legitimate moral interests discussed in earlier chapters of the book, such as concerns about future generations and protection of biodiversity, would again tend to be underrepresented by citizen participation or the lack thereof.

A more fundamental reason to question the appropriate power of citizen participation concerns the broader issue of how elected officials should represent their communities. Depending upon one's particular conception of representation it can be argued that even when every affected individual is involved in the decision-making process, there may be situations where the duly-elected public official has the right, obligation, or audacity to supersede the opinions of constituents. These issues are discussed more fully under the heading of "equality of representation," to follow.

While it need not be the case that participation leads to power and that land-use decisions directly reflect in all cases the expressions of citizen participation, ethical land use does require community consultation and adequate opportunities for public participation. Moreover, maximal citizen participation and formal access to the political processes through which land-use policy is made are clearly important to ensure responsiveness of land-use decisions to constituent needs and a basic sense of fairness. We can broaden our understanding of political equality by considering the other ways in which it might be defined. Here we can turn for insights to the well-developed literatures in political science and sociology on community power.

Equality of Political Influence and Power

Political inequalities are often discussed in terms of the three "faces" or "dimensions" of power described in the community power literature (see Forester, 1982; Gaventa, 1980). A first face or dimension of political power can be seen in the overt decisions about growth and land use which occur in formal decision-making structures (e.g., city councils, planning commissions, state legislatures). Discussion here has historically centered around debates between elite theorists on the one hand (Hunter, 1953) and pluralists on the other (Dahl, 1961; Polsby, 1969). At this level attention is given to the ability of particular individuals, parties, and interests to prevail on relatively structured land-use and development questions (e.g., whether or not to enact a proposed development ordinance). Bachrach and Baratz (1970) expanded this framework to include a second face of power which they call "nondecision-making," in which the focus of attention shifts to the level of agenda-setting and the ability of individuals and groups to inject their concerns into formal decision-making structures. Lukes (1974) identifies a third face of power in which the question becomes one of whether individuals and groups are manipulated in such a way that political demands do not even arise but nevertheless appear on public agendas or are voted upon at formal decision-making levels (see Gaventa, 1980).

There are at least three ways, then, of thinking about inequalities in land-use politics corresponding to these three faces of power.

Equality of Formal Decision-making

While there is much disagreement in political science and sociology about which hypothesis of power (e.g., pluralist, elitist) best describes the current set of relationships at work at the local level, we need not become embroiled in this debate. It is sufficient for our framework to assume that inequalities occur frequently at the level of explicit and formal decisions. In the case of a proposed highway alignment that would displace low-income and minority interests, although the interests of these groups might be clearly articulated, they may simply lack sufficient resources or stature to influence local power relationships. The sources of political power in this type of situation are many, among them money (and all that it buys: experts, direct mailings, television advertising), personal connections, social status, organizational skills, access to media, and control over information. These social and economic resources are often unevenly distributed in the community, and local land-use decisions tend to reflect these allocations.

A strong argument can be made that a more equitable distribution of community power in land-use decision-making should be facilitated through a more equitable distribution of basic political resources. Davidoff has argued eloquently for political and governmental arrangements where all affected parties, such as in the highway case, would have at their disposal planning experts and the necessary funding to pay for such experts. "The plight of the relatively indigent association seeking to propose a plan might be analogous to that of the indigent client in search of legal aid" (1972, pp. 287–88). While a program of advocacy or plural planning such as that proposed by Davidoff need not be the exact institutional approach to an equitable political system, it illustrates the kind of changes that may be appropriate.

We should not forget that this political equality does not merely extend to an immediate decision, but rather can result in a pattern of decision-making over a long period of time. A community group or interest may win one political battle but end up losing the war. The equality ought to extend as well to the ability of community groups and factions to elect local officials who are reasonably supportive of their viewpoints and interests.

Achieving a more equal distribution of political resources in land-use matters suggests the need for better environmental education and awareness as well as certain institutional changes—for example, establishing the kinds of assistance advocated by Davidoff, ranging from the provision of funds for experts to ensuring that electoral systems are not discriminatory. It is particularly important to create land-use planning and policymaking structures which encourage political organization, competency, and empowerment. New forms of neighborhood and regional planning may, for example, do much to facilitate this.

Informed land-use planners, and other public officials involved in land-use policy, can do much to facilitate equality in this realm. The strategies available range from direct political organizing and coalition formation to more passive strategies such as ensuring that a full and complete distribution of technical information occurs.

Equality of Interest Expression

Many land-use issues and concerns never make it onto the public agenda in the first place. This second face of power represents an additional dimension of political equality we must strive to obtain in land-use decision-making. An understanding of this second dimension arose in the late 1960s, largely in response to the inadequacy of the pluralist-elitist debate in explaining local political dynamics. Bachrach and Baratz are credited with developing this perspective—what they called "nondecision-making"—in their classic book, *Power and Poverty* (1970). Their concern was with understanding the subtler ways in which certain political demands and interests are prevented from reaching the level of formal decision-making. They defined these "nondecisions" as actions which result in "suppression or thwarting of a latent or manifest challenge to the values or interests of the decision maker. To be more nearly explicit, nondecision-making is a means by which demand for change in the existing allocation of benefits and privileges in the community can be suffocated before they are even aired; or kept overt; or killed before they gain access to the relevant decision-making arena; or, failing all of these things, maimed or destroyed in the decision-implementing stage of the policy process" (Bachrach and Baratz, 1970, p. 44).

The concept of nondecisions can take a number of forms in political practice. Such agenda-setting might occur, on the one hand, through the generation of political rhetoric. Ideological community rhetoric concerning the sanctity of private property rights, and the economic and other consequences that may result from tampering with these rights, may prevent the voicing of political demands and opinions of a contrary nature. Such nondecisions may occur, on the other hand, through the explicit threats of certain individuals and groups in the community. Individuals in the community may be led to believe that their political support of, say, restrictive land-use controls would be followed by economic and political reprimands by those in positions of local power. Schattschneider (1960) has called this the "law of anticipated reactions."

Delaying and deflecting conflict away from formal decision-making structures constitutes another form of nondecision-making. Bachrach and Baratz describe the political strategy of creating special committees "for detailed and prolonged study or by steering through time-consuming and ritualistic routines that are built into the political system" (1970, p. 45). They describe the use of nondecision-making to systematically neutralize the power of the black population in Baltimore in the 1960s. A number of strategies were used to deflect political demands. In 1966, for instance, when CORE (Congress on Racial Equality) identified Baltimore as a target city for future black organizational efforts, white politicians successfully headed off these efforts by appointing prominent black leaders to newly created improvement committees—in essence coopting them. Ethical land-use politics must be careful to ensure that what might appear to be legitimate avenues for public participation are not used to deflect political demands.

Clarence Stone, who studied the politics of Atlanta, reaches similar findings. He argues that the demands of certain political interests and groups in the community never reached the public agenda because local elected officials were predisposed to favor particular social groups, particularly business and upper-income interests. Stone analyzed a series of urban renewal proposals over a twenty-year period and found what he called a "systemic bias" in favor of business interests desiring to expand the central business district (CBD) and those wishing to locate low-income public housing away from the CBD (but not in or near affluent areas). Concomitantly, there existed strong political biases against low-income and neighborhood interests. Stone found that a high proportion of the rejected neighborhood initiatives failed in the initial agenda-setting stages where they were the least publicly visible. Stone concludes from this that "official decision-makers were strongly predisposed to act favorably on business-supported proposals. Only when the full impact of public opposition was felt, generally at the highly visible stage of official disposal, did decision-makers show any appreciable tendency to reject business demands" (1976, p. 156).

Political demands and interests concerning land-use policy, then, can be thwarted long before they actually reach the formal decision-making agenda. Land-use planning and policymaking must be sensitive to the ways in which certain political demands fail to make their way to the formal decision-making level. Numerous actions can be taken to ensure, at a systematic level, that "equality in interest expression" is maintained, or advanced. As with the first face or dimension of power, planners and public officials must be sensitive to political structures which facilitate the organization of political interests (e.g., neighborhood organizations) and planning and administrative structures which elicit the opinions, viewpoints, and perceived problems of different groups and interests in the community. It may necessitate, for instance, more aggressive outreach programs to ensure that groups in the community that are typically and consistently underrepresented on the public agenda have a voice in shaping it (see Crenson, 1971). Effort should be made to ensure that certain political demands are not unfairly deflected through such local actions as delegating a perceived problem to a study commission.

Equality of Interest Formation

In recent years the limitations of the pluralist/elitist and nondecision-making models have led to the consideration of a third face of community power. Power in this dimension focuses on the largely invisible impacts that certain political actors and institutions can have in affecting whether or not political demands are ever even formulated, or the ways in which these beliefs are formulated. Lukes is often credited with this addition to community power theory. He defines the third face of such power in terms of any action or institution which seeks to modify and manipulate people's perceptions and consciousness. Power is exerted here in such a way that political demands never fully arise:

> Is it not the supreme and most insidious exercise of power to prevent people, to whatever degree, from having grievances by shaping their

perceptions, cognitions and preferences in such a way that they accept their role in the existing order of things, either because they can see or imagine no alternative to it, or because they see it as natural and unchangeable, or because they value it as divinely ordained and beneficial? To assume that the absence of grievance equals genuine consensus is simply to rule out the possibility of false or manipulated consensus by definitional fiat. (1974, p. 24)

Domhoff referred to these types of influences as the "ideology process" in which "members of the power elite attempt to shape the beliefs, attitudes and opinions of the underlying population. . . . The ruling class in America uses this process to instill and reinforce principles and norms favorable to their economic positions, namely individualism, free enterprise, competition, equality of opportunity and a minimum reliance upon government in carrying out the affairs of society" (1978, p. 170). Domhoff offers a number of examples of how this interest manipulation occurs. One example involves the influence of corporate advertising by such groups as the Advertising Council on American attitudes toward environmental policy and the responsibility for environmental pollution:

> Most council campaigns seem relatively innocuous and in a public interest that nobody would dispute. However, as Glenn K. Hirsch's detailed study of these campaigns shows, even these programs have an ideological slant. For example, the council's ecology ads do not point the finger at corporations or automobiles as the prime cause of a dirty environment. They suggest instead that "People start pollution, people can stop it," thereby putting the responsibility on individuals. . . . Thus, the campaign was geared to deflect growing criticism of the corporate role in pollution, as well as to show corporate concern about the environment. Similarly, the council's Traffic Safety Campaign emphasizes drunk drivers rather than poorly designed and unsafe vehicles as the major problem in causing accidents. (Ibid., p. 184)

The strong emphasis of the American economic system on individuality and the ubiquity of economic opportunity often leads individuals to blame themselves for their social and economic conditions, in turn deflecting the formulation and expression of certain political demands. Ryan has described how social forces and structure are downplayed as explanations for social and economic problems: "Educational failure, teenage pregnancies, black unrest, and other phenomena which are best understood in terms of the way our class system operates, are turned into reproaches of the victims for their alleged failure to correct personal defects and take advantage of the opportunities provided them" (1971, p. 183). Sennett and Cobb (1972), in their interviews with working-class families in Boston, identify a similar phenomenon of self-blame, which is seen to account for much of the political and other acquiescence of these individuals.

Gaventa (1980), in his analysis of the political power relations evident in Appalachian coal communities, illustrates the clear importance of this dimension of power at the local level. Gaventa distinguishes between direct mechanisms of interest formation and control, such as the media and its control over the flow of information, and more indirect forms. Gaventa offers three examples of possible indirect avenues of interest manipulation:

1. Adaptive response to continual defeat, leading as well to internalization of dominant values and beliefs.

2. Interrelationship between participation and consciousness. Participation inevitably leads to political learning; those who do not participate are placed at a learning disadvantage.

3. The consciousness of the powerlessness, even when aroused, is likely to be shaped to the context and powerfield in which this occurs. (Gaventa, 1980, pp. 15–19, my synopsis)

How can inequalities in this power realm be detected? How can it be determined that individuals and groups in the community are being manipulated in ways contrary to their true interests? Lukes and others admit that operationalizing this otherwise intuitive concept is difficult at best. One approach is to compare the political outcome of a similar set of circumstances in another political context, which might provide clues to the effects of local manipulation. For instance, if a group of groundwater consumers in one county secures passage of legislation restricting the use and pollution of this resource, but its counterpart in another county with an even worse groundwater pollution problem is completely acquiescent, this may lead us to suspect that the interests of the latter water users have somehow been manipulated. We must be careful, however, not to overlook the other factors and circumstances which might account for the differences in political behavior and demands. Yet comparative analysis may provide prima facie grounds to ensure that a full and adequate understanding of the nature of these groundwater contaminations, and the public policy alternatives available to address them, are held by the more apathetic group of water consumers. Another approach is to work the other end of the policymaking process by trying to judge how specific actions or institutions serve to distort and manipulate circumstances to meet their needs. For example, a highly visible symbolic action (e.g., perhaps a grand concession by a development firm) or a well-funded public relations campaign (e.g., by a coal company extolling the jobs, and other benefits of strip mining) might be analyzed and their impacts on public opinion and political activism traced (e.g., did they serve to modify or manipulate popular opinion in ways which led to political quiescence?).

Land-use policymaking structures can be organized to ensure maximal equality of this type of interest formation. Perhaps at the most fundamental level is the facilitation and encouragement of open dialogue on land-use issues—a dialogue which neither manipulates nor constrains free thought and the development of unpopular opinions. The political structure and its participants must not be so narrowly dogmatic that innovative ideas and political expressions are quelled before they are formulated. For instance, consider a locality where the dominant economic and political class espouses a narrow definition of land-use planning which views its primary objective as the provision of adequate land and facilities for industrial growth. The community is led to view any other notions of land-use policy as inappropriate (e.g., inefficient, wasteful, anti-American). Had there been a more open and free debate of issues, individuals and groups in the community might begin to view other ideas and political demands as equally legitimate: for instance, the need to protect local farmland and sensitive natural areas.

Numerous actions can be taken in practice by professional planners, landscape architects, and elected officials involved in land-use policymaking. One potentially positive approach is the strategic distribution of information and knowledge. For instance, low-income residents may begin to view access to decent jobs, medical facilities, and transportation as legitimate political demands when they are confronted for the first time with the opinions of other individuals who validate such perspectives. They may begin to see what their neighborhoods can and should look like when they learn about the experiences of other neighborhoods in similar economic and social circumstances. For instance, one community interested in (but timid about) establishing a greenway may receive the necessary courage to proceed upon learning that other communities (in-state) have successfully achieved a network of green without infringing upon private property rights or breaking the budget. With information, the community learns that greenways are good for business and community pride as well as for recreation and the environment.

Equality of Representation

Many ethical questions arising in the political context involve different understandings of the concept of representation. Representation is another dimension of political equality—it can be argued that, while elected officials may have no ethical obligation to respond equally to all community interests in their decisions, they have an ethical obligation to provide "equal representation." Presumably all land-use officials acknowledge an obligation to represent their constituents. How do public officials define the concept of representation? How do representatives define their constituencies and the interests of these constituencies?

The questions hinge, in large part, on the particular theory of political representation one chooses to embrace. A classic distinction is made in political theory between a *delegate* theory of representation and a *trustee* theory (see Pitkin, 1967). Under the former theory, land-use officials take the view that essentially they should seek out and consistently respond to the specific opinions and preferences of their constituents, whatever these might happen to be. In contrast is the trustee theory, in which land-use officials view their representative positions as grants from the people to exercise independent judgment about what is appropriate land-use policy. In reality, most public officials fall somewhere between these two positions, finding some validity in each at different times and with respect to different issues.

Edmund Burke, the eighteenth-century British Parliamentarian, perhaps has been the person most clearly associated with the trustee perspective, believing that the job of the public official is far too complicated and judgment-ridden to lend itself to a strict adherence to constituent opinions. As Burke states in a famous 1774 speech to his local constituents: "Your representative owes you, not his industry only, but his judgment; and he betrays, instead of serving you, if he sacrifices it to your opinion" (Burke, 1969 [1837], p. 221).

Political judgment is a matter of wisdom rather than will, so his argument goes. Representatives ideally are competent and intelligent leaders, rather than simply obedient civil servants. An additional and corresponding line of argument is that the electoral process is meant to install leaders who are, in effect, specimens or samples of the populations they are serving, and that it is assumed they will generally act and vote as their fellow citizens would. This argument falters, however, in the face of clear and undeniable contrasts between how the public feels about many issues and how public officials feel about them. The trustee approach implicitly raises a conceptual distinction between what is best for constituents (what serves their interests) and what they think is best for them: "It seems more likely that serving one's constituents does not amount merely to following directions from them, but rather also, and sometimes conflictingly, to benefit them or further their interests, at least in the judgment of the legislator" (Burke, 1969, p. 35).

In contrast, land-use officials who assume a delegate approach attempt to track public preferences and opinions on specific land-use issues in the community and then vote or act as consistently with these opinions as conscience allows. Officials in this role are likely to be concerned more with public opinion polls, community attitudinal surveys, and community opinions as registered at local public hearings, through letters written, and so on. Assuming a delegate role may require the official to support positions that he or she may disagree with and may feel are not in the long-term best interests of the community. This is often a major dilemma for land-use officials.

Consider the following hypothetical example, where support for a project, which may have substantial negative consequences, is great in the community. The coastal town of Sea Breeze is a natural port whose economic base is closely tied to fishing. The town's environs are comprised of a largely pristine, extremely productive estuarine area and a beautiful coastline. The town is small and contains a charm and intimacy lacking in many larger, more developed coastal cities. Despite these amenities, recent economic conditions have hit the town hard. Unemployment is at an all-time high and local businesses, including the once-dominant fishing industry, are suffering. As if in direct response to these serious economic conditions, an oil company proposes to locate a large oil refinery within the town's jurisdictional limits. Analysis of the proposal's impacts by town staff indicates that the plant will provide many jobs for local residents and a major upward boost to the otherwise sagging local economy. Moreover, the city's tax base will expand considerably, permitting the town to undertake badly needed capital expenditures, such as road, street, and park improvements, that have been neglected for some time. The impact assessment prepared by staff also indicates, however, that the proposed plant will create significant levels of water pollution and will likely threaten the long-term integrity of the regional coastal ecosystem. The possibility for catastrophic damages, as the result from an oil spill, also exists. Furthermore, the location and size of the plant will change the character of the community for decades to come.

Members of the business community are anxious to gain swift approval of the proposed plant before the oil company decides to locate its refinery in another state. Public sentiment, as expressed in a series of public hearings and in a citizen questionnaire, is overwhelmingly supportive of the plant. Despite this public approval, several council members take action to block the plant, arguing that it will ruin the town's historically high quality of life and will be regretted by residents in the future. These council members are able to muster just enough political support among their colleagues to deny the project. Are the actions of the elected officials appropriate and ethical? While the public overwhelmingly supports the proposed development, the elected officials feel justified in acting counter to this public opinion and in assuming a trustee's role (i.e., acting on what *they* feel is in the best interest of the community).

The theoretical justifications for acting in ways that may be counter to public opinion can take several forms. First, representatives may feel that their constituents have formulated opinions without a full and complete understanding of the situation—in particular, without a full grasp of the long-term ecological and socioeconomic ramifications of permitting such a development. Perhaps constituents lack complete information about the true environmental impacts, or perhaps information which indicates that the level of benefits to be generated by the project are not as great as predicted. Perhaps the elected officials have identified certain individuals or groups in the community who have not been adequately heard from. Recall Goodin's theory (1982) of "retrospective rationality," which might serve as an additional justification here; that is, the elected officials in the Sea Breeze case may feel their denial is justified because the town and its populace will, at some future date, thank them for their political courage and foresight. Here, as well, we must recall the alternative ways in which the *public* can be conceived and defined. In taking the above actions, the public officials felt that the interests of a broader public (perhaps including the rights and interests of nonhuman species or of other jurisdictions and people who may rely on the same ecosystem) had to be considered. And this book argues that these factors can and should enter into the judgment of public land-use officials who historically have seen programs only in the form of development, not conservation.

Of course, in practice there may well be situations where there are fundamental differences between the land-use views of an elected official and the views of the general public. For instance, the elected official may strongly dislike the proposed design for a new city hall building—a design that the public strongly and cohesively supports. In this particular case, the possible ramifications of following public opinion may not be great, and the possibilities for violating the interests and rights of some broader public not as obvious (assuming the design does not undermine the heritage and integrity of an historic district, for instance). In contrast, consider a situation where the constituents strongly support land-use regulations intended to restrict the entrance of lower-income individuals into a community. Here the negative ramifications of blind adherence to local public opinion are much greater and the identification of the rights and interests of a broader public much easier. The public representative is more justified, it seems to me, in assuming a trustee posture in the latter circumstance than in the former (but even this is debatable, of course). And, even in the former case, the existence of a well-functioning democratic system (and the opportunity to eventually vote the maverick official out of office) may serve to reduce the moral seriousness of the official's action.

Questions of representation are considerably more complicated in circumstances where the public has not developed strong or clear opinions on land-use issues and policies. Here, public officials have opportunities to serve as leaders—that is, pursuing problems, policies, and projects upon which the public is either uninformed or uncertain. The official may believe strongly in the need for a bike system for the community, but has received no firm response from his constituents, either positive or negative. Even after extensive public notice and public discussion, public reaction is still uncertain. Is the official justified in pursuing issues and concerns he perceives to be important *independent* of constituent opinion? For many of the reasons already mentioned, such a role of leadership appears ethical and appropriate.

Returning to how a land-use official defines the relevant public, we find an interesting dilemma in communities where city officials are elected on a ward or precinct basis. For instance, consider a proposed development project which will benefit the constituents in an official's ward yet will harm the larger community. Does the official support the preferences and interests of the ward, comprised of constituents who directly elected her to office, or to the city at large that is guided by a city council which is intended to make decisions for the good of the city as a whole? While the interests of the official's electoral ward or precinct are important and relevant, ethical land-use would seem to require that representatives consider the well-being of the jurisdiction as a whole in making land-use decisions. Burke echoes similar feelings in his theory of the appropriate role of members of the British Parliament: "Parliament is a deliberative assembly of one nation, with one interest, that of the whole—where not local purposes, not local prejudices, ought to guide, but the general good. . . . You choose a member, indeed; but when you have chosen him he is not a member of Bristol, he is a member of Parliament" (Burke, 1969 [1837], p. 221).

Conflicts of Interest and Political Bias

Historically, public land-use decision-making has been seen by many citizens as primarily a way of padding one's pockets and bank account—if one can obtain a public position of authority, such as becoming a member of the local planning commission or city council, this can be converted to personal power or profit. If one can bestow a rezoning or guide public facilities in the direction of a friend or colleague's land, there might be political or monetary rewards. Even more blatantly, perhaps, public officials might vote in such a way that their own land and properties are benefitted, such as building an unnecessary public parking lot on land owned by city council members. These are fairly clear examples of land-use corruption and are obviously unethical as well as illegal. In the United States, there is the tendency to think that such political acts are a thing of the past, but this type of land-use corruption still exists at every level—from the town council to the U.S. Congress.

Actual or potential conflicts of interest represent a major category of unethical land-use politics. Most states have now enacted conflict of interest laws to prevent elected or appointed officials from voting on issues when they have a direct financial interest, but enforcement remains inconsistent. The reasoning from the perspective of political ethics is clear—such interests bias decision-makers into doing what is financially or politically profitable for themselves rather than what the public interest might require. Despite these laws, the problem of biased decision-making in land-use policy remains, partly because the ranks of local planning commissions and city councils are swelled with individuals who have associations with the real estate and business communities, which have a direct stake in land-use matters.

The extent of the financial or political interest that a land-use decision-maker might have in an action will, of course, be relevant. When the interest is direct and substantial, such as in the case of a rezoning for a piece of property adjacent to a council member's land, or an action affecting a business in which a land-use official has partial or complete ownership, there is no doubt that bias will result. Voting or acting in such cases is clearly unethical. The issue may be more ambiguous when a financial interest is small and indirect:

> When legislative land-use decisions are involved, if the financial interest is very small or if the impact of the decision is remote and speculative, there is not likely to be a conflict of interest. An example is a city council member voting on a comprehensive rezoning that affects his or her property in the same way that it affects the property of all other city residents. However, if a particular land-use decision will affect a citizen board member's financial condition in a specific, substantial, and readily identifiable way, the board member would be well advised to refrain from any participation in that decision. (Owens, 1990, p. 35)

Another issue of concern is when elected or appointed land-use officials are influenced by campaign contributions or other forms of assistance given in the political process. Need we say more?

Land-use ethics, then, requires that land-use officials and decision-makers minimize the extent of their conflicts of interest and decision-making bias. This can occur most notably through the public disclosure of a financial or personal interest (see Owens, 1990). Other strategies include an official abstaining from voting or participating in a land-use matter when even the hint of a potential conflict might exist (recusation). It is increasingly common for individual local jurisdictions to enact their own conflict of interest ordinances. In Charlotte, North Carolina, for example, an ordinance states that all council members (and their spouses) must declare all real estate or businesses they own in the county and also identify their employer.

Summary

Ethical land use requires that public decisions about land use will be made through an equitable and fair political process. In particular, ethical land-use politics implies constant diligence so that the conditions of political equality prevail. Political equality in land-use decisions can be defined in several ways, including equality of participation, equality of power and influence, and equality of representation. Ethical obligations exist to ensure that decision-making structures and mechanisms provide reasonable and fair equality at each level. At the level of participation, ethical land use requires that all citizens who are potentially affected by land-use policies and actions have opportunities to become involved in meaningful ways in these decisions, and that their opinions and preferences be solicited in the early stages of decision-making. Ethical land use requires not only attention to the imbalances in political power which may exist, but also that, whenever possible, mechanisms and institutions be created to promote greater political parity in land-use decision-making.

Equality in land-use representation is also required under ethical land use. While land-use officials must surely be sensitive to the expressed preferences and opinions of the electorate, ethical land use requires that land-use officials exercise their own judgment concerning land-use decisions. Such judgments must go beyond narrow parochial concerns and consider the broad array of potential ethical obligations which may be present (e.g., obligations to broader publics, to principles such as keeping promises or preventing harms, or to represent other forms of life). Land-use officials clearly have ethical obligations to ensure that their decisions, and their judgments, are made entirely independent of any possibility of personal benefit. Public officials have moral obligations to extract themselves from decisions when their objectivity may be impaired by gifts, favors, personal and business associations, and other factors which might bias one's attitudes or decisions.

PART V

CONCLUSIONS

15

PRINCIPLES OF ETHICAL LAND USE

THROUGHOUT THIS BOOK it has been my position that the social allocation of land to different uses and activities is fundamentally and inextricably a matter of ethics. Whether a parcel of land is used for low- or
moderate-income housing rather than high-priced condominiums is a
question of ethics. Whether riverfronts are preserved as natural areas for
wildlife habitat, greenways, and other conservation objectives or used for
industrial activities is an ethical question. Such examples of conflicting
land uses are inexhaustible and they occur in every locality and state in
the United States (and indeed in every nation). Thousands of planning
commissions, city councils, and other citizen boards make difficult land-
use decisions on a regular basis. Perhaps in no other aspect of government are there as many discrete decisions to make, with so many different actors, interest groups, and community factions seeking to influence
these outcomes. And, of course, who speaks for the land?

The existing ethical framework, however, is insufficient to provide
guidance in this massive decision-making arena. In most cases land-use
decisions are usually not even considered to be problems of ethical choice,
at least in any explicit way. They are often discussed entirely in economic,
technical, legal, or political terms, with little acknowledgment that such
decisions directly involve moral choices; that is, decisions about right
and wrong, good and bad. The normative framework which *has* developed is largely economic, wrongly narrow in scope, and morally indefensible for many, if not most, land-use conflicts.

Land-use decisions are also political, of course; that is, they occur
within a context of political power and influence, where some individuals and groups are winners and others are losers. Public land-use decisions must be considered political decisions in the sense that they are
made by elected or appointed government officials. Politics can be thought
of in both positive and negative ways. Pejoratively, politics is often viewed
as a process by which unscrupulous politicians seek to amass power and
serve their own self-interests often at the expense of the broader public
interest. While undoubtedly this occurs in land-use politics, a somewhat
more benign view is probably more accurate. Elected officials look for
good reasons to support one position over another, but they are typically

left with a very empty and vacuous ethical dialogue. Frequently officials make decisions about controversial land-use issues by counting and comparing the number of people speaking for and against a proposal. What emerges often in these decisions is a kind of utilitarian logic, with public officials seeking, in the crudest of ways, to support the interests of the majority (as they perceive it). This clearly relates back to the economic view of the world. The best way to promote the interests of the majority is to let the market system work its magic, to do what can be done to push it along.

Politics in land-use matters is not inherently bad. Indeed, it is essential—no public decisions can be made that are not political, but the ethical content and focus of these politics are inadequate. To the extent that there is a reasoned ethical underpinning to land-use politics, it is unnecessarily narrow in focus, largely economic and utilitarian. This is unfortunate and leads to, I think, a need to spur a broader discourse and dialogue on this subject. What is desperately needed, then, is to expand the land-use debate, to begin to recognize that ethical and moral obligations extend beyond narrow economic or utilitarian views. My intent has been to inject new substance and life into the land-use debate. In particular I have argued that a comprehensive theory of land-use ethics must acknowledge a wide range of ethical obligations.

The Key Elements of Ethical Land-Use Policy

What I present in this section is a recounting of the major components of a theory of ethical land use. I reiterate that my conclusions are fairly broad, and they are, admittedly, open to a user's discretion and judgment in their specific application. Indeed some scholars might characterize them more as ethical orientations, rather than specific ethical standards or principles for policy and planning. Nonetheless, they are offered as a starting point, as an initial set of concepts and principles for discussion within the land-use community. Furthermore, they represent a theoretical agenda for the future.

The principles and imperatives that I present below appear in an order that corresponds roughly to the sequence of the book's chapters. As I stated in the beginning of the book, I have sought to avoid presenting a grand all-encompassing moral framework which will, in some logical way, interrelate and organize these different moral concepts. My view of land-use decision-making has, from the beginning, assumed that different circumstances will suggest the relevance and applicability of different concepts and principles. This kind of moral pluralism recognizes the merit of identifying a number of ethical principles which might be helpful or germane to resolving specific ethical quagmires.

Maximal Public Benefit

Ethical land use seeks to promote the greatest quantity of social benefits or welfare, other things being equal. Land-use policy which seeks primarily to promote the interests and welfare of a few, and disregards the interests and welfare of the larger public, should be considered unethical. Utilitarian objectives in land-use policy must be constrained by other important moral duties, including the acknowledgment of certain land-use rights, obligations to distributive justice, and obligations to future generations and the environment itself. Ethical land use requires looking beyond narrow economic and utilitarian reasoning when considering the merits of land-use policies and decisions.

Much contemporary land-use theory is driven by a neoclassical microeconomic model, which views as correct those land-use policies which move us toward Pareto optimality and which achieve "highest and best" economic use. If, according to a well-functioning market system, the highest and best use of a wetland is for a shorefront marina, then this is the ethically preferable use for such land. If, according to the market system, the highest and best use of a mountaintop is for resort condominiums, then this is the morally appropriate outcome. Historically, the planning profession has, unfortunately, largely confined its own notion of good land use to this economic paradigm. Land-use planning—interventions into the land-use market—is often seen as justified only when certain market failures are present (e.g., the externalities generated by certain types of land use). Many land-use planners see themselves as essentially attempting to fine tune the free market allocation of land. This places serious constraints on public land-use discourse. Individuals, particularly professional land-use planners, feel obligated to justify their decisions, indeed their very existence, in terms of market failure.

Distributive Justice

Ethical land-use requires careful consideration, at every stage possible, of the distributive effects of land-use decisions and policy. At a minimum, ethical land use requires that actions be avoided which serve to lessen the social and economic conditions of those least-advantaged in society. Land-use policy can and should be used to improve the conditions of these individuals and groups. In short, land-use policymakers must acknowledge that, in a variety of ways, land-use policy can be influential in promoting a just society.

Public land-use decisions have tremendous impact on the welfare and life-prospects of individuals. Land-use decisions strongly influence the distribution and accessibility of such social resources as housing, jobs, education, parks and recreation, and health and medical services. A just society requires that all individuals be assured access to at least minimum levels of these primary social goods. Land-use policies are clearly unethical when they serve to worsen the conditions of the needy and when they deprive individuals of basic equality of social and economic opportunity. Ethical land-use policy will help to prevent local or regional policies that result in socially or economically closed and exclusive communities and cities. I have argued that cities cannot be permitted to operate like country clubs, but must be open and accessible to all income and social groups.

The ethical imperative of ensuring just and open communities can be theoretically grounded in several ways. I am inclined to draw heavily from Rawlsian theory, in which the principles of a just society are derived through an "original position," where individuals decide on these fair principles under conditions of equality, and in the absence of personal information which might bias the result. There is much to recommend a Rawlsian basis for ethical land-use policy. Other important theoretical bases include arguments from human rights and from equal opportunity, among others.

Preventing Harms

Ethical land-use policy prevents or minimizes the imposition of harms (on people and the environment). The principle of culpability holds that those who cause land-use harms are accountable for them.

Managing land use, at its heart, is often an attempt to prevent uses and activities which are incompatible with surrounding or adjacent uses, or the interests of the community and its environment. Preventing the siting of a cement factory in a residential zone, however, is not simply a matter of incompatibility, but of fairness. Ethical land-use policy prevents this type of activity because it would create certain harms (e.g., noise, airborne pollutants, truck traffic). The principle of harm avoidance is a key underpinning of any theory of land-use ethics. All harms are not avoidable, however, thus bringing into play the principle of culpability. Some land-use harms may not have been foreseeable. For instance, despite assurances to the contrary, a certain permitted use may create certain harms for the broader public—say, the unexpected contamination of groundwater from a particular industrial or agricultural process. Culpability requires the causal agent to bear responsibility (financial and otherwise) for this result, in turn assuming appropriate corrective or compensatory actions.

This element of ethical land use also has relevance to many of the issues confronted by rapidly growing communities faced with dramatic public facility and service needs. It can be argued that because new development is the causal agent, it ought to be held accountable for a significant portion of these new needs and demands. This is also often a matter of mitigating or compensating for harms created. For instance, new development increases impervious surfaces, which generates greater levels of runoff and flooding—harms to many specific individuals and the broader public. Prevention or avoidance of harm may first demand that new development install site-level stormwater controls or minimize the extent of impervious surfaces. Assuming that stormwater runoff is still considerable, culpability will require contribution to the funding of perhaps a regional stormwater or flood control project (among other possible corrective actions).

Land-Use Rights

Ethical land-use policy must protect minimum social and environmental rights due every individual irrespective of income or social position. These rights may be legal or constitutional, or they may be moral. Land-use rights may be viewed as moral entitlements to basic minimum social goods, such as affordable housing, access to transportation and mobility, health care, recreation, and natural resources such as beaches and mountains. Individuals are entitled to be free from certain excessive levels of environmental risk; for example, from air and water pollution, or from hazardous waste disposal. The concept of individual and public rights places parameters on the extent to which government can enact land-use policies designed to maximize social utility or welfare.

All members of society have rights to certain minimum levels of primary goods—basic conditions necessary for a flourishing and healthy life. These include quality public education, unpolluted air and water, personal safety and security, and minimum shelter and health-care. Such a position strongly demands land-use policies that prevent exposure of citizens to high levels of, say, ozone or carbon monoxide.

In addition to protection of basic health and safety, all individuals are entitled to those additional primary goods essential to personal development and fulfillment, including such things as interesting and stimulating visual environments and access to basic recreational opportunities. I find considerable merit in the public trust doctrine and similar notions of common law, that hold that certain environmental resources are of such a public nature and of such public importance that individuals and the broader public cannot be deprived of access to them (e.g., beaches and shorelines). Ethical land-use policy will not permit development patterns which prevent or foreclose the use of such resources by all members of society. Many other types of land or natural resources, including mountains, forests, and rivers, also fall within the notion of public trust and should be protected accordingly.

Environmental Duties

Ethical land use acknowledges obligations to protect and conserve the natural environment, both for humans and other forms of life. Ethical obligations to the environment lie at both ecosystems, species and organism levels. In particular, ethical land-use policy acknowledges that Homo sapiens is not the only species on the planet and that nonhuman life has inherent worth as well. Ethical duties to the environment suggest that land-use policy should be oriented to minimize the extent of the human "footprint," and to allow the proper use of only those natural lands deemed essential for human needs. These ethical duties imply that landownership carries with it fundamental responsibility of stewardship. Thus, there is no fundamental right to abuse the natural features or characteristics of land.

The development of land and the growth and progression of cities has historically occurred with little consideration given to the impacts on regional ecosystems. Marshland in Florida is drained for new housing projects, deserts are paved over in California for new roads and commercial developments; prairie pothole wetlands in Minnesota are converted to agricultural uses: beaches, dunes, and barrier islands are destroyed up and down the east coast of the United States to make way for second-home and resort developments. Ethical land-use policy acknowledges both the intrinsic and instrumental values of the natural environment. Without the basic functions provided by the ecosystem, human survival would not be possible. Instrumentally, ethical imperatives require us to recognize the productivity and importance of wetlands, for instance, and the human benefits they provide (e.g., as pollutant filters, as nursing grounds for many forms of aquatic life, as habitat for birds and wildlife).

Land-use ethics must also acknowledge that a person is but a "plain citizen" on the earth and has no right to use land and natural systems in a wasteful or abusive manner. Rather, we must admit that nature and natural systems have intrinsic value, irrespective of their utility to people. We must reject what Erhenfeld has called the "arrogance of humanism" and seek to minimize the destructive patterns of land development and urban growth. We have a strong ethical obligation to ensure that the human "footprint" is a small one.

Ethical land-use policy takes exception to the commonly held belief that *Homo sapiens* is intrinsically superior to all others, creatures great and small, and that consequently people have little obligation to acknowledge and respect the existence of other life-forms. Throughout the United States and indeed throughout the world, the growth and expansion of human settlements result in the unprecedented wholesale destruction of natural habitats. Ethical land-use policy embraces "biocentrism," which holds that all forms of life, all species on the planet, have inherent worth.

Urban and agricultural development requires that we sacrifice some portion of the natural world for human survival. This broad environmental duty, however, leads to a series of more specific rules of conduct intended to minimize environmental destruction. For instance, it is argued that we should not sacrifice wetlands or other important elements of the natural system for "nonessential" purposes and only when alternative locations or designs are unavailable. This may suggest, for example, that we redevelop abandoned urban centers before destroying untouched natural areas. It also suggests that wasteful, low-density, sprawl-like patterns of growth are unethical and should be stopped. This component of the ethical theory of land use is also highly skeptical of efforts to develop land when it is claimed that environmental damage will be repaired or compensated for. In important and fundamental ways, nature is irreplaceable and such efforts, even when moderately successful, are replacing original works of art with forgeries.

Obligations to Future Generations

Ethical land-use policy acknowledges important obligations to posterity and to generations of people yet to come. Ethical land use acknowledges that current land-use practices and decisions can have substantial impacts on future generations; that is, current practices can so foul the natural environment that life in the future will be difficult or extremely unpleasant. Ethical land use argues that human beings have special obligations to protect landscapes and resources which may enrich the lives of future residents, and to protect important and irreplaceable cultural and historical resources. All land-use decisions today must incorporate consideration of their cumulative, long-term effects.

The land-use ethics proposed in this book strongly rejects the popular view that it is philosophical nonsense to speak of obligations to future generations. Land-use policies and actions have tremendous impacts on people of the future, in both short and distant time-frames. At the most basic level, land-use practices and policies can so foul a community or region that life in the future will be difficult and extremely unpleasant. Land is a finite resource; if it is not conserved and used wisely it can be exhausted before reaching distant generations. Moreover, current generations have tremendous influence over the quality and beauty of future existence. I would strongly argue that people have no right to destroy things of clearly irreplaceable cultural value or historic significance. The same applies to landscapes, natural or humanmade, which may tremendously enrich the lives of future inhabitants (many places come to mind, including national parks such as Yellowstone, the Great Smoky Mountains, and Yosemite; barrier islands and seashores, such as North Carolina's Outer Banks; scenic river systems such as the Columbia River Gorge and the Hudson River, among others). And it is important to recognize the value and importance of our everyday landscapes, such as the neighborhood forest or pond, which influence in significant ways the quality of our lives. Ethical land use acknowledges both the special nature of these areas and our special role as stewards for the future.

These obligations to posterity require that we guard against incremental changes that commit us to land-use patterns that undermine the interests of future generations. It may often be difficult to argue against incremental development and alteration of these special lands (e.g., what will one power plant do to the visual qualities of Shenandoah National Park?). Yet history shows us that incremental changes set the stage for wholesale changes—once a home has been built, a new road to service the house is justified; once the road has been built, pressures for additional services and development are experienced.

Life-Style Choices and Community Character

Ethical land use allows individuals to pursue unique life-style choices. Thus, land-use policy tolerates a diversity of life-styles and assists individuals in pursuing their own fundamental life plans. Ethical land use acknowledges that communities have the moral authority to establish and promote a certain physical community character, but these efforts must be tempered by the need to respect individual rights and life-style choices that directly affect only the individual.

Ethical land use must consider the role and status of individual life plans in the larger planning framework. Recently, substantial and serious conflicts have arisen over such things as the location of churches and parochial schools, the regulation of adult theaters, and unrelated people living in a single-family dwelling. These conflicts raise important questions about the extent to which government (principally at the local level) can take actions to restrict or regulate these activities. The theory of land-use ethics offered here argues that, when there are no compelling reasons to do so, government land-use bodies should refrain from impeding those land uses and activities that are fundamentally tied to one's personal beliefs or life plan. Religious freedoms clearly fall into this category. Adult theaters do not seem to fall squarely in this category but are indeed elements of personal life-style. Individual life-style choices must not be casually squelched without strong reasons. A free society requires a diversity of opinions and interests and a flourishing of personal choice and initiative. Land-use policies should protect rather than stifle this diversity.

In seeking to protect individual life-style decisions, I do not suggest that our land-use ethics will condone choices which violate other principles. Perhaps the most obvious conflict arises when community leaders seek to maintain economically and socially segregated communities. This type of life-style choice, under our principles of ethical land use, would be unacceptable for reasons already specified.

Paternalism and Risk-taking

Ethical land use avoids actions that are paternalistic and situations in which individual assessments of acceptable risk are replaced with society's.

However, ethical land use can constrain individual risk-taking behavior when there are substantial social costs involved and when accurate knowledge and understanding of risk is low; ethical land use can also support social constraints on individual risk-taking when full and complete information on risks is low. At the very least, ethical land use requires the full disclosure of all relevant risks and hazards.

Many land-use policies involve restrictions placed on the extent to which individuals can put themselves at risk to certain natural and technological hazards. Restrictions to building on floodplains, near landslide hazards, and in seismic fault zones, among other sites, are increasingly common. Such land-use actions are substituting society's standard of "acceptable risk" for the individual's, and are often described as paternalistic by those experiencing these restrictions. Do restrictions such as these placed on voluntary risk-taking amount to paternalism? If they do, are there theories or ethical principles that might defend such governmental interferences?

Land-use ethics assumes that individuals generally know best what their own life plans and preferences are. Other things being equal, ethical land use seeks to avoid paternalistic actions that interfere with voluntary risk-taking. However, such land-use interferences are usually not paternalistic because they are intended to prevent the imposition of harms on other individuals or the general public (e.g., allowing construction in a floodplain displaces flood water onto other areas; allowing coastal development in high-risk locations inevitably leads to extensive public costs in the form of disaster assistance and expenditures to repair roads and sewer lines). Moreover, such land-use restrictions are also frequently intended to prevent individuals from placing themselves at risk to forces and hazards not fully understood and when information and knowledge about the risks is low.

Few cases of pure paternalism exist. Land-use officials will, however, likely face circumstances where the social effects of personal decisions may be modest and where full information and knowledge about the risks are present. Here, land-use ethics must also confront the question of society's right (indeed obligation) to step in when an individual's personal choices lead to placing himself or herself at great risk to life and health. The principle of protecting life-style choices requires special care in enacting such land-use restrictions. It does not preclude governmental action, however, and collective decision-making bodies have the ethical authority, and indeed duty, to periodically check the risk-taking behavior of individuals under certain circumstances.

Expectations and Promise-keeping

Ethical land use requires that public land-use authorities keep the promises they make. Land-use ethics requires acknowledgment and respect for explicit and tacit promises made. Ethical land-use policy does not, however, require public land-use bodies to satisfy private expectations formed on the basis of broader economic or social trends. At a minimum, ethical land use requires planners and public land-use bodies to do everything possible to clarify when public promises are made, when they are not made, and when citizen expectations concerning land use are valid and legitimate.

Many land-use disputes involve conflicts between the expectations of different parties. Neighborhood homeowners are indignant when their city council grants a rezoning application permitting the construction of a commercial complex in an area they thought was reserved for low-density residential. Moreover, the city's comprehensive plan and zoning ordinance appeared to state firmly and clearly the city's intention to keep out such undesirable activities. The neighborhood homeowners feel the city has reneged on an explicit promise. The homeowners may have a good case. Land-use promises can also be of a tacit sort. For instance, a retiring farmer who discovers that he is no longer permitted to develop his land after watching his fellow farmers do so for many years may feel indignant. He feels that the rules have changed unfairly.

Principles of land-use ethics acknowledge a public obligation to respect land-use expectations that are legitimately formed through explicit or tacit promises. To disregard public promises is to violate a fundamental principle of ethics. Moreover, it jeopardizes the reciprocity and mutual trust that society heavily depends upon. While public land-use authorities have obligations to respect expectations formed from publicly issued promises, there is no ethical obligation to fulfill expectations based on general social or economic trends. Ethical land-use also requires that public land-use bodies do everything possible to spell out more clearly when public promises are (and are not) issued.

The Privilege of Landownership and Use

Ethical land use views the use and development of land as a privilege, not an inviolable right. Private landownership is necessarily subject to the constraints and restrictions established by society. Diminution of land value due to land-use regulation is a morally relevant consideration, but it must be balanced against the ethical merits and objectives of public restrictions. As long as land is not physically taken by the government, and personal access and use by its owner remain, a declaration of a "taking" does not seem justified.

There has been much disagreement in the United States about what private landownership means. Native American cultures, on the one hand, traditionally saw land as something that could be "used" but not "owned" in a strong proprietary or possessory sense. Since the arrival of European settlers on the North American continent, a considerably different notion of property has been popular—one which sees landownership as entitling absolute or nearly absolute dominion over land. Under this view, land indeed *belongs* to individuals and, thus, entitles them to use and abuse the land. Societal conceptions of property have been changing slowly over time to recognize the collective impacts and nature of land use. Interestingly, there is much in English real estate law, adopted in most of the United States, which supports the notion that ultimate ownership of land resides with society or the collective. This suggests that the use and development of land should be viewed as a privilege, not a right, and must be subject to the constraints and parameters established by society.

The question of when, if ever, government land-use actions constitute "takings" requiring compensation has been a daunting one, and it is far from being settled clearly in the American courts. I find much to support a more narrow interpretation of the takings clause of the Fifth Amendment of the U.S. Constitution. Compensation seems due in those circumstances when, because of government policies or actions, an individual is denied direct personal use or access to his or her land. Otherwise, compensation does not seem automatically required, at least from a moral point of view. This is not to say, however, that the extent of the diminution of land value resulting from land-use regulations is not a morally relevant factor to consider. Such severe economic devaluations are serious and must be justified by important public objectives. In particular, the greatest moral weight should be attributed to land-use restrictions that seek to prevent harms, to protect health and safety, and to prevent the disruption of the basic natural and ecologic systems that may be present on site. In considering the ethics of land-use actions that result in severe devaluation, it is entirely appropriate to balance the extent of these impacts against the seriousness of the social objectives pursued through such restrictions.

Interjurisdictional Land-Use Obligations

Ethical land-use policy acknowledges that no political jurisdiction is free-standing; ethical obligations exist to other jurisdictions, particularly those which are adjacent or surrounding. At a minimum, ethical land use requires one jurisdiction to consult with and coordinate with other jurisdictions, and to consider the impacts of its land-use policies on communities and citizens beyond its borders. Ethical land-use policy implies that jurisdictions have obligations to minimize the imposition of harms on other jurisdictions and have regional fair share obligations, such as to provide minimum levels of affordable housing, waste disposal, transportation, open space, and recreation.

Land-use policy-making occurs at a number of different jurisdictional levels, much of it historically at the local level. There is a natural tendency for elected and appointed officials, and indeed the citizenry in general, to consider only the interests of *their* locality or jurisdiction in making decisions. However, because of the tremendous spillover nature of land-use decisions, an action or decision taken in one jurisdiction may have substantial impacts on adjoining jurisdictions (or even jurisdictions at considerable distances away).

At the most basic level, local land-use decision-makers have an obligation to view their moral community as extending beyond their legal corporate boundaries. There is a basic ethical imperative that each jurisdiction seek to determine, to the extent possible, the impacts of their land-use decisions on other jurisdictions, and to factor this information into the decision-making process. More specifically, jurisdictions have an obligation to consult and inform and, to the extent possible, to seek cooperation and coordination. Just as individual landowners and users are subject to principles of harm and culpability, a jurisdiction has an a priori obligation to minimize the harm it imposes on other jurisdictions in pursuit of its own land-use objectives. It may also be entirely justified for some jurisdictions to demand and receive special compensation when land-use harms are simply unavoidable.

Each jurisdiction also has certain fair share obligations. The provision of low- and moderate-income housing is perhaps a good case in point. Each community is interlinking and interdependent and consequently has certain shared obligations. Affordable housing is one such obligation. Each must share in this burden, and when one chooses to ignore it others must bear disproportionately larger burdens. Regional welfare may also require fair-share sacrifices at the local level in such other areas as waste disposal, shelters for the homeless, streets, roads and other transportation facilities, and rehabilitation facilities.

Fair and Equitable Political Process

Land-use policy and decisions must be formulated through a fair and equitable political process. Land-use policy-making must provide the opportunity for all interested and affected parties to participate. Ethical land use requires that efforts be taken, whenever possible, to ensure that a level political playing field be maintained and that all community interests and factions, and geographical regions, be able to exercise meaningful influence on the outcomes of land-use decisions. As the moral community increases in scope, including, for example, future generations and other forms of life that may be unable to speak for themselves, ethical land use imposes special ethical requirements on elected and appointed representatives to consider them in their decision-making. Ethical land use also requires certain minimum ethical conduct on the part of land-use officials, including the avoidance of conflicts of interest.

Land-use issues are invariably political issues. They involve conflicts between different perspectives and interests and may result in some people being winners and others losers. It is important that land-use conflicts and decisions be resolved in a context of *fair* politics, however, where all interested and affected individuals are able to have their positions and opinions aired. Ethical land use must incorporate the basic principles and precepts of democracy. In particular, land-use ethics must acknowledge and sustain the basic concept of political equality: that each individual in the community has a morally equal or equivalent say in what happens. At the most basic level, for example, this requires that potentially impacted citizens be duly informed in advance of projects or governmental decisions which may adversely affect them. It will also require that, in considering land-use actions, public officials must give full and balanced consideration to all legitimate perspectives.

Ethical land-use policy may require certain programs and policies intended to equalize this political playing field. It might require, as Davidoff suggested many years ago, that public funds or personnel be allocated to otherwise underrepresented land-use constituencies to help them advocate their positions. It may require, as a further example, that we carefully examine procedures used in making public land-use decisions with an eye for how they are biased against participation by certain individuals and groups. (For instance, how do informal neighborhood meetings compare with a jurisdiction-wide referendum?)

The goal of political equality in land use also acknowledges that political decisions must be sensitive to the many constituencies not present and unable speak for themselves in land-use matters, including future residents, nonhuman forms of life, children, the mentally handicapped, and absentee owners, among others.

Developing the Ethical Framework

These broad ethical principles represent a very preliminary listing of the possible components of a theory of land-use ethics. I have presented them in the hope that they will further stimulate debate and thinking in this area. I am certain that there are many different constructions and formulations of such a set of ethical principles, and I have no delusions that others will wholly embrace those presented here. Indeed, I am sure that, as my own thinking and research in this subject advances, the set of principles will expand or contract or undergo modification accordingly.

There is considerable work to be done in developing and refining an ethical and moral theory of land use for the United States and abroad. First, an approach must be developed by which conflicts between these broad principles can be resolved. For instance, a particular land-use decision or policy may protect an endangered species (e.g., setting aside large tracts of habitat) but serve to undermine the economic and social position of the least advantaged. On the other hand, a land-use proposal that elevates the condition of the least advantaged (e.g., the construction of affordable housing) may have deleterious effects on an endangered species. An approach to resolving such conflicts could take the form of either a prioritizing or a lexical ordering of the above principles, or the development of an additional set of principles specifically intended to break such moral "ties." (And, of course, ethical land use requires a searching for policy and planning alternatives that can, at the same time, advance these different standards; e.g., a land-use scheme that protects habitat but also provides affordable housing.)

An additional element is the preparation of a more specific set of rules of conduct which would flow directly from the broad ethical principles presented here. These would seek to make the ethical endeavor a pragmatic one and hopefully provide real and concrete guidance to planners, designers, and policy-makers faced with specific land-use dilemmas. The rules of conduct might be organized by individual ethical principles or could be a free-standing list. Any single rule of conduct might satisfy several, perhaps all, of the ethical principles above. For example, a rule of conduct which prohibits development of floodplains and riverine ecosystems (other things being equal) responds both to principles of protecting other forms of life, to principles of sustaining and protecting the natural ecosystem, and to providing a minimum level of safety to all individuals, among others.

Ideally, what will result from the above principles, rules of conduct, and other more specific elements of the theory will be a tangible vision of ethically organized human settlement patterns. I have no delusions that any one set of principles will be accepted or embraced by everyone. But in the process of developing and defending a set of ethical principles, I hope that individuals and policy-makers involved in land-use decisions will begin to question their own ethical underpinnings. Perhaps the above set of general principles will serve as a constructive starting point from which individuals will be able to craft their own ethical frameworks.

It is appropriate to end by returning to Leopold's eloquent charge in *A Sand County Almanac:* "quit thinking about decent land-use as solely an economic problem. Examine each question in terms of what is ethically and esthetically right, as well as what is economically expedient" (1949, p. 224). As we have seen, land-use policy and planning decisions invariably involve complex judgments about what is and is not ethical. In the spirit of Leopold, we must learn to treat these decisions with seriousness and moral reflection, and to aspire to bringing about ethical land use.

REFERENCES

Alterman, Rachelle, ed. 1988. *Private Supply of Public Services: Evaluation of Real Estate Exactions, Linkage, and Alternative Land Policies.* New York: New York University Press.

American Institute of Certified Planners. 1989. "Code of Ethics and Professional Conduct." Washington, D.C.: American Planning Association.

American Planning Association. 1992. "Ethical Principles in Planning." Washington, D.C.: APA.

American Society of Landscape Architects. N.d. "Code and Guidelines for Professional Conduct." Washington, D.C.: ASLA.

Arnstein, Sherry. 1969. "A Ladder of Citizen Participation." *Journal of the American Institute of Planners* 35: 216–24.

Attfield, Robin. 1983. *The Ethics of Environmental Concern.* New York: Columbia University Press.

Bachrach, Peter, and Morton Baratz. 1970. *Power and Poverty: Theory and Practice.* New York: Oxford University Press.

Bagne, Conrad. 1978. "The Parochial Attitudes of Metropolitan Governments: An Argument for a Regional Approach to Urban Planning and Development." *St. Louis University Law Review* 22: 271–309.

Banner, John W. 1976. "A Constitutional Right to a Liveable Environment in Oregon." *Oregon Law Review* 55, no. 2: 239–51.

Barbour, Ian. 1980. *Technology, Environment and Human Values.* New York: Praeger.

Barrett, Carol D. 1989. "Planners in Conflict." *Journal of the American Planning Association* 55, no. 4: 474–76.

Baxter, William F. 1974. *People or Penguins: The Case for Optimal Pollution.* New York: Columbia University Press.

———. 1986. "People or Penguins: The Case for Optimal Pollution." In Donald Van DeVeer and Christine Pierce, eds., *People, Penguins and Plastic Trees.* Belmont, Calif.: Wadsworth.

Beatley, Timothy. 1984a. "Applying Moral Principles to Growth Management." *Journal of the American Planning Association* 50: 459–69.

———. 1984b. *Political Discourse and Procedural Rationality: A Critical Synthesis of Rawls and Habermas.* Chapel Hill: University of North Carolina, Department of Political Science.

———. 1985. "Paternalism and Land Use Planning: Ethical Bases and Practical Applications." In Thomas Attig, Donald Cullen, and John Gray, eds., *The Restraint of Liberty.* Bowling Green, Ohio: Bowling Green Studies in Applied Philosophy, Bowling Green State University.

―――. 1988. "Development Exactions and Social Justice." In Rochelle Alterman, ed., *Private Supply of Public Services*. New York: New York University Press.

―――. 1989a. "Planning for Endangered Species: On the Possibilities of Sharing a Small Planet." *Carolina Planning* 15, no. 2: 32–41.

―――. 1989b. "The Role of Expectations and Promises in Land Use Decision-making." *Policy Sciences* 22: 27–50.

―――. 1989c. "Towards a Moral Philosophy of Natural Disaster Mitigation." *International Journal of Mass Emergencies and Disasters* 7: 5–32.

―――. 1990a. "Land Development and Endangered Species: A Case Study of the Coachella Valley Habitat Conservation Plan." Prepared for the National Fish and Wildlife Foundation, Washington, D.C.

―――. 1990b. "Managing Reconstruction along the South Carolina Coast: Preliminary Observations on the Implementation of the Beachfront Management Act Following Hurricane Hugo." Quick Response Research Report no. 38. Boulder: Institute for Behavioral Science, University of Colorado.

Beatley, Timothy, and Philip Berke. 1990. "Seismic Hazard Mitigation through Public Incentives: The Palo Alto Seismic Hazards Information Ordinance." *Earthquake Spectra* 6: 57–79.

Beatley, Timothy, and David J. Brower. 1990. "Planning in Austin, Texas: An Analysis of the Representative of the Austinplan Process." Chapel Hill: University of North Carolina, Center for Urban and Regional Studies.

Beatley, Timothy, David J. Brower, and Lou Ann Brower. 1988. *Managing Growth: Small Communities and Rural Areas*. Augusta: Maine Office of State Planning.

Beauchamp, Tom L., ed. 1975. *Ethics and Public Policy*. Englewood Cliffs, N.J.: Prentice-Hall.

Becker, Lawrence C. 1977. *Property Rights: Philosophic Foundations*. Boston: Routledge & Kegan Paul.

Beitz, Charles. 1975. "Justice and International Relations." *Philosophy and Public Affairs* 4, no. 4: 360–89.

―――. 1979. *Political Theory and International Relations*. Princeton: Princeton University Press.

Benedict, Murray R. 1953. *Farm Policies of the United States, 1790–1950*. New York: Twentieth Century Fund.

Bergin, Thomas. 1978. "Needed: A New Theory of Land-use Planning." In Piedmont Environmental Council, *Toward a New Ethics of Land Use*. Warrenton, Va.: PEC.

Berke, Philip, and Timothy Beatley. 1992. *Planning for Earthquakes: Risk, Politics, and Policy*. Baltimore: Johns Hopkins University Press.

Berry, David, and Gene Steiker. 1974. "The Concept of Justice in Regional Planning: Justice As Fairness." *Journal of the American Institute of Planners* 40: 414–21.

Berry, Wendell. 1981. *The Gift of Good Land*. San Francisco: North Point.

―――. 1991. "Living with the Land." *Journal of Soil and Water Conservation* 46, no. 6: 390–93.

Blackstone, William T., ed. 1974. *Philosophy and Environmental Crisis.* Athens: University of Georgia Press.

Bok, Sissela. 1978. *Lying: Moral Choice in Public and Private Life.* New York: Random House.

Booth, Annie L., and Harvey M. Jacobs. Forthcoming. "Ecofeminism: Connectedness and Wholeness in Human/Nature Relationships." *Environmental Ethics.*

Bosselman, Fred, David Callies, and John Banta. 1976. *The Takings Issue.* Washington, D.C.: Council on Environmental Quality.

Brody, Jane E. 1988. "Scientists Eye Ancient African Plant As Better Source of Pulp for Paper." *New York Times,* December 10, p. C4.

Brown, H. James. 1981. "Market Failure: Efficiency or Equity." In Judith I. de Neufville, ed., *The Land Use Policy Debate in the United States.* New York: Plenum Press.

Bullard, T. 1990. *Dumping Dixie: Race, Class, and Environmental Quality.* Boulder, Colo.: Westview Press.

Burke, Edmund. 1969 [1837]. "Speech at Mr. Burke's Arrival at Bristol." In *The Works of Edmund Burke.* New York: Harper.

———. 1969. *Reflections on the Revolution in France.* New York: Penguin Books.

Burke, Edmund K. 1968. "Citizen Participation Strategies." *Journal of the American Institute of Planners* 35: 287–94.

Busby, Fee. 1990. "Sustainable Agriculture: Who Will Lead?" *Journal of Soil and Water Conservation* 45 (Jan.): 89–91.

Caldwell, Lynton K. 1974. "Rights of Ownership or Rights of Use? The Need for a New Conceptual Basis for Land Use Policy." *William and Mary Law Review* 15: 759–75.

Callicott, J. Baird. 1989. *In Defense of the Land Ethic: Essays in Environmental Philosophy.* Albany: State University of New York Press.

———. 1990. "Whither Conservation Ethics." *Conservation Biology* 4, no. 1: 15–20.

———. 1991. "Conservation Ethics and Fishery Management." *Fisheries* 16, no. 2: 22–28.

Callies, David L. 1985. "Regulating Paradise: Is Land Use a Right or a Privilege?" *University of Hawaii Law Review* 7:13–28.

Care, Norman. 1982. "Future Generations, Public Policy, and the Motivation Problem." *Environmental Ethics* 4: 195–213.

Carson, Rachel. 1962. *Silent Spring.* Boston: Houghton Mifflin.

Clark, Stephen R. L. 1977. *The Moral Status of Animals.* Oxford: Oxford University Press.

Coase, Ronald. 1960. "The Problem of Social Cost." *Journal of Law and Economics* 3 (Oct.): 1–44.

Collins, Richard C. 1991. "Land Use Ethics and Property Rights." *Journal of Soil and Water Conservation* 46, no. 6: 417–18.

Comerio, Mary C. 1989. *Seismic Costs and Policy Implications: The Cost of Seismic Upgrading in Unreinforced Masonry Residential Buildings and Policy Implications for Maintaining an Affordable Housing Stock.* San Francisco: George Miers.

Commoner, Barry. 1971. *The Closing Circle: Nature, Man, and Technology.* New York: Knopf.

Conservation Foundation. 1988. *Protecting American Wetlands: An Action Agenda.* Washington, D.C.: CF.

Cordes, Mark W. 1989. "Where to Pray? Religious Zoning and the First Amendment." *Land Use and Environmental Law Review* 1989: 97–162.

Costonis, John. 1973. "Development Rights Transfer: Exploratory Essay." *Yale Law Journal* 83: 75–128.

———. 1975. "'Fair' Compensation and the Accommodation Power: Antidotes for the Taking Impasse in Land Use Controversies." *Columbia Law Review* 75: 1021.

Coughlin, Robert, et al. 1981. *The Protection of Farmland: A Reference Guidebook for State and Local Governments.* Washington, D.C.: National Agricultural Land Study.

Counts, Thomas S. 1984. "Justice Douglas' Sanctuary: May Churches Be Excluded from Suburban Residential Areas?" *Ohio State Law Journal* 45: 1017–39.

Crenson, Matthew A. 1971. *The Un-politics of Air Pollution: A Study of Non-Decisionmaking in the Cities.* Baltimore: Johns Hopkins Press.

Cribbett, John E. 1975. *Principles of the Law of Property.* Mineola, N.Y.: Foundation Press.

Dahl, Robert. 1961. *Who Governs? Democracy and Power in an American City.* New Haven: Yale University Press.

Davidoff, Paul. 1972. "Advocacy and Pluralism in Planning." In Andreas Faludi, ed., *A Reader in Planning Theory.* New York: Pergamon Press.

———. 1975. "Working toward Redistributive Justice." *Journal of the American Institute of Planners* 41, no. 5: 317–18.

Dawson, Richard E., et al. 1977. *Political Socialization.* Boston: Little, Brown.

DeBonis, Jeff. 1991. Membership Solicitation Letter. Eugene, Ore.: Association of Forest Service Employees for Environmental Ethics.

Defenders of Wildlife. 1989. *Preserving Communities and Corridors.* Washington, D.C.: Defenders of Wildlife.

DeGrove, John. 1984. *Land, Growth and Politics.* Chicago: APA Planners Press.

Demsetz, Harold. 1967. "Toward a Theory of Property Rights." *American Economic Review* 57: 347–73.

Denig, Nancy Watkins. 1985. "'On Values' Revisited: A Judeo-Christian Theology of Man and Nature." *Landscape Journal* 4, no. 2: 96–105.

Devall, Bill. 1988. *Simple in Means, Rich in Ends: Practicing Deep Ecology.* Salt Lake City: Peregrine Smith Books.

Devall, Bill, and George Sessions. 1985. *Deep Ecology: Living As If Nature Mattered.* Salt Lake City: Gibbs M. Smith.

Domhoff, G. William. 1978. *The Powers That Be: Processes of Ruling Class Domination in America.* New York: Vintage Books.

Donnelly, Jack. 1989. *Universal Human Rights in Theory and Practice.* Ithaca: Cornell University Press.

Downs, Anthony. 1957. *An Economic Theory of Democracy.* New York: Harper & Row.

Dubos, Rene. 1972. *A God Within.* New York: Scribners.

Durwald, Allen. 1987. "Leopold: The Founder." *American Forests* 93 (Sept./ Oct.): 26–29.

Dworkin, Gerald. 1971. "Paternalism." In R. A. Wasserstrom, ed., *Morality and the Law.* Belmont, Calif.: Wadsworth.

Ehrenfeld, David. 1981. *The Arrogance of Humanism.* Oxford: Oxford University Press.

Ehrlich, Paul, and Anne Ehrlich. 1981. *Extinction: The Causes and Consequences of the Disappearance of Species.* New York: Ballantine.

Elazar, Daniel J. 1972. *American Federalism: A View from the States.* New York: Thomas Crowell.

Evernden, Neil. 1985. *The Natural Alien: Humankind and Environment.* Toronto: University of Toronto Press.

Feinberg, Joel. 1973. *Social Philosophy.* Englewood Cliffs, N.J.: Prentice-Hall.

———. 1974. "The Rights of Animals and Unborn Generations." In William Blackstone, ed., *Philosophy and Environmental Crisis.* Athens: University of Georgia Press.

———. 1980. *Rights, Justice and the Bounds of Liberty.* Princeton: Princeton University Press.

Feld, Marcia Marker. 1986. "Commentary: Planners Guilty on Two Counts." *Journal of the American Planning Association* 52, no. 4: 387–88.

Feldman, David. 1991. *Water Resources Management: In Search of an Environmental Ethic.* Baltimore: Johns Hopkins University Press.

Flaven, Christopher. 1989. *Slowing Global Warming: A Worldwide Strategy.* Washington, D.C.: Worldwatch Institute.

Forester, John. 1982. "Planning in the Face of Power." *Journal of the American Planning Association* 48: 67–87.

Fox, M. W. 1980. *Returning to Eden: Animal Rights and Human Responsibility.* New York: Viking.

Frankena, William. 1973. *Ethics.* Englewood Cliffs, N.J.: Prentice-Hall.

Franklin, Jerry F. 1989a. "Towards a New Forestry." *American Forests* 95 (Nov./ Dec.): 37–45.

———. 1989b. "Viewpoint: The New Forestry." *Journal of Soil and Water Conservation* 44 (Nov./Dec.): 549.

French, Peter A. 1983. *Ethics in Government.* Englewood Cliffs, N.J.: Prentice-Hall.

Fretwell, Sammy. 1990. "General Assembly Debates Dolphin Rights." *Sun Myrtle Beach News,* March 16.

Friedman, Milton. 1962. *Capitalism and Freedom.* Chicago: University of Chicago Press.

Friedmann, John. 1973. *Retracking America: A Theory of Transactive Planning.* New York: Anchor Press.

Gaventa, John. 1980. *Power and Powerlessness.* Urbana: University of Illinois Press.

Gert, Bernard. 1988. *Morality: A New Justification of the Moral Rules.* Oxford: Oxford University Press.

Giltmier, James W. 1990. "On Stewardship Ethics among Land Managers." *Journal of Soil and Water Conservation* 45 (Nov./Dec.): 625–26.

Glass, James. 1976. "Citizen Participation in Planning: The Relationship between Objectives and Techniques." *Journal of the American Planning Association* 45: 180–89.

Godschalk, David R., et al. 1979. *Constitutional Issues of Growth Management.* Chicago: APA Planners Press.

Godschalk, David R., and David J. Brower. 1978. "Beyond the City Limits: Regional Equity as an Emerging Issue." *Urban Law Annual* 15: 159.

Godschalk, David R., David J. Brower, and Timothy Beatley. 1989. *Catastrophic Coastal Storms: Hazard Mitigation and Development Management.* Durham, N.C.: Duke University Press.

Golding, Martin P. 1972. "Obligations to Future Generations." *Monist* 56 (Jan.): 85–99.

Goodin, Robert E. 1976. *Political Theory and Public Policy.* Chicago: University of Chicago Press.

———. 1980. "No Moral Nukes." *Ethics* 90: 417–90.

———. 1982. *Political Theory and Public Policy.* Chicago: University of Chicago Press.

———. 1983. "Ethical Principles for Environmental Protection." In Robert Elliott and Arran Gare, eds., *Environmental Philosophy.* University Park: Pennsylvania State University Press.

Gosselink, James G., Eugene P. Odum, and R. M. Pope. 1974. *The Value of the Tidal Marsh.* Baton Rouge: Center for Wetland Resources, Louisiana State University.

Gradwohl, Judith, and Russell Greenberg. 1988. *Saving the Tropical Forests.* Washington, D.C.: Island Press.

Gramlich, Edward M. 1981. *Benefit-Cost Analysis of Government Programs.* Englewood Cliffs, N.J.: Prentice-Hall.

Greenstein, Robert, and Scott Barancik. 1990. "Drifting Apart: New Findings on Growing Income Disparities between the Rich and the Poor, and the Middle Class." Washington, D.C.: Center for Budget and Policy Priorities.

Habermas, Jürgen. 1976. *Communication and the Evolution of Society.* Boston: Beacon Press.

Hagman, Donald G. 1979. "Estoppel and Vesting in the Age of Multi-Land Use Permits." *Southwestern University Law Review* 2: 545–91.

Hagman, Donald, and Dean Misczynski, eds. 1977. *Windfalls for Wipeouts.* Chicago: APA Planners Press.

Harden, Jackie. 1986. "Is It Natural to Protect Endangered Species?" *Florida Key Bulletin,* July 20.

Hardin, Garrett. 1968. "The Tragedy of the Commons." *Science* 162: 1243–48.

Hare, R. M. 1987. "Moral Reasoning about the Environment." *Journal of Applied Philosophy* 4, no. 1: 3–14.

Hargrove, Eugene C. 1980. "Anglo-American Land Use Attitudes." *Environmental Ethics* 2 (Summer): 121–48.

———. 1989. *Foundations of Environmental Ethics.* Englewood Cliffs, N.J.: Prentice-Hall.

Harness, Cotton, III. 1990. "Brief of Appellant, S.C. Coastal Council vs. David

H. Lucas, appeal to S.C. Supreme Court, Case No. 90–38." Charleston: South Carolina Coastal Council.

Heath, Milton. 1984. "The North Carolina Mountain Ridge Protection Act." *North Carolina Law Review* 63: 183–96.

Hildreth, Richard. 1980. "Coastal Natural Hazards Management." *Oregon Law Review* 59, nos. 2–3: 201–42.

Hite, James C. 1979. *Room and Situation: The Political Economy of Land Use Policy.* Chicago: Nelson Hall.

Hoffman, Stanley. 1981. *Duties beyond Borders: On the Limits and Possibilities of Ethical International Politics.* Syracuse: Syracuse University Press.

Hotelling, Harold. 1931. "The Economics of Exhaustible Resources." *Journal of Political Economy* 39, no. 2: 137–75.

Howe, Elizabeth. 1980. "Role Choices of Urban Planners." *Journal of the American Planning Association* 46, no. 4: 398–409.

Howe, Elizabeth, and Jerome Kaufman. 1979. "The Ethics of Contemporary American Planners." *Journal of the American Planning Association* 45, no. 3: 243–55.

Hubbard, F. Patrick. 1977. "Justice, Limits to Growth, and an Equilibrium State." *Philosophy and Public Affairs* 7: 326–45.

Hughes, J. Donald. 1983. *American Indian Ecology.* El Paso: Texas Western Press.

Hunt, Thomas Charles. 1989. "Mined Land Reclamation in Wisconsin since 1973." Ph.D. diss. Madison: Institute for Environmental Studies, University of Wisconsin.

Hunter, David B. 1988. "An Ecological Perspective on Property: A Call for Judicial Protection of the Public's Interest in Environmentally Critical Resources." *Harvard Environmental Law Review* 12, no. 2: 311–84.

Hunter, Floyd. 1953. *Community Power Structure.* Chapel Hill: University of North Carolina Press.

Jackson, Wes, Wendell Berry, and Bruce Coleman, eds. 1984. *Meeting the Expectations of the Land: Essays in Sustainable Agriculture and Stewardship.* San Francisco: North Point.

Jefferson, Thomas. 1955 [1787]. *Notes on the State of Virginia.* Chapel Hill: University of North Carolina Press.

Jennings, Veronica T., and Fern Shen. 1988. "Bitter Fight Sets Stage for Howard County Vote on Growth Limits." *Washington Post,* December 5, pp. D1, D6–7.

Kavka, Gregory. 1978. "The Futurity Problem." In R. I. Sikora and Brian Berry, eds., *Obligations to Future Generations.* Philadelphia: Temple University Press.

Kelleher, Susan. 1989. "Denver Reviewing 'Living in Sin' Law." *Washington Post,* Sunday, April 30, p. A12.

Kellert, Stephen. 1979. *Public Attitudes toward Critical Wildlife and Natural Habitat Issues.* Washington, D.C.: U.S. Fish and Wildlife Service.

Kelman, Steven. 1981. "Regulation and Paternalism." *Public Policy* 29: 219–54.

Kheel, Marti. 1991. "Ecofeminism and Deep Ecology: Reflections on Identity and Difference." *Trumpeter* 8, no. 2: 62–71.

Kleinig, John. 1988. *Paternalism*. New York: Rowman & Allanheld.

Krieger, Martin, 1973. "What's Wrong with Plastic Trees?" *Science* 179: 446–55.

Krumholz, Norman. 1982. "A Retrospective View of Equity Planning: Cleveland." *Journal of the American Planning Association* 48, no. 2: 163–74.

Kuehn, Robert R. 1984. "The Coastal Barrier Resources Act and the Expenditure Limitations Approach to Natural Resources Conservation: Wave of the Future or Island unto Itself?" *Ecology Law Quarterly* 11: 583–670.

Kusler, Jon A. 1985. "Liability as a Dilemma for Local Managers." *Public Administration Review* 45: 118–22.

Kusler, Jon, and Mary Kentula, eds. 1989. *Wetland Creation and Restoration: The Status of the Science*. Washington, D.C.: Environmental Protection Agency.

Landis, Scott. 1992. "Seventh Generation Forestry: Wisconsin's Menominee Indians Set the Standard for Sustainable Forest Management." *Harrowsmith Country Life*, November/December, pp. 27–33.

Large, Donald. 1973. "This Land Is Whose Land? Changing Concepts of Land as Property." *Wisconsin Law Review* 1973: 1039–83.

Lee, Douglas J. B., Jr. 1981. "Land Use Planning as a Response to Market Failure." In Judith I. de Neufville, ed., *The Land Use Policy Debate in the United States*. New York: Plenum Press.

Lemon, Steven J., Sandy R. Feinland, and Colin C. Deihl. 1989. "The First Applications of the *Nollan* Nexus Test: Observations and Comments." *Harvard Environmental Law Review* 13, no. 2: 585–606.

Leopold, Aldo. 1949. *A Sand County Almanac, and Sketches Here and There*. Oxford: Oxford University Press.

Little, Charles E. 1987. "Commentary: On Loving the Land." *Journal of Soil and Water Conservation* 42 (July/Aug.): 249–50.

———. 1992. *Hope for the Land*. New Brunswick, N.J.: Rutgers University Press.

Locke, John. 1952 [1690]. *The Second Treatise of Government*. New York: Liberal Arts Press.

Lukes, Steven. 1974. *Power: A Radical View*. London: Macmillan.

McCloskey, J. Michael, and Heather Spalding. 1987. "A Reconnaissance-Level Inventory of the Wilderness Remaining in the World." San Francisco: Sierra Club.

McEvoy, James, III, and Thomas Dietz, eds. 1977. *Handbook for Environmental Planning*. New York: Wiley.

McHarg, Ian. 1969. *Design with Nature*. Garden City, N.Y.: Anchor Books.

McPhee, John. 1971. *Encounters with the Archdruid*. New York: Farrar, Straus & Giroux.

Mahar, Dennis J. 1990. "Policies Affecting Land Use in the Brazilian Amazon: Impact on the Rainforest." *Land Use Policy* 7, no. 1: 59–69.

Maleski, David. 1985. "Sociobiology and the California Public Trust Doctrine: The New Synthesis Applied." *Natural Resources Journal* 25, no. 2: 429–66.

Mandelker, Daniel R. 1982. *Land Use Law*. Charlottesville, Va.: Michie.

Manne, Henry G. 1975. *The Economics of Legal Relationships: Readings in the Theory of Property Rights*. St. Paul: West Publishing.

Manning, Russ. 1981. "Environmental Ethics and John Rawls' Theory of Justice." *Environmental Ethics* 3: 155–65.

Marcuse, Peter. 1976. "Professional Ethics and Beyond: Values in Planning." *Journal of the American Institute of Planners* 42, no. 3: 264–74.

Masters, Brooke A. 1990. "Battlefield Development Approved: Culpeper Backs Plan for Brandy Station." *Washington Post,* September 26, p. JA20.

Mattox, Jim, et al. 1985. "Brief of the Appellee, in *Matcha v. State of Texas.*" Houston: Court of Appeals for the Supreme Judicial District of Texas.

Meine, Curt. 1987. "The Farmer as Conservationist: Aldo Leopold on Agriculture." *Journal of Soil and Water Conservation* 42 (May/June): 144–49.

Merchant, Gary E., and Dawn P. Danziesen. 1989. "Acceptable Risk for Hazardous Air Pollutants." *Harvard Environmental Law Review* 13, no. 2: 535–58.

Meyerson, Martin, and Edward Banfield. 1955. *Politics, Planning and the Public Interest: The Case of Public Housing in Chicago.* Glencoe, Ill.: Free Press.

Michelman, Frank. 1967. "Property, Utility and Fairness: Comments on the Ethical Foundations of 'Just Compensation' Law." *Harvard Law Review* 80: 1165–1257.

Midgley, Mary. 1983. *Animals and Why They Matter.* Harmondsworth, England: Penguin.

Mill, J. S. 1955 [1861]. *Utilitarianism, Liberty, and Representative Government.* New York: Dutton.

———. 1978 [1859]. *On Liberty.* Elizabeth Rapaport, ed. Indianapolis: Hackett Publishing.

Mishan, E. J. 1975. "The Postwar Literature on Externalities: An Interpretative Essay." In Henry G. Manne, ed., *The Economics of Legal Relationships.* St. Paul: West Publishing.

Moore, G. E. 1903. *Principia Ethica.* Cambridge: Cambridge University Press.

Moore, Terry. 1978. "Why Allow Planners to Do What They Do? A Justification from Economic Theory." *Journal of the American Planning Association* 44: 387–98.

Morris, Richard K., and Michael W. Fox, eds. 1978. *On the Fifth Day: Animal Rights and Human Ethics.* Washington, D.C.: Acropolis.

Mueller, Dennis. 1979. *Public Choice.* Cambridge: Cambridge University Press.

Myers, Norman. 1979. *The Sinking Ark: A New Look at the Problem of Disappearing Species.* New York: Pergamon Press.

Naess, Arne. 1973. "The Shallow and the Deep, Long Range Ecology Movement, Summary." *Inquiry* 16: 95–100.

———. 1979. "Self-Realization in Mixed Communities of Humans, Bears, Sheep, and Wolves." *Inquiry* 22: 231–41.

Narveson, Jan. 1967. "Utilitarianism and New Generations." *Mind* 76: 62–72.

———. 1987. *Morality and Utility.* Ann Arbor: Bks. Demand/UMI.

Nash, Roderick F. 1985. "Rounding Out the American Revolution: Ethical Extension and the New Environmentalism." In Michael Tobias, ed., *Deep Ecology.* San Diego: Avant.

———. 1989. *The Rights of Nature: A History of Environmental Ethics.* Madison: University of Wisconsin Press.

Nelson, Arthur. 1988. *Development Impact Fees.* Chicago: American Planning Association, Planners Press.

Nobokov, Peter. 1978. *Native American Testimony.* New York: Harper & Row.

Nollman, Jim. 1990. "For the Seventh Generation." *E: The Environmental Magazine* 1, no. 4: 58–59.

Norse, Elliott A. 1990. "What Good Are Ancient Forests? Global Resources, Global Concern." *Amicus Journal* 12 (Winter): 42–45.

North Carolina Land Stewardship Council. N.d. *Principles for Land Stewardship.* Raleigh: North Carolina Land Stewardship Council.

Nozick, Robert. 1974. *Anarchy, State and Utopia.* New York: Basic Books.

Odum, Eugene. 1963. *Ecology.* New York: Holt, Rinehart, & Winston.

Oelschlaeger, Max. 1991. *The Idea of Wilderness.* New Haven: Yale University Press.

Okun, Arthur M. 1975. *Equality and Efficiency: The Big Tradeoff.* Washington, D.C.: Brookings Institution.

Ortolano, Leonard. 1984. *Environmental Planning and Decisionmaking.* New York: Wiley.

Osofsky, Howard R. 1983. "Solar Building Envelopes: A Zoning Approach for Protecting Residential Solar Access." *Urban Lawyer* 15, no. 3: 637–752.

Owens, David. W. 1990. "Bias and Conflicts of Interest in Land-Use Management Decisions." *Popular Government* 55, no. 3: 29–36.

Palm, Risa. 1981. *Real Estate Agents and Special Studies Zones Disclosure: The Response of California Homebuyers to Earthquake Information.* Boulder: Institute of Behavioral Science, University of Colorado.

———. 1989. *Natural Hazards: An Integrative Framework for Research and Planning.* Baltimore: Johns Hopkins University Press.

Parfit, Derek. 1981–82. "Future Generations: Further Problems." *Philosophy and Public Affairs* 11: 113–72.

———. 1984. *Reasons and Persons.* Oxford: Clarendon Press.

Partridge, Ernest, ed. 1981. *Responsibilities to Future Generations: Environmental Ethics.* Buffalo: Prometheus.

———. 1984. "Nature as a Moral Resource." *Environmental Ethics* 6: 101–30.

Pateman, Carole. 1970. *Participation and Democratic Theory.* Cambridge: Cambridge University Press.

Pearce, David, Edward Barbier, and Anil Markandya. 1990. *Sustainable Development: Economics and Environment in the Third World.* Brookfield, Vt.: Glower Publishing.

Pearlman, Kenneth. 1984. "Zoning and the First Amendment." *Urban Lawyer* 16, no. 2: 217–78.

Peterson, Merrill D. 1975. *The Portable Jefferson.* New York: Viking Press.

Piedmont Environmental Council. 1981. *Toward a New Ethic of Land Use.* Warrenton, Va.: PEC.

Pitkin, Hanna. 1967. *The Concept of Representation.* Berkeley: University of California Press.

Pizor, Peter J. 1986. "Making TDR Work: A Study of Program Implementation." *Journal of the American Planning Association* 52, no. 2: 203–11.

Polsby, Nelson. 1969. *Community Power and Political Theory.* New Haven: Yale University Press.

Popper, Frank. 1982. "A Practical Land Ethic." *American Land Forum* 3 (Spring): 8–9.

Posner, Richard. 1972. *Economic Analysis of Law.* Boston: Little, Brown.

Postel, Sandra, and John C. Ryan. 1991. "Toward Sustainable Forestry Worldwide." *Journal of Soil and Water Conservation* 46, no. 2: 119–22.

Prichard, H. A. 1949. *Moral Obligation: Essays and Lectures.* Oxford: Clarendon Press.

Race, Margaret S. 1985. "Critique of Present Wetlands Mitigation Policies in the United States Based on an Analysis of Past Restoration Projects in San Francisco Bay." *Environmental Management* 9 (Jan.): 71–82.

Rawls, John. 1971. *A Theory of Justice.* Cambridge: Harvard University Press.

Real Estate Research Institute. 1974. *The Costs of Sprawl.* Washington, D.C.: Council on Environmental Quality.

Rees, William E. 1990. "Sustainable Development and the Biosphere: Concepts and Principles." *Teilhard Studies,* no. 23, pp. 1–28.

Regan, Tom. 1979–80. "Utilitarianism, Vegetarianism, and Animal Rights." *Philosophy and Public Affairs* 9: 305–24.

———. 1980. "Animal Rights and Human Wrongs." *Environmental Ethics* 2: 99–210.

———. 1982. *All That Dwell Therein.* Berkeley: University of California Press.

———. 1983. *The Case for Animal Rights.* Berkeley: University of California Press.

———, ed. 1984. *Earthbound: New Introductory Essays in Environmental Ethics.* Philadelphia: Temple University Press.

———. 1986. "The Case for Animal Rights." In Donald Van DeVeer and Christine Pierce, eds., *People, Penguins, and Plastic Trees.* Belmont, Calif.: Wadsworth.

———. 1987. *The Struggle for Animal Rights.* Clarks Summit, Pa.: International Society for Animal Rights.

Regan, Tom, and Peter Singer, eds. 1976. *Animal Rights and Human Obligations.* Englewood Cliffs, N.J.: Prentice-Hall.

Reid, Walter, and Kenton Miller. 1990. *Keeping Options Alive.* Washington, D.C.: World Resources Institute.

Renz, Jeffrey T. 1984. "The Coming of Age of State Environmental Policy Acts." *Public Land Law Review* 5: 31–54.

Repetto, Robert. 1988. *The Forest for the Trees? Government Policies and the Misuse of Forest Resources.* Washington, D.C.: World Resources Institute.

Repetto, Robert, and Malcolm Gillis, eds. 1988. *Public Policies and the Misuse of Forest Resources.* Washington, D.C.: World Resources Institute.

Robbins, Roy M. 1941. *Our Landed Heritage: The Public Domain, 1776–1936.* Princeton: Princeton University Press.

Roberts, E. F. 1970. "The Right to a Decent Environment; E=MC²: Environment Equals Man Times Courts Redoubling Their Efforts." *Cornell Law Review* 55, no. 5: 674–706.

Rodman, John. 1977. "The Liberation of Nature." *Inquiry* 20: 3–22.
———. 1980. "Animal Justice: The Counter-Revolution in Natural Right and Law." *Inquiry* 22: 3–22.
Rokeach, Milton. 1968. *Beliefs, Attitudes and Values: A Theory of Organization and Change*. San Francisco: Jossey-Bass.
Rolston, Holmes, III. 1988a. *Environmental Ethics: Duties to and Values in the Natural World*. Philadelphia: Temple University Press.
———. 1988b. "Values Deep in the Woods." *American Forests* 94: 33, 66–69.
Rosenbaum, Walter. 1991. *Environmental Politics and Policy*. Washington, D.C.: CQ Press.
Ross, W. D. 1930. *The Right and the Good*. Oxford: Clarendon Press.
Routley, Richard, and Val Routley. 1978. "Nuclear Energy and Obligations to the Future." *Inquiry* 21: 133–79.
Ruben, David-Hillel. 1972–73. "Tacit Promising." *Ethics* 83: 71–79.
Ruch, Carlton, and Larry Christensen. 1981. *Hurricane Message Enhancement*. College Station: Texas A & M University.
Runge, C. Ford. 1984. "Institutions and the Free Rider: The Assurance Problem in Collective Action." *Journal of Politics* 46: 154–81.
Ryan, William. 1971. *Blaming the Victim*. New York: Pantheon Books.
Salt Lake County, Utah. 1989. "Natural Hazards Ordinance." Chapter 19.75 of the Salt Lake County Code.
Salvesen, David. 1990. *Wetlands: Mitigating and Regulating Development Impacts*. Washington, D.C.: Urban Land Institute.
Salwasser, Hal. 1990. "Sustainability as a Conservation Paradigm." *Conservation Biology* 4, no. 3: 213–16.
Sampson, Neil. 1992. "Editorial: The Critical Question of Sustainable Forests." *American Forests* 98: 6.
Sandel, Michael. 1982. *Liberalism and the Limits of Justice*. Cambridge: Cambridge University Press.
Sax, Joseph L. 1971a. *Defending the Environment: A Strategy for Citizen Action*. New York: Knopf.
———. 1971b. "Takings, Private Property, and Public Rights." *Yale Law Journal* 81: 149–86.
———. 1980. *Mountains without Handrails: Reflections on the National Parks*. Ann Arbor: University of Michigan Press.
———. 1988. "Property Rights in the U.S. Supreme Court: A Status Report." *UCLA Journal of Environmental Law and Policy* 7, no. 2: 139–54.
Scanlon, T. M. 1974. "Rawls' Theory of Justice." In Norman Daniels, ed., *Reading Rawls: Critical Studies on Rawls' "A Theory of Justice."* New York: Basic Books.
Scarfo, Robert. 1986. "Stewardship: The Profession's Grand Delusion." *Landscape Architecture* 77: 46–51.
Schattschneider, E. E. 1960. *The Semi-Sovereign People: A Realist's View of Democracy in America*. New York: Holt, Rinehart & Winston.
Schelling, Thomas. 1981. "Economic Reasoning and the Ethics of Policy." *Public Interest* 63: 37–61.

Schneider, Howard. 1990. "Reforestation Bill Is Cleared by Maryland House Committee." *Washington Post,* March 31, p. B1.

Schneider, Stephen H. 1989. *Global Warming: Are We Entering the Greenhouse Century?* San Francisco: Sierra Club Books.

Schulze, William D., et al. 1983. "The Economic Benefits of Preserving Visibility in the National Parklands of the Southwest." *Natural Resources Journal* 23, no. 1: 149–74.

Schwartz, Amy E. 1990. "Ancient Monuments, Modern Hopes." *Washington Post,* August 20, A23.

Scott, William B. 1977. *In Pursuit of Happiness: American Conceptions of Property from the Seventeenth to the Twentieth Century.* Bloomington: Indiana University Press.

Sennett, Richard, and James Cobb. 1972. *The Hidden Injuries of Class.* New York: Random House.

Shabecoff, Philip. 1988. "Survey Finds Native Plants in Imminent Peril." *New York Times,* December 6, pp. C1, C11.

Shepard, Paul. 1973. *The Tender Carnivore and the Sacred Game.* New York: Scribner.

———. 1991. *Man in the Landscape: A Historic View of the Esthetics of Nature.* College Station: Texas A & M University.

Siemon, Charles L. 1990. "Who Owns Cross Creek?" *Journal of Land Use and Environmental Law* 5, no. 2: 323–78.

Sikora, R. I. 1975. "Utilitarianism: The Classical Principle and the Average Principle." *Canadian Journal of Philosophy* 5: 409–19.

Sikora, R. I., and Brian Barry, eds. 1978. *Obligations to Future Generations.* Philadelphia: Temple University Press.

Singer, Peter. 1975. *Animal Liberation.* New York: Random House.

———. 1979a. "Killing Humans and Killing Animals." *Inquiry* 22: 145–56.

———. 1979b. *Practical Ethics.* Oxford: Oxford University Press.

———. 1979–80. "Utilitarianism and Vegetarianism." *Philosophy and Public Affairs* 9: 325–37.

———. 1981. *The Expanding Circle.* New York: Farrar, Straus & Giroux.

———. 1985. *In Defense of Animals.* Oxford: Basil Blackwell.

———. 1986. "Animal Liberation." In Donald Van DeVeer and Christine Pierce, eds., 24–31. *People, Penguins, and Plastic Trees.* Belmont, Calif.: Wadsworth.

Smart, J.J.C., and Bernard Williams. 1973. *Utilitarianism: For and Against.* Cambridge: Cambridge University Press.

Smith, V. Kerry. 1986. *President Reagan's Executive Order.* Chapel Hill: University of North Carolina Press.

Snyder, Thomas P., and Michael A. Stegman. 1986. *Paying for Growth: Using Development Fees to Finance Infrastructure.* Washington, D.C.: Urban Land Institute.

Solow, Robert. 1974. "The Economics of Resources or the Resources of Economics." *AER Proceedings* 64: 1–21.

Steinberger, Peter J. 1982. "Desert and Justice in Rawls." *Journal of Politics* 44: 983–95.

Steiner, Frederick R. 1990. *Soil Conservation in the United States: Policy and Planning*. Baltimore: Johns Hopkins University Press.

———. 1991. "On Living with the Land." *Journal of Soil and Water Conservation* 46, no. 6: 388–89.

Steiner, Frederick, Gerald Young, and Ervin Zabe. 1988. "Ecological Planning: Retrospect and Prospect." *Landscape Journal* 7, no. 1: 31–39.

Stokes, Samuel, et al. 1989. *Saving America's Countryside: A Guide to Rural Conservation*. Baltimore: Johns Hopkins University Press.

Stone, Christopher D. 1974. *Should Trees Have Standing? Toward Legal Rights for Natural Objects*. Los Altos, Calif.: William Kaufman.

———. 1987. *Earth and Other Ethics: The Case for Moral Pluralism*. New York: Harper & Row.

Stone, Clarence. 1976. *Economic Growth and Neighborhood Discontent*. Chapel Hill: University of North Carolina Press.

Sumner, L. W. 1987. *The Moral Foundation of Rights*. Oxford: Clarendon Press.

Surber, Jere Paul. 1977. "Obligations to Future Generations: Explorations and Problemata." *Journal of Value Inquiry* 11: 104–46.

Taylor, Paul W. 1981. "The Ethics of Respect for Nature." *Environmental Ethics* 3: 197–218.

———. 1983. "In Defense of Biocentrism." *Environmental Ethics* 5: 237–43.

———. 1984. "Are Humans Superior to Animals and Plants?" *Environmental Ethics* 6: 149–60.

———. 1986. *Respect for Nature: A Theory of Environmental Ethics*. Princeton: Princeton University Press.

Thompson, M. 1980. *Benefit-Cost Analysis for Program Evaluation*. Newbury Park, Calif.: Sage Publications.

Thorpe, Francis N., ed. 1909. *American Charters, Constitutions, and Organic Laws, 1492–1908*. Washington, D.C.: Government Printing Office.

Tobias, Michael, ed. 1985. *Deep Ecology*. San Diego, Calif.: Avant.

Tribe, Lawrence H. 1972. "Policy Science: Analysis or Ideology." *Philosophy and Public Affairs* 2, no. 1: 66–110.

———. 1974. "Ways Not to Think about Plastic Trees: New Foundations for Environmental Law." *Yale Law Journal* 83, no. 7: 1315–48.

Tuan, Y. F. 1974. *Topophilia: A Study of Environmental Perception, Attitudes, and Values*. Englewood Cliffs, N.J.: Prentice-Hall.

Turvey, Ralph. 1963. "On the Divergences between Private and Social Costs." *Economica* 30: 309–13.

Tversky, Amos, and Daniel Kahneman. 1974. "Judgment under Uncertainty: Heuristics and Biases." *Science* 185: 1124–31.

Udall, Stewart. 1963. *The Quiet Crisis*. New York: Holt, Rinehart & Winston.

"U-Md. Students, Landlords Fight P.G. Zoning Law." 1990. *Washington Post*, July 14, p. F9.

United Nations. 1988. "Universal Declaration of Human Rights." Originally published, 1948. New York: U.N. Department of Public Information.

———. 1991. *World Population Prospects: 1990*. New York: United Nations, Population Division.

Urban Land Institute. 1986. "It's Your Land: How Americans Feel about Land Use and Development." *Urban Land* 45: 24–25.

Van Der Ryn, Sim, and Peter Calthorpe. 1990. *Sustainable Communities*. San Francisco: Sierra Club Books.

Van DeVeer, Donald. 1979. "Interspecific Justice." *Inquiry* 22: 55–79.

———. 1986a. "Interspecific Justice." In Donald Van DeVeer and Christine Pierce, eds., 51–65. *People, Penguins, and Plastic Trees*. Belmont, Calif.: Wadsworth.

———. 1986b. *Paternalistic Intervention*. Princeton: Princeton University Press.

Van DeVeer, Donald, and Christine Pierce, eds. 1986. *People, Penguins, and Plastic Trees: Basic Issues in Environmental Ethics*. Belmont, Calif.: Wadsworth.

Verba, Sidney, and Norman Nie. 1972. *Participation in America: Political Democracy and Social Equality*. New York: Harper & Row.

Walter, Bob, Lois Arkin, and Richard Crenshaw, eds. 1992. *Sustainable Cities: Concepts and Strategies for Eco-City Development*. Los Angeles: Eco-Home Media.

Warren, Karen. 1987. "Feminism and Ecology: Making Connections." *Environmental Ethics* 9: 3–20.

Weinstein, Neil D. 1980. "Unrealistic Optimism and Future Life Events." *Journal of Personality and Social Psychology* 29: 806–20.

Weiss, Edith Brown. 1989. *In Fairness to Future Generations: International Law, Common Patrimony, and International Equity*. New York: Transnational Publishers and United Nations University.

———. 1990. "In Fairness to Future Generations." *Environment* 32, no. 3: 7–11, 30–31.

Westman, Walter E. 1985. *Ecology, Impact Assessment, and Environmental Planning*. New York: Wiley.

White, Lynn. 1967. "The Historical Roots of Our Ecological Crisis." *Science* 155: 1203–7.

Will, George F. 1985. "It's Government's Business to Build Trust." *Durham Morning Herald*, May 23, p. 5A.

Wilson, E. O., ed. 1988. *Biodiversity*. Washington, D.C.: National Academy Press.

———. 1992. *The Diversity of Life*. Cambridge: Harvard University Press.

Wolf, Peter. 1981. *Land in America: Its Value, Use, and Control*. New York: Pantheon Books.

Woodbury, Stephen. 1987. "Aesthetic Nuisance: The Time Has Come to Recognize It." *Natural Resources Journal* 27, no. 4: 877–86.

World Commission on Environment and Development. 1987. *Our Common Future*. Oxford: Oxford University Press.

Yan, Ellen. 1990. "Disney Firm Neighbors Are Grumpy and Happy." *Los Angeles Times*, April 22, p. B-1.

Yen, Marianne. 1988. "Too Tall in Manhattan: Court Orders Developer to Tear Down Building's Top 12 Floors." *Washington Post*, February 10, p. A3.

Zales, Joan. 1988. "Prairie Dogs Gassed Day before Planned Rescue." *Boulder Daily Camera*, July 20, p. A1.

Zelinsky, Wilbur. 1973. *The Cultural Geography of the United States.* Englewood Cliffs, N.J.: Prentice-Hall.

Zurvalec, Lori A. 1979. "The Duty of a Municipality to Consider the Environmental Effect of Its Land Use Planning Decisions upon Regional Welfare: Judicial Balancing in the Absence of Interjurisdictional Planning Legislation." *Wayne Law Review* 25: 1253–77.

BIBLIOGRAPHICAL ESSAY

The subject of ethical land use necessarily draws from an eclectic and diverse literature in a variety of land professions and academic disciplines. What follows is a brief guide to more important works in land-use ethics which represent good follow-up readings for those interested in particular subtopics. The citations are organized roughly according to the chapters in the book.

General Ethics

Because few books specifically address land-use ethics, readers may wish to begin by consulting a basic treatise on ethics. Several good ones include William Frankena's *Ethics* (Prentice-Hall, 1973); Peter Singer's *Practical Ethics* (Oxford University Press, 1979), and Joel Feinberg's *Moral Concepts* (Oxford University Press, 1969) and *Social Philosophy* (Prentice-Hall, 1973). These general works nicely identify the nature of ethical judgments, the factors that ought to be considered in such judgments, and the range of ethical concepts, standards, and principles useful in guiding them.

Several philosophical journals address ethics, although they rarely deal specifically with land-use matters. Among the journals that explore the more applied dimension of ethics are *Philosophy and Public Affairs* and the *Journal of Applied Philosophy.*

Utilitarian and Market Perspectives

At a philosophical level, numerous treatises have examined and defended utilitarianism, including the classic writings of Jeremy Bentham (*Introduction to the Principles of Morals and Legislation,* Clarendon Press, 1879) and J. S. Mill's *Utilitarianism* (Hackett, 1979), among others. Discussions of how utilitarian philosophy is translated into public policy can be found in numerous public policy and policy analysis texts (see Duncan MacRae, *Policy Analysis for Public Decisions,* University Press of America, 1985), and in more specialized books on such techniques as benefit-cost analysis (see Thompson, *Benefit-Cost Analysis for Program Evaluation,* Sage, 1980).

Discussions of market failure and government intervention to correct for the presence of negative externalities can be found in most basic textbooks on microeconomics. Several books in natural resource economics with especially good explanations include Myrick Freeman et al., *The Economics of Environmental Policy* (John Wiley, 1973), and Joseph Seneca and Michael Tanssing, *Environmental Economics* (Prentice-Hall, 1984). William Baxter's *People or Penguins: The Case for Optimal Pollution* (Columbia University Press, 1974) is a succinct and forcefully argued defense of the use of economic reasoning in environmental policy.

Several good articles and book chapters in the urban planning literature discuss succinctly the land-use implications of market failure. These include Terry Moore, "Why Allow Planners to Do What They Do? A Justification from Economic Theory," *Journal of the American Planning Association* 44 (October 1978): 387–98; H. James Brown, "Market Failure: Efficiency or Equity," and Douglas Lee, "Land Use Planning as a Response to Market Failure," both contained in Judith de Neufville, ed., *The Land Use Policy Debate in the United States* (Plenum Press, 1981); and Thomas Bergin, "Needed: A New Theory of Land Use Planning," in Piedmont Environmental Council, *Toward a New Ethics of Land Use* (PEC, 1978). On the tragedy of the commons, Garrett Hardin's classic essay by the same name remains the basic starting point (*Science*, vol. 162, 1968).

Land-Use Rights and the Prevention of Harms

Land-use rights and the prevention of harms are concepts that express deontological perspectives on ethical land use. In both cases there is relatively little written that applies them specifically to land-use policy and planning. In the area of land-use rights, however, numerous philosophical and policy books address the concept of rights in general, including human rights. On the philosophical side, Joel Feinberg has written extensively, including an impressive collection of essays, entitled *Rights, Justice and the Bounds of Liberty* (Princeton University Press, 1980). Other good basic philosophical texts on rights include Virginia Held, *Rights and Goods* (University of Chicago Press, 1984); L. W. Sumner, *The Moral Foundation of Rights* (Clarendon Press, 1987); and Ronald Dworkin, *Taking Rights Seriously* (Harvard University Press, 1977). On human rights, several good overviews include Jack Donnelly, *Universal Human Rights in Theory and Practice* (Cornell University Press, 1989), and Henry Shue, *Basic Rights* (Princeton University Press, 1980). General discussions of both rights and obligations to avoid or minimize harm can be found in most of the introductory textbooks on ethics cited above.

Land-use rights have been addressed in the area of constitutional limitations to planning and zoning. Several good planning law texts exist, including Richard Lai, *Law in Urban Design and Planning* (Van Nostrand Reinhold, 1988); David Godschalk et al., *Constitutional Issues of Growth Management* (APA Planners Press, 1979); Brian Blaesser and Alan C. Weinstein, *Land Use and the Constitution* (APA Planners Press, 1989); Alexandra Dawson, *Land-Use Planning and the Law* (Garland Press, 1982); and Stuart Meck and Edith Netter, *A Planner's Guide to Land-Use Law* (APA Planners Press, 1983). The public trust doctrine represents one category of significant public environmental and land-use rights, placing restrictions on the use of private land. A good overview of the doctrine is found in Joseph L. Sax, *Defending the Environment: A Strategy for Citizen Action* (Knopf, 1971).

Distributive Obligations in Land Use

A rich and extensive literature exists in philosophy, law, and social policy on distributive justice which has direct relevance to land-use policy and planning. Outstanding conservative treatises include Robert Nozick's *Anarchy, State and Utopia* (Basic Books, 1974). A good discussion of different concepts of equality can be found in Douglas Rae, *Equalities* (Harvard University Press, 1981). Among contractarian views, John Rawls, *A Theory of Justice* (Harvard University Press, 1971), remains the ground-breaking work. A number of attempts have been made in planning and related fields to apply and adapt the Rawlsian framework to land-use issues. Among these are Timothy Beatley, "Applying Moral Principles to Growth Management," *Journal of the American Planning Association* 50 (1984): 459–69, and David Berry and Gene Steiker, "The Concept of Justice in Regional Planning," *Journal of the American Institute of Planners* 40 (1974): 414–21.

Among the land professions, urban (or city) and regional planning has exhibited the most concern about the distributive and social aspects of land use. There is a considerable literature here, including Paul Davidoff's extensive writings (e.g., "Advocacy and Pluralism in Planning," *Journal of the American Institute of Planners* 31 [1965]: 317–18). The work of Norman Krumholz in documenting the implementation of such equity planning is also very useful (see Norman Krumholz and John Forester, *Making Equity Planning Work: Leadership in the Public Sector,* Temple University Press, 1990).

Environmental Duties and Obligations

The literature of environmental ethics has been growing steadily in recent years, and it is now quite extensive. Many good readers and basic textbooks are available, including Holmes Rolston, *Environmental Ethics: Duties to and Values in the Natural World* (Temple University Press, 1988); Robin Attfield, *The Ethics of Environmental Concern* (Columbia University Press, 1983); John Passmore, *Man's Responsibility for Nature* (Duckworth, 1980); Donald Scherer and Thomas Attig, eds., *Ethics and the Environment* (Prentice-Hall, 1983); Donald Van DeVeer and Christine Pierce, *People, Penguins, and Plastic Trees* (Wadsworth, 1986); Robert Gore and Arran Gore, *Environmental Philosophy* (University of Queensland Press, 1983); Tom Regan, *Earthbound: New Introductory Essays in Environmental Ethics* (Temple University Press, 1984); and Eugene Hargrove, *Foundations of Environmental Ethics* (Prentice-Hall, 1989).

Roderick Nash's *The Rights of Nature: A History of Environmental Ethics* (University of Wisconsin Press, 1989) is recommended as an overview of the literature and the different schools of thought in environmental ethics, and their origin and development over time. A good introduction to the key issues and debate in environmental ethics is found in John McPhee's *Encounters with the Archdruid* (Farrar, Straus & Giroux, 1971), which documents the thoughts and feelings of environmentalist David Brower as he interacts with various representatives of development interests (e.g., Charles Fraser, developer of Hilton Head, South Carolina). Different theoretical and philosophical sub-areas within environmental ethics in turn have their own leading works. In the theory and philosophy of animal rights, Peter Singer's *Animal Liberation* (Random House, 1975) and Tom Regan's *The Case for Animal Rights* (University of California Press, 1983), expressing a utilitarian and a rights view, respectively, are two of the most important works. Good discussions of the reasons and rationales for protecting endangered species are found in Paul Ehrlich and Anne Ehrlich's *Extinction: The Causes and Consequences of the Disappearance of Species* (Ballantine, 1981); Edward O. Wilson, *The Diversity of Life* (Harvard University Press, 1992); Bryan Norton, ed., *The Presentation of Species: The Value of Biological Diversity* (Princeton University Press, 1986); Bryan Norton, *Why Preserve Variety?* (Princeton University Press, 1988); and David Ehrenfeld, *The Arrogance of Humanism* (Oxford University Press, 1981).

To a large extent the beginnings of concern about environmental ethics in the land professions are marked by the publishing of Aldo Leopold's classic *A Sand County Almanac* (Oxford University Press, 1949). This is must reading for land-use professionals, especially his essay on "The Land Ethic." Many of the more recent writers and thinkers on environmental ethics draw heavily from, and build upon, the basic foundation outlined by Leopold. More recent elaborations of Leopold's holistic philosophy include Holmes Rolston's *Environmental Ethics: Duties to and Values in the Natural World* (Temple University Press, 1988) and Baird Callicott's *In Defense of the Land Ethic* (SUNY Press, 1989). Perhaps the most detailed and well-developed philosophical treatise on the biocentric view is Paul Taylor's *Respect for Nature: A Theory of Environmental Ethics* (Princeton University Press, 1986). Whether or not readers find its theoretical foundation convincing, this book is impressive in its attempt to lay out a set of ethical principles for guiding human relationships with the environment, and for resolving conflicts between human and nonhuman interests.

The development of what has become known as "deep ecology" begins with Arne Naess's ground-breaking essay "The Shallow and the Deep, Long Range Ecology Movement," *Inquiry* 16 (1973): 95–100, in which he coined the term. Other recent deep ecology books include Michael Tobias's edited volume, *Deep Ecology* (Avant Books, 1985), and Bill Devall and George Sessions, *Deep Ecology: Living As If Nature Mattered* (Gibbs M. Smith, 1985).

There are now several scholarly journals focused on environmental ethics. *Environmental Ethics* is the older and more established. Others include *Trumpeter* and *Environmental Values*.

Future Generations

There has been an active debate in philosophy about the merits of moral obligations to future generations, and the nature and extent of these obligations. Two good anthologies are recommended: Ernest Partridge, ed., *Responsibilities to Future Generations: Environmental Ethics* (Prometheus, 1981), and R. I. Sikora and Brian Barry, eds., *Obligations to Future Generations* (Temple University Press, 1978). Among the best attempts to flesh out the policy implications of concern for future generations is found in Edith Brown Weiss's work, including *In Fairness to Future Generations* (Transnational Publishers and United Nations University, 1989).

On the concept of stewardship, Wendell Berry's *The Gift of Good Land* (North Point, 1981) is an especially good treatment of the Christian perspective. Charles Little's *Hope for the Land* (Rutgers University Press, 1992) is also outstanding. Stewardship has received considerable attention in the land professions in recent years. In landscape architecture, for example, Robert Scarfo has written several informative articles including "Stewardship: The Profession's Grand Delusion," in *Landscape Architecture* 77 (1986): 46–51.

Paternalism and Risk-taking

A number of good general textbooks on risk and paternalism exist. General issues relating to the ethics of risk management are covered well in William Lowrance, *Of Acceptable Risk* (William Kaufman, 1976), and Kristen Shrader-Frechette, *Risk Analysis and Scientific Method* (Kluwer, 1985). Several basic philosophical works address paternalism, including Donald Van DeVeer's *Paternalistic Intervention* (Princeton University Press, 1986) and John Kleinig's *Paternalism* (Rowman & Allanheld, 1984). A number of good articles in both philosophical and policy journals are recommended. Especially good are Steven Kelman's "Regulation and Paternalism," *Public Policy* 29 (1981): 219–54, and Gerald Dworkin's classic essay, "Paternalism," in R. A. Wasserstrom, ed., *Morality and the Law* (Wadsworth, 1971).

Expectations, Private Property, and the Takings Issue

Several books exist that discuss the concept of private property and its different rationales and defenses (e.g., utilitarian, natural law, contractarian). These include Lawrence Becker, *Property Rights: Philosophic Foundations* (Routledge & Kegan Paul, 1977), and Stephen R. Munzer, *A Theory of Property* (Cambridge University Press, 1990).

On the takings issue, an expansive literature exists. One of the most comprehensive treatments, though somewhat dated now, is Fred Bosselman et al., *The Takings Issue* (Council on Environmental Quality, 1976). More recent discussions can be found in Godschalk et al.; Lai; Blaesser and Weinstein; and Dawson, cited above under land-use rights and the prevention of harms.

Considerable discussion in recent years has centered around the need for alternative conceptions of private property in land which better take into account ecological protection, and other important social and environmental constraints. David B. Hunter has written an excellent essay arguing for such a redefinition in "An Ecological Perspective on Property: A Call for Judicial Protection of the Public's Interest in Environmentally Critical Resources," *Harvard Environmental Law Review* 12 (1988): 311–84. On the question of increases in land value, and alternative techniques and proposals for addressing increases and decreases in land value, *Windfalls for Wipeouts*, edited by Donald Hagman and Dean Misczynski (APA Planners Press, 1977), remains the leading book.

Community Character and Duties beyond Borders

On the subject of duties beyond borders, and obligations to regional welfare, much of the existing literature focuses on the nature of exclusionary zoning and regional fair-share housing requirements. Good discussions of these subjects can be found in "Symposium on Growth Management and Exclusionary Zoning," *Journal of Urban and Contemporary Law* (Summer/Fall, 1991); Stuart Meck and Edith Netter, *A Planner's Guide to Land-Use Law* (APA Planners Press, 1983), esp. section 4, "Constitutional Limitations on Land-use Regulation"; as well as the other textbooks on land-use law mentioned above. On the question of regulating aesthetics, see Richard F. Babcock, *Billboards, Glass Houses, and the Law* (McGraw-Hill, 1977), as well as Richard Lai, *Law in Urban Design and Planning* (Van Nostrand Reinhold, 1988), esp. parts 4 and 5.

Ethics of Land-Use Politics

On the subject of political equality, several general introductory books can be recommended, including Charles R. Beitz's *Political Equality: An Essay in Democratic Theory* (Princeton University Press, 1989). The community power literature is voluminous and readers may wish to refer to several good overviews, including John Gaventa's *Power and Powerlessness* (University of Illinois Press, 1980); Robert Waste, ed., *Community Power: Directions for Future Research* (Sage 1986); and Nelson Polsby, *Community Power and Political Theory*, 2d ed., rev. (Yale University Press, 1980). Several good books exist which describe the political process surrounding the planning and development of land, and the actors and interest groups typically involved. Anthony James Catanese's *The Politics of Planning and Development* (Sage, 1984) is one such book, oriented toward the field of urban planning.

A number of good books exist which examine alternative theories of representation and the ethical obligations of elected officials. Hanna Pitkin's *Representation* (Atherton Press, 1969) is a classic and a fine overview of the alternative meaning of representation. Several other volumes exist which introduce the range of ethical issues confronted in the political process, including Norman E. Bowie, ed., *Ethical Issues in Government* (Temple University Press, 1981); Peter A. French, *Ethics in Government* (Prentice-Hall, 1983); and Dennis F. Thompson, *Political Ethics and Public Office* (Harvard University Press, 1987). A modest literature specifically addresses ethical issues in land-use politics, for example on conflict of interest issues. David Owens's *Conflict of Interest in Land-Use Management Decisions* (University of North Carolina Institute of Government, 1991) is recommended.

INDEX

Library of Congress Cataloging-in-Publication Data

Beatley, Timothy, 1957–
    Ethical land use : principles of policy and planning /
    Timothy Beatley.
        p.   cm.
    Includes bibliographical references and index.
    ISBN 0-8018-4698-6 (acid-free paper). —
ISBN 0-8018-4699-4 (pbk. : acid-free paper)
    1. Land use—Government policy—United States.
2. Land use—United States—Planning—Moral and ethical
aspects. 3. Land use—Environmental aspects—United
States. I. Title.
HD205.B43 1994
333.73'13'0973—dc20   93-40870
                                                          CIP